AF225104

Still FILM CRAZY

(After All These Years)

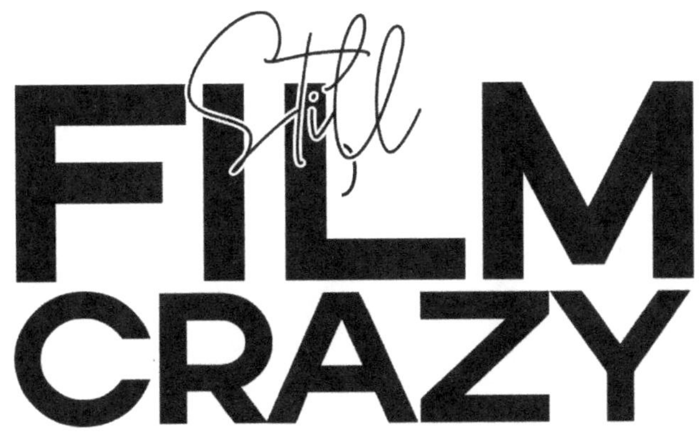

(After All These Years)

Collected Interviews

Patrick McGilligan

Sticking Place Books
New York

© Sticking Place Books 2023

www.stickingplacebooks.com

Cover image: *The Young Girls of Rochefort*
© Hélène Jeanbrau/Ciné-Tamaris

All rights reserved.
No part of this book may be reproduced, stored in or introduced into a retrieval system, or transmitted, in any form or by any means (electronic, mechanical, photocopying, recording or otherwise) without the written permission of the publishers, except in the case of brief quotations embodied in critical articles or reviews.

ISBN 978-1-942782-46-9

For Francesco Zippel
My film-crazy friend in Rome

CONTENTS

Introduction: Himself Interviewed　　　ix

Auteurs of the 1970s and 1980s
Ken Russell (1975)　　　1
Ralph Bakshi (1977)　　　13
Peter Weir (1986)　　　25
Oliver Stone (1987)　　　43

The Business
Boston Bankers (1976)　　　67
Video Visions, Milwaukee (1983 – 2003)　　　81

More Tender Comrades
Anne Edwards (2013)　　　91
Clancy Sigal (2017)　　　105
Peter Davis (Frank Davis and Tess Slesinger) (2020)　　　117

Biographical Subjects
Clint Eastwood (1976)　　　133
LeRoy Collins and Oscar Micheaux (2004)　　　149

Mavericks and Independents
Dean Stockwell (1988)　　　161
Jules Feiffer (1980 and 1990)　　　169
Matt Tyrnauer and Scotty Bowers (2017)　　　179
Barry Alexander Brown and *Son of the South* (2021)　　　185

World Class
Pedro Costa (2010)　　　201
Adoor Gopalakrishnan (2011)　　　209

French Connections

Michel Ciment and *Positif* (1993)   221
Bertrand Tavernier on the American Cinema (1992)   229
Bertrand Tavernier on the French Cinema (2020)   247
Grover Dale! (2022)   263

Notes and Acknowledgements   273

Index   275

Introduction: Himself Interviewed

Although he appears in numerous documentaries, has provided commentaries for DVDs, and has appeared on television's *The Today Show* and radio's *Fresh Air*, Patrick McGilligan claims not to enjoy giving interviews about his work. "As a writer, I prefer to choose my words carefully," he said. "I am never very happy with an interview I give, or my spoken-word commentary." Paradoxically, he has interviewed hundreds of show business and literary personalities and people from other disparate professions. He has made a specialty of the Q. and A. with seven entire books composed of conversations with celebrities in the arts, including five volumes featuring screenwriters who suffered his interrogation. This is his eighth such book of interviews, uncollected, meaning most – though not all – have been previously published but not until this time have they been brought together in book form.

Setting aside his qualms about the format, McGilligan agreed to be interviewed about the lows and highs of "interviewing" in a career of non-fiction stretching back fifty years.

—◦—

Have you always been interested in famous people?
I read grade-school-level sports biographies when I was young, holding the hand of my mother as she walked me to the Madison, Wisconsin downtown library, where I gravitated to the life stories of athletes such as Henry Aaron, a Wisconsin baseball legend, and Mickey Mantle, the same for the Yankees in New York. In time I graduated out of that phase, and I haven't read a book about a sports figure since high school, at least. But I liked true stories about flawed heroes that also taught life lessons.

Then one day Annette Funicello's mother rang the doorbell of the house where I grew up with my family on the shore of Lake Mendota in downtown Madison, asking for directions. Paying a debt of gratitude to my father, she brought Annette, Sammy Ogg and "Moochie" over for a backyard cookout and boat rides in the summer of 1956. The Hollywood folk had descended on our town for an episode of *The Mickey Mouse Club* that was being shot on a farm outside Madison. Annette and the other child actors were superstars to any red-blooded American boy. I suppose that is when the first seeds were planted.

When did you begin to interview famous people?

In college, when I worked for the radical campus newspaper, sometimes interviewing local personalities – some of whom later attained surprising prominence in Wisconsin politics – I fell in with a group of older graduate students who knew more about the cinema than I did and had a lot to teach me. One of them was Gerald Peary, with whom I ran a film society, and Gerry was (and is) an enterprising fellow. He found out the Senegalese novelist and filmmaker Ousmane Sembene was going to pay a visit to campus, and we arranged to interview Sembene. We got our resulting piece accepted by *Film Quarterly*, which was my first published interview with a film person; then we did the same with the onetime head of MGM, Dore Schary, who came to Madison to peruse his own archives for his autobiography.

In those days we researched our subjects as best as we could in the college library (there was no Internet, young readers) and we always went to our interview sessions with many notes and lists of questions and a tape recorder that we had borrowed and that we hoped would not malfunction. Many filmmakers passed through Madison because of the university culture, and I and other people in this film-crazy crowd buttonholed as many as we could. In time I evolved my own interests and my own style of interviewing, but for example, when I wrote my first book about James Cagney the book came almost entirely out of library research without any supporting interviews. Later, when I was living in California in the early Eighties, I went back and revised this book and incorporated interviews with many people I had met or corresponded with, who were once associated with Cagney.

What do you mean by your interests and style evolved?

Well, my interests began to be reflected in my choice of interview subjects, which was dependent more, early on, on chance and the whim of my collaborators. I developed an empathy and fascination with Hollywood writers, for example, perhaps because I also worked as an editor all through my career, and I had an intimacy with and an understanding of writers. While living in Hollywood, I began accruing interviews with retired, successful scenarists that I eventually turned into the first *Backstory*. To create a five-book series was not in my mind, and in fact the first volume was circled off a list of proposed projects by Ernest Callenbach of the University of California Press, God bless him. It paid $500, which I thought generous at the time.

Off and on, during the early and mid-seventies, I had also worked on staff in Boston for the *Boston Globe*, and some interviews (Ken Russell, Ralph Bakshi, and the Boston bankers in this book) were spun off from those assignments. I always did loads of research, and I was always super-nervous about the tape recorder and about asking all the questions on my long list within the allotted time. Sometimes I accompanied Joseph McBride – sometimes he accompanied me – as we sat for hours with Golden Age directors such as Allan Dwan, Rouben Mamoulian and Howard Hawks. Later in life, I took fewer notes and did less research, and I learned to listen to what was being said and to go more with the flow. This is the better approach, I am convinced. Especially when doing extensive interviews for my major biographies I learned also to do my own transcribing – which I hate to do because it's so time-consuming – but it is often true you hear things, little details or passing mentions, which you missed the first time through because you were trapped in the moment.

Were you at all crazy about movies as a boy? Is that why you focused on Hollywood?

No. I saw only a handful of movies before I entered high school. *Ben-Hur* because my parochial grade school class went to see it, and *The Alamo* because my father liked John Wayne. And I had interviewed all sorts of people, and only a couple of screen luminaries, before I was hired by the *Boston Globe*, first for an internship in the arts department in the summer of 1973, and later for an arts staff position. I had some arts qualifications, including flings with acting in summer stock and college, and at the *Globe* – thanks to my editor, Robert Taylor – I was allowed to write about books, music, the stage and screen, but also about political terrorism and the busing crisis and what-have-you. My main beat revolved around the arts. I rode the campaign bus with Ronald Reagan, asking him questions about how his Hollywood past related to his political future. I reported from the sets of *Jaws* and *Taxi Driver.* I had a natural ability to soak up knowledge about movies, probably owed to my upbringing – my mother grew up fascinated by show business – and I also came under the influence of this older group of students, greybeards, when I was a student at the University of Wisconsin.

Many of your lengthiest interviews – in Backstory *and* Tender Comrades *and some in this volume – are obviously transcribed and meticulously edited. What are your editing rules?*

I'm glad you asked! The rules continue to vary and evolve. I learned as a *Globe* journalist not to include every word that someone utters, especially throwaway words. Later, when I worked in Los Angeles as a Senior Editor of *Playgirl,* part of my job was assigning and editing the cover celebrity interviews, although I always like to add that, generally speaking, our "celebrity" was someone on his way up or down in the entertainment field.

I refined what I call my Dolly Parton rule of thumb at *Playgirl.* Dolly says a lot of ums and ahs. Other interview subjects swear liberally. Some interviewers include textual asides like, "May we take a break for a drink of water?" I try to pare the interview down to the essential and the sequential. And if famous people hem and haw, or swear a lot, as a rule of thumb I cut half of it out, so they don't come across as idiots, but I keep half for the flavor. That's the Dolly Parton rule.

I should add that some interview subjects ask to read and vet their transcripts, which almost always causes conflict and stress. Sometimes there are irreconcilable differences. My *Film Comment* editor Stuart Byron took a few incriminating snippets out of the Boston bankers piece in this book because the bankers complained (before publication) that I had told them I was working for the *Boston Globe* but not that I was freelancing the larger text to *Film Comment*. (Byron agreed with the bankers; I did not.) Arthur Laurents insisted I had made up vast portions of my interview with him for *Backstory 3* and would not believe I had simply edited what he had said, even after I had shown him the transcript. He threatened to sue; I ignored him (and we stayed friendly). The strangest request I ever got from a subject was when Oliver Stone's authorized biographer phoned me years after my *Platoon*-era interview, to ask if he could drop a quote into his book but change the meaning of the sentence into the very opposite of what Stone originally said. That was a head-scratcher, and I did scratch my head for a while, but I figured it was Stone's interview – his biography – he is a complicated man – so why not?

I constantly remind myself these extended interviews are a shared experience with the subjects as well as the readers, and I try to honor the subject's concerns when it is a formal Q. and A. (as opposed to an interview conducted for a biography, where it can be more investigative or adversarial). The editing can be laborious but especially with writing professionals most of the time the improvements were priceless. Or put it this way: I should have paid them!

Tell me about this collection.

In 2000 St. Martin's Press issued a collection of my interviews with Golden Age of Hollywood personalities – directors, actors, writers left out, for one reason or another, of the *Backstory* series. It was called *Film Crazy*. This is an informal sequel consisting mostly of interviews with post-Sixties film figures, with some material overlapping my biographies, including interviews with Clint Eastwood, LeRoy Collins, the star of Oscar Micheaux's last picture, and people I caught up with after my *Tender Comrades* book – Clancy Sigal, Anne Edwards, and Peter Davis speaking about his parents, who had been Hollywood Communists. The interviews run the gamut from Oscar-winning to maverick filmmakers, from people in the business end of film to animators and actors. Some of the people I knew for many years before I interviewed them; I went to high school with Barry Alexander Brown, for example, and Bertrand Tavernier was long a close friend, growing closer, before his death in 2021.

Do you have favorite interviews?

They are all favorites, as Robert Altman used to say about his movies, especially those films of his that critics weren't very fond of. I associate the interviews closely with the people, whom I grew friendly with, often, during the interview stages. Even persons you'd think might have much better things to do, like Oliver Stone, phoned me for weeks and months to tinker with the words and get them down on paper in a way that felt good.

I am fondest of the longer interviews, and that is probably why they go on at such length – I let them run on, sometimes, regardless of the relative importance of the subject. Some interviews in the *Backstory* series and in *Tender Comrades* are mini-biographies of people who will never have a biography written about them. The more time you spend with people, the deeper you drill down. The shorter ones are more like snapshots in time.

The ones that will forever bother me are those that didn't work out the way I would have wished. There are people I admire, whom I met, who didn't warm to me in the slightest – George Cukor, for example, or James Baldwin. I was escorted up to Henry Fonda on the set of *Midway* and introduced to him as a correspondent for the *Boston Globe*. I stuck out my hand. Fonda glanced contemptuously at my long hair and Sixties-throwback attire, and sniffed, "He's too young to be working for the *Boston Globe*!" He pushed past. That was a short interview.

I can tell you from experience sometimes if you ask a stupid question it works out just fine because the person you are talking to is an understanding soul. But first you have to wangle your way into the presence of the person, with enough time set aside for the interview, or you don't get the chance to ask stupid questions. After my first book about James Cagney was published, I worked hard over the years to meet him, writing letters to his various addresses, ingratiating myself with his family. I was at William Wellman's house on Cape Cod when Cagney phoned from Martha's Vineyard. When I visited Raoul Walsh in his home in the hills outside Los Angeles, he told me I had just missed Jimmy, who had stopped by the day before. Cagney always wrote back to me, graciously, saying he'd be happy to meet me and be interviewed if the situation could be contrived, but it never happened. So, I can brag that in my time I interviewed John Wayne, Mae West, Katharine Hepburn, Jimmy Stewart, etc., etc., but what I really regret is I never caught up with Cagney.

Patrick McGilligan
Milwaukee, Wisconsin
June 1, 2023

Auteurs of the 1970s and 1980s

Ken Russell

1975
Interview by Patrick McGilligan and Janet Maslin

When this interview was being conducted, Columbia was engaged in a marketing survey that would make it official: *Tommy* would not be the film to secure Ken Russell's reputation with a wide audience after all. Columbia was discovering that the likeliest audience for the picture would be young Who fans, and that if advertising the presence of such Hollywood types as Ann-Margret and Jack Nicholson at the expense of various rock stars in the cast would be a mistake, even mentioning the director's name in the ads would spell disaster.

Russell was, at this stage, still hoping *Tommy* would attract a varied following, and he had no reason yet to suspect trouble – still, he seemed cheerfully resigned. The man whose *The Boyfriend* was recently cut from 140 minutes to 72 minutes for television is accustomed to unexpected disappointments.

Russell points out that, if *Tommy* was great fun to make, it is also one of his sloppier efforts, and deliberately so. The matching mistake that has a brown-eyed child growing up to be blue-eyed Roger Daltrey is especially striking, but throughout the film there are lesser examples of the same thing: curtains that aren't quite sewn together, props that keep changing, glimpses of the leading lady's underwear, even one fleeting shot of the director working a hand-held camera while Elton John sings.

Incidentally, Russell does another brief cameo in the picture, appearing as one of the cripples Tommy promises to (but ultimately cannot) heal. Just why he deemed this sort of role appropriate is anybody's guess.

—◦—

What do you like to do when you are not directing?
Sit on a mountaintop and look at the sun. Yes, and go blind in the eyes. My favorite part of the world is the Lake District where I made *Mahler* and a dozen other films – or bits and pieces of films. It's this sort of great, rejuvenating place. It's a weird, mysterious place that I discovered about eight years ago quite by accident when I was doing some research on a film about Rossetti and the Pre-Raphaelite poets. I happened to read, in my research, that one of the few places he had visited before he died was in the Lake District. I remember going up with my wife in a car in a very off season, March or something. One sort of went through this mountain pass and, suddenly, Shangri-La, the *Lost Horizon* bit. It did seem a very strange place and I began to realize why so many Victorian poets – Wordsworth, Shelley, Keats, Southey, Coleridge and De Quincey – gravitated towards it. It does have a very strange force behind it.

I intend, eventually, to go up there and stay up there and make my own films with a 16mm camera on, say, Wordsworth's "Preludes" – which is about his childhood up there and his mystical feelings about the place.

And never come back?

Well, rarely come back.

What is your routine when in London? Do you see many films?

I never see films if I can possibly help it. I see them for particular reasons – if I hear of an actor and people say, "Well, you're doing a film on so-and-so, so then you should certainly see so-and-so. He's a new actor." Or if I want to satirize something that I hear about – that I'm going to use in another film – like *The Exorcist*, for example, in the Liszt film [*Lisztomania*]. I have a scene where Liszt exorcises Wagner, so I wanted to know what the latest popular conception of exorcism was. So I went to see *The Exorcist*. I saw the tricks and it was pretty obvious how they did them. Hilariously funny, I thought.

I go to films for that reason, or when I'm a captive on a boat. After lunch, there isn't much to do – although I write scripts quite a bit on boats – but if I need a bit of relaxation then I go and see the movies. When I'm actually working in London, one of the last things I want to do when I'm free is to go and sit in the black cinema when I've been in the black studio all day long. Also, I've seen so many films that I don't want to see any more. I've seen enough – whereas I haven't read enough books and I haven't looked at enough sunsets or listened to enough music. I would prefer to do those things as a priority – insofar as they are refreshers and they also help me to make the films I make. Looking at other people's films wouldn't do that at all. I don't want to be influenced by films. I have assimilated all the influences I need to keep me going for the rest of my filmic life.

I've seen a couple of American films by accident. I occasionally go. Everyone kept saying, "*Blazing Saddles, Blazing Saddles* – you must see *Blazing Saddles*," so that was the last time I actually went into a cinema and paid money and sat down and saw. I was very glad I did. On the boat to New York I saw *Mame*, which was better than I thought it was going to be from just hearing the record. Once, when Warner Bros. was in love with me, before they wanted to murder me, they wanted me to direct it. I heard the record and I hated it. It was the antithesis of everything I like. It was despicable. So I was surprised by the film. It was nowhere near as bad as I thought it would be. Then I saw a film that I liked very much called *The Crazy World of Julius Vrooder*. It's about a mental casualty of the war and it all takes place in a mental hospital overlooking the biggest war cemetery one's ever seen. It's a very light anti-war comedy with a very delicate touch. I gather it died the death here – no one seems to have heard of it. That was the best film I've seen in a long time. And I saw a terrible comedy with George C. Scott called *The Bank Shot*. Whew. It's the only film I've fallen off to sleep in in a long, long time. Oh yes, and a quite hilarious film called *The Tamarind Seed*.

Was it intended to be hilarious?

I shouldn't have thought so – not with Omar Sharif and Julie Andrews.

How would you describe your visual aesthetic – the flashy, showy Ken Russell style?

The flashy, showy thing comes from Catholicism. I probably wasn't like that at all until I became a Catholic. Since Catholicism is a very flashy, showy religion, which isn't to say that it isn't devout or sincere or any of those things – but it just is flashy, showy, flamboyant and god-knows-what – I certainly wasn't any of those things until I saw the… film. Film! Until I saw the film! Ha, ha, ha. I mean, until I saw the light. Well, everything's a film – *Jesus Christ Superstar*.

It's a very un-English characteristic, generally speaking, though, of course, there are exceptions. All the films that have impressed me were flamboyant. Eisenstein's films, Fritz Lang's early German expressionist films, early Griffith, *Citizen Kane*, my favorite American film. They were the ones that impressed me the most. It is as if out of kinship towards their way of looking at things. And I suppose, being rather more inspired by music than literature, I can't hear a bit of music without seeing a picture or thinking about one. Since thoughts are pictures, it's inevitable.

—◇—

Where does your love of classical music – and classical composers – derive from?

I suppose it was always there. It came when I was recovering from a slight nervous breakdown after a spell in the Merchant Navy at the end of the war. I just happened to be sitting like a vegetable in an armchair – the radio was on all the time – and, by accident, a piece of classical music came on. I sat up suddenly. I just couldn't believe what I was hearing. I had just never realized that such amazing sounds could be made. It was a simple, old B-flat minor Tchaikovsky piano concerto – the slow movement – which is very beautiful, absolutely sublime. From that moment, I simply rushed out and bought every classical record I could get my hands on. I have done that ever since.

How do you research the lives of the composers you have portrayed in film – such as Mahler?

Whenever you got a record you just looked at the back and thought, "That's interesting." The old program note. I was always curious as to why they wrote that particular piece. From then on, the development is obvious.

By the time I came to do these musical biographies – for instance, with Mahler – I have read his biographies, his wife's letters and everything I could lay my hands on years ago before I ever thought of making the film. Because he interested me. I've been listening to his music for twenty years. So, when the opportunity came for me to make a film, when I felt I was ready – because there are a lot of films that I've put off because I don't feel that I'm ready to do them yet – when it actually came to doing the film, I had obviously been thinking

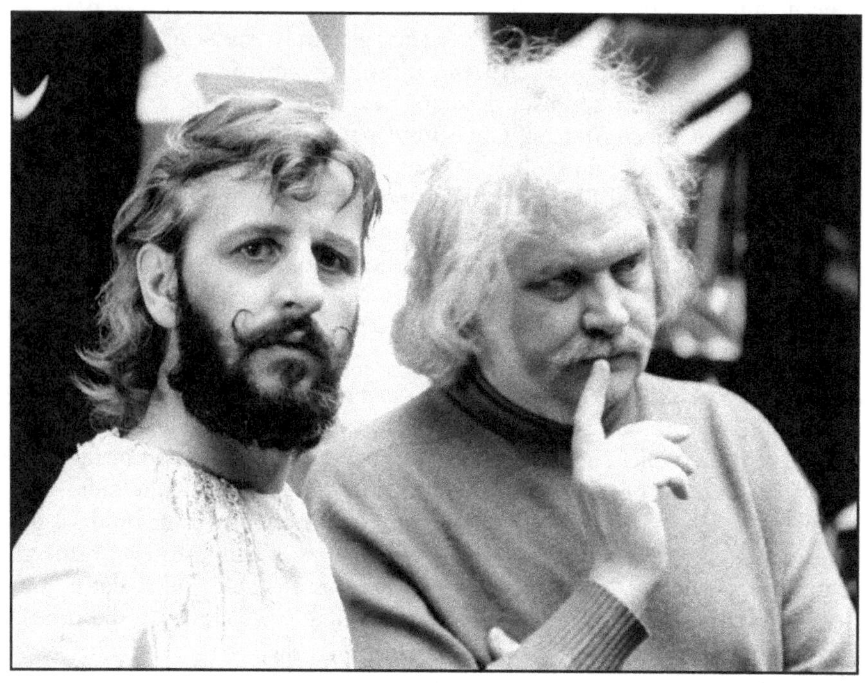

Ringo Starr (playing the Pope) with Ken Russell
on the set of *Lisztomania* in 1975.

about Mahler for twenty years. I just wrote it down, you know? It took a very short time, about three weeks. Given the facts of the man's life, given what he says about the symphonies, given the symphonies themselves and given one's train of thought, that's all one needs. It's sort of like automatic writing. It has to be organized, of course, into a form. I always work with music playing. Or, no matter what I'm doing. I never write far away from the gramophone.

What kind of attention do you give to historical fact?

Well, there are about three or four books on him which more or less repeat the same thing. I met his daughter, Anna, you see, as well – she's still alive. I talked with her a lot about him. And he did say these things were in his symphonies.

When one is doing a film that is one hundred minutes long, it is a question of condensation. The best example that I can give you is that there were about six men interested in his wife before Mahler died, which he knew about. I don't think she had any affairs with them but they came pretty close. She nearly ran off with one of them. The film isn't about that but that's an important part of it. He saw the threat to his marriage in terms of music – as a brutal, tough military march – so I condensed all the lovers, would-be lovers and admirers into one figure, who was the soldier, who represents the military theme. There's a sequence in the film where the love theme comes up and it's disrupted suddenly when this man appears; I just let the music carry on, the military theme comes in, the threat diminishes and the love theme comes back. So that's a good example. I get the facts, think how he handled it in his music, and that usually gives me a key as to how he condensed them in his music and as to how I can condense them into the film.

There is a sequence on the mountain top, where he converts from Judaism to Catholicism. I'm sure he took it with a bit of a pinch of salt, insofar as he thought it was a necessary step in his career as a conductor. He had to convince Cosima Wagner that he was an okay guy, and that's why he did it. It seemed a very cynical move. Since, even in a lot of his religious symphonies – his symphonies about death and so forth – he treats a lot of the things as a joke (I mean, he has scherzos and things, a bit of light comic relief, and he put nature worship before everything else), I treated that conversion in the same sort of way, as almost a joke. I had him jumping through Christian hoops and hammering a Jewish star which he carries into a Wagnerian cross-cum-sword – things like that. It's a lighthearted, almost Charlie Chaplin sort of sequence. It seems to upset some people.

A lot of the film is about his relationship with his wife. I mean, she said, "Oh, I'm just your shadow," and there's a sequence where she is just his shadow, following behind him. I dress her exactly the same as him and put a black stocking over her face; and she's just a vague shadow of herself, ignored by everyone, while the people are all crowding round him.

Mahler was preoccupied with death. She found he was writing some songs one day on the death of children. She was furious. She said, "Why do you tempt providence like that? Why don't you write songs about the life of children, the joy of children?" He says, "Oh no, I've just got to do it." She then throws the music into the lake, and he says, "No, it's still in here," tapping his head. He went on writing, and his youngest child suddenly keeled over and died. These things seemed to happen throughout his life; he was compelled to do things which then happened.

He put a lot of his psychology, a lot of his personal life into his music. When he became jealous of his wife and they were nearly breaking up, she said, "Oh, I'm nothing to you," and he said, "You remember the second subject of the first movement of the Sixth Symphony?" She said, "Yes. I copied it out for you, remember?" He said, "Well, that's you." And it is the most beautiful thing he ever wrote – but it's cut across by a brutal military march. He always associated the threat to love, or the death of love, with a military band. Because, when he was a kid, they lived next door to a barracks. His father was very brutal – beating up his mother and seducing the maidservant – and always, a military band was playing whenever this was going on.

How do you know that?

Well, he said so.

How much of the material is purely subjective – as with Tchaikovsky in The Music Lovers, *things which you simply feel to be true.*

What I've done in *Mahler* is project things into the future a bit, because he was always going on about how no one ever really dies. In a way that's the theme, also, of *Tommy* – a sort of continuing life cycle, spring-summer-autumn-winter, that eternal renewal thing. He was very taken up with Nietzsche's philosophy on that. The fact that he was terrified of death – he kept putting off his Ninth Symphony because he knew that Beethoven had died after his Ninth, and Bruckner died after *his* Ninth – he cheated, and called his Ninth Symphony, "Song of the Earth." But eventually he wrote number nine, which is all about death, and then of course he never finished. So he was right; he did go.

He had a thing about changing his religion, and being afraid of being buried, and then being afraid of being cremated and so forth. He changed his religion just because he had to in Germany at that point, just to get on; the Jews weren't popular even in those days, in 1900. I thought, what if he'd just been a few years later and his music was banned by Hitler? I thought, I wonder what would have happened if he'd tried to change his religion then? It wouldn't have made any difference, he'd have gone to the ovens anyway. So I missed all that, projected all those thoughts about his life, and what happened to musicians like him in the regime that followed – which Cosima Wagner was partly responsible for, because Hitler always said, to understand National Socialist Germany, you must read Wagner's philosophy and listen to his music. All those things subconsciously rose to the surface, and I put them in the film.

Is it significant – to your choice of subjects – that the composers you have portrayed biographically, such as Mahler and Tchaikovsky, are beset by neuroses or some personal disorder?

If they didn't have any neurosis, they wouldn't have written the music. You can't have one without the other. I think most artists have – I wouldn't go as far as to say a neurosis – but they have a different inner life or vision. I've got to like the music. The things that attracted me to Tchaikovsky were the agony of his life that he poured into the Ninth Symphony; I found that very moving, and very revealing. It seemed to tell me more about him, once you've given a clue, than all the biographies you can read put together. Obviously it should, because it's a distillation of his entire experience in forty-five minutes, the culmination of his life, a tortured life.

Symphonies, in particular, seem to be the greatest achievement that man has made in assimilating and putting forth remote human emotions and philosophies in an abstract way. They seem self-consciously, as far as I'm concerned anyway, to open up paths of perception that are denied one in literature. You can read very amazing philosophical books and so forth but, to me, symphonies are almost like inner space science fiction music. It's a trip in the mind. I've never taken drugs, but I imagine it's the same sort of thing; you're in control in a sense, when you're listening to music and, given a clue, you can go on this amazing journey, as it were.

Mahler was interested in things which interest me – like the Third Symphony is an exploration of God through nature. Every moment is what the rocks tell me, what the flowers tell me, what the animals in the forest tell me, what loves me. He also said it could be what God tells me. I'm interested to know what those things did tell him, and so that is why I find his symphonies fascinating. I also find the Sixth Symphony fascinating – which he said was autobiographical. It has the most beautiful theme he ever wrote, but he didn't let on until quite late in life – in fact, he was estranged from his wife by then, and only mentioned it in desperation – that this theme represented her. If he had told her a few years before, it might have helped matters; but he didn't.

His music seems to throw a lot of psychological insight into his own personality, and what moved, affected and shaped his life. I was very fortunate because more so than any other composer, he said what his things hinted, what they were about. It's like this voyage of discovery combined with this sort of detective work to try and solve the mystery behind him. Which one can't do but, at least by exploring, you can throw some light on him.

What is the situation with distribution, in America, of Mahler?

It's been finished over a year, and we did have an American distributor, but...

Ely Landau of the American Film Theatre?

That's the chap, yes. Negotiations went on and eventually came to a close. He came to England and said, "Well, there are just one or two things we'd like to clip out." I said, "Tell me the first one." He said, "There's this conversation of Mahler on the mountain that's in rather bad taste; that would have to go." That's my favorite sequence, it lasts ten minutes and it's the highlight of the movie. So I said, "Don't bother to tell me the rest," and showed him the door.

———o———

How does it feel, then, to have the full backing and spiritual support of a major company like Columbia for Tommy?

Somebody who shall be nameless – some high executive – saw the film and said, "Great, there's only two criticisms I have to make." I said, "Well, what are they?" He said, "There are two yawns in the picture. People in the film actually yawn, and nobody yawns in a Columbia picture."

He also said, "Oh, those black bits you've got on the screen with a few arrows. I appreciate the significance of it but I just wonder about those." I said, "Oh well, of course, that's just a storyboard for how we're going to shoot an optical sequence." I mean, all it was was some black paper with white chalk marks with an arrow pointing to a pinball, to show the direction it was to go. A child would know it was just a guide for the people who were going to shoot the thing, to accompany the music. But *they* thought it was part of the finished product. I don't think they know too much about movies.

Why were you attracted to Tommy?

Again, it's very religious. It's a pilgrim's progress, it's about somebody trying to find answers, it's about masses trying to find answers and the fact that answers are often not to be found in externals, but mostly in internals. It's all to do with "put on your eyeshades, put in your earplugs, put a cork in your mouth, turn inward and play pinball." I mean, that's a very good metaphor, it seems to me. Who wants to do that? Nobody. Very few people, anyway. It's about instant enlightenment, instant answers, an obvious solution, and it's about the exploitation of religion. One of the first straight documentaries I ever made – just cut to music, actually – was about Lourdes. It was the first time I learned to cut films to music, although I sure didn't cut it myself. It was about Lourdes – the pilgrims, the processions, the exploitation; and *Tommy* is about the exploitation of religious ideals, as much as anything else – the way, in this case, that people reject them. Chuck out the baby with the bath water.

Did you hear the Who album when it was originally released?

Yes, it was played to me by some friends of mine who – they knew my interest in visuals with music – said, "You must do this." I played side one and I thought it was rubbish. I couldn't follow the story; I couldn't make head nor tail of it. I was unfamiliar with music of that kind, anyway. Then, a few years later, an album came out which was very badly orchestrated – it had nothing to do with The Who. I hated it, insofar as it was a big symphony orchestra, all bloated, and it sounded more like Leonard Bernstein – at least, though, the numbers were more dramatic. One could follow the story since there was a bit of a synopsis; it became much clearer.

About that time, I was approached by some people to see if I would be interested in doing a script. I met Pete Townshend. Pete showed me all the scripts that had been submitted to him by various promoters over the years, and they were all, without exception, totally horrific. Mostly Julie Andrews-type scripts; some were amazingly awful in that sense. One was set on a pinball table, for some extraordinary reason. They varied from that sort of pseudo-science fiction thing to the Julie Andrews musicals. All the scripts were rubbish; they didn't seem to be what Pete seemed to be about.

I assimilated everything he'd written about the pieces. I wrote a little treatment in which I put forth the ideas I thought he was on about, and then we discussed that, made slight changes – very slight – and then I wrote the script, pointing out various gaps in the storyline which I thought needed opening out and amplifying and explaining, which he hadn't bothered about in the original.

What changes did you make to Townshend's original score?

We both said from the start we didn't want to use any dialogue. So that was that. I wrote the script with the songs where the dialogue would be and the action written against the verse of the songs.

How did you actually shoot the movie without dialogue?

We wrote the script and, naturally, I knew the words for the songs. Occasionally, I said, "Could you alter one line here or so?" – you know, to give a bit of emphasis to something – and he'd say, "Yeah." He'd written the new songs, given me the words for them and so, basically, I had a whole lot of songs.

I told him where I thought there should be instrumental things to accompany visuals to link those sequences, and then we simply went into a recording studio for three months and recorded it, totally out of context. This person would be available, and then Ann-Margret would be flown over and she'd do all her songs. Because we had worked out exactly the way the story should go, I could say to Ann-Margret, "Sing this song yawning, because you are going to be bored with Tommy's problem by this time. Years have gone by, or you've just had a breakdown; put this marshmallow in your mouth and sing with that. Or put a cigarette in your mouth and sing yawning because you're not interested." So it went on like that. Everyone we talked to we filled in, and if they hadn't seen the script, at least they knew where they stood in context to that whole particular sequence.

So we had it dramatically sorted out before we actually got onto the floor; then it was just a question of doing it to playback, and knowing you had to get a certain sequence over by x number of lines. Which was a very good exercise, insofar as it made one very concise. You had to make sure the visuals didn't over-run the music and it stretched your imagination. The impact was greater because it was much more concise and stated in a much shorter time than one would naturally do.

Did you have any trouble working with the musicians?

Only insofar as I was naïve enough at the very start, when we were doing the pre-recording, to suggest to Pete Townshend, "When are we starting? Eight o'clock in the morning, nine?" He said, "I think you should start it a little later." I said, "Ten o'clock?" He said, "Just a wee bit later than that." I said, "Two o'clock in the afternoon then." He said, "Well, if you think so, all right." Of course, I was in the studio at two o'clock, and he came in about five o'clock, knowing nobody would be there, and then we sat there until midnight. Then they started coming in. Well, that's when I got the message that they work a different time scale to filmmakers. Once I got over that hurdle, it was okay.

The last I heard, you had no interest in rock music.

I still haven't. What I've heard doesn't do anything for me. But the fact that *Tommy* is written in a rock idiom is, so far as I'm concerned, beside the point. It's a good piece of music and it's a very good opera. I don't care what style it's in. I mean, in the Twenties, Kurt Weill could write symphonies that sounded like Richard Strauss, but when he came to do his operas they sounded like German jazz. He was just a good musician. Well, Townshend's been brought up with a rock background and has got a rock following. But *Tommy*, at least the film version, will reach those people, and I hope will reach millions more people, who've never dreamed of hearing rock.

How did you cast the film if you are so unfamiliar with rock music?

A lot of names were suggested, as I am not familiar with rock at all. A lot of the people I had never heard of at all. Somebody would be suggested, and one would hear their records and so forth.

I'd never heard of Eric Clapton or Elton John, for example, but I thought any performer who's good at all could play the cameos if it's up their street, as it were.

I do know we needed good actors to play Tommy (Roger Daltrey), his father (Robert Powell), and his mother (Ann-Margret). The mother had to do more singing than anyone else and most people in the film put together. Someone said, "Well, what about Ann-Margret?" I remembered her from the days of *Bye Bye Birdie* and the Elvis things and I said, "Look, she can't act, can she?" They said, "Go and see *Carnal Knowledge*." So I saw it and thought, "Couldn't be better, really super." And she is, I think, very good in the film.

What kind of an effect do you hope to have, with the kind of extravagant visuals you employ in Tommy *and your other films?*

An effect that is going to illuminate music. If we are talking about music – or an effect that is going to illuminate the idea in the fastest possible way, in the most dramatic way, and in the most emotional way – with the most impact, because I like instant exposure to an idea. It doesn't give one time to put up the metal grille of censorship in the mind. The thing about reading – the thing about Aldous Huxley's *The Devils* – is that you can censor it as you go along. By the time you've translated the words into pictures – because one's brain obviously can't be open to horror all the time – there's this censorship thing that seems to operate, and it's transmitted into an acceptable picture. Whereas the thing I like about visual things is that before you get time for the defenses to go up, it's hit the brain; and you have to react simply as you would. There's no time for a sort of wall to go up, and I think that's what I like about it.

Is your wife [costume designer] Shirley Russell an influence on your filmmaking?

Yes. She always reads the script, for example. The first script I wrote for *Lisztomania*, she said, "Rubbish!" and threw it away. I thought it was a masterpiece but then I started number two immediately because I have to work with her and live with her and she's usually right. She said, "Um, getting better." The one I finally ended up with, she said, "Huh, it's alright," so that's good.

We also talk about the effect we want to get over and the best way to achieve it visually. Because we met at the same art school – although she is a dress designer, she actually went through the painting and sculpting bit – I discuss things with her. For instance, there is a sequence with Liszt in hell which I discussed with her, and for which she is going to do the storyboard. Some of Liszt's music sounds like old silent film piano music, rather hearts and flowers, and we're doing a sort of Charlie Chaplin *Gold Rush* sequence. That's just to one of his piano pieces and I've worked closely together with her on that; she suggests things, we mark it in. Yes, she's very crucial to the construction of the whole thing, to the look and feel of the whole thing.

—o—

I wanted to ask you about this week of interviews that you've given in New York City. The press has always been fairly hostile to you; what sorts of questions have you been asked, and what is your impression of their attitude?

Well, they always start off with, "Now, you're called a controversial director…" You can fit in the rest from there, I think.

A lot of people, when they met me, I was told they were going to be cowering in corners and absolutely terrified of facing up to the ogre who was going to come rushing in and probably pummel them to pulp. Most of them said, "Gosh, you look like Santa Claus…" I've got this beard now, and a very benign expression, and I usually have a coat slung over my back, which they think is a sack full of presents. They see the dandruff on my shoulders and they think it's snow. Santa Claus is the new image, but they'll probably still be saying, "I survived the ogre."

I understand you had a bit of trouble on the Tomorrow *show with host Tom Snyder.*

Oh, if I'd have known what he was up to, how boring and dead, what a piece of plastic surgery was sitting in the chair, well, I either wouldn't have done it, or I would have approached it in a different way. That was the first thing he said: "Now, you're controversial…" He'd never seen any of my films – he had no intention of seeing then, didn't really want to. As far as he was concerned, I was just somebody sitting in a fur coat, talking. I think he was an idiot.

Ralph Bakshi

1977

Interview by Patrick McGilligan

Once he was the much-cussed, much-discussed bad boy of animation, today he is practically respectable. The grosses for a squeaky-clean *Wizards* were high, for his epic version of *The Lord of the Rings* they were higher. Could it happen to a nicer guy?

I telephoned Ralph Bakshi one hot summer day in 1977 when he was still working on *The Lord of the Rings* and requested an interview; without hesitation, he invited me over to his high-rise quarters on Sunset Boulevard in Los Angeles for the first of several scattershot bull sessions. Work was not interrupted – we borrowed at times from the end of the day and during lunch hours; with obvious pride, Bakshi escorted me through his artists' chambers, pointing out Hobbit sketches in various stages of completion. He was charming, talkative, infinitely distracted, whimsical, and obsessed. His grin was sloppy and disarming, his trousers faded. We talked for hours at a throw. He would chain-smoke nervously, gaze out the window absent-mindedly. Once, as we talked, I noticed a paperback at his elbow: Ishmael Reed's *Mumbo-Jumbo*. Somehow it was the perfect match-up. Like Reed, Bakshi is driven by the images of his hell-born youth – the knotted visions of guilt, terror, alienation, paranoia, controlled fury, and innocent misogyny. Like Reed, also, Bakshi is a vivid, unmistakable stylist, a maverick, and a loner, whose collected body of work, already at this early juncture, marks him, at least in this country, as one of the foremost feature animators of his generation.

How did you get into animation?

I was a cartoonist because I went to an art school in New York and took a cartooning course. Well, when I graduated from the High School of Art & Design, Terrytoons offered the top student in art a job based on his portfolio. I had no background or knowledge of film. I wasn't a film buff. My thing was to be a comic-strip artist. But I had to earn a living, and that was in animation, and I haven't left animation since.

Were you trained at all in animation?

No, animation comes very naturally. I find animation excruciatingly easy, as compared to, say, illustration or painting. On the other hand, I'm not sure whether it's animation that comes easy to me, or filmmaking.

What kind of cartoons did you draw as a kid in the Fifties?

Garbage. Basically, I was trying to be ultracommercial. My stuff wasn't anything too different from what was being bought at the time. *Li'l Abner* was still pretty big when I was young, as was *Beetle Bailey. B.C.* had just arrived. *Hi and Lois, Buz Sawyer, Prince Valiant.* The standard run-of-the-mill stuff. That was what I grew up with, that I was trying to feed off of, that I was dying from. I didn't even have the background of the forties pulp situation. I started cartooning late.

When you first started working for Terrytoons, it had an extremely poor reputation in the industry.

The worst. The end of the line. But I spent ten years there and finally ended up running the place. A lot of it has to do with my insecurity, and a lot has to do with it being the best job I could ever get in my life, coming out of Brownsville. Understand, I was making two or three grand a week as a 23-year-old kid. I was rolling in women and money.

When I came there, a very talented man named Gene Dietch was running the place. But Dietch was up against it. He just didn't have the right people up front, for the creative work. Animation at that point was trying to lean toward very hip ideas and abstract designs. You have to remember that the action artists were very big in the Fifties, all this abstract and way-out stuff. Jackson Pollock, you know, with his swirls. So cartoons were changing styles to what we call modern design. Guys kept thinking about the way the backgrounds looked and the shape of the characters. But the content did not change at all. Or the approach. It was like a quest ending with nothing. The nothing being the mentality of still dealing with children.

I sat down one day and said very clearly to myself that even if I created the greatest animated short in the world it would be just that and nothing more. And that was already done, as far as I was concerned, by Bugs Bunny, Porky Pig. I said to myself, what am I doing? The heck with Mighty Mouse and Tom Terrific.

The problem had nothing to do with design. It had to do with being honest on the screen. That's it. And honesty on the screen meant whatever I really felt should be put on the screen. With no holds barred.

When we got into story meetings, I would ask writers what they knew about the characters they were portraying. Who is this crow that's dropping a coconut on this elephant's head? I wasn't angry about it. I was really confused. I said, what does the elephant have to do with any of our lives?

As for style, you say you were a reactionary, in the sense that you were always –

Looking backwards.

Away from –

The style of the day. Did I tell you what looking backwards means to me? It's important. There was a period of art in this country before money was king. We're talking about the Golden Age of illustration, from 1890 – 1904. We're talking about guys like N.C. Wyeth and [Howard] Pyle and

English illustrators also, like Arthur Rackham and [Edmund] Dulac, artists who portrayed honestly what they were feeling to produce little masterpieces of art. I'm talking about the Ashcan School of artists, like John Sloan and Reginald Marsh, guys with a far more individual approach.

This was the stuff I just drifted to naturally. I went into the story department at Terrytoons, and on the floor were all these first-edition illustrations, bought over the years, lying with broken bindings and coffee stains. The stuff was so mistreated that I asked if I could take it home. Because I loved the stuff, and they did not care for it.

I picked up the largest collection of illustrated children's books in the history of the world, I'm sure; I had to have a truck pick them up from the studio. And these are the books that taught me about animation and where I had to go.

Did you create any substantial characters in your years at Terrytoons?

I made a thing for CBS [television] called *The Mighty Heroes*, you know, super-hero stuff. There was a character called Sad Cat, which I created. There were also two mean brothers. And there was a latent homosexual that I did but couldn't show.

What about when you moved to Paramount, after eight months as head of Terrytoons?

That was my big break. They gave me a title of producer-director, and I ran the studio myself, without television on my back or anything. Yet what happened there was the same as at Terrytoons. The excitement of totally running my own place and of creating new ideas was there. But the ideas had to fall into the same format: good children's cartoons. So I threw up my hands and quit after six months.

What did you do there within that six-month period?

I was trying to get close to *Mad* comics. I was trying to make the stuff adult. I was trying to do that kind of wacky humor, which was a little bitter. But it was the same characters and the same corny voices doing the same corny sounds.

I did try one thing which was interesting, *Mini-Squirts*, a bunch of kids trying to act like adults. Now had I been able to carry the material far enough, it would have stood a chance. But it just turned out cute, very cute.

What were the big Paramount cartoons at the time?

Casper, Little Audrey. But every studio was trying to create the new wave, and nobody was creating it. In short, everything had been said, goddammit.

—◇—

How did you make the leap to Fritz the Cat *in 1972? It seems like an entirely different consciousness.*

It wasn't. You've got to back up. You have to understand, this is the thing

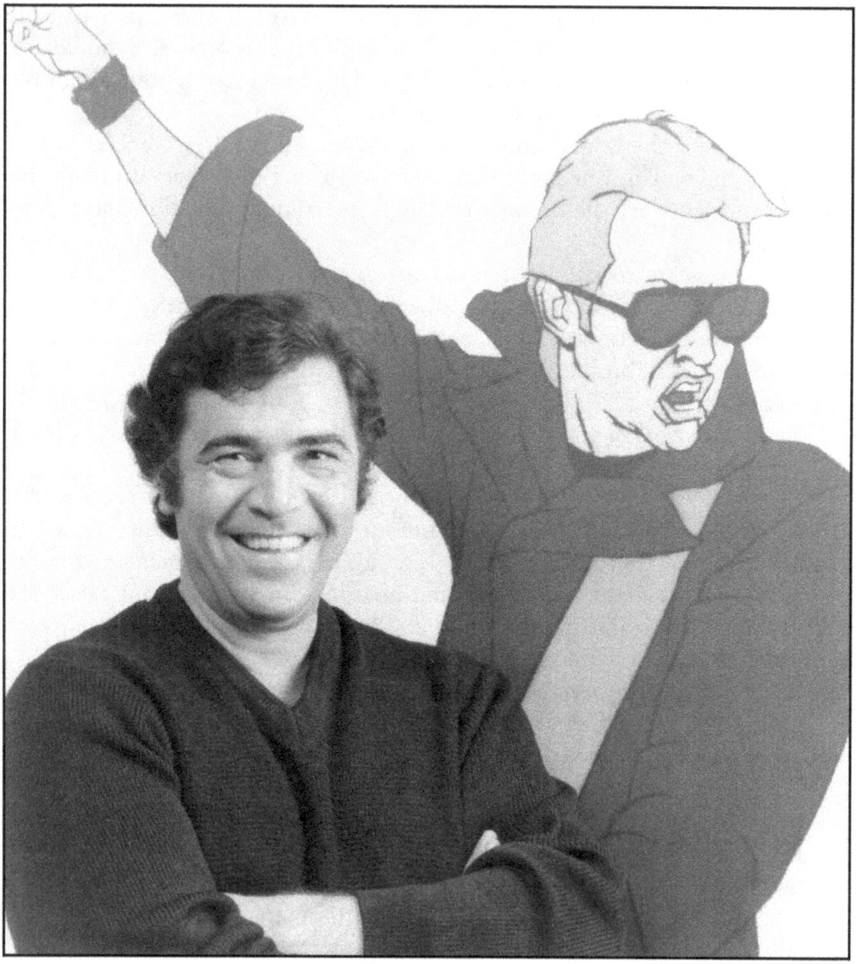

Ralph Bakshi, in 1981, in a publicity shot
for his film *American Pop*.

I wanted to do. I left Paramount in 1969 because I wanted to do cartoons for adults. Now *Fritz* only came about because I loved it: one. But two: it was the tradition of motion pictures to find the book that sold. (I really had *Heavy Traffic* already under my arm, but it had all brand-new characters.) Plus, *Fritz* was a great transitional picture for me. Understand, I was dealing with animals in *Fritz*, which I was familiar with, right?

Had you read R. Crumb's Fritz the Cat?

Oh, I was reading it. I was a fan of all the underground comics at that point. I would say the underground comics pried me loose. Because I got so furious with myself. If they could do it in their medium, why couldn't we do it in ours? What was worse, these guys were younger than me. [Laughs]

Who put up the money?

Warner Bros. put in a little, and then Farley's Cinemation. A lot of private investors. Then we made the film for $700,000. Complete.

How much production was done on the East Coast?

Twenty-five percent. After a few months I realized there weren't enough animators. So I moved it to the West Coast. It was incredible. It was crazy. I mean, to move a whole movie and meet total strangers was nearly a disaster for me.

How did you obtain the rights?

Well, I haven't got the rights to *Fritz the Cat*. I had nothing to do with the business end. That was all taken care of by my partner in the thing. I had nothing to do with the contract on any level, including my own.

Did you meet R. Crumb?

Once. We had a falling out.

At the first meeting?

No, the falling out was when he saw the movie. He didn't like it. The first meeting, I told him I wanted to do it. He said yes. Deep into the film, he decided against it. But the contract was signed, and hundreds of thousands of dollars were spent, and the film *had* to proceed legally. But that's very bitter for me, and I would really like to avoid going into it.

It sounds as though a brick fell on your head.

Yeah, it was like that. My anxiety and anxiousness to do the film propelled me on. I did nothing more than go into a room at nine o'clock in the morning and leave at twelve at night, trying to do this movie for $700,000, and for a year and a half. I have ill feelings about it because I got caught in the middle. I don't know if Crumb believes that totally, but that is the case.

How did the studio react to the picture?

Warner Bros. threw the picture out. The first thing I showed them was the "Big Bertha" sequence, freaky stuff. Cinemation, the distributor that picked it up, was doing this X-rated stuff anyhow. They thought it was the greatest thing in the world. They wanted to see sex in every scene.

The bad publicity helped the box-office?

There's no question about it. It made the distinction between this film and anything Disney ever did. Even the X rating helped, which I fought against vehemently. It deserves [to be taken] off.

How did you approach sex in making Fritz?

I had never done anything like *Fritz*. I had a fifteen-year history of doing just the opposite. How much sex? I didn't know. It was like being the Wright Brothers.

There was a massive fight over another matter: Fritz is going over the bridge in a car; Duck, the black crow, actually *turns* into a crow and flies out of his car, plucking Fritz to safety. I argued, "This is wrong. We're not doing crows." Otherwise, I was back with the format where a character can defy gravity.

How much of the animation were you controlling at this point?

Every scene. Everything. I storyboarded the entire *Fritz the Cat* movie and the entire *Heavy Traffic*. The animators and everyone came to me; all the work was handed out from me. I had total control, except for the dollars.

I think if I have made any major change in animation, it's that I'm directing as a live-action filmmaker would because of low budgets and a small crew. Animated films had been done by two hundred separate people, each with a little piece. Everything was basically a committee choice. The producer was king. That's where Disney got his reputation, and that's where Max Fleischer got his reputation. But starting with *Fritz*, every color, every cut, every determination had to be mine.

How do you write a script?

In outline form. It's not broken down into dialogue unless the dialogue starts to flow. It's almost a poem approach.

It churns for a long period of time and then comes out. My wife tells me this because I say, "God, this went quick." And she says, "Who are you kidding? You've been thinking about it for three years already." What I don't do is polishing. Maybe I'm afraid to look at it, but I don't sit down and go over it. I think that's a major fault of mine. The area I'm concentrating most on now is story. Decent dollars will deliver decent animation, but story is the key.

What happened to you after Fritz *was released?*

Fritz went boom.

All of a sudden, you found yourself king of the world.

Not king of a world I understood. All of this and all of that and Cannes Film Festival and Europe for the first time in my life, and the whole Hollywood hype descended on my head. Then they wanted another *Fritz* from me, another animal film, and my big fight was to do *Heavy Traffic*. I wanted to do what I wanted to do, which is human animation. So I wrote *Heavy Traffic* and, finally, because I didn't do anything else, I sold it.

—◦—

What was your idea behind doing Heavy Traffic?

To make a more personal film than *Fritz*. It had to do with my background, my life, the things which I observed directly. I tried to make a film instead of a cartoon. *Traffic* is closer to film. *Wizards* is a cartoon. *Fritz* will always be a cartoon. *Coonskin* is a film. The thing with *Heavy Traffic* was to make the transition to film. That was the intent.

Were your experiences as bleak and nasty as Heavy Traffic *suggested?*

One doesn't have to be involved directly. If one grows up in an environment, if the environment totally passes him by physically, he is affected by it mentally. I'm not saying that [the character] Ida was my mother or [the character] Angie was my father, but I'm telling you that if they weren't, they were living next door to me. Some other kid had an Ida and an Angie. And there were more Idas and Angies, they were all people I knew. That makes it autobiographical. So I'm saying this is the total effect of growing up in Brownsville, on the screen in *Heavy Traffic*. That's what I was after.

Whatever possessed you to "tackle" Coonskin?

Well, the word tackle is wrong. If you saw *Fritz* and you saw *Traffic*, you'd know it was an obvious extension. Fritz examined the Sixties in a certain way, college and revolutionary types. *Traffic* examined a personal boyhood experience. And *Coonskin* was examining the black experience, examining the Superfly type.

My approach to all three movies was total honesty. These were my observations, my knowledge, right? I didn't have to research black men. I grew up with them.

Did you have any sense of the impending controversy?

No, making this film was the most joyous. You have to understand, the film opened up Bakshi Productions. It also almost closed down Bakshi Productions. But even when the film opened up, it was only attacked by one group.

Whether they were right or wrong in what they wanted, I don't know, because I don't know what it was. But I am opposed to that sort of censorship. I think that's what we're talking about: censorship. I'll argue forever whether *Coonskin* is anti-black. But the line of attack at the Museum of Modern Art was that it would never be shown anywhere in the world, and "we're going to see to that."

This was a group from CORE [Congress of Racial Equality]? What did they say?

Oh, you know, "It's racist." "You can't draw big lips." Mind you, I'd done all this in previous films, too. And, of course, the cliché: "Where does a white director come off doing black characters in cartoons?"

This was the first public screening?

The Museum had seen the film and loved it, a breakthrough in animation. They set up a very special night to screen it for film people. They invited me. I brought the film over. It was the first screening in public. And it was quite surprising – I would have thought any group would have waited until they'd seen the film. But it was attacked almost from the titles.

The room was filled, although there weren't many protesters from CORE there, eight or nine. Screaming, "You can't watch this film!" People pulling people out of their seats. It was that kind of night. The audience was very frightened. They were being attacked verbally throughout the movie. People kept running up and down the aisles in pitch blackness. It was very strange. Very surrealistic.

I was angry. When the lights came on at the end, I was supposed to speak. So I walked down the aisle to talk to the audience. I wasn't going to be chased out. We had a whole battle up there. A lot of pushing and shoving. It was very ugly. Then I went back to Hollywood.

What happened from that point on?

Coonskin was just dropped by Paramount, given to a small distributor over whom I had no jurisdiction, and the distributor went bankrupt in two weeks after the film was released.

It sounds like a crushing experience.

It would have to be. I had a lot of good things to say about how poorly we treat black people. And how poorly some black people treat black people. And it was a good movie. One I love dearly. And one that will remain one of my favorites, not because of the controversy, but because it is a very well-made movie that looks at who really controls the ghettos and why.

How did Coonskin *affect Bakshi Productions?*

Very strongly. I had trained for the project, for the first time in Hollywood, nine black animators off the streets of the ghetto, which I thought was pretty sensational. They left, out of embarrassment and confusion.

The energy of the studio diminished slightly. There was confusion, a lot of anger. A lot of guys had worked very hard on the film. Then the film did zero business, and we had to start from scratch again. It was just a time of, what went wrong?

What was the genesis of your next film, Hey, Good Lookin'? *And why has it never been released?*

It was one of the repercussions of *Coonskin*. Meaning that it was also an exploratory film on the Fifties, on the whole black, leather-jacket gang situation, which was very "big" when I was growing up. It basically dealt with a black teenage gang and a white counterpart. And, obviously, I had to animate some black characters in the film. Is it obvious to you what the problem was?

Not that I had even finished it. I had set the finish with the crew for three or four months away, practically a wrap-up for us. But it kind of cooled at that point. Nobody *told* me they weren't going to release it. Obviously, there was a decision made as to whether a *Coonskin* was going to happen all over again.

I really don't want to discuss it because, at this point, everybody assures me that it is a much superior film to *Coonskin*. We are finishing it. It will be released.

Let's go on to Wizards.

Great. *Wizards* was an attempt for me to cool it. There is a lot of personal pain in doing a *Traffic* or *Coonskin* which I can't explain. They don't come easy. So *Wizards* was an attempt by me to have some fun, meaning to practice the art of animation, do my first PG, let the audiences, too, cool down a little. This is after *Coonskin*, after all.

It was my easiest film. There were no directorial problems, no points I had to clear up in my head. "What do you mean by that, Ralph?" Nothing. And that's how it ended up. Nice. Pretty good. Made a lot of money.

Was Wizards *a dress rehearsal for* The Lord of the Rings, *which came along in 1978?*

You can call it that, but that isn't why I did it. It's a dress rehearsal because I went through some minor fantasy; and, sure, it's going to help *Lord of the Rings*. But *Wizards* compared to *Rings* is like a comic book compared to a great illustration. There's a big gap between the movies.

What's the history of your involvement with Lord of the Rings?

I had wanted to do it since 1956. I kept bothering the motion picture company that owned the rights. As the years rolled on, twenty years, my stature grew, I guess. And the project had fallen apart for them. So on my two hundredth try with the same motion picture company, they said yes.

Now *Rings* is a two-hour epic with a huge cast of characters. This is the most complex animated story ever attempted and for me, it is a matter of how I can increase the art of animation visually, and how I can surpass anything I've ever done.

The first thing I said to myself was: Get a producer who understands this, get a writer, and let's build a team to do it. Well, I got involved with Saul Zaentz, who produced *One Flew Over the Cuckoo's Nest*. And we brought in Peter S. Beagle, who wrote *The Last Unicorn*, and this guy called Chris Conkling, who has never written anything before but who is quite talented.

We're not doing *The Hobbit*, incidentally. *The Hobbit* is a joy, but the *Rings* are what it's all about. Also, we are dividing it into two pictures, a book-and-a-half per picture. We'll finish the first and look at it. And then, depending on what we see, we'll decide how the second one should be approached, if at all.

What will it look like?

It's going to be like nothing you've ever seen. I'm attempting, for the first time, a totally realistic animated film, not only in content but in style. What is a realistic painter as opposed to a cartoonist? Michelangelo and Rembrandt drew real muscles in the right proportions with real painted backgrounds, right? That's the intent of the movie.

I often wonder why your ideas are comparatively different from anything else that's ever been attempted in animation.

I've thought about it. Let me tell you something that is probably totally wrong. There has never been a man who has run an animation studio and who has a background like me. What does that mean? Did Walter Lantz live in Brownsville? *There* has to lie the answer.

—◦—

Could we talk a bit about your background?

It embarrasses me: the poor boy, tough kid of the streets who makes it big. Embarrassing. It's like a B movie. I'll try to give you a visual picture. Immigrants living on the streets. Poor, hustling, trying to maintain some sense of sanity. Their children become gangsters, in the true sense of the word: sinister and powerful men in the neighborhood.

You are talking about very tough, angry black kids in gangs. You are talking about absolute poverty. You are talking about a total ghetto mixed-ethnic-groups situation where you played in the streets and lived in the streets and died in the streets. You are talking about a school system that was just there, basically, to keep you in your seat. Not to teach you anything, because most of the teachers were wrestling with six-foot giants, who they had to subdue with rubber hoses. And this is my school experience. On the other hand, you are talking about a certain sense of freedom and spirit that, I think, was good too. You are talking about a boy's American dream of trying to make it one way or another. You are talking about flashy cars and flashy girls. The sexual approach was always the James Dean approach. Tough, slick, cool.

It sounds like an angry life.

Yeah, I lived very angry without realizing it at the time. My total experience was anger, over which I've probably mellowed a little, I have to tell you. And the films probably helped me.

Did you yourself experience the violence?

It's a small example but it's interesting. Obviously, you can't afford cars in Brownsville. The young kids can't, okay? Three o'clock in the middle of some dark ghetto street, right? These buildings after buildings after buildings.

Like, you drop your girlfriend off on a stoop and you walk home, right? Well, you were liable to walk into anything. A twenty-block walk home on a cold winter night – it's a gauntlet. Just walking in the neighborhood at night is a totally fearful experience, whether someone drags you into the hallway and puts a knife to your throat; or whether some woman walks by and asks you up to her apartment – and what the hell does she *really* want? On and on. Well, do that over an eighteen-year period. I'm not just talking about the walk. I'm talking about all the tributaries of that kind of existence.

What was your lifestyle like, later, in the Fifties? Were you a beatnik?

No, no, I can't say I was anything at all. That includes the Sixties as well as the Fifties. I observed everything. I never became part of anything.

Have drugs influenced your animating?

No, I've never taken anything more than an occasional what we call a reefer. [Laughs] And that was before the drug thing. Back in '53 or '55. But I have no connection with drugs whatsoever. I'm even afraid to take any aspirin when I get sick. I'm totally opposed to dropping pills of any nature. I wish I could learn to take tranquilizers.

So many characters in your films are "high."

Because that's what I observe. Everyone is either high or losing his mind. Cocaine, for example, is running rampant in Hollywood. It's lunacy. Drugs are as much part of our culture now as anything. I can't avoid that part of it.

It's amazing that you are so tuned in to the consciousness of the Sixties without considering yourself part of it.

That's interesting. Other people have said the same thing. But I think one cannot observe the truth when he is enmeshed in the situation. Being a hippie, for lack of a better word, doesn't allow one to see everything that's really coming down. Or being black. It's being separated and not being part of the group, it's the one who lays back and just observes everyone's ideology. In the Sixties I knew who the phony revolutionaries were and who weren't, and a lot of very intelligent friends of mine, involved tooth and nail, could not or would not see beyond the last speech they heard. I don't know why, but I feel that I'm able to observe even the smallest thing, because I am apart from what's happening.

You describe yourself almost voyeuristically.

Yeah, but again, it all ties in. If you are talking about walking down that street alone, you are talking about that attitude carried over into other things. Not the fear – the way of life. Now you may be walking on the outskirts of a bohemian situation. Or you are walking on the outskirts of a drug culture. It gives you a better perspective than being caught in the middle of it, I suppose. Although I could be wrong.

Peter Weir

1986

Interview by Patrick McGilligan

Subsequent to my meeting with Australian-born and bred director Peter Weir, I had the odd experience of being asked, within twenty-four hours, the nearly identical question about him by six, seven, eight people. Was he as searching, as spiritual, as mystical as his films? Well, he seems down-to-earth, practical and rational, and he winces at references to "mystical" or "magical" qualities in his work.

His films, however, include *The Cars That Ate Paris* (his low-budget, first feature), *Picnic at Hanging Rock* (his first U.S. release, an evocative allegory about British schoolgirls who, on an innocent outing, answer the siren-call of the unknown), *The Last Wave* (his foray into apocalyptic dreams and the Aboriginal subculture of urban Australia), *The Plumber* (real Brian De Palma terrain, a psycho-sexual suspenser made for Australian TV), *Gallipoli* (Aussie conscripts sacrificed by British indifference during WWI), *The Year of Living Dangerously* (the power of myth in rebellion-torn Indonesia), *Witness* (B-movie with cop-on-the-run Harrison Ford finding virtue in the arms of Kelly McGillis and the Pennsylvania Amish), and now the adaptation of Paul Theroux's novel, *The Mosquito Coast*.

Weir does not pretend to enjoy interviews, and he does not consent to do many of them. He prefers not to say anything about himself at all. When pressed, he squirms, equivocates, and replies – but with qualifications. His ultimate goal as a "commercial" director is to have his signature become more "invisible." Is Howard Hawks an ideal? Sorry, says Weir, he is not familiar with the films of Hawks. Pressed further, he rather reluctantly says, "Jean Renoir." It begins to make sense.

Of the pack of stylish directors to emerge from the Australian cinema in the Seventies, Weir has managed to "go Hollywood" yet maintain an equilibrium between commercial and artistic demands. His films still course with subcurrents of emotion and psychology. He is drawn to people losing and finding themselves in exotic cultures, to stories of the human spirit transcendent over villainy, politics, and broken relationships. As a "colonized" descendant, Weir seems haunted and propelled all the more, therefore, into these various international contexts. Each motion picture is very different from the preceding one, and yet there are manifest links in their material and accents. Even Weir's camera has rhapsodic moments when it seems to take on a life of its own, floating above and circling round, as if infinitely wise.

His *Gallipoli* was neither as trenchant nor as angry as Bruce Beresford's *Breaker Morant,* yet it is equally involving. Weir lacks Fred Schepisi's piercing iconoclasm à la *Barbarosa* or *Iceman*. Weir seems himself as a Romantic, in the 19th-century meaning of the word. His films do not have vitriol or sting; instead, they convey great muted feeling and passion. They are not likely to inflict pain, but count on them for strange foreboding and mesmerizing pleasure.

Weir sees his limitations in the area of story craft, and he may be right. There are holes in *The Year of Living Dangerously* and *Witness* that spoil the near mastery. That is one reason he has shifted from the realm of the senses and hunkered down to storytelling. Admirably, he can take on big, old-fashioned love stories set against backdrops of revolution and criminal intrigue and still remain true to his instincts.

Theroux's novel *The Mosquito Coast* is a nigh-mystical tale of an American hybrid of Don Quixote and Robinson Crusoe run amok in a remote jungle territory. It is a perverse, hypnotic adventure that beguiles with its charm and lyricism, and then bedevils with its descent-into-Hell third act. Interestingly, Paul Schrader's and Weir's script softens some of the uglier aspects. Gone, for instance, is Theroux's final image of a vulture gulping down the hero's tongue. But Weir (who often writes his own films) has worked more compassion into the script, giving Allie Fox (Harrison Ford) a more rounded character.

I met Weir in Los Angeles, working on the scoring of the film with composer Maurice Jarre. After an Australian career spent in television, documentaries, and short films, Weir is now one of Hollywood's most admired young directors, though he still resides with his family in Sydney. There are glimpses of influences – Freud, Jung, even Scrooge McDuck – in his work that he has picked up, absorbed, and submerged along the way. Some he prefers to eschew, but though Weir would protest, it's all there in his films – unmistakable and difficult to unravel.

We talked in the shaded patio of his suite in the Bel Air Hotel, a watering hole of nouveau Hollywood, miles from the studios and the L.A. tangle. Weir could easily be one of his own leading men – a slighter, more cerebral Mel Gibson or Harrison Ford – boyish and handsome, determinedly low-key, reticent, and casual. If he were to film our brief encounter, the camera would probably not hover on him. No doubt it would creep in on the plastic, gaping beast behind us spewing water into a small fountain.

—◦—

Tell me about growing up in Australia, and how you were influenced by movies.

It was a postwar baby boom experience fairly similar to that of kids anywhere in the Western world, in the sense that the big excitement was to earn enough pocket money, or to be treated by your parents to the Saturday afternoon movies. First, my father used to take me, then I went with the kids from the street. I rarely missed a Saturday, so I grew up with American film culture.

Because the Australian film industry was in eclipse at that point?

That's right – with the exception of the Australian newsreel, and the work of Charles Chauvel and Ken G. Hall. Of course, it was mainly Western serials. It was interesting to see [George] Lucas and [Steven] Spielberg, in various films, revive that memory.

Were movies the dominant aspect of your youth?

No. It was just part of the fabric of life, as much as the beach and swimming. I grew up in a very middle-class neighborhood near the sea in Sydney harbor. It was the pre-television era, when the street was your life, and there were always other kids in the street to play with.

A lot of people grew up with matinee serials, but not every filmmaker chooses to escape into that sort of fantasy and, in a sense, back into boyhood.

It's a very rich line; perhaps it's nearly exhausted. Certainly, it is in the hands of lesser talents. Comics were the other factor in my upbringing, rather interestingly, without making too much of it. I don't know if there is an equivalent today, but you collected comics, you swapped and sold them. Perhaps it was just a craze, but it seemed to go on for years. American comics would specialize in one character or another. I liked the Disney comics, the Scrooge McDuck character – he was so mean – and Gladstone Gander, because he was less goody two-shoes. But also comics like *The Phantom* and *The Blackhawk*, the pilot.

Then television hit in '56 – let's see, I was born in '44 – and I became very interested in America. It was so new, you just sat there fascinated, no matter what was happening.

As much as I try, I cannot see the influence of comics in your work. It is difficult to categorize your film, except as "Peter Weir films." You avoid genres, save Witness, *which really transcends genres.*

Yes. I don't tend to think in categories, really. I think of myself as a storyteller, and I would have chosen another medium if films hadn't been available, presumably writing.

When I was a kid, my father used to tell me serials. He'd make them up. It was a great treat for about three or four years. Because of the active, outdoor life, naturally they'd have trouble getting me to bed. One of the temptations was that my father would give me an episode of his serial. If I really had to single out an influence, I'd choose that experience – the *pleasure* of telling the tale.

His longest running one, which went over twelve months at five minutes a night, was called "Black Bart Lamey's Treasure." Which was pretty clearly a pirate tale, set in the Caribbean. I think he borrowed some from Rafael Sabatini, and God knows who else, but it was a great title, and I can still recall certain passages. He was a very good storyteller – it had nothing to do with his occupation; he was a real estate agent – but he had the *knack* of spinning a yarn. He would always leave it as a cliffhanger. And "Black Bart" was such a success that it went on and on, until finally it did come to an end. He just ran out of inspiration, I suppose. When I begged him for another one, he started a whole story about witchcraft, which my mother banned because it was so frightening I couldn't get to sleep.

Did your father have any artistic aspirations?

During the war, when he was very short of money, doing odd selling jobs and whatever, he wrote for the radio. They were always advertising for scripts for the long-running serials. I found one of his once in a cupboard with a whole batch of radio plays that he'd written for a series called *Dr. Max*, a human interest series about a country GP, each one centered around a specific case. He had two produced, I think.

It was a tremendous discovery. In my whole family background I couldn't find anybody with an interest in culture. Not any real records of who we were before we came to Australia. Which is quite typical of the immigration pattern. There's a kind of veil dropped over the past.

Could this be one reason why, so often in your movies – as in Gallipoli, *or* Witness, *or* The Mosquito Coast – *the movie is observed through a boy's eyes? A boy in the shadow of his father?*

I think that's coincidence. Pure chance.

Does this draw you to a story?

Hmmm. No. Not that I'm aware of.

—◦—

When did you first become aware that films could be art?

That's interesting. I guess with Stanley Kubrick. I was not exposed to any film culture in my late teens. The Sydney Film Festival had started in the late Fifties, but I was not aware of it, not until sometime later. I might have been in my early twenties when I first saw *Dr. Strangelove*, and that led me to see earlier Kubrick films, and to watch out for him. He struck me particularly as being different because, up to that point, I had thought of movies the way most of the public does, as being entertainments. I was quite unconscious of any greater resonance.

I had seen the odd bits of Charlie Chaplin and thought they were *quaint* – he didn't move at the correct speed – and at the time I thought they were a little bit inflated. My father took me to see a couple of Chaplin pictures that were revived in the late Fifties. He sat there, falling all about, while I sat there feeling rather curious. It must be like the music of your parents that you can't quite plug into.

Of course, later in the Seventies, I saw virtually all of Chaplin's work I could get hold of, in some sort of chronology, and I was flabbergasted – and

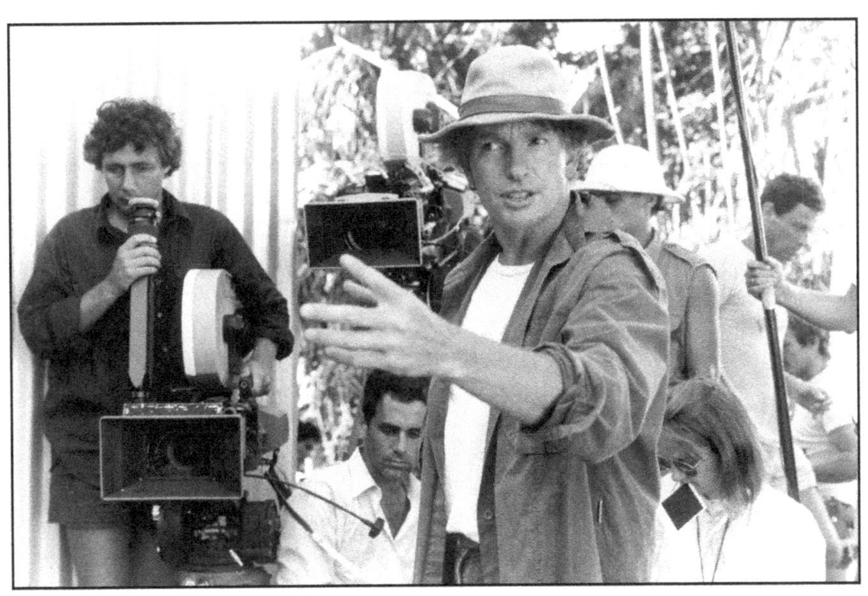

Peter Weir (in hat), on location directing
The Mosquito Coast.

laughing! It has always interested me that you can see something one time and it doesn't work for you, and later on it will. And vice versa. In fact, the reverse is really painful. I got out a Visconti film recently that so inspired and excited me at one period, and I found I couldn't get into it at all. I'll always appreciate it as the work of an artist, but where was the fire? It's a most unpleasant sense of loss. It happens with books too – and music sometimes. I'm sure it happens with people too.

Did this realization about films push you further toward directing?

No, it was really through the theater. I went to London and Europe when I was ten, in 1965. On board ship, going over, I got involved with a couple of other characters doing a shipboard revue. It's a very long trip – five weeks. The days passed very slowly, and there wasn't much entertainment on board, and we did a little television satire on a closed-circuit system.

I got terribly excited by that experience. We met again in London, and various things happened out of that. We became collaborators. We didn't know what we were doing really, but we did manage to appear as a comedy act on an amateur night in a folk club in London. We wrote a book based on one of the characters we invented on board the ship. I later made it into a film, actually – it's called *The Life and Flight of the Reverend Buckshotte*. It belonged to a series of short black-and-white films I made prior to my first feature film.

Prior to this, had you any involvement in show business?

No. I had dropped out of the university. I was a pretty hopeless student. I had some *Student Prince* idea of it all that we'd be laughing and talking and there'd be *girls...*

I got to my first lecture, there were nine hundred of us, and there was an ant down in front with a microphone talking about James Joyce. I looked at the fellow next to me, who became a very good friend, and said, "I can't believe this!" Afterward, we went for a beer, the beginning of many beers and many skipped lectures...

So I went into real estate. My father was glad to see me get out of that time-wasting process; he was looking forward to me joining him. He had a small one-man business, quite successful, and he looked forward to "Weir & Son" on the window. I sold real estate for a year and a half, and I was very successful at it too, especially when I was selling land. I was only a kid of nineteen. I saved up enough to buy a ticket to Europe, which is really what I wanted to do.

Why?

I don't know. Just to get out. Something was building up. Some pressure. It's a rather uncomfortable period to remember. I felt like I was playing a part. I didn't feel like I fit into that rather lovely world I was growing up in. It was part of a whole unrest that was happening all around the Western world.

Were you influenced at all by the Sixties?

I was very much on the edges of it. I went through all the various fashions of the day, and the fashionable ideas and ways of seeing the world, which bring faint embarrassment when you think back on it. A lot of it was just youthful naivete and arrogance, really, and I think it is the arrogance of the times that I find myself uncomfortable with when I reflect. Perhaps all we're left with is some good music.

Certainly you distrust politics, politicians, and ideologies. That comes through strongly in your films.

Yes. All of them. I've never been a joiner.

Is that partly a result of your experience in the Sixties?

Yes, that really confirmed me. I think I burned myself; I don't think anyone did it to me. I'm astounded when I think back on how I allowed myself to be susceptible to the fairly cheap propaganda put out by my peers and comrades-in-arms at the time. But I'm not angry about it, just realistic.

Did what happened prompt the explosion of filmmaking in Australia in the late Sixties and early Seventies?

In my view, very much so. It had to do with the [Vietnam] war first. Not only war, but great social upheaval, if one looks back through history, has always caused great movements in the arts, immediately after or during. Post-World War I France. Post-revolutionary Russia. This country [the United States] after and during the Vietnam War, particularly in movies. A whole generation of filmmakers came out of that period. It was very true in Australia, particularly for a country that had been so conservative in all areas up until the Vietnam War.

There was a debate in the streets – father against son, brother against sister – about the rights and wrongs of the war. That's the only conversation you heard anywhere – buses, trains, lifts. But people were *talking* to each other, and these conservative people would hardly say hello to each other in a doctor's waiting room. There is a certain sort of social stiffness that exists in our country – not so during that period.

Add to that the youth upheaval, the rock 'n' roll, the long hair, the dope, the whole swirling cauldron of change… The excitement and the thrill of chaos produced all sorts of interesting things, some of them short-term, some of them significant. Restaurants for alternative ways of eating, clothes, leaving your father's business to become a…

Filmmaker.

Exactly. I was caught up in it and did all those things, and to my family's amazement and horror, when I came back from Europe in '66, I was *radicalized*, as they used to say in those times. I came back long-haired, antiwar, married, with no money, and determined to go into theater or television. They couldn't believe or understand that. I went away one person and came back another.

So I dug ditches and delivered bread and all sorts of odd jobs until I got a job in television as a stagehand and floor-sweeper. Meanwhile, I was working with two or three friends doing off-off-Broadway-type theater, almost the next stage out of university revue, as a writer-performer. We wrote our own stuff and directed each other. It was not a commune, as such, but there were five or six of us, eventually, and we worked as a group and had a great time.

I began to make little films to put in the shows. It was a period of multimedia, and I used to enjoy taking some of our more complex sketches that we couldn't do on stage and shooting little 16mm black-and-white films. Sometimes I was in them and sometimes I wrote them, but I always directed them. I didn't realize I was directing them. In fact, the first long film I did [*Count Vim*], fifteen minutes long, I put on "produced by Peter Weir."

Was it painful for you to leave the Sixties behind? Is there any residue in your work?

I'm very much another person from who I was then. It was just like you were a pilot in the Air Force, and suddenly your application was selected for not just an astronaut program but for really deep space probe. You were one of six, eight, ten individuals who were going to go to Saturn. That's what happened to me...

It all became irrelevant...

Now, over coffee, I can just smile at these things...

—◦—

When and why did you decide to become a film director?

I went back to Europe in '71 for six months on a study grant from the government film commission. I was studying British feature film production. I saw the *Monty Python* series and I knew it was all over for me as a writer-performer. They were just *so good.* And we were just beginning to break through – at that point we had been commissioned to do a half hour comedy series for the Australian Broadcasting Company. I pulled out at the last minute. I sold my sketches to them and left the group. It was a bitter thing between us.

But I had an instinctive feeling about film. Partly it was my ignorance of film culture and film history that allowed me to have so few inhibitions, to see a future for myself as a director.

I would guess – especially on the basis of Picnic at Hanging Rock, The Last Wave *and* The Plumber *– that you were reading and heavily influenced by sociological, anthropological, and psychological texts throughout the decade.*

Yes, yes, yes.

You seem to wince at that. Why?

Because I have moved on. I was reading Carl Jung, Carlos Castaneda, Immanuel Velikovsky – I can still dip into him – and the Old Testament, among other things. Not so much Freud, whom I am just now starting to read. And not political texts either.

I had concerns then, and though other things besides books influenced me, it was just like finishing with an author; I moved on. But they became part of what I *was* rather than my current state of thinking. Incidentally, a lot of the reading and investigation cleared up my mind on certain points; and if the mysteries were not cleared up, for me their importance receded. Though I remain fascinated by religious philosophy, by spiritual inquiry, by the human condition.

Your films have a preoccupation with dreams and illusions, with the subcurrents of reason, with ancient, forgotten beliefs.

I must say that is abundantly apparent now, but I can't say that I was *aware* of being aware of it at the time. I'm somewhat uncomfortable with that pattern. It gives me no particular pleasure. I don't think there is anything significant about it.

These are just things I got very interested in ten years ago and began to investigate in myself, and to think, read, and talk about. While I did so, I was least in touch with these things. Fortunately, I realized this after some years – that it was best not to talk about them and then they will come back with all of their richness.

Of course, we all have dreams as part of our psychic makeup. There are simply unmeasured abilities we have, forms of communication, or ancient influences that have come through the very genes that make us what we are. It's a subject with no boundaries. But I've explored it consciously enough to decide it's best to leave it alone and to concentrate on craft.

Did the Aborigines become a source of concern or guilt for you?

Yes, sure, though I don't know about guilt. It became personal for me by meeting an Aborigine and getting to know him slightly – [actor] David Gulpilil, who was in *The Last Wave* – and who, as you may know, is a tribal man and a very curious case, because he would go between the two worlds and do his acting in the city, with an agent and a fee, reading scripts, and turning up for make-up calls; then he would disappear for six months, during which time he might as well have been on another planet, or in another time. He goes back in his time machine to his tribal lands, where all the ancient laws apply to him. I met Gulpilil when I was shooting an episode in a television series for a British company, a colonial tale of thirteen episodes in 1973. He made me realize that everything I had been taught in school about the Aborigines was total hogwash. Through long conversations with him, I realized the absurdity of the history books, which teach that the Aborigines were a kind of Stone Age people in the dawn of time, nomadic, without any culture of significant or enduring qualities, that they collapsed in contact with a more advanced, superior, and complex culture.

Talking with David, I realized the Aborigine culture was very much alive, if underground, so to speak. It was simply a different culture, and we had been looking at it with our definition of culture. The Aborigines use the same word, culture, to mean something far richer than what we have come to mean by it. Here was a most interesting case where we had lost something since contact with the Aborigines – something *they* still had. They lost something, too – the land and a lot of tribes.

That began a period of years of reading and talking and eventually of filmmaking, an effort that to me was always a failure, because I captured so little of what I got to know over that period. It remains, to this day, a real frustrating memory for me.

That means you are not satisfied with The Last Wave *as an exploration of those themes.*

No. It's only two or three percent of what I knew. Maybe what I discovered was meant to be personal. Maybe it wasn't something I was meant to put in a film. It was something that interested me, that's all.

One thing about these films of the Seventies – leading up to Gallipoli – *they are intensely "serious" and surprisingly humorless for someone whose professed background was comedy shtick.*

Picnic at Hanging Rock and *The Last Wave* seemed to go together. It was a pretty unfunny time, this tail end of the Sixties, with all its excesses. One of the unfortunate things about a conversation of this kind is that the serious side of me tends to come out, whereas in life I like to think I am a good jokester, and that's there's a lot of humor on my sets. In *Witness*, for example, Harrison and I cooked up some of the comedy while shooting – it's there in the dance in the barn and in the breakfast scene, which was Harrison's idea and comes from an audition he once failed.

Comedy is bloody hard to do, incidentally. But I have not given up on comedy. For the moment, for me, the best comedy springs out of genuine drama. But the type of comedy I would like to do is *Lolita* – very black, tense humor; that's the type that thrills me.

The end of the period of speculation in the Seventies came about in a very sharp, particular way. I was making a documentary in Sydney, which I really did as a favor for a friend, a potter – highly regarded, charming, much loved – who was retiring from teaching pottery after many years at a technical college in Sydney. An arts foundation wanted this filmed record of his work, so I said, "All right, if I can make it my own way."

I found his story very interesting. He had been a prisoner of war of the Japanese, captured in the fall of Singapore; he had endured the hardships and horrors in a Japanese prisoner-of-war camp, and yet, after he came out, he had become a potter. Of course, anyone who becomes a potter has to go to Japan and immerse himself in the history of the great masters of pottery. I found this very interesting – that a man who had experienced prisoner-of-war trauma ended up having this kind of Oriental aspect to his personality, apart from his pots.

Part of this film involved meeting a Japanese potter called [Shigeo] Shiga, a master who was living and working in Australia. I filmed him one night when he opened his kiln and brought some pots out. It was very exciting for me. And over many glasses of sake that night he talked about pottery – about *art* and about *craft*. That conversation that evening came to change my view about filmmaking, and it remains unchanged to this day.

Putting it simply, for him there was no art, it was all craft. He talked about how the great potters didn't sign their pots because it was considered a vanity to do so; how their pots were utilitarian objects rather than something just to be stuck on the wall, like paintings; how you make these vessels to be used, for eating and drinking; how you make each one to the best of your ability – using *Head, Heart and Hand*, which is what I called the documentary – in perfect balance. How you should never think about making a work of art because you would be punished if you did. That the gods choose when to touch your hands, and you will never know when that may be. You must keep working, and every now and again, when the gods do touch your hands, out will come this wonderful creation. It was so fundamentally opposed to the European idea of, simplistically speaking, the artist-as-God.

I loved his approach. Here were movies – which were items to be used and consumed in your daily life and then thrown away. When I returned to feature filmmaking, the emphasis for me was clearly on craft, and to forget about the artistic propaganda trip that I felt had been perpetrated.

Of course, inspiration is still part of the process – head, heart, and hand. The area of the heart, or presumably, the soul, the unknown area, provides that leap of imagination that touches the fires to the brain. But after talking with Shiga, I found I had a kind of pocket philosophy that would get me through some ups and downs, and threw me back into the fray, trying to understand this wonderful craft I was involved in. And I was free of the curse of thinking of it as an art form.

Were you experiencing some crisis as regards filmmaking?

I really had been growing up under the crossfire of Hollywood and the films of the great European directors. I sensed a great deal of pretension coming from the European cinema, but even so for a while that was very influential in my personal cinema. Apart from rare, isolated figures in the American tradition, it seemed as if there were fewer "serious" directors in Hollywood.

But one changes and one's personality changes. For me, it wasn't the influence of films or directors, though someone like Kubrick, who is artistic *and* mainstream, was a model. I don't spend much time in the cinema. It's a cliché – but I was never satisfied. I was always changing, and that is what kept me going. It was frustrating for me, trying to get certain subjects right. For me, it was a question of new territory.

For a long time I had been asking myself: Is film a craft, or is it an art? Should I be making small, serious pictures for art houses or big, expensive ones for large numbers of people? The result of these conflicting thoughts over the years was that craft was the correct emphasis for me. Because I found myself happiest in the Hollywood tradition, and I needed to find a healthy attitude toward what I was doing.

What then?
I had to teach myself how to make movies. I had made three features – but in some ways, the more I went on, the harder it became, the less I knew. I was like a primitive filmmaker.

I stopped filmmaking in 1978 and put myself through a course I was sorely lacking. For twelve months I watched movies; I was in touch with a library with a very good collection of world film culture. I started with [D.W.] Griffith; then I moved from him to the Russians; then I moved to England and looked at Hitchcock's films; then I shot back to the States for Chaplin; then I went across and dipped into France, then Germany, working my way forward up to the period of the Forties movies, which is where I'd begun, through television, to see the great filmmakers.

I was astounded, astonished, and fascinated with the great gift of these films and so glad that I hadn't looked at them earlier. If I had, I don't think I would have made films. Because I was at the bottom of the hill.

Who were paragons for you – then and now?
I don't have any *one*. I have a sort of rogue's gallery, my own Madame Tussauds of living and dead who inspire me. Of the current filmmakers, I will watch anything by Andrzej Wajda. I was particularly struck, recently, by *Danton*, and I'm fascinated by the controversy surrounding it in France, which is as interesting a story as the story in the movie. From this country there is always Woody Allen and Marty Scorsese to watch – and Spielberg. From the past, I suppose from one's much-thumbed book of filmmakers in the back pocket, there is always Jean Renoir.

What was your breakthrough film?
Gallipoli – which came after that film course. It was the first time I think I had real confidence in what I was doing, some understanding of craft, while still being an apprentice. I think my least personal film, and favorite film, is *Gallipoli*. It has the least to do with me, really.

There is still a transcendental quality in the later films as well, The Year of Living Dangerously *and* Witness. *There are soaring passages. Are you familiar with Van Morrison?*
Oh, yes.

These moments remind me of some incomprehensible Van Morrison lyric, which he sings over and over again in some rhapsody. On some level it is gibberish, or just words, but he is striking something deeper, soulful, spiritual, something at once articulate and inarticulate, moving himself and the listener. But one couldn't say what is being said precisely, or – sometimes – what it is you are saying.

Maybe that is some essence of art. You really can stare at a painting, can't you? Particularly when it is a landscape, or some 18th-century English gentleman whose name is not known. You have to sit down and stare at it. You can't put your finger on it.

That's what I've loved to discover for myself in opera in the last ten years. Some I don't like and have propelled me out of the theater. But those I have loved have always been in a foreign language. I'm always disappointed when they announce it will be sung in English or with subtitles. Because I love to *not* know what they're saying, and to just go with the music, really.

Music is the fountainhead, the source of all my inspiration, in a way, if you can generalize. It certainly doesn't have anything to do with words and such. Storytelling is my trade, my *craft*. But music is my inspiration; and my goal, my metaphor, to affect people like music. The images should float over you like music, and the experience should be beyond words.

In the middle of some scenes, the camera becomes sensuous, carrying emotion and subtext, and really transporting the audience to another level.

I think that's true of a lot of films I've done, but I've become so aware of it that I've tried to strip it out of *The Mosquito Coast*. I've attempted to eliminate my own style as much as possible, like some sort of personal cultural revolution. I think style can become inhibiting in a long career.

I have consciously eliminated it from this picture and made it plainer, more straightforward. For other reasons, too – the material and essential ideas of this film are so contradictory to mainstream American filmmaking, are so deeply unconventional, that I felt the form and shape of it should be very conventional, in order not to repel the viewer.

In fact, the opening sequence has some of the plainest opening images I've ever had, even bland. I shot another opening at the same time because I was aware of this problem. Originally, I shot a very mysterious, Peter Weir-style opening with dark figures on the horizon and all sorts of weird things going on, then I very cleverly revealed what it was. I thought it might be too close to *Witness*, but I decided it was just my style. At the dailies everybody was impressed. "Wow. This is really *you* at your best. That music you played over those images – wow! It blew me away." I thought about it and thought about it and dropped it all. It was a symbolic gesture, but it did echo on throughout the film.

Though you have been involved for quite some time, Paul Schrader's script existed before your commitment.

Originally, the project belonged to [producer] Jerome Hellman. He loved the book, bought it, and brought in Paul Schrader to do the screenplay. If you look at *Mishima* and then read *Mosquito Coast,* you'll see the connection. I met the two of them in Sydney and we talked, because I wasn't sure I could bring it off. Paul's draft was a classic example of an adaptation: it was simple, it was true to the material, while transmitting it into the film form. The script was a great attraction.

Though I revised the script, Paul and I never really worked together. We had long talks by phone. In the end we were going to have the credit arbitrated, because I felt I had contributed to my share of the screenplay. But in the editing room, ironically, I ended up cutting more of *my* scenes and *my* dialogue. So the cut that you will see ends up being fairly close to Paul, which is pretty faithful to Theroux.

What attracted you to the story, per se?

The challenge of the story was, for me, that it was a tragedy and very particularly an American tragedy. It's in the great tradition of the tragic form. It reminded me of certain operas, of Shakespeare certainly – of *Macbeth,* which I have always loved, and of *Othello.* My favorite production of both those plays always held me in deep thrall. I've always enjoyed watching this great soldier, Macbeth, watching this ambition awaken in him and consume him, and with Othello, the same with jealousy.

I saw Allie Fox like that and wanted to present a story where you understood what happened to the man and *felt* something, not necessarily for him, but felt something at the end other than anger toward him, which people who read the book felt. It should be as if you are imagining your own father somehow, whom you believed in, and whose weaknesses you begin to see; this giant of a man only gets smaller and smaller as you grow. You have to find a new way to see this person. Then you see the weaknesses in yourself, and it's all wonderfully difficult.

To add to that, the final excitement of the charge: Could one present this form in the American cinema, in the Hollywood narrative tradition? To my knowledge, it has not been done.

The American tradition – and *Witness* served that tradition – is to have the hero, the leading man, particularly these rare people like Harrison Ford, with his great strength and integrity – these people like John Wayne and Steve McQueen, who are part of the fiber of the culture – to have the hero start off with a flaw that is healed or cleansed. At the end, he walks off into the sunset, and he's a better man for the experience. It is as much a part of the American myth as the poor kid selling newspapers on the street corner who grows up to become president of the United States. It's all part of the winning turbine that drives this country to succeed, to triumph, to overcome the odds. But it's left untouched the whole tradition of drama that goes back to the

Greeks and beyond – of *failure* – and of visions that are too limited. Of great men who collapse.

There was the excitement, the challenge, the feeling of fresh ground with the story, to take such a man and see if I could hold that audience.

Is Mosquito Coast *a way of commenting on America?*

No. God, no. I'd cringe at the thought.

Why?

That is the school of propaganda, of sociology, of teachers who feel they need to change society through film. That is just not my approach, which is definitely storytelling. As is Theroux's.

But I think the story is an obvious –

Parable?

Yes.

I think Theroux placed it very correctly as the subtext and didn't moralize in an obvious way about it. I put it out of my mind, and I refused to ever think about it. Because it would always be there and it had to find its rightful balance, and so I never went for a cheap shot in that area, though of course it's there and it's what's driving the whole thing.

Are you a little tentative, in general, about filming stories about America or Americans? Bruce Beresford seemed at home with Tender Mercies *and Fred Schepisi does Westerns like* Barbarosa, *but you seem a little more wary.*

Being from a colony like Australia, it's that much easier to find your way into certain aspects of life here, and to feel quite at home. Then again, every now and then, you strike an area in which people are as foreign as Frenchmen, or as any other country where you don't have language as an apparent way of understanding the culture.

It's certainly easier for us to come here than the English, perhaps because they come here with such a highly defined culture, a known past. Whereas with a colonial people, the dispossessed of the world, the whole country is built on that starting-again notion.

You have a very keen sense of being "displaced," of being a colonial descendant, an uneasiness about what it means to be an Australian.

Most Australians don't think about it and they feel very comfortable about being Australian. I guess I'm just one of that group that has a particularly different view.

It's a very fascinating subject for me, as a European really, whose family was transported, pulled up roots, and moved to Southeast Asia. Australia was built on a series of failures, horrible experiments, and the results of those experiments are still in progress. In recent years there's been quite an accelerated attempt – artificial, almost – to create the Australian character in a hothouse and to get it blooming, so that we can say, "Look, we've got an identity." But that's a very recent acceleration as a result of advances in the media.

This is obviously the empathy you bring to The Year of Living Dangerously, *or to the Amish colony of* Witness. *I see* Mosquito Coast *in the same vein, with Allie Fox as a kind of one-man colonizer with no regard for the native peoples...*

I hadn't particularly thought of him that way, but it's very interesting to see him as setting off to start a new colony...

—◦—

You seem so resistant to any definition. I bring to you examples of motifs in your work: of intuition and madness, of underlying social consciousness, of "lost" individuals transforming themselves in a clash of cultures – and you say, "Partly accidental, partly coincidence."

Totally. I was thinking the other day, "Gee, that would make an interesting film..." some short story I was reading, then I thought, "Oh no, it's another thing of a person going into a foreign culture..." So I decided I can't do that.

Why do you frown at that?

It's too obvious. Also, I like to feel I'm more private than that. I don't take any pleasure in interviews because, like a lot of public entertainers, professional entertainers, absurdly this contradiction exists for me of wanting to stand up and get applause while at the same time wanting to retain privacy.

But as the number of pictures build up, someone with a head on his shoulders can fairly easily sit down and form a portrait of the person who made them. That's not unreasonable.

I talked earlier about altering style, but I think that's something like the clothing you wear. That's something you *can* change. The deeper aspects – you don't really choose those courses, you are just drawn in certain directions. I'm doing what is natural to me.

But I *am* looking for ways to force change on myself. I am trying to drop stylistic aspects, to remove myself further from the film, to allow other influences to come in, to find a fresher approach, and to not become too predictable. I'm looking for a way to eliminate, to simplify, to rely on fewer tricks and gimmicks, and in a way I've been trying to do that for years.

The word I would choose to describe my work, which we haven't fooled around with, is *wonder*. What an interesting word that is! It's certainly a word I would apply to my first viewing of the first film that left me in a state of wonder as a kid, which was *The Wizard of Oz*. That stays with me, the experience of seeing that picture, probably in re-release, when I was ten or twelve.

It was a world I didn't fully understand, which is a part of wonder, and without question I have attempted to do that in my films, and I still do. Because of the pleasure of that wonder. To be made like a child again, really, when you see a film. [Laughs] Not in the sense, of course, that a lot of committees down the road mean it. "We're all kids at heart…"

It's just… *not knowing*… and to come out of the theater into the street and you don't know if it's night or day, or raining, and you bump into people and you get into the wrong car and you go down a one-way street the wrong way. Those are the kinds of experiences in the movies I like.

Are you wary of losing yourself in Hollywood?

No. The only person you have to be wary of, really, *is* yourself. Being a filmmaker, I have this image in my mind as an analogy. There is a movie I can't remember the title of, a World War II story, an American or British picture, about the captain of a small destroyer dueling with a U-boat commander, and the entire picture is this cat-and-mouse between the two vessels. The captain of the ship and the U-boat commander spend the entire movie plotting to kill each other. That's my current analogy. I am both skippers, trying to outmaneuver myself, avoid sinking myself, playing chess with myself. Hollywood is just irrelevant. They just provide the room you play in.

Oliver Stone

1987
Interview by Patrick McGilligan

Has Oliver Stone been getting to you lately? If so, you have plenty of company – film critics, many Hollywood studio executives, and right-wingers/left-wingers (for polar opposite reasons) everywhere.

Not that Stone had been keeping a low profile, previously. If anything, he has courted recognition and controversy from the very beginning. He has not been humble, and he is not in the struggling caste of screenwriters. No, he is one of the best, best paid, and best known.

His career began in high gear with *Midnight Express* in 1978, the brutal, real-life story of a young American imprisoned in Turkey for drug-smuggling, Stone's first, major, produced screenplay (discounting student and low-budget efforts). *Express* brought a hailstorm of criticism from people who believed it depicted the Turks in broad, racist strokes, copped-out on or negatively slanted the prison homosexuality, and in general deviated from Billy Hayes's book, on which the movie was based. There was also a script Oscar for Stone and a similar best script award from the Writers Guild. What some saw as wretched, cartoonish melodrama, others saw as the perverse downside of reality.

Stone next embarked on a series of collaborations with some of the more independent-minded, flamboyant, box-office directors in Hollywood, notably John Milius, Brian De Palma, Michael Cimino and, less memorably, Hal Ashby. (Stone would rather not discuss the botched yet still eminently watchable *Eight Million Ways to Die*.) The result was a number of the more dubious, outrageous, action-filled movies of the Eighties. (Also, some of the more ambitious and fascinating.) *Scarface* and *Year of the Dragon*, particularly, were excoriated by the community organizations against racism and inauthenticity, but Stone doesn't hedge much or apologize. (Defending *Dragon* in one interview, he blamed the negative reaction to the film on "organized Chinese groups" and people like independent filmmaker Wayne Wang, who "doesn't know shit – excuse me – about Chinatown. If Wayne Wang is to be believed, then the Chinese are some of the most boring people in the world.")

Having been tagged with charges of racial insensitivity, Stone might well seem to hold right-wing sympathies. But his subsequent sneak attack as one of the most left-wing (albeit, iconoclastically so) directors in Hollywood surprised a bit, though the town ain't really going to go down in history for the size of its left-wing salon.

Indeed, most of us can be forgiven for not being prepared at all for Oliver Stone, the director. Few will remember *Seizure*, a low-budget horror film shot in Canada by the then 25-year-old Stone, a recent NYU film school graduate. And you had to be up pretty late to see *The Hand*, his second directorial opus in 1981, a grand guignol ditty with Michael Caine haunted by his dismemberment. Not half-bad; in fact, having seen it on Hollywood Boulevard during its very brief run, I thought that it is actually half-good.

It was an open secret in L.A. during the last decade that Stone was a frustrated "cause freak," whose commercial sell-out was a disillusioned "detour into the mainstream" (his words) after more cherished projects had foundered. His long-planned adaptation of Vietnam Vet leader Ron Kovic's *Born on the Fourth of July* came asunder days before shooting was to begin, and his script about Russian dissidents was optioned but never made. Stone was growing rich and fat with assignments but increasingly dispirited by his own stagnation. Around the time he finished *The Hand*, he attended a screening of Warren Beatty's *Reds* and was struck by its vision and daring. Consequently, Stone's own political and creative goals were revitalized.

—◦—

The first fruit of that was *Salvador*, a pell-mell immersion into newspaper headlines and Central American back-alleys that put James Woods and Jim Belushi together in a compressed account of the recent, tragic rending of El Salvador. Even with its flaws, *Salvador* came on like a hammer blow, showing the influence of a comic-fantastical Borges, a high-steam Scorsese, and a polemical Godard. If James Woods doesn't get an Oscar nomination for his hurt, raging, bullying performance as journalist Richard Boyle, there is no justice in the world. But that may have been the point of the movie, after all: There *is* no justice in the world. Even more than *Under Fire* and *Missing* (and they would make a nice triple bill with *Salvador*), Stone's film was the bitter pill of truth about the suppressed story behind the story down there.

Salvador opened the doors, the same year, to *Platoon*, Stone's Vietnam memoirs, written more than a decade ago, and one of those more personal scripts shelved after "dying of encouragement" in Hollywood. Get ready – *Platoon* will not be the only Vietnam flashback in 1986, a year that is shaping up as a trendy nostalgic tribute to the grunts of Vietnam. In good time there will be Stanley Kubrick's *Full Metal Jacket* (adapted from the novel *The Short-Timers*), *84 Charlie MoPic*, a shoestring Sundance project, Lionel Chetwynd's *Hanoi Hilton* (about P.O.W.'s), and James Carabatsos's *Hamburger Hill*, another foot-soldier paean. (Carabatsos, also a screenwriter turned director, did the script for Clint Eastwood's *Heartbreak Ridge*, Clint's way of saying, "Hey, don't forget Grenada, too.")

Vietnam is as personal as it is political for Stone. He is mesmerized by exotic cultures and by the possibilities and truths in America as reflected in its immigrant cultures, and this enchantment crops up recurrently in the settings and concerns of his movies. The headline of one weekly paper in Los Angeles dubbed him: 'The cinema's low-rent Lord Jim." Probably that anonymous headline writer meant a low-rent Joseph Conrad (one of Stone's literary gods), but however inadvertent the reference, Lord Jim is akin to the obsessed, deeply flawed, anti-heroic probers and pariahs that lace Stone's work.

As a Yale drop-out, Stone spent two years in Vietnam teaching Vietnamese-Chinese students in 1965. Then, after an interval of travel and writing, he returned to Southeast Asia to volunteer as a soldier in the War. He served with the 25th Infantry Division near the Cambodian border and was wounded twice. He was awarded the Bronze Star for combat gallantry and a Purple Heart with Oak Leaf Cluster. *Platoon* is from his one-year-plus tour of duty. He says the story of the film is telescoped from his own experiences and that, just like the character of Chris Taylor (played by Charlie Sheen), in Vietnam he did some "morally repulsive things."

—⊶—◇—⊷—

Platoon will likely be controversial for years to come. It charts the dead logic of the "morally repulsive" war: it may be the benchmark Vietnam War movie (from the U.S. point of view), the one by which all films about combat are measured. It takes the futility of the war and the rape of Vietnam for granted, and instead focuses on the scary intimacy of fear and hate; on the psychology of the battlefield; on the civil war-within-the-war; the left-wing versus the right-wing (as it were) of the soldiery and the command. *Platoon's* verisimilitude amazes – Stone has recreated (on location in the Philippines) the eerie, moral chaos, and gotten the period on-target.

Unlike the herky-jerky style of *Salvador*, *Platoon* is very assured, lyrical at moments, even in its grotesque images of battle and death. The film's multi-character ensemble of young unknowns is anchored by three central performances: Willem Dafoe as Sgt. Elias is the conscience of the platoon; Tom Berenger is St. Barnes, the dark angel of death; and Charlie Sheen (Martin's son) is recruit Chris Taylor, Stone's alter ego. Berenger does a riveting 180-degree turn from his *Big Chill* prototype, and Sheen cannot help but evoke his father, similarly mired in *Apocalypse Now*. (Likewise, Charlie is burdened with disconnected voice-over narration – a weakness in both *Apocalypse* and *Platoon*.) Stone, a great movie buff, relishes such resonant connections.

—⊶—◇—⊷—

It's interesting to compare briefly movie directors off the set with the stylistic line spun out in their films. Hawks, cold and witty, dry as tumbleweed; Peckinpah, a poet with writer's block, whimsical and dangerous, whether drunk or sober; Scorsese, manic and hyper, driven intuitively, with no direction home. The best of the auteurs personify their films somehow. It is clear with the back-to-back whammy of *Salvador* and *Platoon* that Stone will be with us as a director for quite some time – the aloof kid with preppie perks, driven to seek the heat and corruption underlying the ordered world.

One-on-one, Stone is intense, tightly reined-in, boiling over, alternating fury with laughter; you can't be sure when he is kidding. Husky and broad-shouldered, Stone has a big Humpty-Dumpty egg-face that is bland and ingenuous. But the eyes blaze, and when the grin cracks open, you half-expect lava to pour out. Ultimately, he is much more studied and thoughtful than the Angry Young (well, actually 40-year-old) Screenwriter I had imagined. Stone evinces the writer's sober intent on coming across, on being precise, on being understood, on making his point. Also, he is funny.

I didn't but I should have asked him what words he might choose for his tombstone. We did fool around with some terrible credos. "Show the ugly!" I suggested. "Yes…" he agreed, "But show the good!" *Platoon* is an ugly, painful, doom-laden film, with much that is honest and beautiful and, yes, good. Apart from its intrinsic historical value as the first feature to be directed by a former vet, I believe Stone when he says his goals in making it were in part modest and private. Rather than affecting a grand, universal statement about men in war, he is content to exorcise his own ghost from Vietnam.

—◦—

You have worked with some pretty disparate directors. Or maybe I should say, directors who have little in common other than personal flamboyance and operatic filmmaking styles: Alan Parker, John Milius, Brian De Palma, Michael Cimino, Hal Ashby. Let's start with Milius and Conan the Barbarian.

It was very difficult and complicated to get rights to the [Robert E.] Howard *Conan* books. [Producer] Eddie Pressman spent a fortune in legal fees, and then I couldn't direct because I had no clout. I begged Ridley Scott to do it. I went down on my knees to him. This was off *The Duellists*, we hadn't even seen *Alien* yet. He said yes and then he said no. It broke our hearts. Instead, he did *Blade Runner*.

Because we were depressed by Ridley's turndown, we turned it over to John and Dino [De Laurentiis, as producer]. Although I like John – I think he's a great raconteur and a John Wayne figure – ultimately, he didn't want to collaborate with me. He rewrote the end and my criticisms were ignored – to the detriment of the picture, I think. He put that whole snake cult stuff in, which I didn't like at all, and which cheapens the story. A snake cult – who cares?

My original draft was a $40 million movie. It dealt with the takeover of the planet and the forces of life being threatened by the forces of darkness. The mutant armies were taking over, and Conan was the lonely pagan – as opposed to Christian – hero; he was Roland at the pass, he was Tarzan, he was a mythic figure. I loved that he had been enslaved and suffered, and that he rose. What was great about the Howard books – actually, thirteen books – was Conan's progression from a peasant to a king. At the end of the movie, in my draft, he is the king, and it means something that he came from these roots. Then he foregoes the kingdom and tells the princess, "I can't be a king this way, as your husband. I can't inherit the throne. I will earn my throne." Then he went riding off to the second adventure, which was supposed to be the follow-up sequel. If they'd done it my way, they would have had a Bond-type series – twelve, thirteen pictures, which is what I had wanted to do.

How did Milius's sensibility clash with yours? De Palma seems apolitical if not intellectually vapid, but Milius seems to revel in being a right-winger, while Cimino has been accused of being one.

Let's face it. John has a certain deafness. He doesn't listen. It was the least successful collaboration I ever had. Whereas with Cimino he listened very well. He *listens* to you. John doesn't. He has a stone wall about him and I guess, being the writer with lesser credits at that point in time, he didn't brook any of my input.

Did his deficiencies have any political connotations? Or was he merely attempting to "masculinize" the material?

I think he masculinized it and went more with his friends – more with the bodybuilding aspect of Arnold [Schwarzenegger]. I think Arnold has a more romantic side. John populated the movie with surfers and bodybuilders. And the look – he made it look like a Spanish Western. I know it was shot in Spain because it was cheaper there, but I wanted to shoot it in Germany or Russia – and to get the whole Russian army, thousands of people in the green, fertile fields of Russia. The picture should have been green; John made it rocky desert yellow, more a [Sergio] Leone Western. It was all cheap – they cut back on the extras, the fights were done on the cheap, the rocks looked like cardboard boulders.

There was no collaboration essentially. I wrote my stuff, and I never really got a second pass. John rewrote. I gave notes, he tore up my notes, and then we never talked about the movie again.

Were you at all simpatico?

Not at all. We used to have tremendous fights. The Panama Canal deal was going down then, and I was saying it's about time we gave it back; and he was taking the John Wayne point of view that this was one of the most traitorous acts in history. But we had a wonderful time – he showed me his gun collection – he's a terrific skeet shooter. I'm quite the opposite. I did all my shooting in Vietnam, and I have never fired a weapon since.

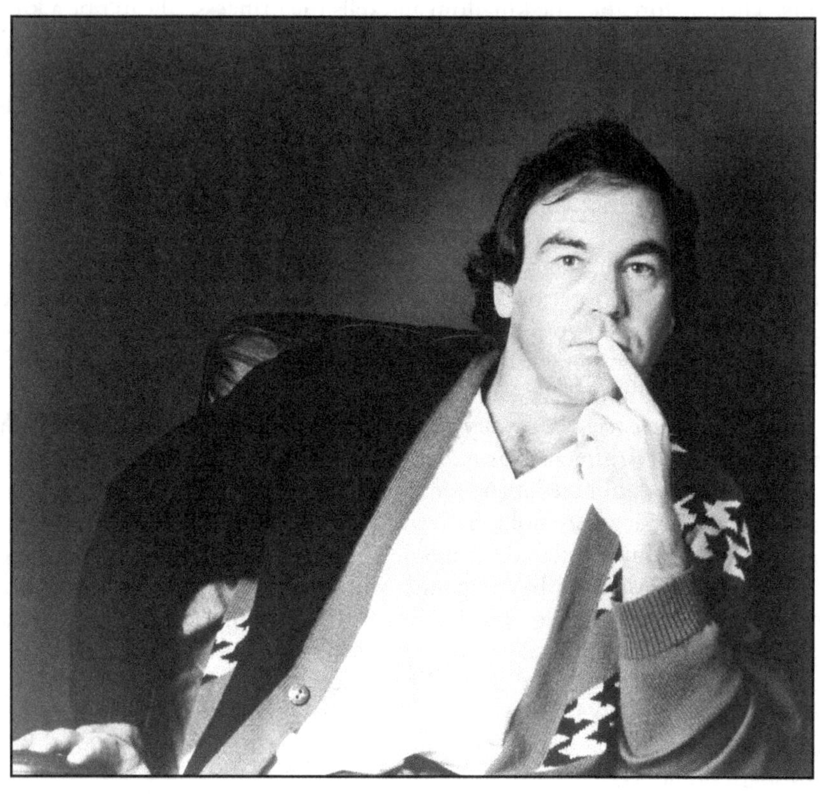

Oliver Stone at the time of *Talk Radio* (1988).

—◦—

You think Year of the Dragon *was a successful collaboration?*

Not ultimately, no. I had a very good relationship with Michael [Cimino]. He wrote the screenplay with me; he was there all the time. He *breathed* me. He shared everything in his life with me. With Michael, it's a 24-hour day. He doesn't really sleep. You get into his skin, he gets into yours. He's truly an obsessive personality. He's the most Napoleonic director I have ever worked with. His gaze is on the future. His gaze is on history. He has no time for pettiness.

For *Dragon*, we did an enormous amount of research. Getting information from the Chinese was very hard. For *Scarface*, it was easy to get the Latins to talk, but I couldn't get the Chinese to talk about gangsters. We went to about twenty, thirty banquets in Chinatown, where we had to eat fifteen-course meals, gorging ourselves, trying to get friendly with these guys who wouldn't tell us the time of day. We got information finally from a dissident gangster group, very on the outs, very unhappy, who took us down to Atlantic City and showed us the inner workings of what was going on in the gambling world, and also showed us what was going on in Chinatown. We met with a lot of the biggies…

How do you react to criticism that the movie is a slur on Chinese people?

The movie is hyped up a bit, but it was essentially honest about the Golden Triangle [i.e., the opium poppy triangle that borders Laos, Burma, and Thailand], the use of youth gangs as the little surface fishes to knock off, to exploit, to run numbers, while the whales deep down are involved in the enormous dope shipping from Southeast Asia. This is serious business. The Chinese are the biggest importers of heroin in this country. They outdo the Mafia, yet nobody knows about it – they do it quietly. There are rarely busts – except this recent one, the United Bamboo Gang. You should read the testimony. It's hilarious. It's right out of the movie.

Who hyped it up? You? Cimino?

I said it wasn't a totally successful collaboration. Dino got his paws into it. For example, the original ending of the movie was brilliant. The Mickey Rourke character had two women in his life. The Chicago Chinese Mafia character, John Lone, was also supposed to have two women in his life – a Hong Kong wife and a New York wife, which a lot of the Chinese have. In a moment of sentimentality, he brings the Chinese wife to the States, because he is having problems with his Hong Kong son. He installs her, separate from his other wife, in a New York apartment. The Mickey Rourke cop character finds out about it and after he can't get him [the Chicago Chinese Mafia character] legally, with a bust or wiretap, busts him for bigamy. He wants to insult him and take away his "face." By taking away his "face," he somehow forces the issues to a head.

Ultimately, it's not in the movie, which is resolved through more conventional means at the shipyard – all the typical, Billy Friedkin-*French*

Connection stuff, which I didn't particularly care for. That's because Dino has a very Fifties mentality, and he demanded to know how could Stanley White, the Mickey Rourke character, the hero of the movie, be an adulterer? How could he be married to one woman and fuck another? We said, "Dino, drop dead, you're living in the Helen of Troy epics you're still doing." Michael won that battle, but, in the process, we lost the other one, which was a key battle.

Mickey Rourke's performance comes across as smug, and in focusing on him, the film lost its authenticity.

I personally think Mickey was marvelous casting by Michael. No actor wanted to do that part. Mickey wasn't even a star at that point. For De Laurentiis and Cimino to bank $20 million on him was a big step.

Why didn't any major star want such a juicy part?

They went right down the list. Certainly it was because of Michael in some cases. And a lot of people didn't like the right-wing, racist nature of the character. He *is* a right-winger. He *is* a racist. That is the way the character was conceived and written. He's sexist on top of it. You had to have a big pair of balls to play that part.

You don't think the film ultimately comes down on his side?

Insofar as he is the protagonist?

As far as being racist and sexist?

You're asking me a very tough question. I condemn vigilantism. I don't believe in it. On the other hand, there's a certain part of me that hates the bureaucracy that prevents the original idea from coming through. I'm a little torn on that aspect.

The fact is, nobody in that Chinatown precinct wants to do anything about the drugs, and this guy is a mover and shaker who wants to rock the boat. That makes him, *per se,* interesting as a protagonist. I don't like the way he does it, his excesses, the unrelenting humorlessness of his character. That's more Michael than me. In *Scarface,* Tony Montana is a nut, but he's funny… I always thought *Scarface* was a comedic *Richard III,* the rise and fall of a petty hood.

—o—

Was De Palma faithful to your screenplay?

To a large degree.

Do you feel Scarface *was successful?*

To a large degree. The dialogue will last. A lot of young lawyers and businessmen quote me the dialogue, and I say, "Why do you remember this?" They say, "It's exactly like my business." Apparently, the gangster ethics hit on some of the business ethics going on in this country. *Scarface* has probably got me more free champagne everywhere in the world than any film I've ever worked on. Gangsters I've bumped into in Paris – gay gangsters – who bought me champagne all night long and said, "How did you *know*?" When I went to

Salvador, I got a lot of my "ins" with Major [Roberto] D'Aubuisson and the right-wing Arena Party because they loved *Scarface*. I was the man who wrote it. I was *muy macho*.

Do you feel they missed the subtlety?

Well, if you really examine *Scarface*, it's very much a left-wing picture. Though Tony Montana [Al Pacino] exposes anti-Communism, he's very much a rebel. Ultimately, he's undone by the establishment when he gets stuck in a bank laundering deal, because he wants to better their deal. He goes to a cheaper fence, which turns out to be a federal operation, and gets busted, which sets in motion his fall. In the end, the only way he can save himself is to blow up a diplomat, which is based on [the assassination of Chilean diplomat Orlando] Letelier, but because the diplomat is with his wife and children. Tony can't bring himself to do it… he refuses.

Am I wrong, or are you in some way obsessed with drug deals and the drug culture? It starts with Midnight Express, *but continues on through* Scarface, Dragon, Salvador, Platoon, *even* Eight Million Ways to Die.

[Laughs] Well, I am the *Big Chill* generation. I grew up with that. And I was hit with drugs in Nam. Certainly, drugs played a part in my life for several years after Nam. But I kicked it all before *Scarface*, which was my farewell to all drugs. I really wrote it off in a big way. What better farewell than a guy falling into a ton of cocaine, and when he looks up at the camera there is all this white powder up his nose. I think it's very funny.

But I saw *Midnight Express* as a story about justice, really. He could have been busted for carrying a pistol. The charge didn't really interest me, it was the sentence. *Platoon* is a realistic assessment of what went on with the drugs in Vietnam, as far as my memory serves me. I wrote it in '76, seven or eight years later, so obviously some things are blurred. But it's a larger theme for me than drugs.

Does it make you nervous delving into non-white, lower-class culture?

No, I find it interesting. As a middle-class white man, I find it very exotic. I did a lot of research for *Scarface* and *Dragon*. I'd been to prison myself on a drug bust prior to *Midnight Express*. Obviously, I cannot be inside the skin of other people – but this is an old argument.

How do you feel about charges that the Turks are treated racistly in Midnight Express, *the Latins in* Scarface, *and the Chinese in* Dragon?

I think the Turks probably had a point. Actually, there was a little more humor in the screenplay. The Turks were shown as a little crazier, not just as torturers. There were scenes with the Billy Hayes character being tortured, then you'd move the camera over to the next cell and there would be another Turk watching TV, or checking out of prison at night, or bringing hookers in; it was like a carnival. There is no sense of values in those jails, no uniformity. I found that hilarious. There was a lot of that in the screenplay. But not in the movie. I think the Turks probably had a good rap on us. It was a little rabid. But we were young.

Scarface, listen, I knew I was going to be in hot water, but I did it because I really wanted to do that whole fascinating South Florida scene. When I was in Miami in 1980, there were something like two hundred drug-related homicides that year – and in fact, there were two Colombians who were killed by chainsaws and carved up worse than in the movie. There was a fascinating theme there of immigrant growth; a kid with two cents in his pocket arrives on the shores of Florida and inside of two years is a kingpin making $100 or $200 million a year. Where else in the world…?

Why are you continually drawn to such foreign or exotic milieus?
I grew up fairly internationally. I traveled a lot. My mother was French; I'm half-immigrant. I've always felt that urge to *rise*, that driven thing that Tony Montana has, coming to a new country. Making my mark – I've always had that hunger. And I'm interested in alternative points of views. I think ultimately the problems of the planet are universal and that nationalism is a very destructive force. Just doing provincial American subjects is really boring. It's just not all I would like to do.

When did you get interested in Asia?
Probably in '65 when I read *Lord Jim*. That was a marker novel for me. It turned my head around. I left Yale in '65 because I really wanted to see another world. Everybody was the same. I felt like a character in [Alan] Parker's *The Wall*. I was being groomed for financial-commercial America. I didn't have any feeling of individual worth.

What was it about reading Lord Jim *that touched you?*
I wanted to see an alternate reality. I felt like I was cut off. There had to be another way – I didn't know what it was, but I had to see the world through different eyes. I knew that *my* eyes were blinding me. I couldn't put my finger on it, but I knew I had to get out, move *physically*, to start to change.

I went to Asia without knowing a soul there. It was great. I remember that first trip like *Two Years Before the Mast*. The first time I was really, really free on my own – it was a great feeling. I was eighteen or nineteen, and I was never the same again.

My father was pissed off at me. He said, "If you go, you're going to screw up your education and you're never going back to Yale." Years later, before he died, I said to him, "See Dad, I did screw up. I never did go back to Yale. But I'm a lot happier now than I would have been if I had stayed."

I did some social work on the streets of Philadelphia before I went overseas. The Hill Christian Association – we used to go down, paint houses and do fix-it jobs, and live with blacks in the ghettoes of Philadelphia. But I was essentially a torn right-winger. My father was right-wing; he hated Roosevelt all his life, and he hated the Russians. I grew up in that Cold War context like we all did, from the Fifties on, learning to fear Russians and hate Communism like cancer.

I reacted accordingly in Vietnam. To me there was no doubt, even when I was a teacher there, that the Communists were the bad guys and we were the good guys, and that we were saving the South from the North. That was my reading of the situation. I felt teaching was good. But now I wanted to see another level, a deeper level, a darker side. What is war? How do people kill each other? How will I handle it? What is the lowest level I can descend to, to find the truth, where I can come back from and say, *I've seen it*? Where can I go for that experience?

You embarked on your career as a writer before Vietnam, with a novel.

I had written a book in Mexico before the war. That was in 1966, when I thought I was going to be the next Marcel Proust. I was furious that no one would publish it. Mostly I was furious with myself and, partly, I joined the Army to obliterate this ego I had devised.

When I came back from Nam, I still had this desire to express myself, but I didn't want to go back to writing that book. Somehow, I felt that novels weren't happening. I was just dealing with the everyday. There was no thought about the future or what was going to happen next. I was just counting the days. I was too tired to do anything else.

Besides, several days after I got back, I was busted for marijuana in Nixon's border war in Mexico and I was thrown in the tank in San Diego. Federal charge, smuggling, five to twenty years. And I was just back from Vietnam, right? I was really pissed off. [Laughs] That's the way they treat the vets?! I got the picture right away. It took some guys years. It took me about five days.

The prison had something like fifteen thousand people and beds for only three thousand, and I had to sleep on a floor for three weeks. The [public defender] lawyer wouldn't even come to defend me. So I called my father and he said, "Where have you been? You were supposed to call." I said, "Dad, I have to tell you something. The good news is I'm out of Vietnam. The bad news is I'm in jail." He called up an attorney and offered him $2,500. This guy showed up that afternoon, beaming, he loved me, rolling his hands – a scene right out of *Midnight Express*. That's where I got a lot of the *Midnight Express* stuff.

He got me off. I don't know how. The charges were ultimately dismissed in the interests of justice, which means they were *bought*. The files were destroyed.

Was coming home a culture shock for you?

Huge. Enormous. Because nobody was fighting the war. That was the problem. It wasn't the hippies or the protestors. They were a very small group. It was the mass *indifference*. Nobody cared. That was what hurt. Nobody realized their sons were dying over there. People were going about the business of making money.

The whole problem with that war is that [President] Johnson never made it a war. Either you go to war, or you don't go to war. You just don't send poor kids and draftees and let the college kids stay in college. That divides the country, *per se*.

—o—

After the war, you drifted for two or three years, according to your official press bio –

I don't know if "drifted" is the word. I was drifting in my head for three, four, five years. My first wife helped me enormously through that period.

I went to NYU film school on the GI bill. Scorsese happened to be the first teacher I met, and he helped tremendously. His energy, his devotion to film, helped me feel focused. Going back to that time, nobody really believed you could study films. Films were exotic pleasures from Hollywood, and I was from the East Coast and didn't know anyone in the film business.

Why did it appeal to you?

Because it didn't seem like work. [Laughs] Because I *loved* movies. My mother had taken me all the time when I was a boy. She was a double-feature freak at the RKO on 86th Street. She used to make me skip school so I would accompany her. I loved it but it wasn't *serious*. It was just something you did.

What was your relationship with Scorsese?

A student. I did three short films in 16mm, black-and-white. He was very helpful with auto-criticism. He knew a lot about movies. I remember him having long, long hair and always being exhausted from having stayed up to watch the late, late show. He'd talk about the movie he'd seen at five a.m. that morning in loving and intimate detail.

I think you can see his influence in your work – you have a lot of his passion and fury on the screen.

That's great.

But your work also has a bitter, angry edge that's sometimes hard to take.

I don't consider myself bitter or angry. I consider myself passionate about the theme. Maybe there was some bitterness after the war about what was going on in America in the Seventies. Hmm, angry… possibly, yes. But I don't like the connotations of bitter.

You're warming up to "angry."

Angry for quite a while in the early Seventies. I loved films like *Taxi Driver*. I drove a taxi in New York and was closer to that character, that personality, after the war. I had a hard time readjusting to civilian life. I was out of sync. I wasn't living in a Larry Kasdan vision of the world. I was living in a much more nightmarish one, and I think Marty Scorsese and Paul Schrader really caught alienation very well in that picture. It really reflected me, too.

I think the anger has dissipated with time. I got married, had a child… life's been good to me compared to other vets.

I catch your sarcasm over The Big Chill *vision of the Sixties. In a sense, you missed out on that decade.*

Probably. The Sixties I thought were horrible. I think the Eighties are much better. [Laughs]

Does that hurt?

I was doing more dope and acid than the hippies. But I was out of touch.

When you see The Big Chill, *is it like a foreign movie to you?*

Oh, yeah.

Platoon *is your* Big Chill.

Yeah.

Does that anger or sadden you?

Not anger at all. Saddened that I missed it – especially the healthy relationships. I never had a coeducational existence. I grew up in that old, pre-war America where everybody went to boys' school and then went into the Army – with more boys. Everything was boy-oriented. I remember the Sixties and the enormous sense of sexual liberation. Women starting to come out of the closet, and fucking was *in,* stylish, fashionable. I missed all of that. I caught up later in the Seventies.

Does that affect the way you write female characters?

I hope not. I've been criticized for that. I like the wife [character] in *Year of the Dragon* very much. I also like Maria in *Salvador* a lot. I know that she's been criticized as simplistic, but that's the way she *was,* and that's the way a lot of those Latin women *are.* Not all. But *some* are – very simple, very devoted to that Latin ethic of being one-man's woman. I *try* to write truthfully.

The material that interests me and the ideas that I've done have all been extreme – Florida drugs, Chinatown drugs, justice in Turkey, civil war in Salvador. These ideas tend to attract male heroes instead of heroines… because they are life and death issues more than Woody Allen issues of angst, acceptance, and love.

Was Seizure *your first screenplay?*

Oh, no, I've been writing ever since film school, but with no success. Robert Bolt helped me enormously on *Cover-Up,* which was a very strong, leftist, anti-FBI script. I loved that screenplay. Bolt, who is socialist and quite leftist in England, helped me write and rewrite it, but we couldn't get it made. Even so, it got me an agent, the first agent I ever had.

By this point, in the mid-Seventies, you are describing yourself as a "leftist"?

I was emotionally disgusted. I thought the cops were pigs. I was with Jimmy Morrison on that one. I was into more radical violence. When they took over NYU, and all of the kids trashed the place, when Cambodia was invaded, I thought they were nuts. I said, if you want to protest, let's get a sniperscope and *do* Nixon. That was my reaction. Why don't we fight instead of this bullshit? I was never really in sync. I was more like Travis Bickle than I was a student protestor. Still, I didn't *politically* see it. I was more into the rock-and-roll.

Watergate was a key turning point. I read a lot of the stuff and began to meet more people and to broaden my contacts in the world. I started to learn. Politically, I was relatively uneducated because I had hewed to my father's line.

Watergate really sort of hammered the point home that the government was a lie. The government lied to us about Ho Chi Minh, and it lied to us about the Vietnam War. I wrote *Platoon* then – in '76.

What compelled you?

To tell the truth as I knew it before it was forgotten.

—◦—

Vietnam is such an obvious subtext in several of your films. It's a sort of bad running joke in Salvador.

All of these guys were in Vietnam. Boyle keeps running into the same guys. Not only were the American troops there, like the Colonel, who says to Boyle, "I remember you! Thieu threw you out!" and Boyle replies, "Then somebody threw Thieu out!" But the Salvadoran death squads were there; Rene Chacon and Jose Medrano, two of the prime movers in the Death Squads, had been in Vietnam studying counter-insurgency techniques.

Salvador *chronicles the Vietnam of the Eighties, and* Platoon *the Sixties. The missing link, the movie you failed to make in the Seventies, is Ron Kovic's* Born on the Fourth of July.

It's a tragedy the picture wasn't made then. We were three days from shooting. I had spent a year on the screenplay, working with Ron Kovic, who had written a terrific book, poetic, a wonderful piece. I saw the whole movie in rehearsals. We changed what we had to change. [Al] Pacino was white heat. [William] Friedkin, the director, had dropped out, which was a real shame, but he had been very ably replaced by Dan Petrie. But then the money fell out. It was one of those crazy half-German, half-U.S. deals – three days before shooting. Al wouldn't wait. He went to do the [Norman] Jewison picture *...And Justice for All.* It was very hard. Kovic was very broken up. I really went into a nosedive. At one point, Cimino tried to resurrect it, but the original costs had mounted to where it was too expensive. That was really a story of the Seventies, Ron's story, very angry.

And nobody in Hollywood would risk making Platoon?

No, not really. It had been sent around by my first agent. People liked *Platoon* but didn't want to make it. So I was put into a really inexpensive movie, *Midnight Express.* [Alan] Parker and [producer David] Puttnam really fought to shoot my screenplay, because it would have been compromised otherwise.

For a long time I gave up on *Platoon. Apocalypse Now* and *Deer Hunter* came out, and there was a kind of lull. It was over. Nobody wanted to make *Born on the Fourth of July.* So I got the message. American didn't really care about the truth of the war. It was going to be buried. Watergate was over, Carter lost, Iran had taken the hostages, liberalism was dead. The truth was dead. I got harder and cynical. So I buried the screenplay.

Actually, I would have left it buried if it hadn't been for Cimino, who came back into my life in '84 and wanted me to do *Dragon* with him. I didn't want to do it. But he convinced me by telling me that after we did *Dragon*, he'd produce *Platoon*. I'd direct it, and we'd get Dino to finance it. I fell for it. It sounded great. And though Dino ultimately did not make the movie, it was Michael who brought it back to life. All of a sudden, he was saying, "It's commercial, let's do it. This is something people are ready to see now…"

When Dino passed on it, I was really heartbroken. I couldn't understand why it was resurrected in order to be killed. But it was alive as an idea. [Producer] Arnold Kopelson brought it to John Daly at Hemdale. Hemdale loved it, and Orion bought into the picture, and we got it made. Orion wanted to do *Platoon* before *Salvador*, but I really wanted to do *Salvador* first – because it was ready to go.

—◇—

Salvador *was one cause you knew very little about.*

I didn't know anything about it. Boyle, I had known for years as a scoundrel, a rascal, and a knave. I had bailed him out of jail a few times over the years. I was going nowhere in my life, creatively. Richard was a breath of fresh air for me. He came down here on New Year's, 1985. We talked, and he showed me notes on *Salvador*. I loved the idea. We got a story, structure, we went to Salvador, we wrote a screenplay from January through March. That's three months – with the travel and everything; because during that period we also went to Honduras, Costa Rica, Belize, Mexico. We were just floating; I was financing the whole thing myself. I said to Richard, "We're going to make this picture starring *you*, Richard…"

And I read Ray Bonner's great book *Weakness and Deceit*. He was the *New York Times* correspondent there before he was fired – Accuracy in Media went after him. I read the book, met the people, and when you're down there and it's six inches from your face – the poverty and what people go through – you *do* get angry. It's a tragedy.

If Shakespeare were alive, he'd probably be a screenwriter, and I bet you he'd be dealing with the canvas of El Salvador. It's such a huge story, and nobody in America really knows about it: 30-50,000 people killed by death squads. Another 500,000 split the country. That's approximately 15-20 per cent of the population dead or gone, because of the right-wing repression, essentially a military mafia supported by the U.S. It's very clear cut to me. And it's very clear cut to the people there, it's not ambiguous.

Did you encounter any political opposition to the script?

Not really. I knew what the reaction would be because I had had problems with other scripts that had been turned down over the years. I had a reputation around town as a "cause freak." On the basis of *Born on the Fourth of July* and *Defiance* – which was a Russian script I did, involving dissidents – and others.

Salvador was just too anti-American for the American money people. Also, the track record on Central American films was real poor. *Missing* didn't do any business in this country, even though it got Academy Award nominations, and *Under Fire* was a total disaster in terms of receipts.

Certain people hated the script. Mostly, studios would "pass," meaning they don't ever tell you why. But anti-Americanism, I heard, was a factor. It took the English [Hemdale] to make it. They had a sense of irony about it. They saw these two scuzzbags [the Richard Boyle and Dr. Rock characters] as funny, almost in Monty Pythonesque terms. I sold it as "Laurel and Hardy Go to Salvador."

I wanted the movie to start that way and then twist. *Dr. Strangelove* was a great model for me, as a kid, because it went from extreme absurdity to extreme seriousness. Another very strong influence was *Viva Zapata!* – because of that liberating pulse beating through it. The movie that most influenced me as a filmmaker, to *be* a filmmaker, was Godard's *Breathless,* because it was fast, anarchic. I'm into anarchy.

Were there scenes you had to sacrifice to get Salvador *made?*

I pulled back quite a bit from a lot of heavier stuff. I pulled a lot of the violence out of it. We weakened a lot in the story. The picture was two hours. It was originally supposed to be two-and-a-half hours. But I couldn't get that version played, so I cut ruthlessly. So this version is a bit choppy – it's been criticized for being choppy – and they're right. It's lumpy.

There are scenes that are abruptly cut; the scene where the Colonel saves Boy's [James Woods] ass, and they all go back into the whorehouse together – in my script that scene develops into an orgy. A Borges-type scene. I wanted it to go from darkness to light. I wanted to have that crazy South American mix of black humor with tragedy. I wanted to play with absurdity as an idea.

I had this tremendous scene: Dr. Rock is getting a blow job under the table. Boyle is fucking a girl while trying to pry information from the Colonel, and the Colonel is so drunk out of his mind that he pulls out this bag of ears and throws the ears on the table and says… "Left-wing ears, right-wing ears, who gives a fuck?" He throws the ears into a champagne glass and proposes a toast to El Salvador and drinks the champagne with an ear in it.

The equivalent of Tony Montana gorging himself on cocaine.

Exactly. I wanted excess because that's the way it is down there. There's a scene at the end of *Salvador* that captures that madness: These guys are ready to kill Boyle, they're beating him up, they're just about to shoot him when they get the word from the Colonel that he's an important hombre, so they let him go. In the next scene, they're having beers together and slapping each other on the back. That's the way it is down there. You can go from light to dark so fast. South American audiences would have understood that scene and liked it.

When we screened the movie for North American audiences, nobody knew how to take that scene. It was too early in the movie. Is this supposed to be a comedy, or is this a serious political movie? Very much an Anglo frame of mind… Why do we have to have that kind of specific intention? Can't we just drift with the movie and see where it takes us? The previewer, an expert on this sort of problem, advised us to take it out.

I also had scenes with [Jim] Belushi in the whorehouse that were deemed too much – a funny scene when he is making it with Wilma – that shocked audiences. It was too lurid. But to me it captured the exact flavor of Central American whorehouses.

Certainly, you didn't compromise on your characterization of Boyle. James Woods portrays him as one of the most repulsive protagonists of all-time.

Oh, Richard is much worse than Jimmy. Richard's a very colorful character. Jimmy didn't want to play him as raggedy and as scummy as Richard really is. Jimmy wanted to make the story more heroic, whereas I wanted to push it in an anti-heroic direction. Jimmy feels he's made Richard more attractive to a larger group of people, although some people would say, "That's attractive?!" Let's say he made him more accessible. But the real Richard is far worse.

You did a fantastic job of telescoping unrelated true events in an almost "living newspaper" kind of style.

I knew no one else was going to make a picture about El Salvador. I really knew it. So I felt I had to tell this whole thing. It's like a War of the Roses, another *Richard III*. I took two years and tried to fit it into two hours, and obviously I was knocked for it. I didn't show [President José Napoléon] Duarte, whom I consider to be a puppet for the military mafia; a false front put up by the U.S. to show there is a democracy. But when Reagan was elected, the entire left-wing of the party – Kiki Alvarez and Juan Chacón and others – were dragged out of the schoolroom where they were meeting, by the death squads, and found three days later with their balls stuffed in their mouths. I wanted to show that scene. I didn't have time. The screenplay was already one hundred and fifty pages long. The entire left was wiped out, the equivalent of the Democratic Party, while fucking Mr. Reagan talks about the fucking Nicaraguans as if they are the bandits of all-time, calling them Marxist and un-Christian, when under the so-called Christian Democratic administration in Salvador next door fifty thousand civilians have been killed, mostly by the military. That's the hypocrisy of American foreign policy. It rouses my anger.

So you're no longer in any sense anti-Communist?

No. Not at all. I've changed totally. I've been to Russia. I've written about dissidents – and I know the story there, to some degree. But I don't see Central America as really being Marxist. I think Nicaragua may call itself Marxist in response to persecution and repression. But even if they are Marxist, which I don't think they are, so what? They have a right to be what they want to be. I don't see a problem. If a Russian nuclear sub can be fifteen miles off the coast of

New York harbor, what difference does it make if the Russians are in Nicaragua? If they are.

It's not a question of Capitalism or Communism when your kid dies of dysentery or diarrhea; it's really a question of health, education, and welfare. And they're not getting it. Next to Haiti, El Salvador is one of the worst offenders in the Western hemisphere. American government officials don't seem to realize that revolution is a response to social and economic conditions, not a Cold War game. It's a North/South conflict, not an East/West one.

It goes beyond that, I think. Mr. Reagan, and various administrations in this country, have truly betrayed our constitution by denying to others the right to revolution and self-determination that we have in *our* constitution. And what the Catholic Church expresses in the encyclicals: "Where there is a manifest, longstanding tyranny, there exists a right of armed insurrection." [Archbishop] Romero called for that, and he's the pivotal figure in the movie.

Obviously, America and Russia are locked in a Cold War struggle, and this thing is determining your life and my life, and our generation's. Until you or I figure out a way to get beyond this Cold War shit, our lives are fucked, we're predetermined to die.

—◦—

How directly did the writing of Platoon *tie into Watergate and the war?*
It didn't tie in politically, really, because *Platoon* isn't about politics, or the government's fault; it's about boys in the jungle. But Watergate was like peeling an onion. There was a sense of liberation, of an oppressive burden being lifted off. I remember this tremendous energy in the country, this sense of pride, and the hope and feeling that the bad guys could be defeated, and the good guys could win. I'd say that, maybe in the same spirit, I was probably saying to myself, "Let's peel the onion, let's get to the truth of Vietnam."
Has Platoon *changed much in ten years?*
It's very similar. The same story exactly. Just minor points. Some characterizations are more rounded, but essentially, it's the same, simple story – probably the least writing I've ever done, more like a newspaper report. Actually, *Salvador* was pretty simple too, because it was more of an explosion about Boyle's life. Very straight. The *Salvador* script took six weeks; *Platoon* four or five. Generally, it just comes in a burst, and I just do it fast – twelve-hour days.
Was it painful to write Platoon?
Once the writing started, no. To get to the point of doing it, yes. I wrote it in a moment when I was broke. I had left my first wife and I was going nowhere. That was in the summer of '76, the 200th anniversary of the U.S., with all this patriotism going on. Getting the pitch was the hardest thing.
How did you get the pitch?
I *remembered* it. That war never went away. Those images you don't forget

that easy. In '76, it was still burning. Then it was a question of organizing the structure of the tale. It's hard to go back. I got very good technical advisors on the movie because to remember details is very hard. To try to get the boys to talk Sixties talk was virtually impossible. They just didn't take to words that were used in the Sixties. But the actual feeling of combat, I think, stayed with me. The fear stayed with me. Also, the difficulty of fighting.

Rambo and *Top Gun* make it look real easy, but I remember the NVAs [North Vietnamese Army] as being terrific fighters. They were always nailing us. I liked *Apocalypse* and *The Deer Hunter*, but as big, mythic movies, not really authentic. They didn't catch the war – not the mood, or the look, or the actual war geography, which is very important. They put bodies into a frame, to fill the frame, masses of enemies. But that's very, very wrong. Perspectives are very important when you fight. You don't see the enemy that clearly.

Did you hold back at all in Platoon?

There's a good taste factor that comes into play. You don't want a head blowing apart because it turns off a certain segment of the audience. I'm aware of that. I want women and children to see the movie. So you don't show the violence as it actually happened. You pull back. You try to do it in a reserved fashion. That's the mode right now. It's not like [Fernando] Arrabal's *Viva la Muerte*. In *Platoon*, I think the power of suggestion is strong. It does the work for you. I've learned that now.

—◦—

What happened to your platoon? How many are still alive?

Oh, I don't know. I have no idea. I tried to get in touch with them when I was working with Cimino, and only found five; three had died, two I went and saw. We were all shipped in at different times as replacement troops. It was not like the old war movies. I arrived in September of 1967, and when I left in January of 1968, out of the original one hundred and twenty men in the company, I recognized maybe ten faces. Some of them were dead; some of them were wounded; some had been shipped back or replaced. But the company got pretty badly beaten up from September of '67 to January '68. I was wounded twice. *Platoon* covers that period. I took characters from four different units and telescoped them.

What were the problems in writing or casting your alter ego?

It was like fate. When Charlie Sheen walked into the room, in ten seconds I knew he was the one who was going to do that role. The eyes, the look, the mood, the feeling, the face – it was just right. There was a *rightness* about him. It *flows*. When Charlie walked in, it flowed.

I had long discussions with Charlie. I tried to get back to that quality of distance that I had when I was in Nam. I wanted to convey the fear I felt in the jungles for the first time. And I wanted to convey to Charlie what the two sergeants in control meant to me. To me – Sergeant Elias, played by Willem Dafoe, and Sergeant Barnes, played by Tom Berenger – they were gods. I was thrown into a war, just a kid from New York, and suddenly everything I had read in Homer was coming true. I was literally with warriors. Barnes was Achilles, a truly great warrior. Elias was Hector, and I was with them in another world. What I wanted to convey to Charlie was my sense of innocence that changes as the movie develops. That's the key to the movie.

The hardest thing to get on paper was the character of Elias. I loved this guy. He was a free spirit, a Jimmy Morrison in the bush. Handsome... he was our god. He was killed in a very freak accident. How do you capture the spirit of someone who was mythic when you were a younger boy? I think we got some of that spirit, but it was hard.

The movie is very close to *Midnight Express*, insofar as it deals with a young man and with innocence. Whereas *Salvador* deals with an older man who is unredeemed – *unredeemable* – although we *tried* to redeem him. Pauline Kael pointed that out in her review. It's not just about El Salvador, it's about salvation. Salvador means "to save." It's about saving Richard Boyle; that's what she said. And she's correct – it's really not just about saving Salvador, but how really hard it is to find salvation in the world. Richard tries to con Maria into marrying him, he becomes a good guy and even goes to church; but it's not so easy – the Archbishop gets shot; then, when he finally gets her out of the country, she gets arrested and gets sent back. Always, Richard is being disappointed, defeated. It isn't *easy*. That's the point of the movie. The country is damned.

Do you see any conflict in directing your own scripts?

I don't see any conflict. I see it as a natural progression, to take it from writing to directing. Sometimes, as a director, I think you need another writer; it would be helpful to have a second voice. But the writer and the director are really two different people, two different parts of the self. The director is more the host, the emcee; the writer is the quieter side, the introspective side, the miserable, depressed, and lonely side. Writing's probably the hardest of the two because it requires more loneliness and isolation, and that's harder to put up with. Directing is more arduous physically; but mentally, writing is harder. It requires concentrated thought over a long period of time. But I don't see them in conflict. They go hand in hand.

—◦—

Stylistically, Salvador *and* Platoon *run counter to the glossiness and form of Hollywood war movies.*

In *Salvador*, the style extends the urgency of the character. The camera is always moving, trying to give tenseness to the situation. The movie is always on top of you, going on *now*. *Platoon*, we pulled back more, stylistically. It's more period. 1967. We didn't shoot right on top of you. Although we still did a lot of hand-held, there's more dolly work, and more crane work. We also had a little more time.

I hate those cleaned-up war movies. Nothing is real. Scorsese, Coppola, and Friedkin in the early Seventies tried to break out of that mold, and Altman, too, was great – his playing with perspectives in *Nashville* was an eye-opener. Those realistic modes influenced an entire generation.

Their credo might be the same as yours. Show the ugly…

Yes, but… show the good! There's a great line I agree with that I read somewhere. Renoir, I think, said, "If it's not to the greater glory of man, don't make it…" I remember seeing *Reds* after making *The Hand* – in which I was trying to show the horror and disintegration of a man, but ultimately you don't win with that kind of movie. I remember seeing *Reds* and thinking, "Goddammit, that man [Warren Beatty] is right…" I don't care how much money he spent, he went out and did something that he believed in and cared about. You have to make films as an idealist. You've got to make them to the greater glory of mankind. Then, even if you fail, even if the film doesn't work, you do not have to be ashamed, because you tried… But if you try something that's small and negative and you fail, then you're really in deep shit.

Are you still a "cause freak"?

Oh, yes. But you have to keep people off balance. Keep dancing. I might surprise you. I might turn around and do a comedy with all women. A remake of *The Women*! [Laughs]

My style is going to change. I might go back to a very low-budget film, like *Salvador*. I still have that in my blood. I'm dying to do something about Nicaragua. I was very interested in South Africa… but it's breaking as we speak. The largest cause perhaps is American/Soviet relations, which I could try to assess, maybe improve. If films *can* help – I have only small hopes that films can help the political climate.

I've grown with each of my films. This is only my fourth movie – two of them admittedly were learning experiences. None of them has been a waste of time for me. That's important. I've educated myself. I've gotten better. I've learned more about my craft. I'm just at the beginning of a road. I'm learning how to make movies.

The Business

Boston Bankers

1976
Introduction by Stuart Byron
Interview by Patrick McGilligan

Though the cry "The banks got me!" seems to have been heard in the film industry since nickelodeon days, relatively few of the nation's leading commercial banks have ever been involved in financing pictures to any considerable extent. The reasons are not really hard to deduce. There is, in truth as well as song, no business like show business, and a banker is likely to be more confused than enlightened by a look at a film company's supposed assets and liabilities. It's relatively easy to understand the continuing value of a product like Kellogg's Corn Flakes, which has achieved strong consumer identification, and similarly easy to adjudge the worth of such a tangible as oil reserves. But what is the typical banker to do with a company that has twenty different, entirely new "products" a year – all of which have commercial potential for at most eighteen months? How is he or she to estimate the worth of something so nebulous as "television residual value"? As William F. Thompson, one of the bankers interviewed here, once observed: "Your normal banker could very well look at the balance sheet of the most profitable film company and conclude that it had no assets at all."

Thus, the very particular expertise that is a requirement to be a lender to the film industry has been developed as a specialty at no more than a dozen banks, and only two have ever been real giants in the field: Los Angeles's Bank of America and the First National Bank of Boston. If proximity to Hollywood is a reasonable explanation for the emergence of the former, First National's entrance was largely the innovation of one man, the legendary Serge Semenenko, now retired after a lifetime's career at the bank (he ended up as vice-chairman).

Looked at with a kind of simplistic schematism, these two banks seem to represent antithetical positions in American banking. The attitudes expressed by senior vice-president Thompson and his assistant George Bruns seem a benign version of those expressed by the stuffy colleagues of such celluloid banker-rebels as Walter Huston in Frank Capra's *American Madness* and Fredric March in William Wyler's *The Best Years of Our Lives*. The boys at First National may come off as quintessential "Eastern bankers," interested only in the bottom line, while the Bank of America and other California bankers, who continue to some extent to finance individual movies, have an aura of being more concerned with creators. Capra, after all, based his Tom Dickson on A.P. Giannini, the founder of the Bank of America: "All the other banks thought he was absolutely nuts, lending money on character. He'd take collateral if you had it, but if you didn't and you had character, he'd lend you money anyhow," Capra is quoted in Richard Glatzer's book, *Frank Capra: The Man and His Films.*

But real life, as always, is a lot more complicated than reel life. A person who lends you money based on "character" is assuming, if only implicitly, a right to interfere with the conduct of your business – to tell you what to make, with what cast, at what cost. California bankers have rarely been accused publicly of doing this, but anyone familiar with the industry knows how nervous even the implied threat of it can make creative people; at the very least, film bankers at Los Angeles institutions have made themselves highly visible, giving speeches and writing trade-paper articles expostulating on industry trends. Ironically, the "Eastern" impartiality of the Boston bankers may result in the hands-off attitude from financiers so essential for creativity.

———○———

Which studios does First National bank for?
WILLIAM F. THOMPSON: We're the main bank for Warner Bros., Fox, and Columbia Pictures.
Why did First National become involved with financing movies in the Thirties? Was it entirely due to Serge Semenenko?
THOMPSON: Certainly, a great deal was due to Serge. He got us into it in the first place and, as his skill became apparent and his reputation grew, other studios sought us out. However, what made our continuing and growing involvement with the film industry possible was the fact that the resources of the bank are far larger than New England can use. One of our former chairmen used to say: "We're like the hospitals in Boston: we have many more beds than the city needs." As a result, to keep our money profitably employed, we have long had to look outside the region, both nationally and internationally, for interesting situations where we could play a part. In the course of this, we have developed certain specialties where we feel we have marketable expertise. The film business is certainly one of them, and it's been very good to our bank.

As I got the story – this was way before my time – Serge knew a fellow who was at American Theatres [Corporation], a Boston exhibitor, no longer in business. Serge handled a loan for American, and was introduced to the people at Universal at the time. I think that was our first studio loan, in 1938.

GEORGE BRUNS: Many of the names you see in the old credit files are long gone; Columbia is about the only one still in existence that goes back to the Thirties.
Can you capsulize the bank's history of involvement?
THOMPSON: Serge was the banker for Universal, until MCA took it over in the Sixties; we financed the Decca-Universal situation, when Decca bought out Universal in the Fifties. And he was the banker at MGM; he set

up the first private placement that had ever been done for a movie company with insurance companies – what was then Loew's, Inc., the parent of MGM. Columbia, all along; Warner Bros. has been here for years, probably since the late Forties or Fifties; Fox came in after Serge left the bank.

BRUNS: We were the bankers for both Cinerama and National General during that time in the mid-Sixties and early Seventies, when they were involved in production and distribution.

THOMPSON: Dick Smith, the head of General Cinema, the big theater chain, is doing some co-production deals, basically with ATV in England, another customer of ours.

—◦—

How do you decide which companies to lend money to?

THOMPSON: Lending to movies is really no different than lending to a chemical company or paper company in terms of credit principles, although each industry obviously has its own particular characteristics. We look at the corporate balance sheet of the entity we're lending to. The qualification would be if we had a company that had other assets. For instance, we're the main bank for ATV, Britain's largest commercial television network. Lew Grade has built up not only a very profitable television network, but he has a big record company, music publishing company, and owns the most prominent legitimate theaters in London, as well as real estate in the Midlands. I'm describing to you an asset base that is completely separate from the movie business. We began financing him eight or ten years ago in television production, because he produced series that were bought by networks in this country, as well as around the world. That's a more predictable sort of thing today; it's cost-plus today, you can't really lose too much if you've priced yourself right and done the deal right. But then he decided to get into feature motion pictures. Well, yes, we're putting up the money for this, but we have other what I call fallback positions; so far he's been very, very successful, and he's picked the right pictures and done very well. But we have to let him take that risk.

BRUNS: This type of analysis has led us, not exclusively, but generally, to the major studios. Now every one of them is diversified to some degree; some of them are splendidly diversified. If their movies were totally unsuccessful, they would get along quite nicely. These major companies have built other operations generally related to the entertainment-type business – broadcasting, publishing, records, music publishing, and so forth – and recently, in fact, have come up with more businesslike management than the old moguls.

THOMPSON: They are very pragmatic businessmen. To me, their activity is not dissimilar to ours in making loans. They are making pictures. The acts of lending money and making pictures are really pragmatic. In the sense that you take what comes along at the time, don't you? They can't say, we'll create a lineup that has two comedies, three Westerns, and one musical – because maybe there is none of some category available this year. So if you see a book like *All the President's Men* and Robert Redford has bought it, you think, that's going to be a commercial movie. You go ahead and act as quickly as you can to sign it up.

All these studios today, more or less, are in the hands of businessmen. The age of the mogul is over. These businessmen are out to make a profit, because they know – history tells them – that if they don't, the shareholders will throw them out and somebody else will come in.

BRUNS: Furthermore, if you think of it as a return on investment, what business do you know of where the return can be so gigantic, as it has been, for example, for Universal with *The Sting* or *Jaws*? That's a huge return. When it's run right, in terms of product selection and keeping the costs in line, your risk-reward ratio is huge. I think this is where the new generation of businessmen are acutely conscious; once they've selected the product, they pay a lot of attention to budgeted costs. There's not this abandon that there was in the mogul days of, "It's good, let's spend money…"

Do you have any input into the release schedule of each studio? Would you, for example, warn against a certain subject or genre?

THOMPSON: I think it's very dangerous for the banker to play moviemaker. In the final analysis we lend out money, we want our money back – because it isn't our money, it's our depositors' money, of course – and we cannot be in the position of saying, "Don't make this Western, make this actioner." Because how do *we* know?

Do you ever discuss the movies in terms of director or cast?

BRUNS: They tell us, but only for interest.

Somebody told me that Los Angeles banker Peter Geiger appeared on a public panel, and said that Liza Minnelli is no longer "bankable," now that she has appeared in one utter flop, Lucky Lady. *That seems to be an awfully short life span.*

THOMPSON: I wouldn't make that kind of judgment; I'd rather have [Warners President] Ted Ashley tell me whether he wants her in a movie, because I don't care whether she's in a movie or not.

BRUNS: That use of the word "bankable" is unfortunate here. What Geiger was talking about is whether the *studio* thinks this person, for whatever reason, is a draw. For many years, John Wayne never made a film that was a total flop; he never made a *Jaws* either. The studio felt it could depend on John Wayne. *They* made that decision, *we* didn't. *They* were banking on him, not *us*.

THOMPSON: It may sound strange to you, but bankers are not operators of a business. I don't care what business they're lending to; you can live vicariously, if you will – and a movie business is obviously more glamorous than stoves – but I think it's highly dangerous for a banker to

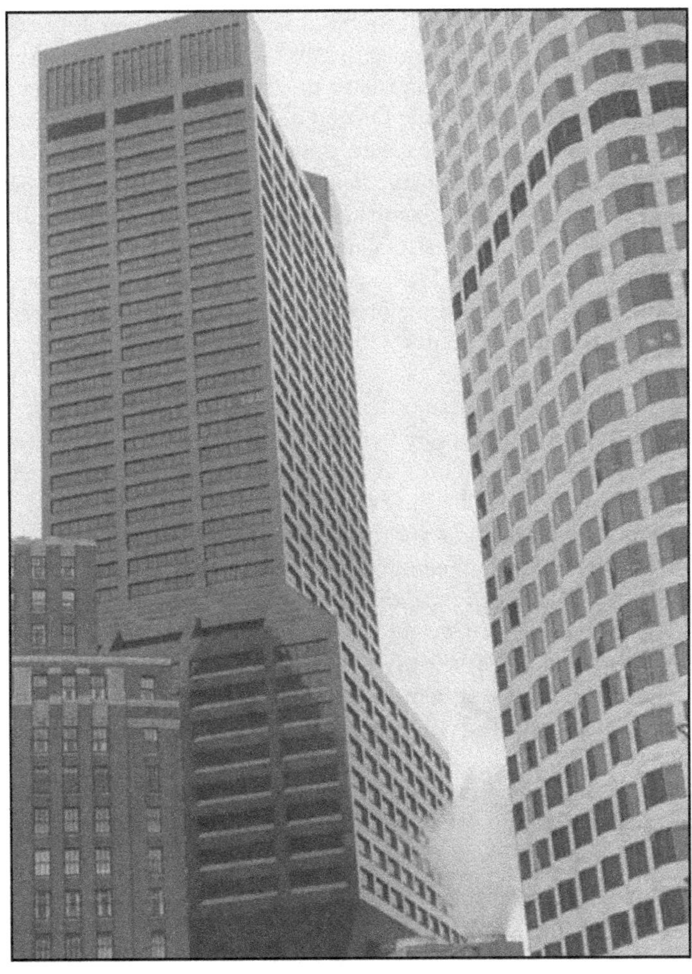

First National Bank of Boston, 100 Federal Street,
Boston, Massachusetts, 1973.

be quivering from stem to stern because he's lending money on movies. To mix in with these creative people, I think bankers would meddle at the peril of their loan; really, from a legal standpoint, we must not be in a position of running the company. All we have a right to do is demand our money back.

Is banking more important to the industry today than before?

THOMPSON: I don't think so, because there are fewer companies that really depend on banks. Universal extinguished their debt. Paramount is part of Gulf + Western, and they don't have to depend on banking. I'm not that familiar with United Artists, but Disney doesn't have to depend on banks. Really, Warner Bros. doesn't have to depend on banks; they have a bank credit outstanding because management believes in it, although they don't have to. Whereas a generation ago there were bank loans outstanding on, I dare say, all of these companies to a greater or lesser degree. I'd say banking plays a lot smaller role today. Not only have companies been managing their assets better, but the cost of money today has become much more significant in their profit-and-loss statements than it was when the lending rate was three or four percent.

Don't forget, a lot of banks have heard about losses in this industry because there *have been* losses by banks that have lent on single pictures, and they've ended up with those movies in their vaults. The coming of television helped those banks greatly because those pictures became worth something. But that's not the way banks want to get their money back. They want to get it back in the time frame agreed upon, and by normal mechanisms.

You never finance an individual picture?

THOMPSON: No, but we get approached all the time. We get a call from some fellow who has a marvelous – in his mind – script. We patiently listen and say, "Look, you'd better take this to somebody who's going to distribute the picture because, first of all, the picture has to get playing time…" It's too risky a business. If you look at the statistics, it's not the kind of business where you can justify making a loan for a single picture. Serge laid down the principle, forty years ago, that we not lend on a single picture, and that is something we have followed throughout. We test that policy from time to time, but it has stood us by pretty well.

I can think of one instance where we lent to a producer for a single picture, but he had an awful lot of securities as marketable collateral. This particular individual – it was he and his wife – were bound and determined to make a movie, and they were warned ahead of time that the securities formed the only basis upon which we were making our loan, because we knew, if the roof fell in, we could still come out okay. Well, the fact is that that movie never saw the light of day. They took the completed film from company to company, from the big ones down to the small ones, and nobody would even invest advertising money. It has never been released. Nobody would take it on for distribution, and we had to resort to the collateral.

But some banks do this regularly?
THOMPSON: That's my impression.
BRUNS: My impression is that it's done less now than it used to be.
Which banks?
THOMPSON: Bank of America has done a great deal on individual pictures. Security Pacific used to do more than they do now; they were active more as the Bank of America was, reading scripts and knowing who is in the picture, all this kind of stuff – assessing the so-called star value.

—◦—

What is the credit situation at 20th Century-Fox?
THOMPSON: They have a substantial line of credit available from us but are using only a part of it. With assets of some $300 million, they're really pretty comfortable.
Is 20th Century-Fox diversified?
BRUNS: It has a vast holding of foreign theaters, principally in New Zealand and Australia, but to some degree in Europe. They own three television stations; they have a small music-publishing operation; they have DeLuxe General film processing lab; they have a small record company; they operate Marineland. They *are* diversified.
THOMPSON: In 1974, half of Fox's earnings came from its non-movie activities. Last year, that percentage dropped because *Towering Inferno* and *Young Frankenstein* were so gigantic that it pushed the movie part up. Non-movie earnings are a steady and growing source of revenue for Fox.
Columbia seems to have made a tremendous comeback.
THOMPSON: It's certainly going in the right direction. Obviously, it'd be nice if the balance sheet gets beefed up some more, but when you think of where this company was three years ago, and where it is today – I haven't lost any sleep over it, let's put it that way.
We're very proud of the job [Columbia CEO] Alan Hirschfield has done; he has really put vitality into it. This is a people business, there's no question about it. Alan has brought new blood to a company that was really getting somewhat tired. The record speaks for itself. They were swamping in oceans of red ink, and Alan really did an outstanding job.
He's a very able chief executive, but one man can't do it alone. He brought in David Begelman for the films. Clive Davis – the record business Columbia had was virtually going down the drain – new heads of distribution and advertising. And those people, in turn, have brought in others. It's really been revitalized from top to bottom.
BRUNS: It's an attitudinal thing, too. He has developed a feeling in the company. The people, when you talk to them, are very enthusiastic about what they're doing, and they bring that enthusiasm out into the creative side.

THOMPSON: I think that the current management of Columbia is more in touch. Not that the old one didn't try to ascertain what the market is, because I go on the premise that all these companies are managed by people who sincerely believe that they have judged the market correctly; they're not fools, they are very intelligent men who run these companies, and a lot of anguish and effort goes into trying to select the release schedule. But as the Columbia management aged, they did lose touch with the marketplace. Hirschfield, being younger, has brought in a lot of younger people. It's not necessarily that youth knows everything, but certainly the moviegoing audience, statistically, is from fifteen to thirty years of age. You have to have some appreciation of what those people want to see, not just now, but a year and a half to two years from now, because that is the product cycle.

Isn't one of the reasons for Columbia's revival its pioneering in shared-risk investment? Tax shelters as opposed to bank loans?

THOMPSON: You had a disastrous balance-sheet situation when Alan Hirschfield took over. Alan realized that the banks weren't going to put up any more money, so he began doing these tax-shelter investments that, in effect, shared a risk, and this was critically important to the survival of the company.

BRUNS: They are now regarded as pre-eminent in the field; they know more about it than any other company, really.

THOMPSON: To me, it makes abundant sense, if you accept the principle of high-risk business, to use the tax laws, as far as the law allows, to share the risk with other people. If you're a movie company, I think it's better to have a smaller percentage of a profit not yet in hand than one hundred percent of a loss.

Basically, Columbia is a movie company; their record company, under Davis, is doing nicely, but it's early in the game there. Bit by bit, Columbia has sold off its television stations.

BRUNS: They still have two, three radio stations.

And Warners? That studio, of all the studios, seems to be the most reliable in terms of its product.

THOMPSON: I can't speak about product reliability. If you mean acceptance at the box-office, all I can do is look at the figures. I think Ted Ashley and his crew there are top-flight people; they are really pros at this business; their record speaks for itself. Overall, it's a highly profitable company. Of course, as you know, the bulk of its earnings are coming from its record business; it's really a record company that happens to make movies.

Does the film division make money?

THOMPSON: Oh, yes. They'll have their losers, just like any company. But they make enough on their winners there to make a very, very respectable profit.

Do you find that these companies have individual characters?

THOMPSON: Each company is different. Its tone is set by the character and attitude of the chief executive officer of the company. Ashley, to me, is like an orchestra conductor; each one is playing a solo, or each one thinks he is playing a solo, and that's the artist in Ashley to let them think so. Yet they're all a team.

With Columbia, Hirschfield is in New York. [David] Begelman, on the Coast, sets the tone for the movie part of Columbia, obviously taking his cue from Hirschfield. Begelman has an entirely different style. I think of David more as the boss, although not in an autocratic sense. Ashley never appears to have the iron fist; it's there, but it's in a nice velvet glove.

United Artists really turned out to be the bellwether of the future, because you don't really need a studio. Remember, these companies – and we keep using the word studios – have eventually evolved into financiers of pictures. Now why do they finance pictures when the risk of loss is so great? Because they can't get the distribution rights to these pictures without putting up some or all of the capital. They make their money on distribution of these pictures, rather than on production, if you can separate the two – and it's pretty hard.

The standard formula is: If you bring the picture to me, and I'm Universal, say, I'll take thirty-five percent of the money the picture earns as my distribution fee in the U.S., after prints and advertising, which I'll put up, and forty percent foreign. Well, it doesn't cost thirty or forty percent to do it; these percentages are embedded in time someplace, God knows how. There is where there's an element of return for one of these seven major companies. The production money that they have to put up, which is – what? – $50 or $60 million per company per year in current dollars, is the capital that they must put at risk in order to get the distribution fees on these, let's say, $100 million of film rentals domestically or, let's say, $100 million foreign, or whatever.

Of course, no film company can have a profitable year from distribution fees alone; unless some of your films go into the black, you don't make money.

The consent decree via which the government forced the major studios to divest their theater chains is now about twenty-five years old. Any thoughts?

THOMPSON: I think it's outlived its usefulness. Obviously, it had a place in our history. The little exhibitor, who started all this sort of thing, couldn't get pictures – because only Universal and Columbia were without theater chains, so the little exhibitors were relegated to the leavings; the other five majors all just filled up their own theaters. So I think there was a reason for it. But look what happened to the industry with the advent of television: the fall-off of the number of people going to the movies, the terrible trauma that all the production companies, all of them except Disney, have gone through. Now you have a situation that, if you put up $50 or $60 million a year, and exhibitors don't want to bid for your pictures, how are you going to get playing time?

The cry of exhibitors today is that there isn't enough product. They've built all these movie theaters everywhere, but my guess is that, if by some miracle another $200 million would be made available to the seven major companies – buying another fifty pictures, at an average of $4 million per picture – I dare say the management of these companies couldn't find fifty more pictures they wanted to make at that kind of money. Secondly, they wouldn't want to borrow $200 million to put into movies; they'd rather buy television stations, start a record company, or go into an amusement park. Because the risk-reward ratio isn't there. It's too iffy. Look at the Christmas pictures last year – and again, I firmly believe that the management of these companies looked sincerely hard at things like *The Hindenburg*, *Lucky Lady* and *Barry Lyndon*; this makes them shy a little bit.

Have independent producers made significant inroads into the domination of the major Hollywood studios?

BRUNS: They're making more films but...

THOMPSON: Generally, they're having to utilize the services of a major to get their product distributed. There are other companies: Avco distributes pictures, American International, Cinema 5 – there are these people. But realistically, if you are putting up the capital, you want to be sure that your picture is going to get all the playing time possible because that's the only way you're going to get your money back, and so you'd be inclined to go to a major.

Here's where the continuing relationships between major distributors and exhibitors play an important part. The major distributors continually have the promise of important pictures, such as *All the President's Men*, coming along. Thus, the exhibitors are more apt to give a break to the films of independent producers, [but only] when the majors offer them.

I understand... I read a report in Variety *that said Columbia was forbidden by its lenders – that is, you – to pour more than a certain amount of money into any one film.*

THOMPSON: I think *Variety* made a mountain out of a molehill. This is not an unusual covenant. Because if you have, let's say, a $60 million credit agreement – Columbia's happens to be significantly more than that – would you want all $60 million to go into one movie? Generally, you'd like a diversification.

BRUNS: That's an exaggeration, but films did cost $25 million. For example, *Hello, Dolly!*

THOMPSON: *Tora! Tora! Tora!*

BRUNS: *Cleopatra* was over $40 million.

THOMPSON. This was one of the old Fox management's problems. They spent $250 million to make eleven movies; those eleven movies generated the biggest percentage of box-office gross in the industry in the years in which they were released, but they proved the old saw that you can buy all the sales you want to buy, if you don't care what it costs you to buy them. It is not an illogical banking concept to set an upper limit. I have never, on the other hand, seen us unwilling to waive that upper limit, because a banker can't know what a film company knows. What is Columbia's ceiling?

BRUNS: Five million dollars, but they have overrides for a number of films per year.

THOMPSON: Let's say they want to make an $8 or $9 million movie; we would almost certainly go along. In the twenty-two years I've been with the bank, I can't remember a time when we didn't accept management's judgment. If I heard a client of ours was going to make a $15-million epic or something, all I would say is, "Do you really want to put $15 million into one movie?" That's as far as we would go – "Are you sure?" – because it may prove to be the best thing since sliced bread.

What we are is another checkpoint. When your head of pictures – in this case, David Begelman – wants to make a deal, he has to first get Hirschfield's approval, as head of the company, and Hirschfield presumably has restrictions from the board of directors as to what he can and cannot do. Since, as I say, the bank, historically, has usually gone along, you may as well ask, why do we have the ceiling at all? The fact is, it makes you stop and think twice.

BRUNS: It is, by no means, limited to Columbia.

I recall reading that [producer] Irwin Allen's latest disaster movie was dropped by Fox because it was too expensive. Were you involved in that decision?

THOMPSON: No, but we were told, because this was one of those budgets that was originally over the permitted budget in the Fox agreement. First we were told they were going to breach the budget there, and then that they had decided to abandon the project. But we did not participate in the decision.

BRUNS: Their permitted limit is also $5 million, but again, like Columbia, the company is allowed a certain number of films each year that go above $5 million and below $10 million.

Irwin Allen's budget was above $10 million, if I recall.

THOMPSON: It was optioned over to Warners. Irwin Allen had, I think, a three-picture deal with Fox: *Poseidon, Towering Inferno* – which they did jointly with Warners – and this third picture. As I recall the details, Irwin Allen had agreed to go over to Warners at the conclusion of his three-picture deal with Fox. When he couldn't come to a satisfactory conclusion with this movie, why, they just decided to let him go over to Warners.

Warners does not have a limit. Their situation is a little different. If you look at the consolidated Warners Communications balance sheet you will find over $200 million cash or equivalent; secondarily, you have a company that makes something like $50 or $60 million after taxes, basically from its record businesses. A bank is not likely, with that kind of liquidity, to put in the kind of covenants that you would with another company.

Does money ever run out in mid-production. [Director] George Stevens once told me a funny story about funds drying up during the making of The Greatest Story Ever Told.

THOMPSON: Bank of America, which was financing a lot of individual pictures at that time, started with that, and Security Pacific picked it up midstream. United Artists did have banking problems with it. *The Greatest Story Ever Told* went over budget, and the bank was asked to increase the loan – millions of dollars. The Bank of America said, "This is ridiculous; it's costing too much money, and we don't want to stay involved." The company, after all, had a half-done movie at this point; they had no choice but to find somebody else who would put up the money. You can't be a little bit pregnant; you've got to go all the way.

Are sky-rocketing budgets causing deep concern in Hollywood?

THOMPSON: You put your finger on it. First, there was this settlement with the unions last fall – that's going to put increased costs below the line. Second, you do have pressure for the star salaries. I don't know whether you've heard the story – I can't vouch for its accuracy – but I heard that Steve McQueen turned down $3 million from Joe Levine for three weeks' work in *A Bridge Too Far*, the Cornelius Ryan book. I have to ask myself, "Do you really think anybody is worth $3 million for three weeks' work?"

I thought this was partly the credo of the New Hollywood, the make-it-or-break-it syndrome, pouring all your money into one star.

THOMPSON: I don't think that's true. If you sat down with Ashley or any of these people we've been talking about, they would say they deplore this. Remember, they are pragmatic and prudent businessmen, and they're not going to jeopardize the company by having a $25 million negative with every star they can think of in it. It's just not sound. And they know that stars don't bring the people to the box-office.

I thought it was generally agreed that you can't go wrong with someone like Paul Newman.

THOMPSON: You may remember a picture of Newman's, *WUSA*. That's a cause picture; he likes these cause pictures, and if he can get a studio to finance him in these causes, he'd love to do it. That's where the picture-picker better be careful. Do you want to be advocate of a cause on the screen, and with your stockholders' money? You can catch the public fancy with what I call "problem movies," but I think you've got to be awfully attuned to what the public is going to like two years from now.

I think the public basically doesn't go to see cause-type things. They go to be entertained. You can go to the *theater* to see gripping drama. But people in Peoria want to laugh or be frightened to death like *Jaws*. They don't care about drugs or homosexuality, really. I think those kinds of causes, if you will, are better left either low budget, if you really have a yen to make those things, or better yet, on Broadway.

BRUNS: On the other hand, there are always exceptions to this general proposition. Take *Easy Rider*, for instance. Abe Schneider, then president of Columbia, took a very dim view of the whole thing. It was such a radical departure. But his son Bert, who produced it, went ahead with it anyway. When he saw the first cut, Abe simply loathed it; so did his wife. Later, of course, when it was a success, Abe was very proud of his son and the picture.

Video Visions, Milwaukee

1983 – 2003

Interview by Patrick McGilligan

When I moved to Milwaukee in 1983, one of the sanctuaries for film-lovers on the east side of the city was a store called Video Visions, which was around the corner from the Oriental Theatre in a small mall that no longer exists, where there was also a Marcus Cinema with three screens. People drove to Video Visions from all over Milwaukee County, and indeed from all over southern Wisconsin. In almost every good-sized city throughout the U.S. there was a store like Video Visions. Quentin Tarantino worked in one in the mid-Eighties, in Manhattan Beach, California, where he and fellow employees and enthusiasts held marathon viewing and discussion sessions and made lengthy oral and written recommendations to their customers based on their own likes and dislikes. "When people ask me if I went to film school," Tarantino has been quoted as saying, "I say no, I went to films."

Greg Kolp, the store manager of Video Visions for the entire span of its operation, knew the video rental business, he knew every regular customer, and he could tell you about any video in the inventory because he had watched most of them at least once. After the store closed and he moved to Las Vegas, Kolp came back to Milwaukee to visit, and over several trips we tape-recorded his recollections of the video rental and sales phenomenon, and of the little independent store beloved and mourned by its east side customer base.

—o—

GREG KOLP: Video Visions began, like many other video stores, in 1983, just as the business of selling videos to the mass public got going strong. The two original co-owners [Jim Howard and his partner] were involved with a record store on nearby Brady Street, which had been renting the new product of videos. Originally the price points of videos were high, and the market for sales was slow to take off. *Casablanca* cost $79.95, for example. The lowest price for any title was $49.95. One of the future co-owners of Video Visions, who had been a University of Wisconsin in Milwaukee film student, convinced his partner to include videos in their record store by buying single copies of new videos and renting them out, a practice that had already begun elsewhere on a trial basis. The idea arose to sell memberships and especially what was then called an "executive membership," which was priced at $500 but negotiable down usually to $300, entitling the purchaser to three free rentals of any video every week. Surprisingly, a significant number of people found this arrangement attractive, and the store's investment in the future with more and more videos became the seed money that enabled the expansion of their video library and saved the record store from financial disaster when its dominant interest – selling music recordings, in those days still LPs – began to falter. When the music business continued to deteriorate, the partners bought out the record store owner, converted entirely to video, and with a bank loan of $25,000 moved into the Prospect Mall.

More and more people started to buy VCRs to tape their favorite movies off television, and more and more people now wanted to rent videos for weekend enjoyment, and the studios began to release more and more motion pictures in video format. When, that same year, 1983, *Raiders of the Lost Ark* was released in VHS, it drove the rental business into a frenzy like no other title before it; and because *Raiders* was released at $39.95, the sales made a big difference and its price set a marker. *Raiders* proved there was a fan base willing to pay the initial cost of new videos as long as that cost was affordable. There would have been less urge to buy the video if it had been priced at $79.95. All of the early marketing was done partly on a research basis to discover what would maximize the return to the studio. The success of *Raiders*, in video, both VHS and Beta, and later Video-Disc and Laser-Disc, demonstrated the wide possibility of a sell-through market. From its beginning, therefore, the home viewing of videos was closely linked to the mass appeal of the biggest blockbusters and their closely associated wide openings, which provided instant gratification for the largest audience.

Video Visions was in a different business from the other independent stores within the vicinity in Milwaukee, in large part because it had a constituency that boasted striking differences from other parts of the city. The immediate east side area had a high population density concentrated in rental units. While many University of Wisconsin-Milwaukee professors lived in the area, so did a high number of students. This meant the population had a lower median age than the rest of Milwaukee. From being quicker to adopt new media to having eclectic tastes, this younger subset of the east side population helped set the tone for our inventory.

For one thing, smaller, independent home-viewing stores like Video Visions tended to fall back on the adult (XXX rated) video market. Most smaller chains had set aside pornography sections, with a lucrative sub-section of gay pornography. The censorship concerns of video store operators in Milwaukee, as well as of those located elsewhere in the state with similar concerns, led to the formation of a local chapter of the Video Software Dealers Association to defend storeowners that felt threatened by proposed anti-pornography statutes. Video Visions and others joined the association as a supportive gesture. But unlike the smaller chains and other independent video stores with a single site, adult films were always only a small part of Video Visions, with pornography claiming only about five per cent of its titles. Most porn videos dropped fast in wholesale price; what once sold at $40-50 dropped quickly to $15-20, and the price fell even lower if you were unconcerned with the degree of quality, or if you were among those who found compilations of old porn films acceptable.

From the beginning, Video Visions was more a place for the worthwhile and the non-mainstream. The customers who frequented the Oriental and Downer Theaters, part of the Landmark chain on the east side, and other like-minded filmgoers in the Milwaukee area, wanted alternative entertainment but not necessarily pornography. There was a lucrative family section at Video Visions, but the primary draws were oddities in the classic film section, horror suspense, the black comedies, the cheesy science fiction, the foreign pictures that flew under the radar and were unrated, and the music videos that were unavailable elsewhere because their owners had no background in the music business. As a general rule, foreign films comprised fifteen per cent of the Video Vision titles and contributed approximately fifteen per cent of revenue. The same could be said of science fiction and horror, although the latter accounted to closer to twenty/twenty-five per cent. Of course, the main category driving the business was always new releases. Mainstream movies priced for the rental market soon stabilized at $59.95, with volume discounts, and slowly rose over the years up to the $65 area. What affected this segment of the market was the studio's drumbeat of having just enough copies to satisfy demand. Of course, everyone knew this was a game to the studio's advantage but their publicizing of it drew attention away from a permanent catalogue and opened the door to the squeezing of the independents, especially the undercapitalized. Business decisions had to be made less according to the worthiness of a particular new release, say an arthouse movie, or a blockbuster sequel. The Video Visions niche would eventually become overwhelmed by the major studios' drive to build a market to advantage the contemporary operations of the movie industry. Flush with cash from the video business, the studios began churning out less than stellar product at higher prices that continued to climb.

The peak video year, according to the Video Vision owners, was probably 1985-1986, and after that came a plateau for about a decade, with fluctuations. The store started out with about five hundred yearly members, and two hundred lifetime members, and the number rose to over two thousand members. One Christmas Eve day Video Visions rented out one thousand titles for one day, with six to seven thousand rented out for the holiday week. Their titles were alphabetically listed on 3x5 cards in small boxes, and removed from the box when they were rented, with the boxes spread around the store in categories to browse. The staff, most of whom had some background in film at UWM, knew the movies and discussed them with customers. The inventory eventually rose to some twelve thousand titles, largely due to expansion of classic titles, foreign-language films, and the implementation of multiple copies to satisfy viewing demands. At its peak there were more than one thousand five hundred foreign films, and more music – rock, opera, classical and jazz – than any other Milwaukee outlet. Video Visions expanded to several rooms at the Prospect Mall, and it got to the point where they had to limit inventory because of physical limitations.

During this peak and plateau period the store operators recognized the first indications that the implementation of multiple copies to satisfy viewing demands, which followed the advance publicity and promotion of presumed hit titles, had a downside. The store was so successful that salespeople visited from Hollywood, offering promotional deals and big cardboard cut-outs to go with advance copies of latest releases. The space and attention given over to the hottest, latest Hollywood film attracted a different crowd. Video Visions had always been famous for its mingling of professors with students, families with lone aficionados, young and old, all sexualities and races. Now within this group there grew a subset we began to call the Watch Once and Done crowd. The Watch Once and Done crowd responded fervently to the increased advertising budgets of the studios and the displays of forthcoming releases. Free studio advertising for the store – in exchange for a guarantee the store would stock new titles – created a customer excitement in the store. But the business was getting tougher and tougher, with more of the stores and chains beginning to cater openly to the Watch Once and Done crowd. A Blockbuster store, for example, would bring in as much as possible in the classic and foreign categories before opening, but within thirty days remove almost all those titles when they did not obtain the level of rental fees required for retention in inventory. Customers that had long patronized Video Visions for specialized product would change stores for the convenience of a Blockbuster location, and then ask Video Visions to open another outlet nearer their residence, because Blockbuster had removed the videos they were more interested in. Gradually, the owners of Video Visions understood that although niche inventory was supposed to give you a certain edge, it only gave you that edge if you could rely upon your niche population. Its niche was constantly trending younger and being wooed away, with the watch-once crowd happy for a more convenient store.

Other independent video stores, envious of the critical acclaim that media and customers gave to Video Visions, and envious of the size of the market on the east side, considered moving in. The arrival of Blockbuster to the Milwaukee area changed the equation, with its chain formula known to everyone: the massive stocking of new releases, special attention to children's videos, elimination of entire categories of films from inventory if a desired rental rate was not achieved, and putting as much pressure as possible on distribution channels to gain an economic advantage. Much of Blockbuster's strategy was analogous to McDonald's, from getting the customers young to slimming down to a compact, instantly intelligible menu. Sell more hamburgers – rent more new releases. Blockbuster's policy towards product

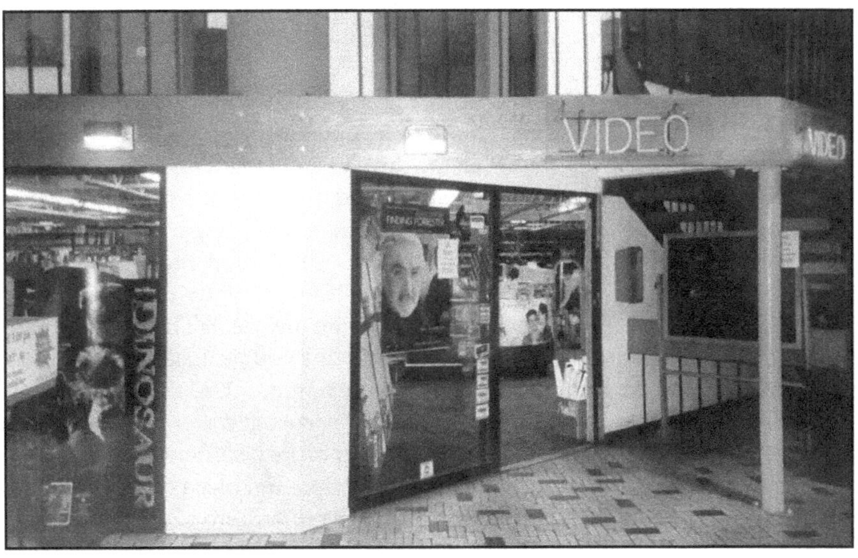

Video Visions on the East Side of Milwaukee
(photo by Max Knowlton-Sachner).

varied, and the chain dealt directly with the studios as well as buying directly from distributors. Either way Blockbuster was always seeking volume discounts, better terms and return privileges. Distributor reps began to tell Video Visions they were forbidden to approach individual, independent stores, or even regional offices. Blockbuster wanted only to deal at the highest levels to squeeze the most possible profits out of each individual franchise.

In the late Eighties the wholesale price for a video had meanwhile stabilized at $59.95, with a volume discount that lowered it to about $56.00 retail. But that only lasted a while because the studios raised their prices at first to $84.95, then $88.95, $92.95, or $94.95, then no retail list price with the cost set by the seller. This was to make as much profit as possible from the rental market, and then to allow, shortly after release of a title – approximately four to six months later – a sale price drop to $19.95, tapping into the new consumer purchase market. There were pricing categories used by the studios – mass market (Best Buy, Target); distributor; and wholesale when dealing directly with the studio. The biggest discounts and the most liberal return policies were reserved for the mass merchants.

Most of the people employed by the video divisions of the studios came from the mass merchant class, or their suppliers. They were not interested in sustaining small local outlets with their products, and many were even resentful of the indie rental market. Blockbuster would buy directly from a studio if they could exercise enough leverage on any deal. They would also approach the distributors, telling them, "We want you to make a profit" but make sure that profit amounted to an absolute minimum. Many distributors would accept Blockbuster's terms and then realize they were not going to survive, because they were paying too much to make a sufficient profit.

Why did distributors take stores on as accounts and bleed them dry? One reason was to take them away from a competitor distributor. Another was to build up their own standing with studios. The studios kept distributors on a quota system. Distributors had to order a set figure of any release to maintain their status. If they did not sell that release in sufficient quantity they had to eat the rest. Once a year there would be a conference of distributors, at which the studios would pitch upcoming product and hold private meetings with distributors, evaluating each for their sales performance and providing cash rewards. Sounds great, but the bills always had to be paid on time and the pressure was such that even the distributors could foresee their arrangements with Blockbuster could never be sustained.

The death knell sounded for Video Visions when a Blockbuster, one of thirty-five that opened in Milwaukee in the late Nineties, opened two blocks away from us. It became quickly obvious that people in the neighborhood had an alternative. Their first choice of a video for the night had two locations. People would check out the title with Video Visions and leave for Blockbuster if the title was not immediately available. It also meant customers would not be satisfied with an older catalogue if they mainly wanted new releases. Other factors that affected rentals were the longer hours that Blockbuster was able to stay open, the drop box system the Blockbuster stores used, and the fluid inventory. At this time as well, cable television began to look at the video store as its main competition, and the Internet was starting to make pornography available in the home. Thus, there were factors in the direct competition with Blockbuster as well as factors external to that competition that began to negatively affect Video Vision's rental business.

At approximately this time, the mid- to late Nineties, the studios finally took note of the pricing they had employed and saw it as limiting the exposure of their offerings. They were tuned into the economic model that had been used for theatrical release. Their displeasure with the old system of first sale had led to higher and higher pricing that eventually had negative repercussions. The beginning of the closure of smaller independents was becoming more common. Warners announced a program for stores that offered rental titles at two different prices. One employed the usual high prices and the other offered much lower pricing in exchange for a share of the rental dollar. This involved a report detailing the number of rentals of the titles involved, and the dollars that were generated. The studio had to be paid weekly on the basis of that report. After a period of time, let's say ninety days, excess copies had to be returned to the studio. Supposedly the video stores would be able to meet demand by having super quantities of a title. This was always questionable from the viewpoint of the independent video store, and that was made even more so when the studios gave Blockbuster an exclusive on this program when it first started up, lasting for months. That is when a really noticeable decline in Video Visions rentals occurred.

A lawsuit was started by a dealer in Texas with financial support from other independents, but it went nowhere as the studios prevailed. By the time the two-tier plan was made available to independents, the damage had been done. Similarly, when the first DVD was ready to be marketed, in 1997, the studios pushing the format – Warners and Sony – picked select outlets in select markets to have the product, gravitating to the chains and further isolating the independents. The decline was slow but steady and the plug should have been pulled long before, except for the gradual building-up of a sell-through market, though that was limited for stores like Video Visions by under-capitalization and the need to use the return from that market to prop up the sagging rental market.

Once again, the pricing was a factor. Typically, the margins were not better; a video with a list price of $19.95 might have a wholesale price of $14.95. Any volume discount dropped the price by a dollar and some change. Growth happened at the beginning of the sell-through boom, but the mass merchants took notice, and the studios proved eager to gain that quick market profit. They felt that rental stores did not push sales, and the few outlets that did received no favors. What became common was the advertising of product by the mass merchants at price points that were lower than what the distributor had received from the studio. By the year 2000, the life of the independent video store had become imperiled, just as the independent bookstores and independent record stores before them also had been imperiled by the mass merchants.

All these changes and practices and trends meant Blockbuster increasingly became first choice in the shopping mainly for rentals. Video Visions closed in 2003, after twenty years in business, selling its 10,000-plus inventory of titles in a thronged sale lasting several days, during which the foreign language titles were the first to be sold down to the last. Many of these titles, manufactured in the first excitement over video, have still never been released in DVD. Now the mass merchant is fighting for their lives as the Internet chews away at their customer base. As they ran the independent record store out of the business, so too are they chased by the specter of the digital download and the free shipping with no sales tax. The latter aspect is under siege, and it will be interesting to see what effect this will have.

The Blockbuster stores in Milwaukee, thirty-five at its peak, included six on the east side. The last of those six, on Oakland Avenue in Shorewood, which was run independently as part of the franchise, closed in 2013, when Blockbuster shuttered its remaining three hundred U.S. stores, ending an era for a chain that once had nine thousand stores and sixty thousand employees. Video Visions had half a dozen. The cries that local businesses are being hurt by the megatron Amazon seem familiar. The video store that tried to be a repertory theater for home viewing, that wanted to duplicate the urbane offerings of the east side entertainment district in Milwaukee, that wanted to bring a bit of the country's cultural centers to the locals, could not be sustained because of many different factors, from the inside and the outside, from the psychology of the owners of Video Visions to the concerted effort to drive such operations out of business, from the decisions that took place in the studios and the technological changes that would put the movie rental business in the dustbin of history. Were mistakes made? No doubt. Would it have mattered if they had not been made? Not at all.

More
Tender
Comrades

Anne Edwards

2013

Interview by Patrick McGilligan

Perhaps best known as a biographer of the rich and famous from across the spectrum, Anne Edwards has told the life stories of everyone from screen figures Shirley Temple, Judy Garland, Vivien Leigh and Ronald Reagan (her book *Early Reagan* was a Pulitzer Prize nominee) to the dynastic sagas of the DeMilles, the Grimaldis of Monaco, the Aga Khans, and the royal family of Great Britain. She also has written popular children's books, bestselling novels, and scripts for television and film.

Born in California and raised in the shadow of the film industry ("Uncle Dave" ran Chasen's, a restaurant for the Hollywood elite), she was a young divorcee with two small children when she was blacklisted by the House Un-American Activities Committee (HUAC) for her political beliefs and activities. Among her sins was being related by her first marriage to writer and director Robert Rossen, one of the original "Hollywood 19," who eventually became a cooperative HUAC witness.

Script work overseas led Edwards to two decades of living in England, France, and Switzerland. She tells her story in *Leaving Home: A Hollywood Blacklisted Writer's Years Abroad* (Scarecrow, 2012), a powerful memoir that weaves the history of the blacklist and her own intimate and professional experiences into a moving testament of integrity and survival. The honest pleasures of this book include many capsule portraits of prominent as well as overlooked blacklist victims. Among these characters are Rossen, who made the Oscar-winning *All the King's Men* before the blacklist and such pictures as *The Hustler* after his "friendly" HUAC testimony, and who is treated by the author with dignity and complexity. The great screenwriter Sidney Buchman (*Mr. Smith Goes to Washington*) comes across as a wise and sophisticated soul, with a personal backstory that is unforgettable and poignant. Many less-familiar names receive fascinating close-ups.

—◦—

I can't help but notice that in the memoir you are somewhat vague about your politics before the blacklist. Were you a Communist, and if you were, why don't you talk about it? If you weren't, why were you a target of HUAC?

I say clearly in the book that I was never a member of the Communist Party. Of course, hundreds of others were not and were still a target of HUAC. In my case, I can only assume what appears to be the most obvious: I was closely associated with several well-known writers/directors/actors who were prime targets – names that were well enough known, as were their credits (movies) – to be desirable additions for HUAC to persecute and so gain headlines (or at least major media coverage). I lived with the Rossens (Robert and Sue, my in-laws) for a lengthy time during the difficult early period of HUAC when Bob was denying any association with the Communist Party. I had close association as well with John Garfield and numerous other famous members of the Hollywood community, who HUAC was anxious to have named (even if they had been named before).

Also, my credits, however few, dealt with stories putting forth strong, liberal storylines. Mainly, I suppose, my original screenplay, *Riot Down Main Street*, sold to 20th Century-Fox, based on the true story of a Texas town that had refused to bury the remains of a returning fallen hero of the Korean War who, though an American citizen, was of Latino parentage... and the town's cemeteries were for "whites only." The mortuary wanted the casket to be moved forty miles to be buried over the Mexican border. (He was finally buried in Arlington.)

The studios all had HUAC "workers" cooperating from inside. The development of my screenplay was immediately cancelled.

I had also sold an original screenplay, *Quantez*, to Universal, a Western about a standoff between an Indian band and a group of "teacherly" whites who had occupied a ghost town on their sorry travel westward. The Indian's side was handled with some sympathy. In 1957, it was eventually adapted by Robert [R. Wright] Campbell with the attitude decidedly reversed to become a shoot-out film [*Quantez*], although a lot of my scenes did remain along with the original title of my screenplay.

I had contributed what little I could spare to several causes that seemed in some mad way to raise red flags. They would seem very common to charity foundations today – and did to me at the time.

HUAC often speared people like myself (not well-known but well-connected) for the direct purpose of badgering them into naming names that would be well-known to the general public. The phrase "guilty by association" was like a deadly virus at that time, poisoning the Hollywood community.

I thought I would ask you a little about actor John Garfield, who is one of the most famous names affected by the blacklist. You talk in your book about how the blacklist actually "killed" some people, and I know this is true, but I don't think people today understand this at all. Garfield seems someone not unlike yourself in his politics – engaged, committed, active – never a Communist, yet tortured to death by HUAC. You say in the book that you knew him well at a certain point. What more can you tell us?

Jule [John] Garfield and his wife Robbie [Roberta] were somewhat like family members. They were both supportive of me from the time of my engagement and marriage to my first husband [Harvey E. Wishner] and, after Jule's tragic early death at thirty-nine, Robbie remained a good friend. The Rossens and the Garfields had been close since their pre-Hollywood New York years. Jule and Bob had started their careers with the Group Theatre, came to Hollywood at the same time and were both signed by Warner Bros. Bob wrote several screenplays that starred Jule. When the Rossens were abroad (late Forties, early Fifties), my husband and I moved in with the children (three: the oldest, Carol, eleven; I was twenty-two). Robbie was somewhat my surrogate mother to go to, Jule my creative adviser.

I was already on the start of my writing career (screenplays, at that time). Jule was interested, helpful, concerned. He liked to tell me stories about his own life, his memories of growing up poor in a New York ghetto, the troubles he got into as a kid, his hitching rides on freight trains and being tossed out without a cent, and having to struggle to get a meal (this was at the height of the Depression). His criticism was always constructive. He wanted me to understand the characters I engaged in my writing, to have in my head a solid backstory. And he was great when it came to sharpening dialogue. I don't know why he didn't write – maybe if he lived longer he would have done so.

What was he like? As you can see from the above – generous with his time – as was Robbie (they had two very young children: Julie and David). Jule had a charismatic personality. I can still hear his voice and speech pattern in my head. He looked you straight in the eye when he spoke to you. He could get passionate over the simplest things. He also could be cynical. He was, as you probably have observed, short and feisty (as was Bob R.) and had boxed as a kid (as had Bob R.). I think he fought for a cause – certainly leaned left – but was never a joiner. He died (1952) before Bob went before the Committee and gave names. Instinctively I feel that would have ended their friendship.

In his last few years Jule formed his own company – in part, I am sure, because it was the only way he could work. It was tough going for him in those last two years. As I knew him, I never could see him as a womanizer. He and Robbie seemed a very together couple – he was a loving father – proud of his small children. I think everyone who really knew them was shocked at the manner of his death (by a heart attack in bed with a young woman). But he was under extreme pressure from HUAC, his work, his future, etc. I considered him a victim of HUAC and those terrible times when no one knew who was a real friend – and when your career would become [suddenly] past tense.

I retained my friendship with Robbie. Her second husband was [my second husband] Leon's attorney and business manager [film and labor lawyer Sidney Cohn]. In the early Sixties, David Garfield came to London to attend RADA and moved in with Leon and myself for a time. He, tragically, also died young – even younger than his father.

I enjoy the fact that you are so warm in the book in your feelings towards Lester Cole, one of the Hollywood Ten. Often, he is maligned in other accounts as a "B" screenwriter or political hardliner. (I knew him and always liked and admired him.) Since he is the member of the Hollywood Ten that you appear to have known best, can you tell us a little about his talent and personality and the circumstances of your friendship?

Well, I met Lester in Hollywood (can't remember how). Then, in London, we both worked on a project for fellow expat, writer-producer Carl Foreman. Lester was at times a very angry man. Neither of us received a fair wage from Carl – who had managed to procure a secret session with HUAC, clearing the way for him to make films under his own name and release them in the States. It ate at Lester – along with his year in prison (he still had nightmares about it) for refusing to name names. His wife divorced him, and none of his so-called old friends came to his aid (or so he said – bitterly). He was bruised deeply, and despite his ferment I liked and believed I understood him. His problems went back before HUAC really but were bolstered by it. He felt he had never got the good assignments in Hollywood and had not been able to make the name for himself that he thought he deserved, and now he was deep into mid-life and could not see how he was going to "rise up from the ashes" when he could not use his name.

He mellowed considerably once he married his second wife – Kay, a very nice, sophisticated, comfortably well-off lady about his own age. I believe she was from San Francisco; at least, once he returned with her to the States, that is where they settled. He had short stays with me in both the South of France and Stockbridge (when Steve Citron, my third husband and I had the inn*) – while Kay was off visiting family or some such.

When I asked Clancy Sigal to tell me about some of the blacklisted London community, he mentioned the names of several people I had never heard of – people like comedy writer Reuben Ship, that's one I recall. You say in your book there were hundreds of blacklistees there in the Fifties and Sixties. I assume many of them were not well-known publicly, or in terms of their credits. Can you pick one out that you didn't profile in your book, and tell us a little about him/her and of people's struggles to create a new life for themselves?

Yes, there were well over a hundred HUAC victims in London (and their families). It was the country to go to. I knew a fairly large number and heard word of many others. I mainly remained close to the writers, directors, etc., whose names were familiar to the press. But there were fine cameramen – sound men (no women in these categories that I know of) – editors, etc. It was a little easier, however, for blacklisted technical personnel to find work on foreign films as their knowledge of modern film technique was badly needed and credit was not as important in those technical jobs.

The actress Betsy Blair was in London – she had been nominated for an Academy Award for her lead role in *Marty*. Her marriage with Gene Kelly was a shambles because of her left-leaning beliefs (he was at the height of his career and did not want to see it crumble, and of course he was not, at heart, as political as Betsy was). It was most difficult for actors to find work in their

* See *The Inn and Us* co-authored by Anne Edwards and Stephen Citron (Random House, 1976).

field, as obviously they could not hide their familiar face behind a new name. Betsy was remarried to the director Karel Reisz (a Czech who came to England during the war and had made a tremendous name for himself in the mid-Fifties to the Sixties as a director of what was then called "The British Free Cinema"). Betsy wrote a very good memoir about her own situation [*The Memory of All That*, Knopf, 2003]. She died only a few years ago but never returned to the States.

There was Ben Barzman and his wife Norma (who also lived in the South of France when I did), but we never became friends (no special reason that I can recall). And Bernhard Vorhaus and his wife – who used to have late "picnic" lunches at their house in London – after the baseball games in Hyde Park. If I haven't included the stories of other people in my book it is because I did not know them well enough to do so, or that I did not think they would have liked me to include them.

I confess I hadn't known the name of Leon Becker, your second husband, who started out in the business as a sound man for Anthony Mann, and who was blacklisted; but then, as you write about in the book, he had an amazing career overseas and ended up working with the Beatles.

Leon had many years of credits denied by the blacklist between Tony Mann and the Beatles. He was Wyler's "ears" (Wyler's quote) and "the man almost always by the director's side" (so said Kirk Douglas) for four of Wyler's films: *Carrie* (where his association with Laurence Olivier began – and was picked up in England years later with *Bunny Lake is Missing*), *Detective Story*, *The Heiress* and *The Best Years of Our Lives*. When Leon got to London, he could not use his name, and Carl Foreman, who had just had his cleared, wanted to start up a production company and had no technical experience whatsoever. He pulled Leon in as a partner in Open Road Productions – for a percentage – where he could handle many of the actual details of making a movie, which Carl often wrote and produced and raised money for. Those films included *The Key*, *The Guns of Navarone* (which was a big moneymaker), *The Victors* (a bomb) and *Born Free* (the script that Lester and I worked on). Carl and Leon broke up shortly after (Carl, incidentally, had just married Eve, Leon's secretary for the previous two years), and then Leon teamed with Walter Shenson for *The Mouse that Roared* (a very big moneymaker and Leon had a good percentage), the two dreadful films I write about in the memoir [*Don't Raise the Bridge, Lower the River* and *Welcome to the Club*], and then *A Hard Day's Night*, in which I personally felt his brilliant musical knowledge managed to hold the film together. Whatever went wrong in our decade-long marriage, I have never been able to dismiss the elephant in the room – the effect the McCarthy years had on each of us.

I am struck by how hard you are on Carl Foreman in the book – for his deal with the Committee, but also for his personality and character – as compared to how conflicted or more understanding you are of Robert Rossen, who cooperated publicly with HUAC and behaved badly in his private life as well. Did you have a general feeling about informers that was sometimes mitigated by knowing the people under sympathetic circumstances?

Yes, I was hard on Carl. I believe he knew how I stood during the years that we were closely associated. I do not have a "general feeling" about informers. They are individuals as we all are with their own difficult histories. They were as much victims as the rest of us. Not everyone possessed the steel it took to defy the Committee. Many were terrified of what their life would be if they did not give names. They made a choice, one that more often than not proved equally hard to live with.

Carl worked hard for his success and was not going to let go of it. I don't criticize him for that. It is who he was. He was also bright, seemingly good-natured, and talented. But he took advantage of those very people who had not had his sense of self-preservation. I don't care to go into it. But I never was able to whitewash him in this matter. It did not change my feelings that other American producers abroad were also paying the blacklisted writers, etc., half the money that was paid to others, which helped bring in a picture on, or under, budget.

I can't compare Carl with Bob Rossen. I never knew Carl as I did Bob. I was deeply disappointed in Bob for naming names, and he knew that I was. But I could see that it ate him up, as it did not seem to do to Carl – at least that was evident to me. I lived in Bob's home, his wife a good friend, his parents were like grandparents to me. He had deep feelings for his heritage and for his family. To my knowledge, he never took advantage financially from those who had been blacklisted, and privately – as I knew him – he never got over the personal guilt he felt in giving names to HUAC. Some of what he felt might be gleaned from his films. Especially, *Body and Soul* (in my opinion one of the greatest boxing films), where Garfield climbs his way to becoming champ by devious methods, which causes the death of the one boxer who had been his friend.

As Bob was a family member, I knew him better than Carl – I knew his history. Perhaps it was hard to put things in their proper perspective, but I do think I tried.

Was there a special character and personality to the London blacklist community, as compared to say the French group? Were there circles within the community? You don't mention Chaplin, or the many people associated with him that were blacklisted, and I notice you only give quick mention to some other well-known people like Joseph Losey...

There was not a large blacklisted community in France, for obvious reasons, even during earlier times. Few Hollywood writers/directors were fluent in French (the exceptions being Sidney Buchman, Jules Dassin and John Collier, who was English but had spent time in Hollywood). There were some latecomers to the Riviera like myself who had lived in England, yet who I had

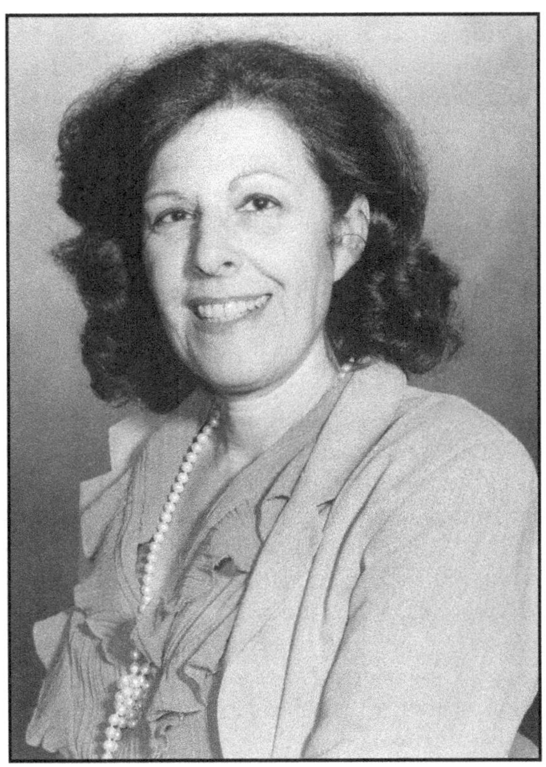

Anne Edwards in 1983.

not previously known – but they did not form a "colony." As it was 1970 by the time I lived there, the blacklistees could have gone home if they had so wished, and perhaps they had journeyed southward because the dollar (taxes) and the pound were high, and at the moment the franc more welcoming; Europe now seeming, after so many years, more like home. Nonetheless, people did come (Paul Jarrico, Lester Cole) but like me, did not stay long. The Riviera – at least, where I was – could have been called a way station during the late Sixties and early Seventies for the former Hollywoodites.

The expat community in France was not large enough for "circles." It was quite different in the Fifties and early Sixties in London, when so many of us landed on English shores. Charlie Chaplin, although I recall he made *A King in New York* there, otherwise seldom came to London, as he lived in Switzerland with his wife and numerous children. Joe Losey was not much of a "mingler." I found him stand-offish and gloomy. I was friendly with one of his ex-wives (not a good report). I believe he nurtured his unique film style in England – pessimistic tales, obtusely lit, claustrophobic settings. He never attended gatherings or the baseball games in Hyde Park. My husband Leon was somewhat friendly with him so there were a few social evenings.

There were many other Americans floating around London and Europe. European production was at its peak during the late Fifties and Sixties, and many American filmmakers had made an exodus abroad, where stories could be shot for much less on "location." European crews were less highly paid, and with the favorable exchange of the dollar a wave of talent was lured from Hollywood to England, Spain, and Italy. They then came back to England to cut, splice, add music, dub, etc. Most went back home after the film was ready for distribution. They seldom became a part of the expat community – which as I see it now – was pretty tight.

I see your book as a feminist statement, although you don't really wave that word around. Was there a sisterhood in the blacklisted community?

I am a feminist. I admit it most proudly. I am also a great many other things. I think of myself more inclusively as a humanist and being a feminist is only one part of the equation.

The fact that there were few women working creatively behind and beyond the camera in Hollywood in the Thirties to the Sixties gives a clear picture of how anti-feminist the industry was. Mostly, women were either actresses, or they were script girls, secretaries, or in the wardrobe department. There were a few women film writers employed at studios – my friend Vera Caspary was one (blacklisted), Lenore Coffee, Isobel Lennart (she was called by HUAC and gave names), Marguerite Roberts and Sonya Levien (who had problems but seemed to have survived in Hollywood). Sonya's daughter Tammy Gold and her husband Lee Gold were part of our London group. Those are all I can think of. Studios bought a great many novels written by women and then had them adapted by men.

Although several actresses were blacklisted, I think Betsy Blair was the only one who came to England. So – no – there was not a sisterhood of female writers, etc., living as expats in London at that time. The women in the blacklisted community consisted mainly of the wives and daughters of the men. Perhaps there was a sisterhood among them, but I was never a member. This was by my choice. I was a working mother of two children with little spare time for lunch meetings, shopping, etc. But they were always gracious in including me in some nighttime social events. I never felt any animosity toward me on their part. They were mostly a generation or more older than I. I can't remember any of the wives I knew who worked. But then they might not have had access to what in the U.S. we call a "green card."

In the beginning, I was sponsored by [producer] Raymond Stross (who brought me to England), and I was able to go in for renewals thereafter. But except for a time when I did some work for the BBC I was [usually] employed by the foreign office of an American company under an assumed name.

Part of the book, your life story, takes place in Gstaad and Klosters. Were there many blacklistees living in those places? I was taken aback by your mention of Salka Viertel, Garbo's friend and frequent scenarist, as being blacklisted. I had assumed she was "graylisted," but as you knew her well this must be my ignorance. Such a great lady – and role model. Was she bitter?

I went to Gstaad after living in Klosters (where Salka lived). Neither town was really a gathering place for the Hollywood victims of HUAC. France, at least, had a film industry and studios. Klosters had drawn more literary types like Irwin Shaw and Peter Viertel (Salka's son). Klosters drew many filmmakers there, but mostly on visits – to see Salka, to ski. Salka was a handsome, wise, enchanting woman – always vital. People took strength from her. She was not American. Polish by birth, European by design. She was in her 60s and a concerned grandmother when she moved to Klosters – concerned about the welfare of her granddaughter – the child of her son, the writer Peter Viertel. His wife, the child's mother, had died in Switzerland in a tragic fire. Salka was a stable and wonderful influence on the young girl (the same age as my daughter).

Her advice was always sound and fair. She was never bitter. She could be sharp-tongued if needed. She displayed no interest at all in returning to Hollywood (or the States). Her family was close at hand. People (famous, talented, old friends) just naturally traveled to see her (Garbo and Chaplin included). Visit Switzerland – see the Alps and Salka Viertel.

Gstaad was a complete opposite to Klosters. Yes, there was skiing and Julie Andrews (and Blake Edwards). Also, Elizabeth Taylor and Richard Burton and many more famous folk. Leon's longtime friend (from childhood) Yehudi Menuhin, the great virtuoso violinist, lived there as well – and in the summer there were these wonderful concerts in a church nearby. The town was filled with celebrity and society. I would have preferred Klosters, but my daughter had graduated from the school she attended near there and was now enrolled in the American school near Gstaad to get American credits to use towards U.S. college entry. Nonetheless, I fell in love with Gstaad and even the marvelously dull Swiss and better yet, wrote well there.

There was a large expat community in Gstaad – but not my friends and colleagues from London. They came from all over the world and were there for reasons that would probably have fueled an entire studio's story file. I found that fascinating. Gstaad was much more cosmopolitan than Klosters. It had fine, beautifully lit restaurants serving their somewhat stodgy but delicious cuisine, a mountaintop club, and the swank Palace Hotel. There was also a terrific international bookstore. It was also twice as expensive as Klosters (or at least was so at that time). I had many friends visit me from the States – but except for Sidney [Buchman] – none that I can recall from my buddy expats.

The term "graylisted" gets bandied about. I would define it as "temporarily" or even "mistakenly" blacklisted for a short time, until the person comes to an understanding with HUAC or the studios. Do you agree? It never happens to a real blacklistee, or former Communist, right?

You will not find the word "graylisted" in the dictionary, and for good reason. If one was listed at all it meant that certain inalienable rights had been denied to you, and once you were on a "list" (given to the studios by HUAC or *Red Channels*, etc.) that was an immediate end to your freedom to work in your chosen field in the country where you were a citizen.

The *American Heritage Dictionary* (where "blacklist" unlike "graylist" is an accepted word) defines a blacklist: "A list of persons or organizations that have incurred disapproval or suspicion or are to be boycotted or otherwise penalized."

Once your name was on a list, that list was placed in HUAC's hands to use on a to-call basis. The Committee could then draw from that list to order someone to appear before them as fit their current agenda, which generally was: what bigger names could be gotten by bringing that person before them? Therefore, someone could be passed by if HUAC did not think they would be of strong service to them at that time. This did not mean that one's name would come off the list. More often it remained "for further consideration." Therefore, the person's name remained on the "do not hire list" at the studios. To circumvent that, the victims used false names.

For about a year or two after Senator McCarthy's death in 1957, there was a lull in the activities of HUAC, and the lists were apparently revised. But HUAC came alive again in the early Sixties. In my case, I had since married Leon Becker, who had not only been blacklisted but who had given up his American citizenship to become a British subject. That rang bells. (See my letter from Leon in *Leaving Home*, page 184.)

I did not include in the book the difficult time we had earlier when he had accompanied me by plane from London to New York, and Passport Control refused to allow him to enter the country. Two guards marched him into a private area where I was not allowed to enter, and then escorted him onto a flight taking off to London. By the time I was in the hospital (in L.A. a year or so later) he managed to get clearance to come to my side (medical emergency) on a limited visa. That was in 1969.

To end the discussion of "gray" or "black" – for most of the victims who finally were able to work in Hollywood again, time had played a mean trick. The Hollywood they had known hardly existed. They had been gone years in most cases without legitimate credits, and unlike me they had not been able to write a bestseller [*The Survivors*, Holt, Rinehart & Winston, 1967] to take them on a new successful road.

I wrote that novel forty-seven years ago and by choice I have never sought screen work (or had to) since then, although [the producers] Richard Zanuck and David Brown (who became my mentors) bought my first book and then engaged me to write a sequel (book form) of *Gone With the Wind*, which they planned to have adapted and filmed when the book was published. (That's a long story – not for this interview.*) Then somewhat later they twice tried to tempt me to try my hand at a screenplay, but both my heart and my head rejected the notion.

You are best known nowadays perhaps for your celebrity biographies. Was it hard or easier knowing some of the celebrities you have written about? I know your firsthand experiences with Judy Garland are written about extensively and poignantly in your memoir, but I am thinking also about people like Ronald Reagan, who is so central to the history of the blacklist (and to your biography career) but who doesn't turn up in your memoir...

It is equally difficult for a biographer to write about someone they never met as one with whom they had a friendship – or perhaps quite the opposite. The subject's celebrity or non-celebrity status has little influence. A serious biography (not an "as told to," etc.) usually takes about two years to write and often as long to research. (That figure does not include multi-volumed works like Robert A. Caro's masterwork on LBJ, or Leon Edel's on Henry James.) It depends a lot on whether the writer has an advance that covers at least some of the travel and secretarial, or research assistant costs. There were always expensive copying costs, photo research, etc. Now, with the technical abilities of the modern computer, it's easier and less costly.

If you do your job well before you have started to write, you have come to know your subject "personally" even if you have never met them. (Let's face it – most biographies are about a person who is dead – and possibly has been for a long time.) I cannot imagine beginning to write about someone's life without examining what I can of their life before I start. Something about that person has had to "speak" to you. There must be questions that need answers.

* See *Gone With the Wind*: *Vivien Leigh: A Biography* (Simon & Schuster, 1977), *Road to Tara: The Life of Margaret Mitchell* by Anne Edwards (Ticknor & Fields, 1983) and *Scarlett and Me* (The *Gone With the Wind* Marietta Museum, 2011), also by Edwards.

You must feel (at least I must) that I have something to say about that person that has not been said before – at least coming from the viewpoint I may have.

Ronald Reagan had no role in my memoir because our lives had not really crossed at that time, and I was not yet writing biography. (We did have a curious connection.) Many years later, when *Early Reagan* had been a success and I had returned to California and was embarking on a second book, *The Reagans*, taking him into the presidency, I did a large amount of my research at the Reagan Library here in Simi Valley. One day Nancy's assistant came to tell me that Mrs. Reagan thought I might be interested in seeing something that was in the basement of the library. Of course, I was. She led me down to this vast cave where all presidential gifts and memorabilia were kept and then across the space to a corner where a red-upholstered restaurant booth was placed. There was a note from Nancy that explained that she had bought the booth at the auction when Chasen's [my uncle Dave Chasen's famous restaurant] was closed, as she and Ronnie had sat in this booth when he had proposed to her and she had accepted.

How hard was it to write this book, your memoir? (Compared, say, to a novel or a Hollywood biography.) How did you research your own life? It's a very intimate book; how did you make the decisions about how far you would go?

There comes a time, and I am at that age, when you have to take your life in your arms and hold it to you to keep it breathing. So, no, it wasn't hard writing the memoir. It was a necessity. Writing is a lifeline to me. I need it to breathe. Also, I felt I had a story that had not, and should be, told. There had been a great many books, films, TV documentaries dealing with the active years of HUAC showing the destruction wrought in the immediate wake of the hearings. But little was known of what happened in the years after HUAC to those men and women who had their lives so cruelly upended.

I wanted – *needed* would be a better word – to tell that story.

I knew it had to be a personal story, *my* personal story – because that was the only way I could tell it.

It was important, I thought, to relate this in strong human terms. I was never really a political person, or an activist. I was a woman and writer who felt things deeply and who found my outlet in writing.

Yes, biography has been a frequent choice of mine in the past. But it requires tremendous travel, hundreds of interviews, and weeks – sometimes months – in dark, damp, or humid archives, which I can no longer endure. Anyway, I was driven to write *Leaving Home* as a memoir for the above reasons and because I believed I had a strong personal story that would connect with readers today.

Research, well… I have always kept a yearly journal or diary – many lost in transit – but I still have a shelf-full. I started doing this in my teens. I still make a special trip to the stationers in December to buy my journal for the coming years. Then , during the year in which *Leaving Home* is set, people wrote letters – many letters! I saved an amazing number, which are quoted in the book. Best of all, my two children – who so closely shared those years with me – were there to consult whenever I was in doubt of when a particular event occurred, etc.

Yes, it is a very intimate book. Because it is my life, and that did not give me leave to recuse myself from writing of incidents, emotions, affairs that I would uncover if I was writing a biography. Otherwise, how could the true person ever be understood?

How far should I go was always an important concern. I picked carefully through the experiences of my life – which ones to relate – which had any true bearing on the thrust of my life – at least these chronicled years as a single woman raising two children under difficult circumstances in countries not of our birth. We were the reverse of the immigrant family who comes to America. I kept to the main influences, the people who I knew had the strongest impact on my life. I don't respect memoirs that drop names and ooze gossip that have no relevance to the personal story being told. Nor do I care to read about their sexual behavior behind their bedroom doors. I applied these same criteria to myself. I included who and what I felt (still feel) deeply about.

Nowadays you are living back in Hollywood, close to where you lived your formative years. Is there still a blacklisted community of any number that you stay in touch with? What message do you have for young people today who see the blacklist as ancient history? Why is it still relevant? What are its lingering effects on American film?

There are no longer enough victims of the blacklist alive to form a community in Los Angeles or anywhere else. I do occasionally hear from their children or grandchildren. I feel somehow like that old, aged Indian in a long-ago Western who, with much relish, tells stories of the days when the Indians (Native Americans) had to be cleansed from the land and how tough it had been for him to survive – but here he was at 101, recounting his tale.

The thing that has settled deep in me is the lack of attention that has been paid to the McCarthy years in school history books, that America's youth are mostly ignorant of those darkest of years. Relevant? Darn tootin'! That was a time in America when freedom of speech, of the right to the pursuit of happiness, of justice under the law was almost lost. We need to be reminded that if power does get into the hands of those who live for power alone and can see no viewpoint other than their own, it could well happen again and perhaps be even more devastating.

Clancy Sigal

2017
Interview by Patrick McGilligan

Clancy Sigal's semi-autobiographical novel *Going Away* was published in 1961 and nominated for a National Book Award. The eloquent howl of a burned-out talent agent who is fed up with the Old Left, the film business, and America, hence he is "going away" to England, it remains among my favorite Hollywood novels, although Hollywood is only its jumping-off point. Sigal has led an eventful life and written other acclaimed autobiographical fiction including *Weekend in Dinlock, Zone of the Interior* and *The Secret Defector*. Returning to the U.S. in the Nineties, Sigal started writing for film, the medium he has danced around and worshipped since a boy.

He also launched a series of non-fiction memoirs with *A Woman of Uncertain Character: The Amorous and Radical Adventures of My Mother Jennie (Who Always Wanted to Be a Respectable Jewish Mom) by her Bastard Son* (Carroll & Graf, 2006) that continues with the publication, in late 2016, of *Black Sunset: Hollywood Sex, Lies, Glamour, Betrayal and Raging Egos* (Soft Skull Press). *Black Sunset* picks up where A *Woman of Uncertain Character* left off chronologically and can be seen as a true-life prequel to *Going Away*. *Black Sunset* recounts the blacklist years in the mid-Fifties in Hollywood when Sigal, a former Communist doing his best not to get caught in the FBI and HUAC sweep, represented talent for the Sam Jaffe Agency.

When did you go to work as a talent agent? How did you get the job?

I got hired by the Sam Jaffe Agency a little after the Rosenbergs' execution in 1953, which traumatized Jews and Hollywood liberals. That's around when I also got fired and blacklisted by Columbia Pictures, after Harry Cohn caught me at night using "his" mimeograph to make anti-Joe McCarthy and "Nix on Nixon" leaflets that a friend of mine and I would drop all over town from his rented Piper Cub plane. Cohn's fixer and v.p. of security, B.B. Kahane, had FBI agents on the studio payroll who told him I'd written unpatriotic editorials in college – these guys really do their research. Plus, it was rumored that my own union president (Screen Story Analysts Guild) had done the dirty and was rewarded with a screenwriter job. In the fog of the blacklist wars, rumors passed as fact, and facts were fungible. The Guilds (actors, writers, directors) were torn apart by the "Red issue."

Kahane was polite and tolerant of his stubborn employee and gave me a weekend to decide whether to "come in and name names." I was tempted; I really had no taste to join the "blacklist community," but in the end the affidavit he asked me to sign was just too absurd. For one thing it had been created for a man twenty years older than me – a boilerplate everyone was expected to sign, regardless of gender and age.

By this time, the FBI, deluded on no evidence that I was a big-time Communist operative, got into the habit of chasing me out of jobs. I was broke, and literally eating out of garbage cans (albeit high quality, Nate 'n Al's in Bev Hills) when one of my girlfriends, a Jaffe secretary, told me they were hiring. What do I have to lose?

My interview with one of the agency's three partners, Mary Baker – my savior and mentor – was a disaster. She immediately knew I was lying about my industry experience but liked my "balls," a word she often used.

At the time, there was no such thing as a learning curve or starting in the mailroom. You were thrown in the deep end to drown. During the first interview Baker tossed me her phone to negotiate a deal with [producer David O.] Selznick for a Jaffe screenwriter, as I recall Charlie Lederer. I'd no idea what an agent does, or what to say, so just kept blathering out of a personal history of loving movies and having total recall of even small screen credits. Selznick was furious to be passed on to me but made the deal, which cinched my new job.

I met Bogart that day and almost fainted with awe.

My last paid job had been as a "banana fiend" on the San Pedro docks (courtesy ILWU) at $2 an hour.

I was totally ignorant of what an agent does, I had to pick it up from my friend Paul Jarrico (whose work I later tried to sell under the table) and eavesdropping on senior agents, like Evarts Ziegler and Bob Goldfarb, both ex-servicemen like most Jaffe agents. Easygoing Bob was especially helpful. I was paralyzed with a goggle-eyed fan's respect for Jaffe's client list of talent who'd made the movies that formed and corrupted me. In a crisis I'd race into Goldfarb's office for him to hold up fingers to indicate the 'quote' I should negotiate for a client. (My poor clients!) Saved my life a thousand times. Ziegler, the top lit agent, was funny; patrician, well-liked, ex-OSS, handled only the "best" studios while I was assigned the Valley, Universal, Warners, Republic and a whole boulevard of fly-by-nights sin the grubby end of Hollywood (Allied Artists, Monogram, etc.).

Timing is everything. The industry was thriving and could afford a Candide like me; jobs plentiful in the postwar boom; and Jaffe needed to fill a niche for a literate "bullshit artist" who could persuade restless clients not to stray – my specialty, as it turned out. Not a smooth ride, I always felt high-strung and nervy and lived on dexxies and whatnot – they lived on old-fashioned martinis and office sex – but though we were competitive with one another there was no backstabbing. Collegiality was a Jaffe trademark. A little lying at staff sessions maybe. "Tomorrow I'm bringing in Ava or Marlon as a Jaffe client." Yeah, sure.

It took me a while to figure out why Jaffe kept me on despite the blacklist, phone calls from Columbia's Kahane, and pressure from the Jaffe family to fire me. Much later, as Mary and I were on our way to Martin Gang's office to "clear" a client (Frank Davis, as I recall, nailed because of his dead wife Tess Schlesinger), Mary confessed they kept me on because I had "steel balls," would go anywhere and do anything for a deal, made a good impression on literate clients… and I was the agency's "sacrifice to the gods" for Jaffe having been cowardly in the purges by dropping all their left-wing (and highest-paid) clients, thus cutting agency income by a half. Before the blacklist Jaffe and Mary Baker had a corner on most of the left-wing writers, directors, and actors because, as Sam used to say, "They were the best, best money, best deals, best people."

Memory is fallible but I stayed at Jaffe from just after the Rosenbergs to October 1956 on the eve of the Soviet crushing of the Hungarian Revolution and the West's invasion of Egypt over the Suez Canal, which almost got us World War III.

God bless my colleagues Bob Goldfarb, Ronnie Lubin, Ziggy, and above all Mary and Sam who knew, without wanting to know, how I spent my nights, meeting with a small bunch of Hollywood refuseniks the FBI tagged as "Omega: The Cell Without a Name." The FBI were such doofuses!

All through the years I never lost touch with Sam and with Mary and Bob, who later became my own agent.

This was in the midst of the Hollywood blacklist. How close had you been to the Communist Party?

I can precisely date when I became a Communist and departed, from the summer of 1942 during the Nazi offensive vs. Stalingrad, to March 1948 when Communists murdered the liberal Czech foreign minister Jan Masaryk by throwing him out a window. Joining the Communists was an act of solidarity with the besieged of the Volga city; quitting was an act of solidarity to myself. Known as a "friendly drop," I kept my Communist friends and still have them. In the Party I was a million miles from the big-time Hollywood Reds like [Dalton] Trumbo, [Ring] Lardner [Jr.], [Edward] Dmytryk and [John Howard] Lawson. Except at UCLA, where I was in a Red branch with children of the jailed Hollywood Ten. What glamour!

What I know about the Hollywood Communists I got from Paul Jarrico, whose Party task was to go around all the movie branches to collect dues. He was a hardliner then, and we fought night and day. Some friendships are funny. Whenever I got fed up with my agency job, Paul urged me to stay on because, "We don't need any more heroes, just an inside man to sell our work."

An awful lot of below-the-line people I knew in Hollywood had been Reds and then quietly dropped out, out of boredom, or the HUAC thing. Right-wingers are correct that Hollywood, at certain levels, tends to be left-liberal. During and just after the war there was a kind of movieland "Red culture," where certain Progressive, Leftish or "Reddish" opinions and attitudes were taken for granted.

The people, especially men, who suffered most from the Red purge were closeted gay men. The several secretly homosexual Communists I knew *all* vanished without a trace. They desperately sought anonymity in a culture of naming names. The FBI and immigration put enormous pressure on Red Gays to recant and betray. Communist Gays had to hide in several closets, against the prevailing homophobic culture, from J. Edgar Hoover, and from the CP's security apparatus that expelled you for "deviance."

The only Communist leader I kept in touch with throughout the "Hollywood years" was the southern California chair Dorothy Healey. She knew Ronald Reagan when he was a pro-Soviet liberal. She was a member pro tem of our "Omega," liking us personally and frowning at our "lack of discipline." Dear Dorothy.

Can you give me a word-picture of the agency at the time? Where it was located? How many agents? Type of premises? Daily activities? Stars dropping by?

8553 Sunset Blvd in West Hollywood, a small tranch of L.A. policed by even more corrupt sheriff's deputies and not LAPD. What I call a "Streamline Moderne," a three-story, purpose-built, white concrete building on the corner of Sunset and Alta Loma. Actor's agents like Ronnie Lubin, Phil Gersh and Sam on the ground floor; TV and literary agents on the second floor; a lawyer in the attic.

We were situated between what later was the Viper Room (and later Tower Records) and Mocambo and Ciro's, and just east of us Mickey Cohen's menswear shop.

Agents are licensed through the state of California as the money pipeline to artists. Jaffe had thirteen or fourteen agents. Aside from Mary, no female agent. I can only think of one other woman agent at the time – Meta Rosenberg, an informer.

Yes, stars dropped by all the time, either to schmooze or more likely to nudge us into finding them jobs. Jaffe specialized in high-prestige Academy Award winners like Fredric March, Joe Cotten, [Barbara] Stanwyck, Ray Massey, Claude Rains, etc. Jaffe expected me to bring in younger talent because the "youth market" was exploding under our feet.

Remember, I'd grown up idolizing a lot of these people, Rains as the Invisible Man, Errol Flynn's Robin Hood, March as Jekyll/Hyde, Joe Cotten in *Citizen Kane*. At business meetings I'd gawk and call Paul

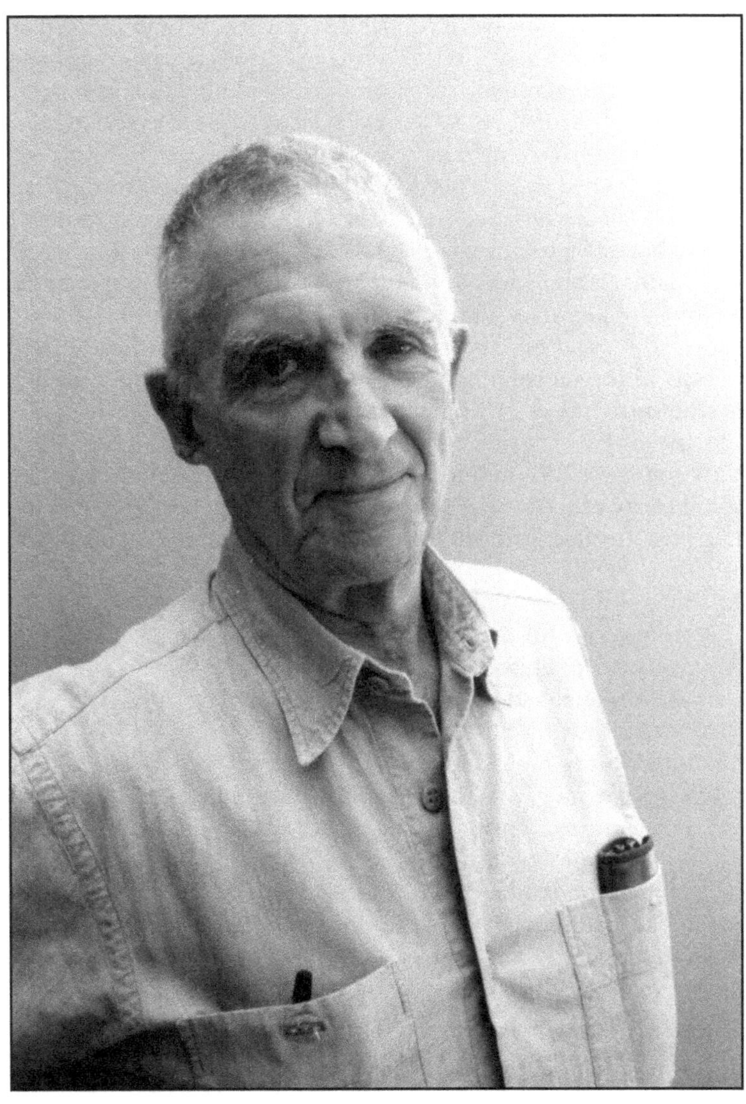

Clancy Sigal
(photo by Ron Colby).

Henreid "Victor" after *Casablanca*, Vincent Price "Shelby" from *Laura*, etc. Mary used to tick me off for this amateurish "civilian" compulsion. I also had a bad habit of quoting dialogue from my favorite movies starring them, which almost always disconcerted actors, because they'd moved on of course. When I met Farley Granger I spewed whole masses of his dialogue from *Strangers on a Train*. Smiling, he thought I was nuts.

My personal favorites who dropped in were Donald O'Connor, who always did back flips over the office rail; Peter Lorre, who I lunched with and who complained bitterly we found him only horror-ghoul parts; and a cowboy star Dale Robertson, a real sweetie. Does anyone remember Cornel Wilde? He became a friend.

The "daily routine" was normal corporate stuff. You stumbled in from a night out, looked over the previous day's "activity reports" we swore we'd done to remind me of what (I hoped) I'd done and had to do today, phone calls in the morning, and hit the new freeway around noon to the Valley studios to knock on doors, pick up gossip and, at Warner Bros., say hello to any of "my" writers at work. I loved hanging around the sound stages. When I was too intimidated to go out to the studios in the midday heat, I hid in my office to read scripts. My wonderful secretary Addy-with-a-y, a former Ziegfeld girl, had to muscle me out the door some days to get the job done.

At some point Sam and Mary appointed me "associate producer" of a TV Western series for Stanwyck; I don't think we made more than one or two, maybe three episodes, co-starring Stuart Whitman. Stanwyck was great, so professional and respectful on the floor. The show doesn't appear in any of the records.

Agenting was a high-stress, results-oriented job. Everybody except Sam was on something, including me. Miltown (anxiety pill) and martinis. And sex in the office. No such thing as sexual harassment. See *Mad Men*. Everyone was to one degree or another an "alcoholic," certainly Mary, who began drinking Bloody Marys at 10 a.m. and boasted she didn't trust anyone who wasn't an alcoholic. Smashed or not, we performed; Sam would never have tolerated falling down drunks.

Religious faith: all client calls to be returned THAT DAY!

Every agent had his own trademark. Bob, casual and easy; Ziggy, Princeton *de haut en bas*; Ronny, steel claw inside the velvet; me, "brass balls," whatever that means. Probably desperate to keep my job and wondering when the FBI would come calling again.

Our big rivals were Charlie Feldman (John Wayne's agent), Wasserman's MCA (Reagan and his sweetheart deal), Abe Lastfogel at William Morris, and the universally-liked Ben Benjamin at Famous Artists. Swifty Lazar was like a guerrilla sniper out there picking off choice clients before we woke up in the morning.

We had no black or Latino clients that I know of.

Was everyone in Hollywood at the time hyper-aware of the blacklist? Or was it a word never to be spoken? Or were most people just apolitical?

Yes, you'd have to be dead from the neck up not to be fully aware of the blacklist. It touched everyone from the big stars to the grips and carpenters. A plague. Hardly anybody spoke openly about the "blacklist." It was a given, an assumption, a cloud in the sky, the weather. We all became "good Germans," making our own quiet personal adjustments. Always aware, and unless directly confronted with it, *schtum*. A temporary insanity. Sam Jaffe, the wealthiest and most secure of us, was most open about it. But neither he nor anyone else ever used the word "blacklist." Euphemisms. "Hey Sam, Lee has a problem." "Is he cleared?" We'd talk about it and never mention it.

The blacklist and war fever drove most people apolitical. Who likes trouble? There was an almost universal sense that an innocent act like signing an ACLU petition could bring a storm down on you and your family's head. So why do it? Family comes first. There were many people I knew who were pro-union and had picketed in the big postwar labor struggles but saw no reason to make trouble for themselves or their families. But everyone knew without "knowing."

A memory: After threatening us to get me fired, Bubbles Kahane at Columbia reneged a little and bargained with Sam: OK, we won't make trouble for Sigal, if he stays away from Columbia. I suspect that Sam negotiated something there, to keep a favored employee. E.g., we won't raise Gloria Grahame's quote if you... etc. In other words, in some circumstances there might be a way around and past the blacklist, often a matter of pure luck.

Reds, near-Reds, Red-friendly liberals were part of southern California's culture. When the bad stuff happened, people didn't necessarily forego or forget their political passions, but sweated it out until the heat died down and they could surface to become active again in things like the Caryl Chessman case.

There were blurred lines between the U.S. Communist Party and the state Democratic Party. An ease, a relaxed sense, that we were three thousand miles away from the Party bureaucrats in New York – almost without exception idiots. This gave the southern California atmosphere a really nice free and easy feeling about "Reds." Sunny undogmatic California is not 13th Street in NYC.

How could you stand to be in a meeting with someone like Martin Gang where the scenarist Frank Davis was being asked to smear his own dead wife? It would make my skin crawl.

How could I be in a meeting with Gang? How could I not be? I wanted to survive, keep my job, and felt a sense of loyalty to Mary Baker and Sam, who resisted a whole lot of pressure to fire me. And at night I went home to crank out, distribute, and in one case fly with a friend over the studios to scatter anti-blacklist propaganda. It's called schizophrenia. Self-contempt is an easy out. Bill Alland (see below) had lots of that, and he simply used guilt and shame to enhance his ego. I repeat Jarrico: "We don't need heroes or martyrs, we need an inside man." Were there mixed feelings? O boy.

I take it you represented more than one "fink." Who was the most sympathetic fink and why? Who was the creepiest cooperative witness you came across?

There's a whole chapter in *Black Sunset* about the informer Bill Alland at Universal. You want creep. We enjoyed each other's company. (He played the reporter in *Citizen Kane*.) He was a customer, a buyer, and always twisted me in the wind, but from time to time he'd buy something, which is an agent's reason for living. He compulsively spoke, again and again, as if testing me and himself, of his HUAC testimony. Had a bad habit of hiring left-wing writers, then informing on them. I was probably the only blacklisted person who would talk to him, which he felt a validation; and he was too productive an executive for me to commercially ignore. A very complicated guy, as many informers were. Never turn your back on him. Jarrico had a strong stomach but always wondered how I could "enjoy" Alland.

Were you ever deceived by a "front," or did you always know upfront they were fronting? Was there such a thing as a typical "front"? I have this vague idea there were enough fronts around Hollywood to fill a big bus. Or was it not that common to run into one?

There was no deception. Everyone's front was Phil Yordan, and it was assumed, not always correctly, someone like Bernie Gordon or [Ben] Barzman, etc. had written it. None of the agents I knew ever admitted they were handling fronted material. There was an assumption. I don't know why but this was not an issue for me, perhaps because old-time blacklistees had previous relationships with Jaffe agents they trusted, and who was I? Around some scripts there was a deliberate vagueness, best not to inquire. My guess is that if I'd ever gone to ask my friend Bob Goldfarb, he simply would have smiled and changed the subject. I'm sorry he's gone, he would have known where all the bodies are buried. It's a little possible that the last person a fronted writer would go to would be me, because I was known as a blacklistee in their community, and why ask for trouble?

Dalton Trumbo and Bernie Gordon were the most prolific blacklisted writers operating under pseudonyms – that I know of. Were there others? Who was the most impressive or likeable personally of the blacklistees hovering around Hollywood at the time? Did you know any of the incredibly tragic examples, people like Sam Ornitz?

Honestly, blacklisted people did not come to me, by the time I arrived all my writers and the actors like March, Rains, Massey, Palance, and the writers, etc. had been cleared; even when they didn't need clearing, they were cleared anyway, in case questions were asked. The fury of the blacklist had run its course by the time I arrived; it was an established and unquestioned institution and cultural trope – on the verge, though we didn't know it, of being dismantled by Otto Preminger and Kirk [Douglas]. I'm not hiding anything. My guess, and it's only a guess, is that other agents like Goldfarb, Ziegler, Lubin and Mary herself had much more direct contact with blacklisted people. We were even past the wink and a nod stage. There is also the possibility, I just thought of it, that Mary and Sam deliberately kept me away from the tainted.

Also, I was a small fish and didn't travel in the lofty social circles of celebrated blacklistees. They had a rigid class system. How many awards, credits, what was your previous quote, etc. I knew one of the celebrated blacklisted screenwriters' sons who was permanently enraged because, in his eyes, his Dad's Academy Award-winning friends put him down because he became a "mere" stagehand.

The lofty exception was Paul Jarrico. Paul was my friend, and part of my bloodstream for so long, I've even forgotten how we met. At the time he was a *shtarker*, a strong-willed Stalinist, I was an active anti-Stalinist, anti-anti-Communist socialist (sorry). Maybe we spent the first year or two yelling at each other. We kept reconnecting with each other. He had an extraordinary gift for friendship overriding political differences, at the same time he was unbendable on his principles. I'd feed him information from "the inside" and he'd feed me information from "inside" his situation. All through my "agency period" he helped me navigate the shoals. Of all the top Reds I met or dealt with he (along with Dorothy Healey) had the best sense of humor. We'd disappear from each other's lives, and then meet again in Paris or London or back in LA, and he'd changed course on Stalin, but – and this says a lot about Paul – used his credibility as a Strong Party Man to lobby the Soviets and East European regimes on behalf of their "spies and traitors," i.e., dissidents. Took a lot of balls to do that. I guess he had what Mary Baker always (wrongly) insisted I had, "steel balls." He should have been a Marine, never leaving a comrade behind. Up to the very end, after he attended a WGA tribute and, fatigued, crashed into a tree, he fought, fought, fought for recognition and credits and residuals for all the *other* blacklisted writers. Or as Dietrich says about Welles in *Touch of Evil*, "He was some kind of man."

I know Black Sunset *ends where* Going Away *begins. It sounds as though you were leading a very conflicted life. What are the actual facts or circumstances of you quitting Hollywood and the agency and leaving "the business"? Why did you do it, and when?*

Two reasons come immediately to mind. Mary Baker suggested I didn't have "blood on my teeth" for the business anymore, and maybe I should take time off to "be a bohemian" and come back refreshed. Plus, and here's an answer interviewers hate because it's so off-point: 1953 and the Rosenberg execution coincided with a workers' uprising in Soviet-dominated East Berlin. I paid close attention, from afar, to "events" in East Europe and could see the sparks of an anti-Stalin revolution, which in my secret heart I'd been waiting for. My thing at the time was to rescue Marxism from its jailors. Mr. K's 1956 "secret speech" and resulting rebellions encouraged me to go to my Red friends, saying now is our time to create a democratic socialism free of cant and ancient dogma. When things blew up in Warsaw, Prague, Berlin and then Budapest I had an overpowering hunch to get there. Ignorant me, all this time, in my own country, the Civil Rights thing was starting to happen. I'm a slow awakener.

I am now going to skip about four decades... all that time you were overseas, a period that you have written about extensively in many novels and memoirs. What year did you return to Hollywood? What was your view of the place politically after all that time? Did you have warm reunions with agency veterans and blacklistees both?

I kept getting journo assignments to bring me back to the States and always liked checking in with Hollywood. I visited in the Sixties and Seventies and returned for good around 1990. By then the blacklist was just a blip, and as before hardly anyone talked about it. Who cared? Oh yes, Dalton and Ring have a credit, yawn yawn.

On my visits from London, I liked getting together with Bob Goldfarb and sometimes with Ziggy Ziegler, and in the late Nineties Sam lived around the corner from us and gave us a tour of his condo with all the photos of the Silent and not so Silent babes he'd dated. In London I'd have dinner with Mary Baker, and one night with her and Ava Gardner I spent the whole evening, as usual, gawping. As "ballsy" as I was supposed to be, show me an old-time star and I faint.

I can't let you go without asking you about your two film credits... the Hemingway film In Love and War (1996) *and the Frida Kahlo biopic. For someone who admires your politics and knows your life story, through your fiction but also nonfiction such as* Black Sunset, *what parts of those films do you feel are "yours" as a writer? What parts of those films are you proud of and do you still like, when you see those scenes at the end of the day?*

My film credits are a bit of a cheat. My friend Michael Elias (*The Jerk*) first "broke my cherry" when I collaborated with him on a wonderful script, *The Man in the Maze*, from a Bob Silverberg sci-fi novel. We sold it to Mel Gibson's Icon [company]; it's in turnaround. Until then, I'd always worked alone; it was hard getting used to working tandem, and Michael was a wonderful teacher and hard taskmaster. Slowly I realized it was much easier to work as a team, and since then Janice Tidwell and I have been partners. Jan and I worked 50-50 on *Frida* (2002) and *In Love and War* and other stuff.

The Hemingway film: Richard Attenborough, the director, met with Janice and me about a new project, in a Vancouver hotel. Before we get down to business he says, "You know, *In Love and War*, if I wasn't old and didn't have arthritis, I'd get down on my knees and beg both of you to forgive me for fucking up your picture…" What a sweetie.

About *Frida*: Fact is, the most memorable scenes – the ones you remember – were written by Janice while I fronted the meetings.

Are you working on any additional memoirs?

Here's a rough, small slice from my next book. The story begins when I arrive in England as a visa-less, passport-less illegal immigrant:

THE BIG SHUN

Spasms of homesickness for "something American" inspires me to reach out to other London Yankees where I'm bound to find a welcome among the exiled Hollywood blacklist community, people like me who came here first. Hoping to be noticed I hang out on the grassy verge of the weekly Sunday softball game in Hyde Park (see Glenda Jackson and George Segal in A Touch of Class) *by expat film directors, actors and writers, some my former agency clients. They ignore me. Not to be put off I pay friendly calls on a couple of celebrated blacklist Hollywood exiles who shut the door in my face. What's up with that? Ah ha, the penny drops. The airlessness of émigré politics. It naturally follows that I'm an FBI informer, a CIA agent, a police spy. Who knows how this stuff starts? At first a painful shock, the Big Snub turns out to be a blessing since it forces me to connect only with the natives.*

P.S. Eventually a blacklisted writer exile friend confesses he's the culprit responsible for spreading the lies. "Yeah, who knows why? But hey, I'm talking to my analyst about it."

Peter Davis
(Frank Davis and Tess Slesinger)
2020
Interview by Patrick McGilligan

People of a certain age know and admire Peter Davis for *Hearts and Minds*, his Academy Award-winning Best Feature Documentary about America's toxic involvement in Vietnam. "It's ironic," Davis said in his acceptance speech at the 1975 Oscar ceremonies, "to get a prize for a war movie while the suffering in Vietnam continues." The fall of Saigon was three weeks away.

Davis had a background as a top journalist and television documentarist, and after *Hearts and Minds* he made other nonfiction films (including the multiple Emmy-winning PBS series *Middletown* about the effects of changing times, technology, and culture on the citizens of Muncie, Indiana). He also wrote non-fiction books and, in 2015, a first novel called *Girl of My Dreams*, drawing on his inside knowledge of the film colony as the firstborn (his middle name is "Frank") of the novelist and scenarist Tess Slesinger and the movie producer and writer Frank Davis. Told in the first-person by a young screenwriter, *Girl of My Dreams* takes place in the early Thirties in Hollywood and revolves around the nexus of the Depression, the U.S. Communist Party, and the studio system.

Although his parents had separate careers before marriage, their best-known writing collaboration was the adaptation of Betty Smith's novel *A Tree Grows in Brooklyn* into the motion picture of the same name directed by Elia Kazan. Slesinger died from cancer at age 39, just as *A Tree Grows in Brooklyn* was being released in early 1945, and she did not live to know their script would be nominated for an Academy Award. There is no biography of Slesinger, and only limited information in the usual reference sources about Frank Davis. Their son agreed to talk about their backstory – their lives, films, and politics. Both were Communists who, at different points in history, had their livelihoods threatened by witch-hunts and the blacklist.

⸺◇⸺

Your father was born in Chicago, making him a Midwesterner in his roots, right? There is very little biographical background on him at IMDB, nor any Wikipedia page, and I couldn't even find a decent New York Times *or* Los Angeles Times *obituary for him. Can you sketch, for me, his early life, background, education, and training pre-Hollywood?*

My brother and I talked recently about trying to create a better IMDB page for our father. And possibly a Wikipedia page too. There were no obituaries because he didn't want one, nor a service when he died. One of his best friends, Edmund North, the Oscar-winning screenwriter of *Patton*, among other films, did write an obit for the Writers Guild publication. Somewhere I have that, but not here in California where the coronavirus has marooned me.

My father grew up in Chicago, was a great athlete already in his teens, and was an only child of my grandfather, an Englishman, and his mother, a Scotswoman. When he was fifteen, they moved to New York because of my grandfather's business, and after one semester at Horace Mann, a private school in the Bronx, his parents separated and they moved to Fresno, California for his mother's poor health. He starred in football and baseball at high school in Fresno, and after he graduated, he enlisted or was drafted into the Army as a result of World War I. He was eventually sent to France but did not see combat. At the time of the Armistice, he was in France in officer's training school.

When he returned to California and was discharged, he entered the U of Cal Berkeley and was a running back on their freshman team, which was so good they beat the varsity. He did very well academically too and was pledged into a fraternity, Phi Delta Theta, an experience that, to his chagrin, followed him the rest of his life. He ended up disliking the fraternity for several reasons. He found the hazing process both childish and barbaric. He discovered they were anti-Semitic and didn't like the exclusionary process in general. He disliked being contacted by them for decades later, but this was only an annoyance, not a terrible bother.

As a football star, he wasn't hazed at initiation, but his best friend was held under water so long he developed a lung problem. My father didn't like the fraternity, and he didn't like going to college with kids two years younger because they hadn't been in the Army. Somewhat to his later regret, he quit college after one year. His football team went to the Rose Bowl (a big deal in those days) three years in a row. I can't emphasize enough what a superb athlete my father was.

By the time he quit college his mother had moved to Santa Monica, so he came down from Berkeley to live there. He heard there were jobs at one of the studios for cutters (i.e., film editors), and he got one at MGM. He began as an assistant cutter, and through his editing experience really learned how films were made and how much timing mattered, how (as he explained to me when I was making documentaries) if you have a boring expository scene and lose the focused attention of the audience, you have to work twice as hard in later scenes to win the audience back. He thought Erich von Stroheim's *Greed*, a silent movie from 1924, was the best film he ever saw. From being a cutter he worked his way up to being an assistant producer.

I see that he has his first vague writing credit as early as 1927, on a Tim McCoy vehicle for MGM called Western, *directed by W.S. Van Dyke, from a story by Peter B. Kyne, with titles by Marian Ainslee and Ruth Cummings.*

Marian Ainslee was a girlfriend of my father's, so that might help explain it.

IMDB lists him as a producer for MGM beginning in 1930, often, in the first couple of years, Spanish-language versions of studio programmers. The book Luis Buñuel: The Red Years: 1929–1939 *by Román Gubern and Paul Hammond (University of Wisconsin Press, 2012) documents how Buñuel, on a six-month posting to MGM in late 1930/early 1931, was assigned to your father's care and supervision, and that they developed a friendship. Your father's assistant, according to the book, a writer named Thomas Kilpatrick, followed them around, translating. Bunuel's six-month try-out ended prematurely when MGM temporarily suspended its Spanish-language-version program, and your father wrote Buñuel a fond send-off. Again, in 1938, your father tried to help Buñuel out by getting him back into the U.S. and again on a job for MGM on a film about the Spanish Civil War that never eventuated. In his memoir,* My Last Sigh *(Knopf, 1983), Buñuel writes that remembering his MGM sojourn, and thinking of your father and Kilpatrick, always flooded him with "good, warm feelings."*

That may all be true, but I never heard my father mention Buñuel.

Did your father have a facility for the Spanish language? Or was that entirely the job of Kilpatrick?

Thomas Kilpatrick, always called Tam, was one of my father's close friends for many years. He met him during his one year in college. In fact, Tam is the person who had a lifelong lung problem that he and my father both felt began with the hazing into the fraternity they pledged – Phi Delta Theta. Tam Kilpatrick grew up on a ranch in New Mexico (after being born in Missouri), and he did speak Spanish. My father may have known a few words but didn't speak Spanish.

How and in what way was your father radicalized?

I believe it was the times themselves that radicalized my father. He felt the Depression was highlighting the inequality in America and in particular the shortcomings, the plain cruelty, of the capitalist system. He went to the Soviet Union in 1935, and he told me he was well aware he was being shown Potemkin Villages and show factories. Yet he was convinced that Communism paved the way to a better existence for more people than capitalism did. He returned from Moscow very sympathetic to the Communists, and I don't know exactly when he joined the Party, but it was probably around that time.

The Spanish Civil War, which began a year or two later, may relate to your question about Spain and Buñuel. My father sent money to the Loyalists and was always vehemently against Franco. In addition to money he sent to the Loyalists themselves, my father paid for a number of Americans to come home when they had no money for boat tickets. After World War II, when Americans once again went to Europe, my father would not go to Spain while Franco was still in power.

Did your father perhaps visit the Soviet Union with Ring Lardner Jr. and Maurice Rapf? In Rapf's autobiography Back Lot: Growing Up With the Movies *(Scarecrow, 1999) he mentions your father among the young people who learned how to produce films under the aegis of his father, MGM executive and producer Harry Rapf.*

He may have. I don't know. My father and Maurice Rapf were good friends, and my father even visited him when he came to New York to visit my wife and me and our sons.

I know your father worked closely with Irving Thalberg, the production head of the studio, who died in late 1936.

He revered Thalberg, said he was the best producer he'd ever seen. Their politics couldn't have been further apart, so obviously it was something about the way Thalberg worked with scripts and directors and film editors.

For much of the Thirties, your father stayed an MGM producer, mostly of B-films, doing very little credited writing for that decade.

My father did not like being a producer, nor working at MGM, but he did stay there seventeen long years [1923-1939]. He met my mother at MGM, Tess Slesinger, when [in 1936] she was lured out by Thalberg to write the screenplay of *The Good Earth*, Pearl Buck's novel about life in China. I think there's a plague of locusts somewhere in that film, and I remember my father telling me how that was done with special effects. It's possible he assisted Thalberg on the movie in a minor way.

My mother and father started writing as a team, and they wrote as a team until she died in 1945. L.B. Mayer tried to keep him on at MGM (Thalberg had died by then) and offered to double his salary. My father wouldn't take it and Mayer exploded, said he'd never work again at MGM. And he never did.

When your mother first came to Hollywood, where did she stand in her life and career?

I don't know much about my mother's first husband, Herbert Solow, whom I met only once. Politically he was a Trotskyist, and my mother was or became more of a straight Communist. (Neither of my parents nor any other former Reds that I've known ever referred to themselves as Stalinists; that was a term applied to them by anti-Communists.)

My mother had written a successful novel, *The Unpossessed*, while she was still living in New York, possibly while she was near the end of her marriage to Herbert Solow. The following year, 1935, she published a book of short stories, *Time: The Present*. It has been republished a few times, but the publisher has changed the title by using one of the short story titles, *On Being Told That Her Second Husband Has Taken His First Lover*. The idea, obviously, is to sell more copies that way. The book was written while she still lived in New York, well before she met my father, who was her [actual] second husband.

She was successful and well known when she came to work at MGM,

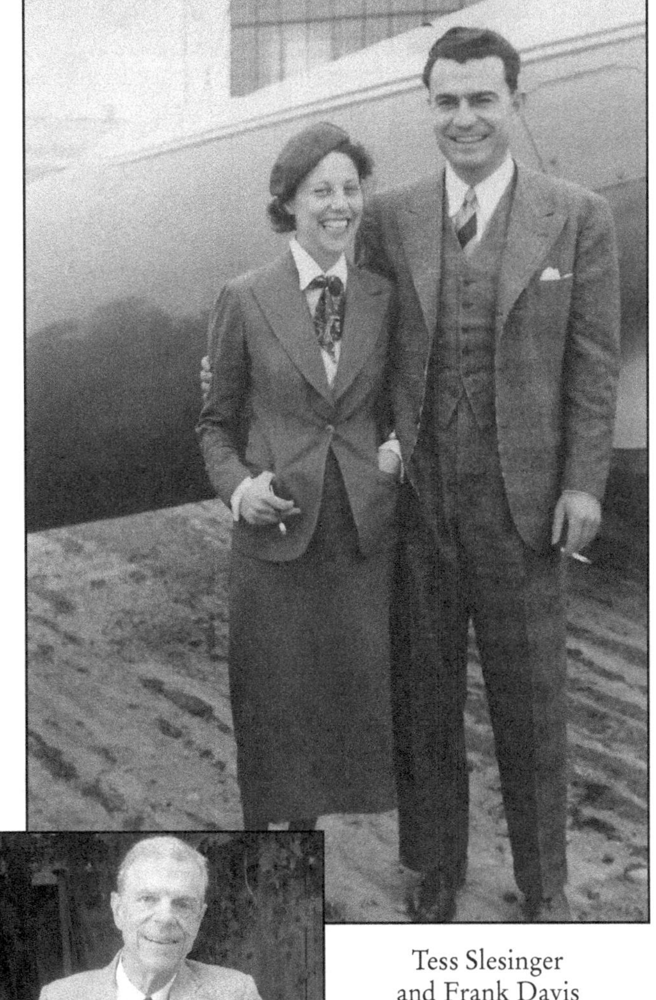

Tess Slesinger
and Frank Davis

Peter Davis
(photo by Alicia Anstead).

but I wouldn't say famous. Her first boyfriend in Hollywood was Clifford Odets, whom she had probably known a little in New York. Odets married the star of *The Good Earth*, Luise Rainer.

My mother was a New Yorker, Jewish, and irreligious. My father was brought up in Chicago, made by his English father to be an altar boy in the Episcopal Church, and he was also irreligious. They had different backgrounds, as you can see, and seem to have been attracted to one another as soon as they met.

Your mother has interesting early credits after The Good Earth. *She very quickly got connected to Dorothy Arzner, virtually Hollywood's only female director in the Thirties and Forties, who was under MGM contract. Your mother helped write Arzner's 1939 film,* The Bride Wore Red, *and then the first film she wrote in collaboration with your father, after he gave up producing for writing, is* Dance, Girl, Dance *in 1940, one of Arzner's last and best-known films. Did she or your father ever speak about Arzner?*

I was too young to hear my mother speak about Arzner, but my father told me they hadn't particularly liked the movie. You said she "got connected to Dorothy Arzner." Not sure they ever even met. Please remember that in those days the ultimate creative force, the true maker of the movie, was almost always the studio, not the director.

What do you remember about their social life, growing up?

While my mother was alive we lived in Upland [east of Pasadena in San Bernardino County], on a small ranch in the foothills of Mt. Baldy. Their friends were both from Upland – they enjoyed the local people a lot – and from Hollywood. The Hollywood friends who visited my parents at Redwoods, as our place was called, were mostly writers, I believe, who would come out for weekend stays at the large old ranch house we lived in. Tam Kilpatrick and his wife; David Hertz and his wife Michael; Nathanael West and his wife, Eileen McKenney, the "sister" of *My Sister Eileen*. Hardly a Who's Who of Hollywood.

Do you have any idea of how your mother and father wrote together? Who had the different strengths? How their talents complemented each other working on scripts?

The image I always have is of my parents sitting across a large table from one another, my mother typing by touch, my father hunting and pecking. He told me later that my mother's strength was dialogue, and his strength was construction. They both cared a lot, he told me, about character and felt that character should drive the plot. The fact that my father had begun his film career as a film editor made him very aware of the need for a structure that would hold an audience. That is, even if you have dazzling dialogue, you didn't want to make the scenes too talky.

Some sources say your mother was active in the struggle to form the Writers Guild.

Yes. Tess was, as you say, involved in the forming of the Screen Writers Guild, as it was then called.

Their first brush with HUAC came in 1939, when a predecessor congressional committee under the leadership of Texas Democrat Martin Dies came to Hollywood to make headlines denouncing Communist influences in the motion picture industry. Your mother and father were among a handful of writers named as Communists or sympathizers, and through their agent, Stanley Bergerman, they issued a public statement decrying the "absurd allegations made concerning our purported 'overwhelming contributions to the Communist Party,'" The statement continued: "We have never been, nor are we, at present, nor have we any intention of becoming members of the Communist Party, or in any way affiliated with it." I'm assuming this is the first example of what your father also managed to do later, in 1955: lying brazenly...

If they denied being Communists through their agent, Stanley Bergerman, then they were surely lying.

Quite apart from A Tree Grows in Brooklyn, *did they have a good opinion of any of the other scripts they worked on as a team which became films?* Remember the Day *in 1941,* Are Husbands Necessary? *from 1942, or* Claudia and David *in 1946?*

They did like their work on *Claudia and David* [a marital drama starring Dorothy McGuire and Robert Young and directed by Walter Lang]. I don't think I ever asked my father about the others.

On A Tree Grows in Brooklyn, *do you know if they worked for either the producer Louis Lighton, or for Darryl Zanuck? I am wondering if they had any opinion of Zanuck, since they did a couple of 20th Century-Fox pictures and he was supposedly good with writers...*

My father told me their work was with Lighton, not Zanuck. But perhaps when he gave me his assessment of *A Tree Grows in Brooklyn*, he meant not just Lighton but the entire executive corps, which of course included Zanuck. His assessment was that, and I can clearly recall his saying this, "*A Tree Grows in Brooklyn* was a great film that the studio made into a good film." Since the studio had control of the script, casting, directing, editing, music – everything, in other words, connected to the filmmaking process – it's pretty clear who had what they call the final cut.

Kazan boasts in his autobiography that he never met with the writers of A Tree Grows in Brooklyn. *But I'm amazed your parents – with their other connections to Odets and the Hollywood Left – never crossed paths with Kazan. Or did your father have any encounters with him, ever?*

Many years later my father met Kazan at a cocktail party, and they shared their memories of *A Tree Grows in Brooklyn*. I think it was a pleasant exchange, but I have no idea whether they complimented one another, or shook their heads about the studio.

I do not recall my father speaking about Kazan as an informer. He may have. He did talk about a number of informers, especially the infamous Martin Berkeley, but my father did not speak bitterly about people. The friends of his whom I knew had not been Communists, though they were all liberals and against the blacklist. As for Kazan, my father actually enjoyed meeting him at the cocktail party, not because Kazan was prominent, but only because of the fact that they'd shared making a movie together without ever having met. My father spoke very admiringly about [Kazan's 1957 film] *A Face in the Crowd*, a collaboration between Kazan and Budd Schulberg, both former Communists and both informers. Although my father thought it was awful that the name-namers ruined other people's careers, he did not disparage their work.

I think it would have amused him that, many years after his death, I exchanged letters with Budd Schulberg, who had written a memoir I liked that had ended when he was about nineteen; in other words it was simply his boyhood as a Hollywood child. I mentioned my parents in my letter. In his answer to me, he was very gracious and mused a little about having known my father when he was very young and my father was at MGM. Then, oddly, he actually named my parents as Communists, informing on them as it were, decades after their deaths. But my father was not a bitter man.

After Tess died in 1945, two years later my father married Isabelle Fair Wrangell, who did not have a profession, per se, but she had worked in a bookstore in Beverly Hills after divorcing her first husband. The bookstore was the famous Hunter Books, owned by her friends, and my father's friends, Marian Hunter and Dick Kilpatrick (brother of Tam Kilpatrick). Hollywood intellectuals, writers as well as stars, bought their books at Hunter's.

Isabelle and my father were married in Dick and Marian's garden. They'd known each other since the Thirties, and Isabelle became my second mother. About a year after that the family moved to Beverly Hills. A year or so later we moved to Brentwood, then to Pacific Palisades. In Pacific Palisades their friends were mostly screenwriters, a couple of directors, a couple of producers. They included Charles and Pamela Kaufman, Franklin and Monique Coen, Julian and Florence Blaustein, and Edmund and Collette North. Like my father's and Tess's friends, hardly a Who's Who of Hollywood, but they were all interested in ideas, literature, politics. Julian was a writer before he became a producer, and he liked writers.

Your father continued writing films without a regular partner. I notice he has credits on some interesting films after World War II... including he worked with Jean Renoir on The Woman on the Beach, *released in 1947. In his December 21, 1946 correspondence to Robert Flaherty (Letters, Faber & Faber, 1994), Renoir says, movingly, "He [Frank Davis] used to write with his wife, Slesinger – they were a team. Her death two years ago hit him very hard. His work with me is the first he has done after a long retirement from which he could not make up his mind to emerge. Our getting together is very important to me, because I think that, in him, I have found my ideal collaborator. Here in Hollywood it is pretty hard to fight single-handedly for the pictures one would like to make. Two minds with the same tastes and ideas are better than one when it comes to defending the thing desired."*

Yes, my father worked with Renoir on *Woman on the Beach*, and in fact he took me to the set one day. He and Renoir became good friends. They liked each other, hoped to work again together. They didn't do so, but I have no idea why. Perhaps because *Woman on the Beach* was not a success, or because Renoir moved back to France shortly after.

HUAC came along in 1947. Was your father personally friendly with any of the Ten?

I think my father knew several, perhaps all, of the Ten but was not close to any of them.

In the October 23, 1947 issue of *Variety*, which I read in research for my novel *Girl of My Dreams* my father and Tess (who by that time had been dead two and a half years) were described as "having championed a Red Constitution" for the Screen Writers Guild by a writer named James Kevin McGuinness. That's not the same thing as being named before HUAC. It was just a *Variety* reporter doing a story on possible Communist influence in Hollywood. At the same time, as you know, the HUAC hearings were going on in Washington, D.C. *Variety* at first opposed those hearings as a witch-hunt, and later moved more to the right.

I know your father briefly tried going to Mexico to escape the growing blacklist after 1950. When did that happen?

What I know is he went to Europe in 1950 with Isabelle and another lifelong friend. A very happy time for them. They were gone three months, and my brother John was conceived in Europe. I remember they came home just in time for the father-son softball game at my school.

My father then went to Mexico a few years later after being named by one or more people, including Martin Berkeley [who became one of the most prolific informers, in 1951 and 1953 testimony, naming as many as 161 people according to Victor Navasky's *Naming Names*]. I don't think he connected with the other blacklisted writers who were there. He may have seen Hugo Butler briefly, but he and Isabelle were in Mexico just a very short time before his agent, again Stanley Bergerman, called him with a job offer at Warner Bros. Jack Warner was no friend of the Reds as you know, but for some reason my father was upgraded to a little-known "graylist," meaning he could work at some studios but not at others.

I think the job was [the 1952 film] *The Story of Will Rogers*. My father was friendly with Will Rogers Jr., who played in both *The Story of Will Rogers* and the film that followed, *The Boy from Oklahoma*. I don't think [Michael] Curtiz [director of *The Boy from Oklahoma*] or anyone else thought Will

Rogers Jr. was much of an actor, but he was a likeable guy. When my father was working on the story about Rogers's father, he took me to his ranch one day, and we saw Rogers Jr. do some amazing rope tricks. I saw Rogers Jr. a decade later in Washington while doing research for a documentary, and he remembered my father very fondly.

My father also worked on *Lucky Me* in 1954, a Doris Day musical, uncredited, during this period. He liked the producer Henry Blanke very much, and he took me to meet him one Saturday when he was delivering a script to him at his home in the San Fernando Valley. He also liked Curtiz, who directed the Danny Thomas version of *The Jazz Singer* in 1952 as well as *The Boy from Oklahoma*, both with scripts by my father; and I do remember one funny anecdote he told about Curtiz, who had been born in Hungary. Curtiz and my father were talking one day, and Curtiz asked him if he knew how a Hungarian recipe began. My father of course did not know. Curtiz said that a typical Hungarian recipe starts with the instruction, "Steal two eggs..."

Someone must have alerted HUAC that your father was working on the "graylist" at Warners, and he must have been subpoenaed. Or perhaps Warner Bros. had to get him cleared.

My father and HUAC had a very interesting relationship that, even now, I don't entirely understand. Pardon me if this story takes a while to tell. He told me about it at the time that he was being questioned, that he really abominated the name-namers. His testimony is easily obtainable by looking up the HUAC records of their interviews in 1955.

My father did not [want to] take the Fifth Amendment, which would have rendered him unemployable. The Committee had done a pretty thorough investigation of my father and had all kinds of information about him, some of which I myself knew because he'd told me. He also told me that both he and my mother, Tess Slesinger, who died in 1945, had been members of the Communist Party. Here's the fascinating part of his testimony. He simply lied – again. He admitted to having a subscription to the Communist newspaper; he admitted to having what amounted to Party meetings in our home; he admitted to giving all kinds of financial help to the famous Abraham Lincoln Brigade that fought on the anti-fascist side in Spain. But he denied he'd ever been a member of the Party.

In the mid-Thirties a Communist named Stanley Lawrence was sent out from the East Coast to recruit members in Hollywood and raise money from them. According to my father's testimony, Lawrence tried to get him to become a Communist. It became a running joke between them, my father told HUAC. My father said Stanley Lawrence tried again and again to get him to join the Party, but he always refused. Lawrence was very passionate about the Loyalist cause. Somehow Lawrence fell out of favor with the leaders of the American Communist Party on the East Coast. He was replaced as their top representative in Hollywood and told to go to San Francisco. He was angry and refused. Lawrence went instead to Spain to fight for the Loyalists. He was killed there in 1937. There were rumors that the Communists themselves had ordered his killing, but I have no knowledge of that. Anyway, there was no jeopardy to mentioning Lawrence because he was long dead.

The Committee somehow knew that my father had even donated a car to the Party, but he denied he had done that. I used that little episode in *Girl of My Dreams,* where a famous actress gives her car to the Communists but disguises the way she does it so that it can't be traced to her. In his testimony, if I'm recalling it accurately, my father said he sold his car across the street from the studio at a used car lot. The Committee had done their homework, but perhaps my father made them doubt they had been given accurate information about the disposal of the car.

My father was also lucky. There was another Frank Davis, in California, a Frank C. Davis not in the film business [he was a UCLA psychology professor and outspoken activist], who was a member of the Party; and my father definitely benefitted from the confusion this seemed to create in the minds of the Committee. He'd also been in World War I and kind of had a sterling record as a leader in the little town where we lived when my parents wanted to move away from the Hollywood area yet still work as screenwriters. Zero Mostel, who gave courageous testimony on the day before or after my father, telling them to go to hell and taking the Fifth Amendment, apparently admired what my father had done, or gotten away with, because he gave him one of his famous paintings of a cat.

Years ago, three different women approached me because each of them wanted to write a biography of my mother. Two of these women had obtained my parents' FBI files under the FOIA. When they abandoned their project on my mother, they gave me copies of the files, which actually concern mostly my father. It turns out he was on J. Edgar Hoover's list for potential "preventive detention" from 1941 to 1959, an amazing amount of time. I think this is because my father, who had traveled to Russia in the Thirties, which HUAC knew, became kind of a recruiter for the Communist Party in Hollywood, and organized events for the Party, which the FBI seems to have known [but neglected to tell HUAC]. My father never knew he was on a list for preventive detention. Probably because he was under surveillance by the FBI and had also been named as a Communist by HUAC witnesses, however, my father's passport was taken away in the early Fifties. He hired a law firm in Washington, D.C., he told me, and paid them $1500 to get himself reinstated as worthy of having a passport, and he did indeed get it back.

The screenwriter Robert L. Richards, a onetime Communist, moved to Mexico when the blacklist descended. Your father wrote the film The Indian Fighter *in 1955, almost simultaneous with his HUAC appearance. The story was credited to "Ben Kadish," who was actually Richards, who never returned to the U.S. and who died in Mexico City. Did they have a friendship?*

I've never heard the names Robert Richards or Ben Kadish, which doesn't mean my father and Richards didn't know each other but only that I haven't heard the names. I do know that Ben Hecht was the second credited screenwriter on *The Indian Fighter*, and he and my father certainly knew one another, but they did not work on this film at the same time. I remember coming down from college to New York while this movie was playing in Times Square, with a huge ad trumpeting its arrival. I was so proud to see my father's name in the ad.

Your father wrote a number of Westerns beginning in the Fifties. Did he have affection for the genre, or did he just fall into this market in television and films?

I think he liked Westerns, when they were serious films like *High Noon*, written by another blacklisted screenwriter [Carl Foreman], because they showed major conflicts and a good deal of the reality in American history, but no, he did not have a special affinity for Westerns.

Did he have a particular relationship with the director André De Toth, for whom he wrote two pretty good films in the Fifties – Springfield Rifle in 1952 and The Indian Fighter in 1955?

No, I think De Toth simply liked his work.

Tell me about his frequent writing partner Franklin Coen – the only regular collaborator he ever had besides your mother – on several films in the last part of his career. How did they get together, and what was Coen like?

Frank Coen was a very close friend of my father's for a long time. I can't tell you much about him, except he was a very nice man, even a man one could call sweet and he wouldn't be embarrassed by that. His wife Monique was a special friend of my mother's (Isabelle, not Tess) and the two couples were frequently together. I really know nothing about Frank's early or later life.

Your father's best-known credit nowadays, because it frequently shows on cable, is probably The Train in 1964, starring Burt Lancaster, but with a handful of writers also contributing to the screenplay uncredited. I have a clipping here from an interview with the director John Frankenheimer in the November 4, 1994 Los Angeles Times, in which Frankenheimer ignominiously disparages the credited writers, your father and Franklin Coen, saying they only received credit after an arbitration and that "I never used one line, not one word" of their script.

Of course, that is a ridiculous claim by Frankenheimer that he didn't use a word of my father's and Frank Coen's script. Burt Lancaster had the original director, Arthur Penn, fired; he had brought in a terrific screenwriter, Walter Bernstein (who later became a friend of mine), to help justify the action scenes Lancaster and Frankenheimer wanted. But the Writers Guild was right to accord the two Franks sole credit because they discovered and wrote the original story, structured the entire film, and devised all the relationships in the film. When I say they "discovered" the story, I mean that they went to Paris and actually found out about the art train itself from a friend of theirs, Alain Bernheim, who lived in Paris. The credits read that the film is based on a 1961 book [*Le front de l'art* by Rose Valland], but that book was written *after* my father and Frank Coen had already written the original script. The film actually should have been [nominated] in the "Best Original Screenplay" category at the Oscars rather than in the "Adapted Screenplay" category. I don't mean to imply that it would have won if it had been in the Original category, only that that's where it belonged.

The Train *was also your father's last credit. What happened to him in his last twenty years between then and his death in 1984? I'm surprised he retired after such a high- profile success...*

Screenwriters don't really retire. They simply stop being sought after and possibly stop having ideas for originals. Despite *The Train*'s success, he wasn't really offered any new screenplays. And he and Frank Coen had finished their screenplay several years before it was made, as I have explained.

My father, as I've told you, was a great athlete, a magnificent physical specimen, period. He went with some younger friends on a two-week rafting excursion down the Colorado River when he was 85, claiming to the raft company that he was only 69. It took him weeks to recover from the exhaustion and sun exposure, but he did recover. He played a lot of tennis right up until he was stricken at 86 with multiple myeloma, a dreadful form of cancer. He died two months after his 87th birthday, not of multiple myeloma but of congestive heart failure. He collapsed on the way into a movie theater with Isabelle and two very close friends.

Until he became ill, my parents traveled a good deal. When he was at home, he read a lot, both fiction and non-fiction. He did research for me on my film about the Vietnam War [*Hearts and Minds*], watching old Hollywood films that might have anti-Asian prejudice or hysterical anti-Communism in them. He did make passes at writing stories, but I never actually saw any of them so I can't tell you what they were about. And he was a passionately devoted grandfather to my four children.

Biographical Subjects

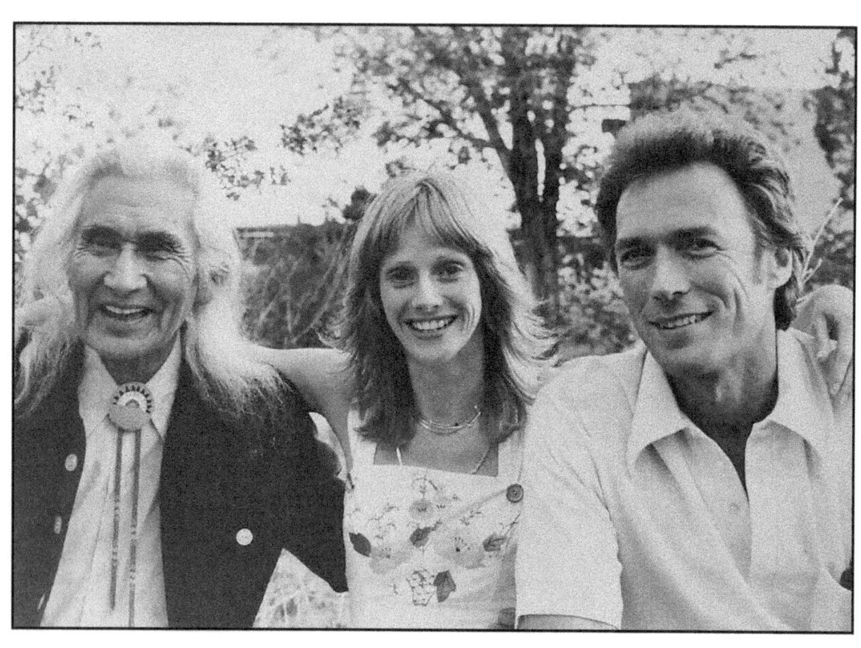

Chief Dan George, Sondra Locke and Clint Eastwood
on the set of *The Outlaw Josey Wales.*

Clint Eastwood

1976
Interview by Patrick McGilligan

April in Burbank. The Malpaso Company is no longer at Universal City – some chagrin over miserable promotion there. Instead, it is located in a Spanish-style bungalow on the Warner Bros. lot. There is nothing like its serenity in all of madly urgent Hollywood, with its ascending leafy-green plants and muted crossworks of brown timber, and a kitchen with water cooler and strewn-about books on Indian folklore. Relaxed, friendly, almost mellow, as different as Southern California is from Northern California, Malpaso takes on the qualities of its number one star and executive, Clint Eastwood, who gravitates between the two distant worlds. He commutes.

Usually – most happily, one presumes – he is with his family several hundred miles north in Carmel – far away from Hollywood. Today, on a late Friday afternoon, he is working on post-production for *The Outlaw Josey Wales*, his latest picture, a Western he also directs. He agrees to an interview. He is dressed in a white T-shirt and blue jeans; he is brown, sinewy, rangy, and handsome. The obligatory press agent is dismissed (a rarity), and Eastwood sprawls into an easy chair in his inner office decorated with posters of Coogan, Dirty Harry, The Man With No Name, etc. A secretary enters, pours herbal tea, exits. Sunlight arrows into the room through tiny shutter apertures, making funny kaleidoscopic patterns on the darkened ceiling.

Eastwood says that he does not like to talk. But in a surprisingly soft and composed voice, coming from across the room, he effortlessly talks the afternoon away…

—◇—

Can you tell me a little bit about The Outlaw Josey Wales?

This film I just finished is a little like *The Good, The Bad and the Ugly*, although it's not satiric. It's a saga. It's about the character I play, whereas in *The Good, The Bad and the Ugly* the only character you got to know – somewhat – is the Eli Wallach character. In other words, Josey Wales is a hero, and you see how he gets to where he is – rather than just having a mysterious hero appear on the plains and become involved with other people's plight.

Are you reacting against the mysterious hero?

No, it was just written that way. I'm not sure that this wasn't written under unique circumstances. This was written by a guy who had never written a book before, a half-Cherokee Indian with no formal education – including grammar school. He's a terribly self-taught person who became famous as an Indian poet and teller of stories. Somebody talked him into writing one down. So he wrote this Western, and it was published down in Arkansas by a publishing company called Whippoorwill Publishing. They put out about seventy-five copies – that's all – hardcover.

He sent it to me unsolicited. Sometimes you don't like to take unsolicited scripts without having them registered with the Guild or an agent, because of possible plagiarism. Anyway, this was sent to me. It sat on my desk with several other things. It was called *The Rebel Outlaw: Josey Wales*. The jacket on it was not too interesting but there was a letter attached to it. My associate, Bob Daley, read the letter one night after I left the office. The letter was such a reaching-out kind of thing – it had such a nice feeling about it – that he figured, "Well, I've got to give this at least a twenty-page read and see if it's going anywhere." So he sat down to read it and ended up reading through dinner and reading through the night. He called me the next morning and said, "God, this has so much *soul* to it that it's really one of the nicest things I've read." I was up in Monterey at the time – at Carmel. So I said, "Get it up to me right away, I'll read it." I read it and felt the same way about it. We called down there where he was living at that time – then in Arkansas, now he lives in Texas – and bought the screen rights.

What is his name?

Forrest Carter.

Is he an older man?

About 40. After we bought the screen rights and began to make the picture, Delacorte brought it out as a paperback, and they changed the name to *Gone to Texas*.

I like Rebel Outlaw.

I didn't like *Gone to Texas* [as a title] because it puts it into a specific region. *Rebel Outlaw* I didn't like because there are so many AIP pictures about motorcycle gangs.

Your Westerns always seem to be more allegorical, more mythic in a sense, rather than specific to a region or history.

I'm attracted to that sort of thing, although I don't think this one is – as much. This one is more of a saga, rather than *High Plains Drifter* where the hero drifts in, you don't know anything about him, and you don't know where he comes from. In this one, you pick him up prior to the Civil War on the Kansas-Missouri border, when the people of Kansas were talking about going to the North and the people of Missouri were talking about going South. He becomes an outlaw because of the war; it shows what the war has done to him.

Are you tending more towards directing nowadays?

I have been for the last few years, but I've started to pull back a little bit. I ended up doing this one because of various circumstances.* I like the story very much too. It just depends. I don't intend to direct every picture I make. In fact, I'd like to lay off a bit, directing. It's a terribly mind-fatiguing job to be both actor and director. Just being a director is a very consuming job – the

---

* Philip Kaufman began the direction but left, after quarrels with Eastwood over his handling.

pre-production and post-production especially. It really isn't the eight or nine weeks it takes to shoot the film that is the problem – it's all the time afterwards. If you direct films, you really can't act in too many films.

You'd rather act?

There's no way you can set a plan; scripts come and go, ideas change, and you see one you'd like to direct and another you'd like to act in. Right now, my feeling is I'd like to hold back for a year or two on directing, and then – unless I find something along the way I want to do – eventually pull out of acting and just direct. If I was doing a part that was more of a departure, a larger challenge, maybe I would prefer not to direct. But, for instance, to do a film like *High Plains Drifter* wasn't that difficult – because I had been familiar with that character for a long time. There was no problem.

—∞—◇—∞—

When did you first decide you wanted to direct?

Back when I did *Rawhide*. When I was up on location one time, we were shooting some vast cattle scenes – about two thousand head of cattle. We were doing some really exciting stampede stuff. I was riding along in the herd, there was dust rising up, and it was pretty wild really. But the shots were being taken from outside the herd, looking in, and you didn't see much. I thought we should get right in the middle of this damn stampede. I said to the director and producer, "I'd like to take an Arriflex [portable film camera], run it on my horse and go right in the middle of this damn thing, even dismount, whatever – but get in there and really get some great shots, because there are some beautiful shots in there that we are missing. Well, they double-talked me. They said, "You can't get in there because of union rules" – which isn't true at all, because if you're doing a shot the normal camera operator can't do, if he's not a horseman, then there's no reason in the world why you can't do it – in fact, I've done it a lot of times and there is no union rule against it. But they kind of double-talked it away. I could see they didn't want to upset a nice standard way of moviemaking.

Finally, later on I went to Eric Fleming [co-star of the television series] and said, "Eric, would you be averse to my directing?" He said, "Not at all, I'd be for it." So I went to the producer, and he said great. Evidently, he didn't say great behind my back, but he said great at the time. He said, "I'll tell you what, why don't you direct some trailers for us – coming attractions for next season's shows?" I said, "Terrific. I'll do it for nothing and then I'll do an episode." And I did the trailers. But they reneged on the episode because, at that time, several of their name actors on other television shows were directing episodes, not too successfully. So about the time I was getting set to do it, CBS said no more series actors could direct their own shows. So I called it a day.

Then I went over to work with Sergio Leone. He didn't speak any English, I didn't speak any Italian. So my agreement with the producer of the show was that

I could rewrite the story. The stories were all the same, but the dialogue was terrible because it was interpreted by an Italian into English. I said, 'You've got to let me rewrite some of this stuff." They said, "Fine." So I got more actively involved in the production over there. Leone had only done one movie before, and we got along terrifically. I started getting interested – because he was a younger man than some of the guys I'd been working with, and a little more imaginative. And working on the European scene sort of inspired me to get back into directing.

A lot of established Hollywood directors were working in television in the early Sixties. Do you remember observing any particular director or directors?

There were a lot of people who had made very nice films – like Tay Garnett (who made *The Postman Always Rings Twice*), László Benedek – guys from another era who had done some nice films along the way. After seven-and-a-half years – different people every week, 200-some odd episodes – you get to see a lot of people. You get a lot of ideas about what to do and about what not to do, because you come across a lot of turkeys – at least, in my opinion – guys that didn't know as much. You end up seeing how they paint themselves into corners.

Is Leone an extremely classical director? Does he plan every shot with enormous care?

Leone isn't the most planned guy; he's very flexible. He's not super-planned like, say, Vittorio De Sica [for whom Eastwood appeared in a segment of *The Witches* in 1967]. He [De Sica] and [Don] Siegel are the two most planned-out guys I've ever heard of. They're very flexible guys, but they're extremely well organized. Leone isn't that organized but he has a very good concept of what he wants. He's very good with compositions; he has a nice eye. He's very good with humor, a very funny guy – his humor is very sardonic. He's not very good at directing actors, he's only as good as his actors are – but most directors aren't very good at directing actors. The most a director can usually do with actors is to set up a nice atmosphere in which to work.

Did Leone work with you in terms of acting?

No. We couldn't even communicate or speak the same language.

Do you communicate today?

Today, I speak Italian in the present tense, and he speaks English in the past tense.

It's amazing to think of A Fistful of Dollars *or* The Good, the Bad and the Ugly *being put together by people who don't even speak the same language.*

The first picture was a German-Spanish-Italian co-production. The German co-producers were down there, and I could speak with them because they could all speak English. I didn't speak any Spanish. I had never taken any languages.

Was the entire mythic quality of the "dollar Westerns" written into the original script, A Fistful of Dollars?

Yes, it was fairly written into the script. I brought all the wardrobe and everything from here, and I had ideas about the character. The character talked a lot more in the script; I took a lot of his dialogue out. My point of view was, the more the leading character talked, the less mystique he had, and the more dissipated the strength of the film. There were many more expository-type scenes written that we took out.

That's the character's real strength – you just wait for him to do or say something, anything.

You are mystified by him. It was played approximately the same way in *Yojimbo*, which it was stolen from or taken from.

Were you conscious of that at the time?

There was never any doubt. When we got over there [to Italy], they told me it was a remake of *Yojimbo*. I said fine. When I first saw *Yojimbo*, I thought, geez, this would make a great Western, only nobody would ever have the nerve to make it with this style. And then when the script came through several years later, I thought this might be an interesting project. A European might not be afraid of it – like Leone – where an American would be afraid of approaching a Western such as *Fistful of Dollars* with that kind of style.

For instance, there were rules in Hollywood years ago, unspoken rules, that you never tied up shots of a person being shot. In other words, you never shot a tie-up shot of a man shooting a guy and another person getting hit. It's a Hays Office rule from years ago, a censorship deal. You'd cut to the guy shooting, and then cut to a guy falling. That was alright – the same thing – the public isn't counting the cut. But you could never do a tie-up. We did because Sergio didn't know all that. He wasn't bothered by that. Neither was I. I knew about it, but I couldn't care less. The whole object of doing a film with a European director was to put a new shade of light on it.

—◦—

Even before Rawhide, *were you attracted to the Western?*

I always liked them, even as a kid, and that's the only way I ever judge a film.

Are you aware of qualities about the Western that attracted you, and that you can articulate?

It's a tough question. I don't know whether I could answer it, although the Western is one of my favorite genres. I don't know whether I can intellectually answer it, because I don't try to approach things in that sort of vein. I try to approach film emotionally, how it moves me. But particularly, in retrospect, I think there's a certain escapism, like to a less-complicated era, a more do-it-yourself era, so to speak. And the excitement of the movement lends itself…

Did you, for example, like John Wayne when you were young?

I liked him as a youth, depending on the film, but I was never a fan of any one particular actor outside of James Cagney.

That surprises me.

I've only met him once.

Robert Redford told me the same thing: the only actor he admires is James Cagney.

I love him. I love his early films. I always try to watch them on television.

That's funny. In a sense, he's the opposite kind of actor from you – he's convulsive and you're so restrained.

He isn't at all like me. When I first started out as an actor, all the secretaries used to call me Coop, because they thought I resembled Gary Cooper, kind of a backward kid – quite a few years ago.

But Cagney… I always like Cagney's style and energy. He was fearless. Most of those guys were, though; they were fearless. Going back to the most famous thing, sticking grapefruits in people's faces, they weren't afraid to do things that were outrageous. A lot of actors get wrapped up in images.

Do you have any sense of working in the same tradition as people like Gary Cooper and John Wayne?

I've approached things totally differently, and I think I come off extremely differently than they do. My films are distinct from theirs – in their time. I mean, because who knows what they might be doing if they were in my generation today. They might be doing similar things. I don't know.

But although you say you approach film emotionally, many of your Westerns have an intellectual or satiric quality about them.

I *can* intellectualize, sit down and talk about them for hours with somebody if they want to sit and exchange symbolism, or whatever. But I don't approach it that way; I start out on an animalistic level, and after I've got the script totally in mind, then I can move on to it on almost any kind of level. But I prefer to be drawn to it on that emotional level; if you start out on an intellectual level, I think you're starting without the nucleus. The instinct and motivation is the thing that will tell you whether it's going to be successful or not; if you have good instincts about a play, and it moves you on that level, then obviously your audience is going to be moved on that level, because the vast majority of the audience doesn't want to intellectualize it, they want to emotionalize along with it. They may want to intellectualize afterwards, particularly if they are film buffs.

Obviously, you yourself intellectualize though – to the extent of pondering the distinctions between saga and myth. Have you ever reflected upon what you, Clint Eastwood, mean to people?

I think I appeal to the escapism in people – the characters I play, let me put it that way. I like those characters myself; that's why, maybe, I carry them to other extremes than my predecessors. In other words, in the complications of society, as we know it today, sometimes a person who can cut through the bureaucracy and the red tape – even if I'm playing in a modern film – a person who thinks on that level is a hero. A person who can do that, such as a Dirty Harry character, a man who thinks on a very simple level and has very simple moral values, appeals to a great many people. I think that's one of the great frustrations in the world. People see things as becoming more complicated. Every time you go to do something – every time you go to register your car – it becomes more complicated. You're waiting in longer lines every year.

For major drama, for major conflicts like crime, they like to see a guy who can hack his way through all that. A very self-sufficient human being is almost becoming a mythical character in our day and age.

Does a sense of history intrigue you about the Western?

Yeah, I think so. It's always nice if you can tie it in – although a film like *High Plains Drifter* didn't have to be a Western, it was just a small morality play. It's probably been done in other forms and fashions over the years – it just seemed as if it played itself out well as a Western. It wasn't intended to be a true saga Western – the winning-of-the-West kind of thing – the saga of men and women who pioneered the West; it was just a vignette of a certain attitude.

Do you do a great deal of historical research?

No. I read books on the West a lot, and sometimes on a certain film I'll look for something specific. On *Josey Wales*, we tried to find as much information as we could about the outlaws of Kansas. We've all heard about the Missouri guerrillas – a lot has been written about that, Bloody Bill Anderson and the group down there – but there hasn't been too much written about the Kansas Red Legs. They were actually sanctioned – legal – by Missouri; they were a state militia. They were like a vigilante group who, under the guise of protection, did a lot of bad deeds.

—◦—

Can you articulate what you've learned from Don Siegel?

Well, I'm a very good friend of his, and I think I've learned a lot from him in the sense that he's a man who does a lot with a little – so therefore our philosophies are pretty much akin. He's a man who's done a lot for very little money with budgets over the years; he's a very lean kind of director – he usually knows what he wants and goes in and shoots what he has intended to shoot and doesn't protect himself, like a lot of guys; there's a lot of guys that shoot thousands and thousands of feet, many and many takes of the same thing. They cover themselves every which way so they can't make a mistake. Siegel laughs about that himself. He says, "Those guys always end up making the 'Best Picture.'" He was brought up to work under a certain economics; he had never been what Hollywood considered a "name director," the handful of guys who always got the big stars.

Coogan's Bluff is very underrated as a picture.

That's the first picture we did together. It was a fun film to do in the sense that the project started out with another director, and Don and I didn't know each other. We started out a little butting heads together and, as it turned out, we ended up with a great working relationship.

Coogan's Bluff started out as a story, not a complete story, but I thought it had potential, and so I signed a deal with Universal to develop it. It was assigned to a guy named Alex Segal, who had just won an Emmy, I believe, for doing *Death of a Salesman*. He and another writer sat down, we had a meeting and put some pretty good work in on it, but we got to a certain point and were stymied. They didn't know where to go with the character – I never did find out the full details. We had a limited time in which to shoot the damn thing – and the agency and the studio said, "You've got to find another director."

So they said, what about so-and-so, naming two or three guys; then they said, "What about Don Siegel? You're out of European films and although he isn't, he's got a sort of cult following in France, he's well thought of in those groups." I said, "I'll look at anybody." So we looked. I said I liked his work – I had seen several things he'd done – he'd obviously shown that he could execute certain things. He heard that I was looking at his films, and he hadn't seen the "dollar films," so he said, "Fine, but let me see his work." It was kind of an ego thing. [Laughs] So he looked at mine and he liked those films; we got together and talked.

Then he went off to New York and wrote a script with kind of a different concept on it that I liked. Originally, they were playing the guy much more as a bumbling type – I'm not saying that's wrong, it might have worked out. The writer working with the first director saw the guy as a guy who's always losing his wallet and being taken by all the people in the big city. Well, I thought that had been done a lot in the past, with James Stewart and a lot of guys. I felt, what happened if it doesn't mean anything that he's a small-town guy? Maybe he was in the war in Korea, he's traveled a bit around the world, and he's been exposed to other things – just because he's not a New Yorker doesn't mean he's a clod. Plus the fact that maybe his kind of prairie cunning might work well for him against a big city background. We got together, hashed it out, and Siegel liked that idea. I liked some of his ideas, we kicked it around, and came to a meeting of the minds.

But he was the only director to do shooting?

Oh, yeah. In fact, somebody told me about Mark Rydell, and I was talking to him as a possible director for it. And Rydell asked, "Who else are you considering besides me?" I said, "Don Siegel and a couple of other guys." He said, "I'll tell you something. If you want to do it in a month's time, there's only one guy that can do it. I can't do it – I don't have the knowledge or the background to do it." He said, "Don Siegel would be the greatest." I thought that was rather admirable to say that, because other guys would say, "Give me another month or two of preparation, and I'll do it." But Mark Rydell said, "No, in the amount of time you want to go, there's only one man who is really capable of doing that, Siegel. He'll do it much better than I would."

—◦—

I think Dirty Harry *is Siegel's best film.*

I thought he did a nice job with *The Beguiled*. Of course, I was the one who hired him for *Dirty Harry*. When I came over here [to Warners], it was tied into somebody else, and the script was going in another direction. I got Siegel involved. My agreement with Warner Bros. was, "I'll do it if you'll let me hire a director like Don Siegel, and we'll take the story back to its original concept" – which was

Harry Julian Fink's screenplay. They had taken it off in another direction.

I wonder if you know that a lot has been written about the film – pro and con.

To emotionalize things doesn't mean I drop any sort of intelligent thought about it. A lot *has* been written about it, pro and con. There are people who line themselves up with the political overtones of the film. But there are none really. Those people are crazy.

Even Siegel has said that, ultimately, it's a very liberal film, as opposed to being right-wing in nature.

The people that call it a fascist film don't know what they're talking about. They're just mouthing off… there's nothing like that in there. The guy was just a man who fought bureaucracy and a certain established kind of thing. Just because he did things a little unorthodox – that's the only way he knew how to handle it. He had so many hours to solve the case and, as far as he was concerned, he was more interested in the victim than the law.

He says, in the picture, he is a man of high morals. Then the law is wrong if this person [the killer] can be let off on a technicality like that. Well, the laws are changing – they're always changing back and forth in the courts, the pendulum is always swinging back and forth, right and left. Once in a while, the court gets too loose on one end, conservative on the other, and it changes every ten years.

We, as Americans, went to Nuremberg and convicted people who committed certain crimes because they didn't adhere to a higher morality; we convicted them on that basis – that they shouldn't have listened to the law of the land, or their leaders at that time. They should have listened to the true morality. We sent them to jail on that basis. That is how it is with this man [Dirty Harry]. Somebody told him this is the way it is, too bad, and he said, "Well, that's wrong. I can't adhere to that." That isn't fascist, that's the opposite of fascism.

I understand a third Dirty Harry *is in the works. Will Siegel have anything to do with it?*

Well, I don't know. It depends on his availability. We're still at a script stage right now. If it works out script-wise, we'll do it, and if it doesn't, we won't. I don't want to do a character just to continue it.

Is it fair to say that Dirty Harry and The Man With No Name are essentially the same character with many common qualities?

No, I don't think so. But they're both moved by passions. Dirty Harry is a man who is callous, seemingly hard on the surface. I think The Man With No Name is much more satiric, it plays on more traditions of the West, and breaking the taboos of the West. Dirty Harry had a much more straight mind – he had a job to do that he became emotionally involved with. The only thing similar about them is that you don't know too much about the background of Dirty Harry, although you get a hint of it – you get a hint that he's had a certain personal life. The Man With No Name – other than in *The Good, the Bad and the Ugly* – doesn't develop too much, and you don't know anything about his background at all. That wasn't always true. In the original *Fistful of Dollars*, we did have a background scene – it was kind of a prelude to the film – but it was better without it.

The thesis of a book I wrote on Cagney is that an actor's work can be approached as seriously as a director's, and that an actor's personal life can often be traced in relationship to his films. Cagney, for example, was very socially involved as a young contract player, and his Thirties films, such as The Public Enemy, *reflect that. By the Fifties – thanks to the patriotism of World War II,* Yankee Doodle Dandy, *and the fact that he is getting richer and more comfortable in life – Cagney's films change greatly. It seems to me that, to a certain extent, your career can be understood this way. You are* The Man With No Name *in your private life, an enigma to people, and very often a reflection of the character you play in film.*

Certain things that come out of the collage of characters you play *are* you; certain elements of the person can't be withheld. I suppose I feel that way, I suppose that's why I play it well. Other people can't play that. Open people, more extroverted people maybe, can't play that kind of character because they don't feel that way. They don't feel alone, and they're lonely alone, if you know what I mean – they're not happy alone. They act real well in circumstances where, maybe, there are a lot of people and relationships going on. I guess that's somewhat because of the way I am. My personal life… I don't care to have it exploited, I get no satisfaction out of having it exploited.

—◦—

I've seen you in movies as far back as The First Traveling Saleslady *in 1956, but I'm not aware of your acting background. Did you go through any formal training that made an impression?*

I've gone to a lot of acting schools, the same as anybody else. I drifted around in my early days before I could get jobs. That era you're talking about – *Traveling Saleslady* – before then, and even after then I went through periods where it was very hard to get work, but I would go to acting classes at night and work on various projects and scenes in groups.

Are you aware of any influences or techniques that you have inherited from that experience? From a coach or another actor?

I've never felt myself influenced by any particular actor, no. I've never felt I played a scene like anybody, otherwise I'd probably be acting like Cagney – but that wouldn't fit with my physiognomy or total being. I've always interpreted things the way it felt to me, not the way it came from an outside source. I've studied in acting groups, but the basic fundamental of learning acting is to know yourself, know what you can do. That's one big advantage of doing a series, if you can. You get to see yourself a lot, get to see what you can do, wrong or right. You get to looking at yourself on film so much that you can almost step away with a third eye, or as a second person.

I think if you take all the books written by Stanislavski, [Michael] Chekhov, or whoever right down the line, the basic function of any teacher is to teach yourself. There's no way you can learn out of a book. You can learn to learn it – if you know what I mean – by learning certain techniques or tricks, the basic concentration. I went through all that scene. And I managed to live through the Fifties when everybody was imitating Marlon Brando. There was a period there when every actor, whether they were playing neurosurgeons or not, always talked like ex-fighters.

Brando's very good, he's a terrific actor. I think he's done some of the finer performances on the screen – especially *On the Waterfront*. But there was a tremendous imitative thing starting with [James] Dean and moving on down, that they have got away from now. This is an era more akin to the Twenties and Thirties when every individual had their own things. You take the major personalities in the business today: they are much more distinctive as personalities than they were in the Fifties. The guys coming on are not as influenced by one guy.

Did you see the [Paul] Mazursky picture, *Next Stop, Greenwich Village*? I saw it the other night. It's so very true. He hit it right on the nail. The whole deal where the character [Larry Lapinsky, played by Lenny Baker] lied about having been at the Actors Studio… because everybody was with that, since Brando had been there a month or two. Everyone was on that scene.

I was up for a picture once, and the producer said he really wanted me for it. But he said, "I have to give the director the last choice." I think Sterling Hayden and Anita Ekberg were the stars; this [part] was for the younger brother. I thought I was really right for it, everybody thought I was really right for it. But the director got some plumber who got off the train from New York, some guy who [mumbles], and the director said, "Man, he's great, put him in the film."* They snapped this guy up, and it's typical of what Mazursky is saying there. You got to the point where, after a while, you said, "Jesus, do I have to say I'm from this funky studio to get a job?" Everybody had to say that to be anybody, to be in on the vogue of the moment. I didn't do that, but I saw it happen. I lived through that era. It was very true the way Mazursky laid it down.

On the other hand, it strikes me that Dirty Harry is almost an entirely different person from Clint Eastwood in some ways – the Clint Eastwood who, for example, practices transcendental meditation. The character on the screen is part of a split personality.

Well, it's a character you play, and sometimes you play a character; it has a certain impact, and people think you are that character. It's a left-handed compliment, in a sense, because you do the character to the point where they think, "Hey, maybe he's a mad-dog killer. I really believe him, that's the way he is, he's gotta be that way." The Man With No Name, same way. "Wow, he must be like a guy who never says anything…" Maybe I am. There are elements of privacy in my life but, obviously, I can shoot my mouth off if I get to feeling in the mood. I've got to admit I'm moody about it, though.

Getting back to directing, what is your relationship with your producer?

* The film was probably *Valerie* in 1957, in which Peter Walker played the brother.

When I first started as a contract player, at Universal, Bob Daley was in cost analysis. Then he became a first assistant and a unit manager. He always thought the way I did, trying to keep as much of the cost of the film on the screen as possible, rather than having it in limousines, etc. So when I was forming this company to do films like *Hang 'Em High*, I needed somebody like a producer in the old sense who knew budgets and schedules. There was a period there where producers were just promoters; they would go out and buy a story and put their names on it as producer and sell it. Today, a producer is a guy who produces – who knows something about the filmmaking aspect. So I hired a guy who had a good background in film rather than just a salesman I didn't need.

When was Malpaso Company formed?

Right after *The Beguiled*. He was working with me during *Beguiled*, preparing for *Misty*.

What does "Malpaso" mean?

"Malpaso" means "bad pass" in Spanish, like a bad pass in the mountains. Or "bad step" – like if you're going to trip over something.

—◦—

Let's talk about Play Misty for Me. *When I was in college that film was a very big moneymaker on campus. Funny. I went to school at the University of Wisconsin in Madison, which is or was a hotbed of the New Left. Yet your films were always popular.*

The only time I've been associated with anything political is by innuendo, or by people's assumptions that I have certain political aspects. Probably – actually – I'm the most moderate person, politically. After Watergate, I'm like everybody else – thinking – "Oh Jesus, politics, keep me away from it." I'm reticent. I've supported Democrats and Republicans in California. It depends on what the guy stands for at the moment.

Didn't you support Nixon in 1968? I seem to recall your picture on a poster, along with people like Henry Aaron and Wilt Chamberlain.[*]

Yeah, that was a while back. Like everybody else, you vote for who you think is right, with the limited amount of knowledge you have at the moment.

Anyway, Play Misty For Me *has an unusually good script.*

That was written by a friend of mine, a girl, Jo Heims, who surprisingly writes both men and women well. She did *Breezy*, too. She wrote the man's part in *Breezy* very well; she captured the whole feeling of a divorced businessman's doing fairly well, swinging along with chicks, but totally disconnected with everything, who sort of rediscovers life through the eyes of this young girl.

I had optioned *Play Misty For Me* when I was doing *Where Eagles Dare*.

[*] The 1972 "Youth for Nixon" poster ("Nixon's the One!") did have Wilt Chamberlain (and Green Bay Packers quarterback Bart Starr) on it, but not former Milwaukee Brave Henry Aaron.

I talked to the author and optioned a sixty-page treatment. Then I went to Europe, doing *Where Eagles Dare,* and Jo had an opportunity to sell it – I had just an option on it, very little money, so she called me and asked if she could sell it, she needed the dough. I said, "Go ahead, because I don't know when I'm going to get out of here, or what I can do with it." I had taken it to Gordon Stulberg at CBS, and he said, "We're doing a film here called *The Sterile Cuckoo* with Liza Minnelli. It's too much like that." I said, "It is? Okay." I took it to Universal – they said, "I don't think so." I took it to David Picker at United Artists, and he turned it down. Everybody turned it down. At that time, I was just starting to come into my own with my films, but I was still the kid from Europe. I didn't have quite enough juice to pull it off.

I was working in Oregon in *Paint Your Wagon,* then I came back down to do [*Two Mules for*] *Sister Sara* for Siegel at Universal, and I signed a deal to do three or four films with them. All of a sudden, it hit me one day: "Whatever happened to that *Play Misty For Me* that you guys bought?" They said, "Well, it's on the shelf, it's not going anywhere, nobody's going to do it anymore." I talked to Jennings Lang and said, "You know, I'd like to make that film." I didn't tell him I wanted to direct it at that time. He said, "Jesus Christ, who in the hell wants to see Clint Eastwood play a disc jockey?" I said, "Who in the hell wants to see him play anything? I don't know… it just seems like a good story. It's got a lot of conflict; elements of it could happen – elements of it have happened to me." I identified with it…

So I went to Lew Wasserman and I told him, "You've got a thing on the shelf here that I'd really like to develop, and I think I can make it very cheap, all on natural sets." He said, "Great, take it and run with it." I know exactly what they were saying behind my back, probably saying, "We'll let the kid fool around with it. He'll do that, and then he'll probably do a couple of Westerns for us, or some other adventure-type film that will seem more commercial at the outset." The other thing they weren't pleased about is… they said, "Why would you want to do a film where the woman is the best part in the film?" I said, "Well, what difference does it make? The guy is the victim, he's the subject certainly. I think it's maybe more conflicting to have a man who handles himself in a more physical situation stuck in a situation where he can't handle it physically, a frustrating situation." But they didn't see any of that.

Then I went to Don Siegel, and I told him, "Don, I've got this little picture that I'm working on now, and I'm really thinking seriously about directing it." Siegel said, "Go ahead. I think it'd be great. I'd kind of like to sign your director's card." You have to have two guys for you to join the union. So I have to say that Siegel was very influential.

So I went to Wasserman again and said, "I've got the script fixed. I want to do a good film and I want to direct it." I had to haggle with him to do the film at a certain price. They said, "Well, could you act in it for nothing, just on a percentage, instead of your regular deal, since we don't consider this a commercial property?" I said, "Fine, I just want to do the picture." They were pleased. My gross percentage turned out to be better than if I had taken the salary. *Misty* came out and did well, despite their advertising. There wasn't much concentration put into it; it was just [put] out. It had tremendous re-release, too; the exhibitors I talked to said they had great luck with it on the second or third run. And they got a really good television sale on it, because the film took off. It made a lot of money, they were happy, and I was happy.

Breezy was also poorly distributed, although many people like the film very much. Wasn't it shelved by Universal and then released a year later? Some bad reviews, initially, virtually killed it.

You can't blame it on reviewers because, if a film's good and the reviewer doesn't see that it's good, that doesn't mean the public will stay away from it. The public stayed away from it because it wasn't promoted enough, and it was sold in an uninteresting fashion. Good reviews would have helped that type of film. There's some films that reviewers can unanimously rap and still do business. But this was a small film – it was just the story of the rejuvenation of a cynic. I thought that was an interesting subject, especially nowadays in the era of cynicism...

William Holden gives a strong performance, and Kay Lenz is really a terrific, underrated new actress...

Yeah, she was nice.

—◦—

Did you do Breezy *deliberately to break pace with* Dirty Harry *and* The Man With No Name? *Are you interested in other genres?*

I'm interested in them but, at the same time, you have to be constantly conscious of the fact that you want people to see the films. One of the films that got the best notices of those I did was called *The Beguiled*. It was a disaster at the box-office, very poorly distributed, and very poorly advertised. That had a lot to do with its lack of success, but the fact is they sold it to the Man With No Name audience – it would do good the first few days and then fade out terrifically. Because they never sold it to the audience who would like that kind of film.

That's Universal. They have a terrible advertising department, they're not smart. Look what they're doing now to *Gable and Lombard*. I don't care what kind of film it is. The ad campaign is terrible. No particular logo or anything, just a spread-out bunch of squares. Horrible copy: "They had more than love, they had fun." That's just about the worst copy I've ever read in my life.

Do you try to oversee your own advertising as much as possible?

I try to keep an eye on it, but there [Universal] it was a harder thing to do. Here [at Warners] it's easier, because they're much better. For instance, the *Dirty Harry* and *Magnum Force* campaigns, both made here at Warners, were, I thought, laid out very nicely.

The script seems very weak in your latest picture, The Eiger Sanction, *although the visuals are very exciting.*

It was more on a visual plane than *Play Misty For Me*. It didn't have the kind of story you could tell with that kind of impact and excitement. The only excitement you could do was on a visual level and that is the way it was written. I would have liked, in a way, to have done *The Eiger Sanction* as a not-so-satiric, maybe serious adventure story with tremendous characters, and conflicts between the characters, and still do it with that same visual thing. You could really make something special. This bordered on a Bondish sort of thing in certain areas.

Play Misty For Me, on the other hand, was fun because it had elements of a Hitchcock-type thing, but at the same time it was unlike Hitchcock. A lot of the time in his films – like *Psycho* – the story part doesn't mean anything until you get to the impact of the psychotic thing. In *Misty*, you have that interpretation of commitment between individuals, and how this interpretation takes people in certainly different directions. I think it was a much more contemporary thing for people today, because so many people go through this in various relationships – not just, as in the case of the picture, where the man is a victim, but there are women too who become suppressed or choked by an individual just because somebody has different ideas about a relationship.

Did you get into The Eiger Sanction *too quickly to develop any ideas in the story, thematically? The characters all seem to be so thinly, almost absurdly, drawn.*

That is just the way it was done. I took a book Universal owned – a bestseller – and I couldn't figure out what to do. The book has no ties. In other words, the character who is killed at the beginning has no relationship to anybody else. I just took it and tried to make the guy relate to the hero, so the hero had some other motivations. The way the book was written, he had no motivations for anything. He just went there [to the Eiger] strictly for monetary gain, no other motivations, period. At the end, he's not with any of the people he started out with – including the girl. It just rambled on that way. But it was a book (Trevanian wrote it) that was especially popular with people who like escapism.

The visual aspects are impressive, nonetheless. I thought there was a long shot the movie might get nominated for an Oscar.

If you wanted to get on that kind of bandwagon, but it wasn't that kind of a movie. The music [by John Williams] was almost up [for an Oscar]. But they had a panel that chose, and they chose *Jaws* because *Jaws* was the movie of the year. The same guy [Williams] did this score, and *Eiger*'s was probably better than *Jaws*.

Also, the challenge of it for me was to actually shoot a mountain-type film on a mountain, not on sets. The only ones done in the past were all done on sets; the mountains were all papier-mâché mountains.

I understand that a technician died during the filming…

Yes, we lost someone… the Eiger is a mean mountain. So it was a great challenge to pull off that type of film – it was a tough film to make. *Josey*, which I just finished, is a much more intelligent story – in a classic mode. It isn't what you would call a standard Western, it has a classic saga feel – I'm not too articulate…

LeRoy Collins and Oscar Micheaux

2004
Interview by Patrick McGilligan

LeRoy Collins was a movie star only once. But the movie was *The Betrayal*, the very last production by the African-American director Oscar Micheaux, shot in Chicago and parts of the Midwest in 1947. That makes Collins one of the last witnesses to an era and a man whose mystique has never been greater. Moreover, the part Collins played was Micheaux himself – that is, the lead character, as drawn from Micheaux's 1943 novel *The Wind from Nowhere*, and whose name in the film is Martin Eden, in honor of Micheaux's literary hero Jack London.

Collins was in his early twenties, attending Roosevelt College in Chicago, after having served in the military in World War II. Though he had only acted passingly ("In my senior year, I was on the high school football team, and when the season ended, I got bored and joined an amateur theatrical group at a community center"), he was picked out of a line of job applicants. "You are Martin Eden," Micheaux flatly told Collins, upon hiring him, "and Martin Eden was me."

The son of emancipated slaves, Oscar Micheaux was raised in Illinois, but as a young man he homesteaded on the plains of South Dakota, writing novels. The novels gave him solvency, and he turned film director.

Micheaux ultimately published seven novels, and between 1919 and 1948 made over forty films with "all Negro" casts that catered largely to segregated, all-black audiences. He produced, directed, and wrote the scripts of his films. While entertainment-oriented, Micheaux's films insistently explored issues such as poverty, courtroom injustice, miscegenation, and prejudice. *Within Our Gates* was made in 1919 as an explicit response to D.W. Griffith's *The Birth of a Nation*, while *Symbol of the Unconquered*, in 1920, excoriated the Ku Klux Klan. Micheaux's 1925 film *Body and Soul* launched the screen career of Paul Robeson.

Micheaux is increasingly celebrated as a pioneering individualist who attacked racism in his films while working outside the official, segregated industry. The Directors Guild of America honored him posthumously in 1986. The Producers Guild gives an annual Oscar Micheaux award, and the trailblazing African-American filmmaker even has his own star on Hollywood's "Walk of Fame." His life and career have become a growth industry for academic scholars.

Like many Micheaux films, *The Betrayal* was concerned with inter-racial romance. The film had a reserved-seat premiere in New York City, where Micheaux advertised it as "The Greatest Negro Photo-Play of All Time." It is the only Micheaux production to be critiqued in the *New York Times*, where Thomas M. Pryor, in his brief June 26, 1948 review, found it noteworthy that its story "contemplates at considerable length the relations between Negroes and whites as members of the community as well as partners in marriage." Yet Pryor faulted *The Betrayal* as "often confusing," with "sporadically poor photography and consistently amateurish performances."

But the film met with great success before "Negro only" audiences in the Deep South, relates Collins. Only three years later, Micheaux would be dead, and the era of "race pictures" and segregated theaters began its slow fade. The star of *The Betrayal* never acted professionally again.

After *The Betrayal*, Collins served for twenty years as principal of the George W. Goethals Upper Grade Center public school in Chicago. He still resides there in the South Side neighborhood of Chatham. His recollections of Oscar Micheaux and the making of *The Betrayal* are all the more fascinating, given that all prints of the picture – like so many other Micheaux productions – have disappeared. In his mid-70s today, Collins is still trim, and still sports a thin mustache, like the strikingly handsome young man whose face stares out from the lobby cards of *The Betrayal*. "Playing Oscar Micheaux" started, for him, as little more than an intriguing summer job.

—◦—

What happened when you met Oscar Micheaux for the first time?
During the summer of 1947 – even though I was in summer school – I was looking around for a job to supplement my income. Someone found out they were going to do a movie in the city [of Chicago], and they were interviewing people for different types of jobs – stagehands, prop men, and whatnot. A couple of us who took the same classes went over to the studio they had rented on 29th Street, and they started interviewing us for these various jobs. I was called aside by one of the assistant directors who said, "We'd like you to read for a part."

I was taken over to meet Mr. Micheaux. He asked me some questions about myself, and then I read for him. All he said was, "I want you to read for a part that you might be able to play." I said okay. So I read a page, and then he had me read another page. Then he looked at his wife [Alice B. Russell] and said, "I think this is the one." That was it. I was cast.
Why do you think Micheaux chose you?
I got the part because I looked like Oscar Micheaux wanted me to look.
Did he give you any advice for your audition?
Nothing. Just: "Read it in your own style."
Were you being camera-tested at the same time?
No. I just read for him, and he was the sole evaluator.
What did he look like?
He was in his 60s, elderly, mature, with salt-and-pepper hair. He always wore a suit and tie – and I think maybe he smoked an occasional cigar. He had some physical problems: he kind of limped, and if I recall correctly, sometimes he carried a cane. He had medicine that he had to take.

He was staying in a nice hotel on 51st on the South Side with his entourage. I went there later to discuss my contract and sign it. He had made money on his books and his earlier pictures – especially because there was no middleman on his pictures, and he was the distributor – and he had a chauffeur with a big black limousine who was also a kind of general handyman and assistant.

You said his wife, actress and producer Alice B. Russell, was with him when you met him.

She was always with him. Alice was refined, well-educated. She had a role in the film, and she would help by holding the script and keeping track of scenes. She was always there on the set and would correct any lines that weren't being done right.

What was this studio like, that he had rented for filming?

It was an old radio news studio. He had furniture and equipment brought in for the filming, and then he used buildings outside for shots of Chicago. Sometimes we went to Wisconsin or Michigan for scenes, especially for the farms and ranches of South Dakota.

Can you describe – for people reading about The Betrayal *for the first time in this interview – your role in the context of the larger story of the film?*

This picture was the autobiography of his life. I played *him*, Oscar Micheaux – although the character's name in the script was Martin Eden. I was the lead actor. I had to memorize a big thick script, and I was in seventy-five percent of the scenes.

Weren't you daunted by the challenge of playing a director in his own life story?

No – although I was told later that forty or fifty people before me had read for the role, people like Oscar Brown, who was a well-known writer, singer, and all-around entertainer.

Had you yourself ever heard of Oscar Micheaux, prior to meeting him?

Never heard of him.

Had you seen his movies?

Like everyone else, I went to movies. I may have seen his, but I didn't attach his name to any that I saw.

Had you read any of his books? Had you read The Wind from Nowhere, *the book on which the film is partly based?*

Not beforehand. I did eventually read *The Case of Mrs. Wingate* and *The Wind from Nowhere.*

In order for you to play the part, didn't Micheaux require you to read his books and do some research about his life?

No. He didn't say anything about that to me, or to anyone else in the cast. Some of the cast were professional actors from Chicago who were in radio. One was a character actor who had been in Hollywood pictures. One young lady [Myra Stanton] I knew because we grew up together. Another actress, Yvonne Machen, had been on the stage in New York; she had played the lead in *Anna Lucasta.* Harris Gaines, another lead, had had a top role in a radio drama in New York.

We had three or four weeks of rehearsal before we shot the film – just reading through the script, because it was a long, drawn-out movie. The cast was all there, at a YMCA or community center he rented out. There were maybe twenty of us who had big speaking parts. We sat around with the script, but it was like a theater situation, and those who had lines would come up to the front of the room and stand. I was up there most of the time because I had more involvement than everyone else. He'd intervene to tell us to speak up, or read a line a certain way; he'd correct you. He wanted to get it down to a fine point before you got into costume, because he was spending a great deal of his own fortune to do this movie.

—o—

What was his manner with actors?

Very gruff. Not what I would call polished. He was very to the point, matter-of-fact, no put-on. He didn't have any patience with people. If he wanted something done, he wanted it done correctly, right then and there. He knew exactly what he wanted – and his manner wasn't pleasant. He'd shout at people. He never shouted at me – not once. He was gentle with me, with the leading ladies, and with two or three other ladies. I think he was quite the guy with the ladies.

Why do you say that?

Because he put so many women into the story of his life – they are out of context sometimes, just in one scene sometimes. There was the white lady in the Dakotas he was in love with, and a black lady in Chicago whom he marries, and another lady in another place that he's romancing… etcetera. It wasn't done in the same way they do things now, but you got the idea that this guy wanted people to know he saw quite a few ladies in his day.

But you didn't see any evidence of him womanizing during the filming?

No, he was older, and all business. His attitude was, "This is my money we're spending, and let's do it quick and get it done with."

I remember he never called us by our real names. It was always by the cast name. I was Martin. From the first moment he laid eyes on me he didn't call me anything other than the name of the character in his book. It was always Martin this, Martin that. I just assumed that identity as far as he was concerned. I don't think he knew my other name except when he wrote the check out.

Your character was named Martin Eden after the Jack London novel – did Mr. Micheaux ever talk about his affinity for Jack London?

No, but it was in his books. If you read his books, you'd see that. Most of his autobiography, and most of his early life, involved living out on the Dakotas on ranches. He was the only black in the area, and he started writing books, and I think he more or less used Jack London as his image. That idea motivated him. There he lived a sort of Jack London isolated existence – a very different kind of existence for a young black man at that time.

Did he confide anything to you about his life at that time?

No, and he never referred to the fact that this was his life.

Wasn't that a bit odd, considering?

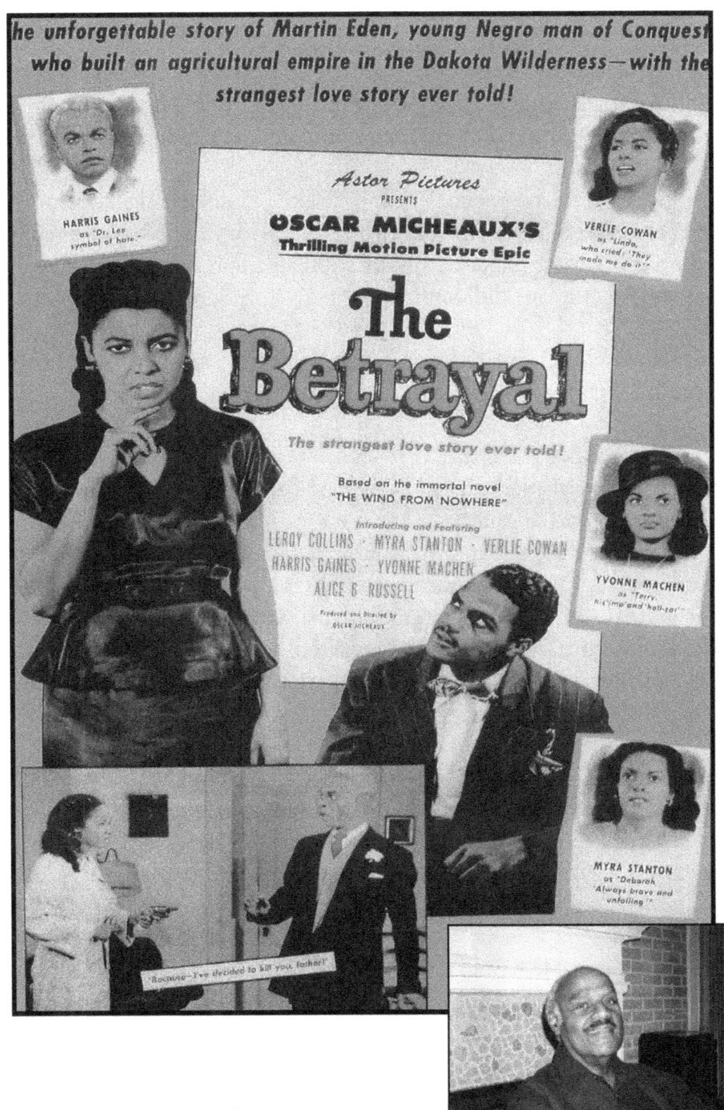

LeRoy Collins in 2004
(photograph by
Patrick McGilligan).

Well, everyone knew it, so there was really no reason for him to say it. He said to me, "You are Martin Eden, and Martin Eden was me," and that was it. We understood: "This is my life story. I lived the way Martin Eden did. These are the people I associated with, and these are the life experiences I had…" and the dramatization of that story is the only thing that changed. He fictionalized parts of it, built it up, although some of these things possibly did happen.

You say he was kind to you.

He could be gracious if he liked you. If he liked you, he had charm, and I was one of the ones he liked. I was allowed to improvise, for example, and I remember that the other actors wore make-up but he stipulated that at no time was I ever to use any make-up. Everyone did, but me.

Why?

I don't know what the reason was. He said it wasn't necessary for me to have make-up on. I guess he wanted me to look more rugged, like he was as a young person.

Did he give you any acting advice?

He told you a few camera clues: "Never look at the camera" – things like that.

That's a pretty good clue, actually!

It all came natural to me, and that's why he liked me, I guess. He said to me, "Be yourself," and I was pretty much natural in the part. I could have survived in the part except that some of the surrounding cast were so weak because they were amateurs, and plus the parts were so badly written. So I went ahead and improvised a little, and he never interrupted me. But he didn't let the others improvise. He'd shout at them if they did.

Did he compliment you if you did it right?

His attitude was, "I expected you to do that." One day the professional actor from Hollywood said to me, in front of the whole cast, that I had a marvelous memory for having committed the script to memory – which I had. But Mr. Micheaux's attitude was, "I expected that."

What did he do on the set? Did he walk around, gesture, look through the camera?

He did everything. He would set up the angle. He would direct the movements. He'd sit on a stool and watch, but he would be in command, directing the troops.

He had a crew there to do the actual filming. It wasn't a big crew, but it was a crew. A crew to do the filming, another crew to move the sets around, and another to do the audio part. All the crew, the cameramen and whatnot, were white, incidentally. He was not very patient with them either.

Why were they white?

Oh, those were union jobs.

Did you have any sense that it was a low-budget production? Were you paid fairly?

I wouldn't know what was fair. There was no job I could have gotten as a college student that would have paid me more money.

Was the budget tight in any way?

Probably, but I had no feeling about that because I had no experience – no frame of reference. He rented a lot of things out.

How was the camerawork? Was the cameraman good, and was Micheaux interested in the visual quality?

It was pretty good, but Mr. Micheaux would usually try to do things in the quickest way and the cheapest way. By the time we got to the photography, we had gone over the script for three or four weeks, and everyone had their parts down to perfection, in terms of memory. He would do as few takes as possible. If he liked it, he'd say, "That's it," and if not, we'd shoot it again.

In the evening he'd have the cast sit down, and they'd run the rushes from the previous day. We'd look at those rushes. If he saw something there he didn't care for, we'd reshoot the scene, because it had been done just the day before. If anything was off, it was reshot the very next day – because the costumes and people were still there.

So he'd try to work quickly, but he was willing to reshoot.

Oh yes. We looked at rushes, and even several months after all the filming was done he had several of us – particularly me, because I was the lead actor – go and shoot a scene that had to be reshot. One of the scenes was on a train, so the assistant director, the cameraman, and some actors and myself went up to the North Shore somewhere and shot a scene on a train that had to be redone. We did that for two or three scenes.

Micheaux himself wasn't there?

No, it was handled by his assistant director.

—◦—

Considering that The Betrayal *is a lost film, and people can't see it nowadays, can you recall any particular scenes – either good or bad? There must have been some interesting stuff going on in a three-hour-plus movie.*

Yvonne and Harris were very good actors. She played a hellcat, and she acted that role very well. He was her pompous, dignified father, who wanted to break up the marriage of Martin Eden to her sister. They were very effective in their scenes together.

I had to wear a Western costume with a big hat and boots at the beginning of the film. In other scenes, when visiting the city, I'd be wearing a suit. But I remember the Western costume, and being up on a horse at one point, saying goodbye to a friend in the West, and then riding off into the sunset. That was a pretty scene.

There was a scene in which the wife has a gun, and Martin Eden is struggling with her – done first in long shot and then with closeups – a good scene, as I recall. And I remember a scene where I was walking in the Dakotas, and the wind from nowhere – the title of the book – came roaring up. They had huge fans blowing on me, and I was supposed to be walking in one direction, but the wind was so strong that it pushed me back, very realistically – almost like a tornado. It even knocked me on the ground, which it was supposed to do. Things like that I remember, but this was over fifty years ago now.

When was the last time you saw the picture?

I saw it only once, at the premiere here in Chicago. The theater was packed. I went with some of my fraternity brothers, and we slunk down in the last rows.

Mr. Micheaux opened it on Broadway – it was the first all-black movie to play Broadway, but the press clippings were not good. For one thing, they said it was too long and the dialogue was drawn-out. Even though I was in it, I knew that. If I could have improvised better, the picture would have been better, because I had taken speech classes, and I had some success at speechmaking. Even I knew that the dialogue could be improved.

Were the characters speaking in some kind of studied fashion?

The dialogue just didn't come natural to a lot of the characters, and the scenes just went on and on. It was like someone saying, "Here is my philosophy, here is how I feel, and I'm going to say it all through this character right now, all at once."

Was he using the dialogue as a platform for his ideas, is that what you mean?

As I have said to other people, I thought he was a pompous and self-serving man – but I respected him, because he was doing something that very few people could do. He had the wherewithal and the knowledge to do it, too. He was a very good businessman, but…

How about "artist"? How much of an artist was he?

He lacked a true artistic touch. He just related his life experiences and put them into a written form and then brought them into a moving picture format. He depicted life, his life, and things that he wanted to be heard about – but I would be highly critical in terms of quality. In terms of *The Betrayal,* certainly, though the quantity was there; the film was *long.*

He certainly saw himself as an artist.

He did, he did. And he was a pioneer, no question about it. He was bold, saying just what he wanted to say. His attitude was, "Get out of my way – this is what I'm going to do."

I remember, one day, we were driving down the road in Michigan, looking for a farmhouse. There must have been four or five cars and trucks in a row, like an Army convoy. He was up front in one car with the cameraman, with me and some actors in the back. He saw the right farmhouse and told the cameraman, "I want a picture of this exterior scene." Well, there were people in the window of that house looking out at this line of cars and trucks – and he yelled at them to get out of the window. Told the people to get out of their own window!

He had boldness, brashness, and I always say he was a – quote – character. He was a unique person of his time.

The advertisements for The Betrayal *seem to court controversy over the interracial romance angle, boasting "The Strangest Love Story Ever Told."*

That was in the Forties, and in most parts of the country that [interracial romance] was unacceptable. The theme was very bold for its time – it was a controversial issue – which goes to the genius of the man. How was he going to achieve something that was sensational? *Create* something sensational; that was intentional. He exploited situations in order to gain notoriety, and on the basis of that came his success. He was selling something – and that was his strategy: making a big issue of it, getting people to talk about it. He knew exactly what he was doing.

When they showed *The Betrayal* throughout the South, the lines formed for blocks outside the theaters. I later saw newspaper pictures of the lines. The picture wasn't a hit in New York on Broadway, but it was accepted by the black audience in the South. It only played on Broadway for a week or so, but that was so Mr. Micheaux could advertise "Direct from Broadway" when it played in all those other places.

You have to realize that in this time blacks could not go to white theaters throughout the South and various other areas; or they could only go on certain days – like only Wednesdays – so Mr. Micheaux rented those theaters after the regular performances were over, at nine or ten o'clock at night; and that's when *The Betrayal* would be shown. That was a hurdle he had to leap – and his greatest attribute, if you ask me. You really have to admire the man. He took on the very formidable task of becoming a distributor at that time, when there were no black distributors. But that is where the money is; money isn't in making the movie, it's in how you get out and use your resources to distribute it and reap the benefits. He was highly competitive in that sense and took the movie around like a road show picture, from one town and city to the next.

—◇—

Did you do any further acting, after The Betrayal?
No. That wasn't my dish. It was fun being with the people, and it was fun to make-believe, but it was also hard work. You got up early and you worked all day, and when you got home it was dark. It may sound glamorous, but not when you're going through it. After that picture I finished college and then went into my field of education. I was a teacher and junior high school principal, here in Chicago, for twenty-four years.

Did you ever see or hear from Mr. Micheaux again?
Not really – but I married my leading lady, Myra Stanton. She was my first wife; we are long since divorced. We had gone to the same high school but didn't start dating until we were making the film. Afterward we got married, and then we had to laugh, because for our wedding gift Mr. Micheaux sent us one of his books, signed.

Mavericks
and
Independents

Dean Stockwell

1988

Interview by Patrick McGilligan

In his book *Negative Space*, critic Manny Farber writes about Hollywood "sideliners," screen players whose fringe characterizations stand out, like raisins in rice, whether in good, bad, or in-between movies. "Standing at a tangent to the story and appraising the tide in which their fellow actors are floating or drowning," Farber says, "they serve as stabilizers – and as a critique of the movie."

One of our best sideliners, nowadays, happens to be Dean Stockwell.

Born of show business troupers (his father, the publicity notes invariably mention, was the voice of Prince Charming in Walt Disney's *Snow White and the Seven Dwarfs*), Stockwell has had a long, intermittent, richly varied and at times climactic career. The first stage of that career was as a popular, ambiguous, glittering-eyed juvenile performer at MGM in the late Forties and early Fifties. By the time Stockwell was fifteen, he had acted in some twenty-two movies, including such pick-of-the-lot properties as *Anchors Aweigh*, *Gentleman's Agreement*, *Kim* and (on loan-out to RKO) Joseph Losey's allegorical *The Boy with Green Hair*.

Stockwell makes no bones about detesting the MGM experience, then as now. After finishing high school at the studio, the teenaged Stockwell quit acting, enrolled in UC-Berkeley, dropped out, then, after shearing his trademark tousled hair, roamed the U.S. for roughly five years.

Hardscrabbling persuaded him that acting was maybe not the worst way to make a living. Back in harness, as a young leading man Stockwell acted in programmers, until he was cast as one of the two killers in *Compulsion* on Broadway, which led to his repeating the role in the film version, and other stellar performances during a flurry of motion picture activity in the late Fifties and early Sixties. For *Compulsion* and for his emoting in the screen adaptation of *Long Day's Journey Into Night*, Stockwell received ("shared cast") Best Actor honors at the Cannes Film Festival.

But Stockwell was still unhappy with acting, with society, and with himself. He was married, for two years, to actress Millie Perkins. He abandoned acting again, embraced the Sixties, and recreated, sex- and drug-wise, legendarily. When he was not keeping company with Beat Generation artists and intellectuals, he was hanging out in Topanga Canyon with Jack Nicholson, Neil Young, Eric Clapton, and longtime pal Dennis Hopper, with whom he has often worked.

By the time Stockwell had opted for a second comeback, the parts for a middle-aged renegade child actor with an out-there reputation had dried up. In the Seventies, Stockwell's moody, offbeat presence could be glimpsed more reliably in dinner theater and episodic television than in the obscure films he made that were barely released. This nowhere period was capped by such projects as co-writing and co-directing Neil Young's anti-nuke, rock-and-roll comedy *Human Highway,* and by Stockwell's bit as an Anglo military advisor in the Oscar-nominated Nicaraguan feature, *Alsino and the Condor.*

Again, Stockwell was discouraged. After meeting his second wife, Joy Marchenko, at Cannes, a place with a lucky association for him, he decided to move to Santa Fe, New Mexico and to take up the sure thing of real estate. In 1983, the following advertisement was placed in the trades: "Dean Stockwell will help you with all your real estate needs in the new center of creative energy." A telephone number in Santa Fe was listed.

Fortunately for moviegoers, fate intervened in the persons of David Lynch, who cast Stockwell as the fiendish Dr. Yuch in the science fiction extravaganza *Dune,* and German director Wim Wenders, for whom Stockwell played the common-sensical brother of drifter Harry Dean Stanton in *Paris, Texas,* which won the Palme d'Or at Cannes in 1984. Needless to add, the actor never did sell much real estate.

Since *Paris, Texas,* it is clear that Stockwell is in the middle of an improbable and fecund third comeback in his career. The roles have included the pansexual weirdo who lip-syncs Roy Orbison's "In Dreams" in the den of iniquity in David Lynch's *Blue Velvet,* and the hard-bitten career soldier of Francis Coppola's *Gardens of Stone*; there were memorable sightings in *To Live and Die in L.A.* and *Beverly Hills Cop II*; and upcoming (this summer) pivotal roles in Jonathan Demme's *Married to the Mob* and Coppola's *Tucker,* in which Stockwell plays none other than Howard Hughes. ("Surprisingly, I look a lot like him!")

Manny Farber also writes about "centered" acting, which entails "deep projection of character," as opposed to an "uncontrolled, spilling over quality."

It is this "centeredness," this uncompromising revelation of a faceted self, which has made Dean complicit with audiences and a boon to filmmakers for forty years. In silly business like 1968's *Psych-Out,* with Jack Nicholson fronting an acid rock band in the heyday of Haight-Ashbury, Dean's eerily tranquil characterization (and the sacrificial death of his character) provides the only authenticity in what was, even at the time, a garbled time-piece. In *Blue Velvet,* his thoroughly oddball performance as Ben provides a sideliner's window onto the edgy surrealism of the rest of the movie.

Stockwell's resurgent joy in acting is found in the range, the looseness and the vitality of his parts in the Eighties. In director Demme's new picture, Stockwell takes a rare leap at comedy as the cold-blooded, loose-zippered Mafioso Tony "The Tiger" Russo. It is a sly, full-bodied, captivating performance, the kind the Motion Picture Academy remembers come statuette-time. It may be misinterpreted as a way-out departure, whereas like everything else he has done, it is very Dean.

When we met at a chic restaurant in Santa Monica, Stockwell was still recovering from an all-nighter of filming Dennis Hopper's latest (with rockers Neil Young and Bob Dylan in the cast). He was wearing blue jeans, cowboy boots, turquoise jewelry. He chain-smoked during lunch. An unlit cigar dangled in his shirt pocket for afterwards.

—◦—

Did it help you as an actor that your parents were professionals in the business, and presumably, role models? Does your acting approach come out of your home at all? Or does it come out of being honed at MGM?

Well, my father [Broadway actor Harry Stockwell] wasn't there. My parents had split up by the time I was six, so he was not a role model at all. My mother [Betty Veronica Stockwell] had given up her career, which was as a dancer-singer-comedienne in vaudeville and *George White's Scandals* – that type of thing. So her career really had very little bearing on the type of thing I was doing. I was the first film actor in my family, per se. My home and my environment was MGM.

I don't think working at MGM influenced me, as far as my acting goes, at all. I think that my acting was strictly intuitive, from the beginning, and has always remained that way. I resisted any attempts by anyone to assist me. Even when I first started acting, when I was six or seven, I always knew, when I was doing a scene, if it was right. I don't know how I knew, but I knew.

How did you think about acting, as a boy, when you thought about it at all?

When it's intuitive, that's a bypassing, really, of the thought process. It's a source that's just prior to or more original than the thought process. When I did think about it, I thought about it in terms of honesty, or truth, or self, or how I would react, how I would feel, what I would do, and what I would say.

Did MGM have acting coaches and classes in which you were constantly worked over?

They had an in-house acting coach for years, named Lillian Burns. I used to have to go into her office, and I hated it. I felt it was just such a waste of time. I had to sit there while she took the script and read the role and cried and laughed and did all this shit, while I just sat and nodded and wanted to get the hell out of there. That was my only coaching.

You talk about MGM in such measured terms. What was the upside of being there, for so many years, when you were growing up?

Well, the only upside that I can really tell you about pertains to where I am now, many, many years later. I have a profession that I'm more comfortable with, that I'm proficient at, and which I need to support my family – my two children and my beautiful wife. I have no idea what I would have done –

I might have been a lawyer, I might have been an artist, I might have been a physicist. Who knows? But at the time, when I was a child, I didn't see any benefits, and in retrospect, I don't see any benefits now.

You were unhappy at the time?

A great deal of my childhood was not there for me, because I was working. I was doing two, three pictures a year, and in between I was going to school on the lot. It was the full-bloom fruition of the motion picture industry. It represented the pot of gold for most people who were striving to achieve this big payoff of fame, glamour, and money. A lot of demands were placed on me that should not be placed on a child, at all, ever.

When you look back on those pictures at MGM, do they give you any gratification at all, after all these years? Or do you experience a different kind of twinge?

Some of them do give me gratification, in retrospect. But the ones I appreciate now, or have some affection for now, I also appreciated to some degree at that time. Occasionally a picture like *The Boy with Green Hair* came along. The war was all around us, constantly, so I took that film very seriously, very purposefully. I felt a certain sense of pride in that film, and I still feel good about it. A lot of people involved in that film were blacklisted, including the director, Joseph Losey. It was my first radical film project. [Laughs]

—◦—

You stopped acting altogether after high school and dropped out of show business for roughly five years. Why?

Well, I desperately needed to get out of the whole thing. I didn't really formulate it in my head that I had to find myself or see the world, I only had to get away from MGM.

I used a different name – my real first name, which is Robert – and I cut all my hair off. I had to earn whatever money I lived on. I was doing a lot of odd jobs in California and New York. By the time I was twenty or twenty-one it became clear that I had no tools to go into any profession. My education was poor at best because it was geared towards accommodating the work. There were only three hours of school a day, which was constantly interrupted by having to go in and do the shots. I had to re-teach myself to read later on.

So I thought I would try acting again, and contacted my agency, MCA. I got a little part on a religious show in New York that paid me $150, which got me back to L.A. I did a number of live television dramas, a couple of stupid movies, and then in part through a friend, or a lover as it were, a wonderful actress named Janice Rule, I was cast in *Compulsion* for Broadway.

You went to some acting classes during this period.

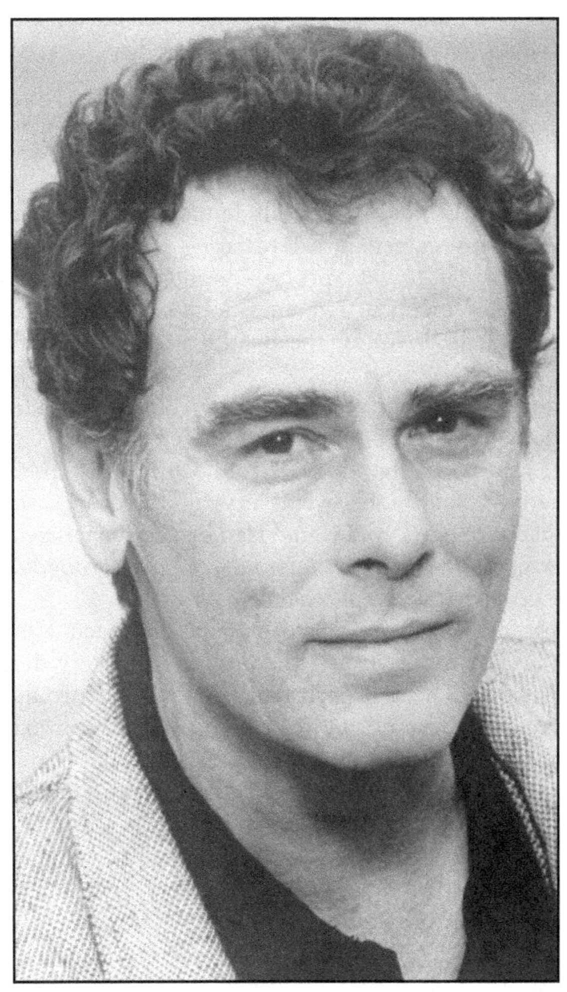

Dean Stockwell in 1989.

I went to some classes around town, and I went once with some people to the Actor's Studio in New York. Lee Strasberg was conducting something, and I walked out after about fifteen minutes. I thought it was horrendous. I was going to classes, to be perfectly frank, looking to get laid.

You were not at all insecure about your acting?

No. And I didn't like the classes. I did not like that highly critical atmosphere which is damaging to an actor's sensibility.

How did the Sixties affect you?

In a positive way, I think. It certainly looked, for a long time, as though the Sixties affected my career in a devastating way. For anyone who was there, who remembers it, it was a profound time that stretched clear around the world: of enlightenment, of awareness, of a critical view of society. The flower children and the love-ins, the Beatles, were the childhood I didn't have.

So I quit working. I told my agent I wasn't going to work for three years, and I didn't. I just participated in that, and I loved it.

The sexual aspects of the Sixties I found incredibly positive. When I arrived at puberty, sexual mores were very rigid and unreasonable. It was frustrating. When it opened up, I found it to be very beneficial.

Can you extrapolate what it is about having gone through the Sixties that has changed or deepened your approach to acting?

Nothing has deepened my approach. The approach was always deep because it was always intuitive, and the intuition is a very deep part of the self. Very mysterious. The approach remains constant throughout. But the instrument of the self becomes more rich and varied as it experiences life. The Sixties were the richest and most varied experiences that I had, so I unhesitatingly say that they had a very positive effect on my work now.

When you returned to acting, in the late Sixties and early Seventies, it must have seemed like a time warp, with all the old studio moguls dead or dying, and the studio systems changed and in disarray.

I was very happy that all of it was disappearing. Independent filmmaking allowed more freedom of expression, more diverse talents to emerge. The films made today are as good or better than those made in the classic days of Hollywood. There are a lot of lousy movies being made now, but also a helluva lot more experimentation.

But you also had trouble landing parts.

All through the Seventies I couldn't get arrested half the time. I was averaging $10,000 a year in income.

Were you going in for a lot of readings?

Yeah. But I never got a job I read for in my life. Never. So I don't read anymore.

Sometimes I'd ask a producer or director I knew if they'd check around and find out if there's a bad rap on me, or if I was on a modern-day version of a blacklist, or what.

Did you have a reputation of being difficult on the set?

No. Never. I'm a total professional. The only filmmaker I ever had a problem with was Henry Jaglom [director of *Tracks* in 1976].

Nowadays you gravitate toward the offbeat, fringe material.

Strangely, the gravitation works not from me to that material, but from that material to me. The only project I sought myself was *Dune*.

Why is that?

I knew you were going to ask about that!

Let's talk about some of those cutting-edge directors. What about Dennis Hopper, with whom you've now worked twice, and with whom you are filming another picture. He has been your close friend since the Fifties. Is it a case of him starting a sentence, and you finishing it?

Sometimes it can be like that, yeah.

How would you characterize Dennis as a director?

Number one, it's a job. The fact that it's Dennis's project makes it a wonderful job. Because Dennis is at the top of the talent side today, as a focused filmmaker and as an actor. He doesn't work with any formula. He's knowledgeable about film history. He is very respectful of all the great filmmakers who have preceded him. He has learned from all of them. But he creates a fresh film each time. It always has Dennis's stamp on it.

What does he do to help you as an actor?

He leaves me alone. If a director leaves me alone, I do my best work.

What about David Lynch?

David and Dennis share a certain facet of their vision – although I'm not sure either one would agree with me. Both of them have at least a streak of surrealism in their souls, and I have always been partial to surrealist art, to surrealist thought, to surrealist being. I think *Blue Velvet* is surrealistic, and Dennis's film *The Last Movie* is definitely surrealistic – and a great movie, incidentally. In [the 1988 Dennis Hopper film] *Colors* there is a little surrealism, but it's there, if you know Dennis.

—◦—

How do you prepare for your roles?

When I first read the material, nine times out of ten what I am going to do with it falls into place at the first reading. Or at least eighty percent of it does. The remaining twenty percent falls into place by itself over a period of time prior to when I start shooting.

How do you feel about rehearsals?

I hate rehearsals. I have always hated rehearsals. You have to do it out of respect to the director, the other actors and the material, sometimes. When it comes to, say, a piece like *Long Day's Journey Into Night,* which was taking a play verbatim and translating it onto the screen, you have to rehearse a lot. I have found ways to rehearse positively now. But I would still rather not do it.

It goes stale for you in rehearsals?

No. It's just a waste of time for me. I don't like to do what I do unless the camera is rolling. Any good film actor has to be able to do ten takes of something and to get very close to hitting what he is after each time, but it is always going to be a little bit different. I hate the idea of doing something, knowing it is right on, and that it is rehearsal.

—◦—

Do you think of yourself, these days, as having a certain persona, in terms of what you give off the screen, the connections you are making with the audience?

I think about that quite a bit. Because I think there's a certain point in the life of an artist when his work begins to communicate most fully. I seem to be approaching the height of my communicative powers now. I find I am able to do less and communicate more with greater ease than ever before. I feel almost a sense of power about acting, now.

The new role, in Jonathan Demme's Married to the Mob, *is a very playful one for you – you are teasing the audience as well as the character – and the performance is less intense than what we have seen in* Blue Velvet *or* Gardens of Stone.

No character has every come as clearly, as easily, and as fully as Tony "The Tiger." It was almost as though I had done it before in another life. I don't know whether it is because I'm half-Italian, or that I've never had the opportunity to do this type of role before – a woman-chasing, amoral, top-dog Don. But I just lit up the minute I read it, and I didn't have to touch it. There! Solid. Completely.

But I get the idea that, in Married to the Mob, *at least, acting isn't work any longer, it's fun for you.*

It should be fun. It wasn't for years and years and years. Now, in this third stage of my career, all that has completely turned around and good luck is still with me. Now, I am finally able to enjoy it.

Jules Feiffer

1980 and 1990
Interview by Patrick McGilligan

Malta, 1980

Almost everything about the live-action, family-oriented musical version of *Popeye* seems unorthodox – beginning with the choice of a scenarist, Jules Feiffer, the occasional screenwriter, off-Broadway playwright, and eastern urban intellectual cartoonist who agonizes, in his work, over the future of sex/love and life.

Yet as with the other ingredients of this bouillabaisse, which include producer Robert Evans, director Robert Altman, pop-rock composer Harry Nilsson, American television star Robin Williams in his screen debut as Popeye, Altman regular Shelley Duvall as Olive Oyl and Paramount Pictures in its first co-producing arrangement with Walt Disney Productions, the choice of Feiffer turned out to have a sort of interior logic.

For one thing, Feiffer knew and admired the work of E.C. Segar, who created *Popeye* as a daily comic strip for newspapers in 1929. And Feiffer was ripe for another foray into screenwriting, having concentrated on theater and fiction and his own syndicated strip since writing the original script for *Carnal Knowledge* in 1971.

When producer Evans telephoned Feiffer three years ago, locating him at a dinner party in New York City, and asked him if he would like to write a movie about the comic strip sailor, it was, to put it mildly, a pleasant surprise. With qualifications, Feiffer said yes.

"I had the general impression," Feiffer recalled, "that Evans was the traditional type of Hollywood producer which, of course, I didn't think very highly of, and that it would be difficult dealing with him. I found out that I liked him and got along with him right from the start.

"I said, 'It's a terrific idea, but only if you're talking about Segar's *Popeye*, not the animated Popeye [of the Fleischer brothers and in film cartoons]. He said, 'I want you to do whatever you want to do.' Now sometimes you'll hear that, and it'll turn out to be bullshit. In this case it wasn't, not because I overwhelmed him, but because Segar so clearly made sense."

Feiffer was given a free hand, with one stipulation from Evans, that Popeye's existential credo, "I Yam What I Yam," be preserved as the moral of the story. "That's the one thing I wanted Jules to stick with," explained Evans. "Everybody can relate to that today, much more so than in the Thirties." That suited Feiffer as well, since he saw the picture as an opportunity to pay tribute to one of the great, unsung cartoonists.

"Right from the beginning," said Feiffer, "I saw myself as being Segar's agent on this picture. To have this come out of the blue – to allow me to pay homage to the great talent whom practically nobody has heard of anymore except cartoonists

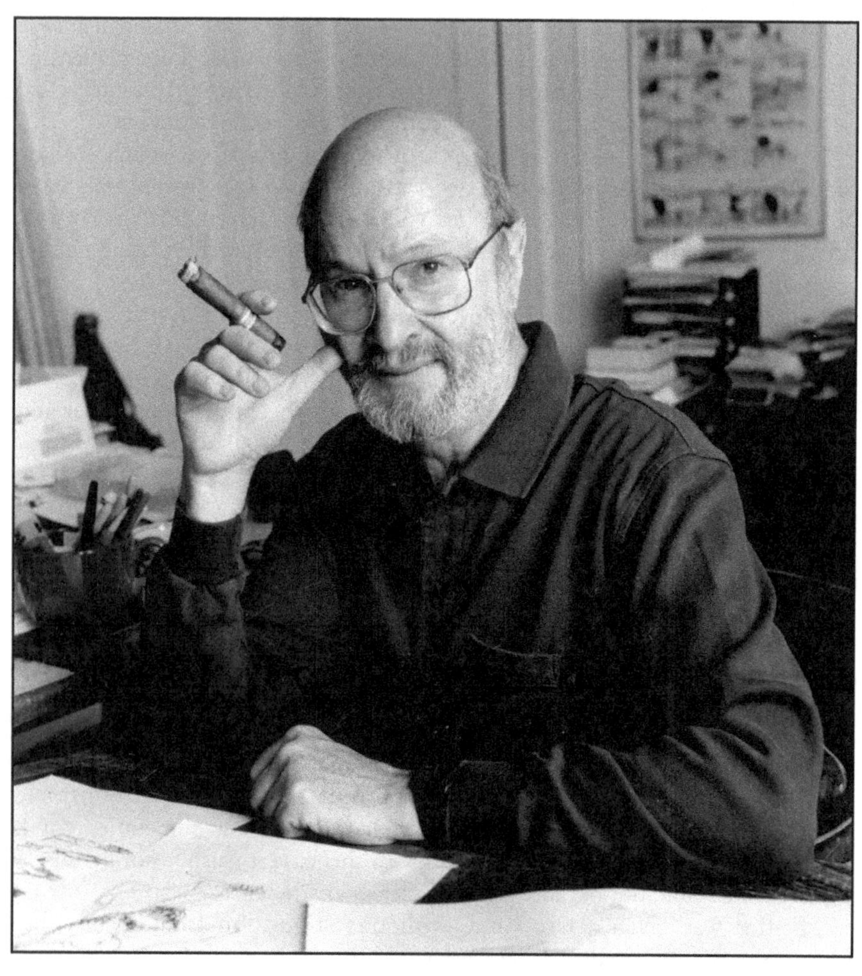

Jules Feiffer in 1990
(photo by William B. Winburn).

– was like a boon to me. Also, the idea of giving me the opportunity to write in someone else's voice – someone with whom I felt compatible – and to do what I wanted to do with his characters, seemed very exciting.

"What I loved about the tone of Segar's Popeye is how civil he was about the awfulness of everybody. He lived in a world in which every character was corrupt, jealous, greedy, and did terrible things to each other – all except Popeye. And somehow he was not mean-spirited. It was not the world of Al Capp, where ugliness really seemed ugly. There was genuine charm, and a word that keeps coming back to me – a *civility* towards his view of the universe."

Feiffer borrowed lavishly from Segar in his original treatment but created a world of his own in the make-believe town of Sweethaven. The story was to revolve around the romance between Popeye and the spindly Olive Oyl. Sweethaven is ruled by the Commodore, an evil presence who turns out to be Popeye's long-lost father. Early drafts had elements of magic and special effects, but eventually, as Feiffer puts it, "the scope was reduced to the personal relationships."

Dustin Hoffman was signed as Popeye; Lily Tomlin was announced as Olive Oyl. This match made in heaven collapsed shortly after prospective director Hal Ashby, Hoffman, and Evans went out and drank vodka and ate caviar to celebrate doing the picture together. For when Feiffer met privately with Hoffman to discuss the evolving script, things ended up, in Feiffer's words, "very messy." Evans backed Feiffer, to the surprise of many, and Hoffman withdrew from the project.

"Evans takes chances," allowed Feiffer. "From my experience with him, he takes risks. He's highly supportive of the people he works with, very loyal and very moving in that way. I just find the kind of support he's given me, earlier when Dustin wanted me off the picture, and then with Altman, rare and impressive to say the least."

—∞—◦—∞—

With the "bankability" of the picture in jeopardy, Evans suggested casting Robin Williams, television's popular Mork of *Mork & Mindy*, as Popeye, and got another green light from Paramount. Then New York agent Sam Cohn sent a copy of Feiffer's script to Robert Altman, who met with Evans and impressed him with "a vision of how to do it that no other director had."

Again confounding expectations, Evans backed Altman to the hilt until Paramount, which was nervous because of the critical shellacking that Altman had suffered on recent pictures, finally gave in. Altman and Robin Williams brought pop-rock iconoclast Harry Nilsson aboard to compose the "walking music" that is heard throughout *Popeye*. And when Gilda Radner continued to be lukewarm about the project, Altman convinced reluctant Paramount executives that Shelley Duvall, his alter ego in *3 Women* and other pictures, was "born to play the part of Olive Oyl."

But there were still a number of "rocky points" ahead, according to Feiffer.

A stickler about the integrity of his writing, Feiffer was suspicious of Altman's reputation for free-wheeling improvisation on the set. His concern was fueled by his own previous experiences of collaboration with directors – on the screen adaptation of Feiffer's play *Little Murders* and on *Carnal Knowledge*.

Although they were (and are) friends, Alan Arkin, who directed the film version of *Little Murders*, barely consulted Feiffer during the shooting – and the results disappointed the writer.

"One of my problems with the film [*Murders*]," said Feiffer, "was that Alan, who did an extraordinary job in interpreting and directing the play off-Broadway, only intermittently found the right style for the movie. Sometimes it worked, and sometimes it didn't. It was his first movie [as director]. The characters were there, the lines were there, but I didn't see the images on the screen the way I wanted them to be seen. I thought much of it was overstated."

Conversely, Feiffer was integrally involved in the filming of his original script for *Carnal Knowledge*, and his contribution there was more gratifying. "[Director Mike] Nichols shot the script," Feiffer said, "but always in consultation. He didn't want me on the set though, because he said I made the actors nervous. Maybe it was him I made nervous, I don't know. In any case, he didn't cut me out either. He wanted me there for dailies and discussions, and he behaved marvelously throughout."

Feiffer had been deeply involved with choosing the actors for *Little Murders*, where he proved to his own satisfaction casting was not his forte, and "every conceivable mistake that could be made was made, with the exception of Elliott Gould." So on *Carnal Knowledge* he deferred entirely to Nichols, who organized the ensemble of Jack Nicholson, Art Garfunkel, Ann-Margret and Candice Bergen. Feiffer thought they all gave "wonderful" performances, true to what he had written, perhaps Nicholson especially, whom Feiffer had never met before the actor was cast as Jonathan, a character he had "imagined as a Jewish boy from the Bronx," rather unlike Nicholson, who is a lapsed Catholic kid from New Jersey.

Feiffer was a non-fan of *Easy Rider* (the film, not Nicholson's performance), which was the budding star's main calling card at the time. He was surprised by the actor's studious approach to Jonathan. Nicholson talked over the details of the way he should look with Nichols and was insistent about not wearing any kind of hairpiece, although he was already starting to go bald. ("On some level, Jack's got enough sense of himself that he doesn't need to disguise himself, or feel he is disguising himself," said Feiffer. "He just wants to do it. To act the part. Be the character. Do it.") Nicholson even gave up pot-smoking during the filming, Feiffer said, because the actor didn't think it was right for the complexity of the character.

The only thing the scenarist helped Nicholson with was a few Jewish pronunciations. Nicholson kept saying *shmook* or *smuck*, instead of *schmuck*. "I gave him *schmuck* lessons," Feiffer said proudly. The actor completely won him over in person and on camera. "Nicholson was thoughtful and absolutely serious in a way that someone like myself, from New York, would expect from a stage actor, not a movie actor," Feiffer recalled.

"There were a couple of scenes in the screenplay that I thought would be very difficult for an actor to play. The first is the one where Bobbie [Ann-Margret] asks, 'Do you think we should shack up together…' and Jonathan tries to wriggle out of it. He says, 'Well, we've got a good thing going here…' When I read that on paper, as the writer, the scene is so full of irony and terror and evasiveness – it has many values. I didn't believe any actor could get it all.

"Then comes the fight with Bobbie, in which there is so much going on in the scene. That scene is funny and savage, with an expression of rage and contempt and self-pity and, again, terror. My recollection is that in both scenes Jack got all the stuff on the first take; particularly I remember the shacking-up scene, watching that during the shooting, or at dailies. I couldn't believe Jack's simplicity, directness, and intelligence. He got everything."

Another thing that impressed Feiffer was Nicholson's consideration towards the other actors and the film as a whole. "There is that final scene with Candy [Candice Bergen] on the telephone, which ordinarily would be done with Mike shooting Jack and somebody feeding Candy's lines to Jack; the camera is on Jack and we don't see Candy. Then Mike shoots Candy. Jack came up with the idea – I'm sure it was Jack – that Mike set up a phone line so Jack could be off-camera talking to Candy. Then Jack simply over-acted like crazy when he was talking to her [on the phone line]. He got emotional in a way we don't see on camera in the scene, but his emotions forced her out of her reserve and forced that performance out of her, which was, first, invaluable to the film but also incredibly generous."

—◦—

Feiffer knew Altman and had admired his work as far back as 1971, when he was part of the *Carnal Knowledge* company filming in Vancouver, Canada, only a few miles away from the set of *McCabe and Mrs. Miller*. In fact, the two casts socialized, and Feiffer introduced Nicholson to Warren Beatty, whom Feiffer knew, for the first time. But Feiffer's and Altman's initial conversations about *Popeye* left him vaguely worried, and the writer wondered if Altman was more interested in the townsfolk of Sweethaven than in the principal characters, Popeye and Olive Oyl. Also, they had "severe arguments" about Harry Nilsson's music.

When the three of them – Feiffer, Altman and Nilsson – arrived in Malta for location planning in September 1979, each was privately convinced the situation was impossible.

Canadian production designer Wolf Kroeger and his crew of carpenters and artisans were busy erecting the town of Sweethaven on a secluded bay on the northwest tip of the principal island of Malta. A production complex was being assembled on the high ground, including a six-track recording studio for on-location sessions.

With tension in the air, Feiffer and Altman finally got down to "very tight, very detailed" story sessions – "which Altman hates to get into, it takes forever to get him to agree to it" – and the results left them both considerably buoyed, their differences temporarily smoothed over.

Shooting began in January. Back in the States, rumors were swirling – among the most titillating, that Evans and Altman were at each other's throats. It made sense, the two of them being "the weirdest possible combination," in Altman's words. But besides not being true (they got along famously on the island), it was the least of the problems in Malta.

Actually, if there had only been a typhoon, the story of the shooting of *Popeye* would rival that of *Apocalypse Now* for its many "rocky points." The filming was complicated by miserable weather, an upwardly spiraling budget, special effects problems, serious accidents and injuries, and the usual real and imagined friction behind-the-camera. None of this is out of the ordinary for a location "shoot," but all of it on one picture was a bit of a dose.

At the outset, Feiffer simply tried to enjoy himself and to figure out why he was there. The troupe assembled by Altman included off-Broadway types, jugglers and acrobats, Italian stuntmen, a circle of British and L.A. musicians, numerous stock company dependables – and family and friends. This Fordian-like community of loyalists inhabits the imaginary world of Altman's movies and becomes a reservoir of fortitude on location.

"I had much more the feeling of putting on an off-Broadway play than of putting on a multi-million-dollar Hollywood musical," Feiffer commented. "There was very little sense of hierarchy, or pecking order. There was a kind of relaxation about it, an openness."

But as the screenwriter, well, Feiffer had to be worried. Altman's modus operandi is mysterious even to those closest to him, but his ideas tend to accelerate during the actual experience of shooting, taking the variables of location into account in ways that are often surprising.

At first it seemed as though the director was spending too much time with the cartoony "extras," developing their individual personalities and their "pick a tick," while leaving Popeye and Olive Oyl to their own devices. The comedy was taken in a very physical direction. The song-and-dance aspects were treated in ragged fashion, with only Altman aware of the final form.

When, early in the filming, Robin Williams began to improvise freely, embroidering Feiffer's script with muttered one-liners, there was a private conversation between the screenwriter and the director that erupted into what seemed like an untenable breach.

"That threw me," Feiffer recalled, "because I felt a relationship was not being established (between Popeye and Olive Oyl), because Robin was monologizing and improvising an ending stream of chatter, some of which was quite good but which taken altogether operated against the sense and emotional conflict of the scenes. When I expressed that to Altman, he said that was easily taken care of in the editing.

He didn't want to interfere with the actor as he was developing his part. He didn't like to do that as a director."

Then, as he is so capable of doing, Altman unexpectedly reversed himself, spoke confidentially with Williams and invited Feiffer to do likewise. At the same time, Feiffer was brought into the cutting room to watch-dog the script with editor Tony Lombardo. Finding Altman "generous in surprising ways" such as this, plus the exciting contagion of the dailies as filming progressed, ultimately won Feiffer over.

In March, when I visited the set, Feiffer was cheerfully doing what he probably never, in a million years, expected to be doing – not only rewriting pages overnight but rewriting the ending of *Popeye* because "the way Altman shoots sometimes alters or makes unnecessary later scenes in the script. It seems to me that the script is now tighter, that the scenes that have been rewritten and have replaced other scenes are really better scenes, and that all of that comes from watching him shoot the film. It couldn't have been done from New York, out of town."

Every day, Feiffer would trundle up the winding path from his bungalow to the set a mile away seemingly as merry as a bumblebee. He was a familiar figure in his sports cap with a copy of the script tucked under his arm – available on the set, in dailies, in the editing room, in the recording sessions. His affection for Altman had grown, and he had willingly surrendered "fifty per cent" of the movie to the momentum of the director.

"He's a very unique, interesting guy," Feiffer explained. "I've gone from not trusting him to trusting him. That doesn't mean that I'm not still critical of him, or that we don't still have differences, but now I'm confident of the working relationship because it's been tested. There's no question in my mind that my presence has contributed something and that that contribution is welcome.

He added: "Remember, I'm coming out of a cartoon world where I do everything. It's exciting to move into a world where others don't simply duplicate your vision in another form, because that's not very interesting, but add to it, round it out, put something of themselves into it, which coheres with your vision and makes it more complete. When that works, it's thrilling."

In April, Feiffer returned to New York. Difficult months lay ahead – another month of ensemble shooting, then a month of precarious underwater footage with Popeye battling an octopus, then months of post-production. Altman continued to take it on the chin with 20th Century-Fox's one-city release of *Health*, which didn't raise anybody's spirits at Lion's Gate, Altman's company.

At the "first cut" screening of *Popeye* in Los Angeles, nobody was very satisfied (as these things tend to go), and a disconsolate Feiffer winged back to New York, wondering if all the work would ever add up. Then, late in October, Altman took a "print in progress" to New York and set up a screening for Feiffer. When the screenwriter arrived, he discovered "a mob of people" and realized that it was one of those Altman gatherings of notables like those Feiffer himself used to attend. In the crowd were people such as author E.L.

Doctorow and director George Roy Hill.

As the lights dimmed, his fears rose. "My viscera was unable to respond," Feiffer recalled, "although something in my head was saying, 'Oh, my god, it's good!' I wish I could see it without being so close to it. I was so terrified of what I was going to see." Yet the response was "effusive," and a reassured, gladdened Feiffer had to admit "the sweetness of the story, the emotion had returned. The look and sense of it was wonderful."

So how should we classify it – an Altman picture, a Feiffer picture, a semi-Disney picture, or perhaps a Segar picture?

"When I saw *Carnal Knowledge*," the screenwriter reflected, "I couldn't tell who wrote it, or who directed it, or who acted in it. It all seemed to come out of one head. It seemed to be a completely unified piece of work, and I was totally satisfied. If *Popeye* works, it'd be the same thing."

—◇—

Whatever the consequences, more movies for Feiffer are not likely to be in the immediate offing. He is working on two plays presently, one for Robert Brustein's company at Harvard for May production, and one targeted for off-Broadway in the future. He considers himself a cartoonist first, then a playwright, then a screenwriter.

He did just finish an "urban political comedy" for Fox, but it's in "turnaround," a distinctly American, quasi-moribund condition. "I've never been in turnaround before," he said with a grim chuckle. "Fox thinks the script needs more development. I think Fox needs more development."

Turnaround, development, bankability – these are things about the movie industry that make Feiffer shake his head. He didn't even have a "deal memo" to write *Popeye*. He wrote it on spec, rightly figuring that nobody could imitate or rip-off the Feiffer way of looking at the world. And when you're talking about movies, you're raising the question of Los Angeles, too.

"It's not my favorite place," allowed Feiffer. "I rented a house in Malibu once and spent a month there trying to write. I wrote six lines. I walked on the beach and ran into Ronald Reagan, who was just retiring as Governor. He looked like he was in better shape than I was..."

—◇—

Chicago, 1990

Jules Feiffer and Alain Resnais are another two names that do not normally go together.

Feiffer's celebrated syndicated comic strip explores attitudes of love and sex, issues of headlines and politics, and the certainty of growing older and feeling depressed about the state of things. He has written plays and novels, and the occasional film: *Carnal Knowledge, Little Murders, Popeye.* "I think Resnais is one of the most brilliant filmmakers of all time," Feiffer says, "yet a lot of his movies are so forbidding that you can't get at the core of them. The ones that work are remarkable, like *Last Year in Marienbad.* Others leave me out in the cold."

So how could they ever collaborate on a movie? Feiffer's thoughts exactly, when Resnais telephoned him out of the blue from the hotel where he was staying in New York. Resnais's English is not very good; Feiffer speaks no French. Yet Feiffer found the formidable French auteur "pure and sweet" and discovered that he liked him immensely.

In Chicago, where he has been nurturing a production of his new play *Elliot Loves*, directed by Mike Nichols, Feiffer talked about *I Want to Go Home*, the film he subsequently made with Resnais about an elderly has-been cartoonist.

"Resnais said that he was a fan of my cartoons, but that's not why he was coming to me. He liked my second novel, a book called *Ackroyd* [published in 1979], about a kid who loves Sam Spade, so he becomes a private detective. No one has read that book, including my wife. Just like the French!"

Resnais said that he wanted to make an English-language film about America, to be shot in France. Did Feiffer have any ideas? Feiffer did not, but he liked the idea of going to Paris to toil on the project. "I thought of this thing as 'Operation Resnais-Scam.' I was going to get my family over to Paris, we'd have a good time, but this thing would fall through. I couldn't think of Resnais as being funny, or how we would fit together."

Months passed. More vague, pleasant meetings in New York. One day Resnais phoned and said that plane tickets to Paris would be approved by the producer Marin Karmitz once Feiffer had come up with an actual story kernel. "I came into Resnais's room and said, 'Jerry Lewis.' A comedian who is a has-been in the United States. He goes to Paris, and the French intellectuals make a big thing of him, and the story goes from there. That's the only thing I knew about the French and the Americans and how to bring them together – this odd business of the French loving what the Americans reject. Resnais liked the idea very much."

Feiffer, wife, and child flew off to Paris. Right away, Resnais informed Feiffer that he was having second thoughts about a Jerry Lewis type ("too close to somebody identifiable"). Feiffer had a back-up position: an elderly cartoonist who goes to Paris for an international exhibition, where he is festooned with honors. The cartoonist is also attempting a reconciliation with his daughter, who has fled to Paris to study Flaubert. She thinks her father is a vulgarian. Her hero – the professor played in the film by Gérard Depardieu – turns out to be a fanatical admirer of her father's strip "Hep Cat."

Although Feiffer is a friend of Adolph Green, it was Resnais who suggested Green, the writer (with Betty Comden) of such vintage musicals as *Singin' in the Rain* and *The Band Wagon*, for the lead role. Green has recently done colorful small parts in films (*Simon, My Favorite Year*). "But Adolph had, until this movie, maybe ten minutes on screen in his entire life, if you add them all together," says Feiffer. They didn't bother to tell Green they were writing a film that would revolve around him. "I wanted to exploit him as a character before I presented it to him. I didn't want to deal with Adolph, who might even say no. It helped enough that I could write a character who sounded like Adolph. It gave me a character instead of a type."

—◦—

Months later. Many trips back and forth to Paris. "Resnais taught me something about how he works. He said the way he believes a movie should be made is that there are only one or two characters from whose point of view you are shooting. Everything has to be seen through their eyes. If they are offscreen, nothing happens. So you have to find a way to tell the story through the eyes of these major characters – in this case, Adolph and the daughter. I don't think I agree with that, but I thought it was a wonderful way of working. It was good discipline, and I got a better script out of it."

Filming began in France in autumn 1988. The director broke the hard news to Feiffer that for the first time he was not going to be welcome on the set. "Resnais said it would make the cast nervous – but he meant himself. I was offended, but I knew he wasn't playing games with me. This was the way he worked."

No matter. His script was fully realized, he says, with "some minor changes and emendations for budgetary reasons." Feiffer saw the finished film, known by its English title *I Want to Go Home*, in Paris. "To my amazement, it left me in tears. I was deeply moved by it. It was a very strange approach to my work because the pace is quite different. Americans would say it's all wrong. As far as I am concerned, it works. It is not Resnais, it is not Feiffer, it is itself. It comes together. You like the people and you care what happens to them. And it's funny."

At the 1989 Venice festival *I Want to Go Home* prompted a standing ovation, and Feiffer received the Best Script award. The response has been largely downhill since then. The film has not been widely distributed; in the United States it remains "unseen and unseeable," in Feiffer's disillusioned words. "The why of it is a mystery to me. I'm as proud of the film as anything. It's probably a better movie than *Popeye*. It's more personable, more approachable."

Feiffer has had no better luck with Hollywood in general in the last ten years. During the Eighties he wrote four scripts for various producers; he also worked for a long time with Volker Schlöndorff on a "very funny" film about civil litigation/credit liability. That and other scripts are in limbo or "turnaround." Perhaps directors know of his reputation for fiercely protecting the words of his scripts. "The problem with me and Hollywood directors, in most cases, is that they can't do a script by me and pretend they are the auteur. They would have to settle for co-auteur, and that can be hard for a Hollywood ego to deal with."

Matt Tyrnauer (and Scotty Bowers)

2017

Interview by Patrick McGilligan

Although familiar with the Scotty Bowers legend from sources for my 1991 book *George Cukor: A Double Life*, I didn't know what to expect from Matt Tyrnauer's *Scotty: The Secret History of Hollywood*. I was woefully ignorant of Tyrnauer's earlier work, which includes *Valentino: The Last Emperor*, shortlisted for an Academy Award in 2009; now I plan to catch up with as many of his documentaries as possible.

His new film tells the life story of Bowers, prolific 'trick' to the stars and cheerful celebrant of sexual freedom. Tyrnauer mixes a patient *vérité* approach with bracing home movies, archival footage, and surprising interviews with Scotty's numberless extended circle, all of it framed by film history experts including William J. Mann (whose 2006 biography *Kate: The Woman Who Was Hepburn* was a similar shock of fresh air). With *Scotty*, Tyrnauer joins the first echelon of American documentarists; he should be an Oscar contender for this film, which is at once a brave corrective to Hollywood fairy tales and a mesmerizing human portrait.

—◇—

How did you convince Scotty (and his wife) to accept such an intimate portrayal of their lives? Your hard work really shows in the verité footage and research. You obviously don't pull punches with the details of his life, then or now. How did the decision come about to use the clip of him masturbating, for example, which is really a startling and courageous image in the film?

I met Scotty through Gore Vidal, whom Scotty met at his gas station in 1946. Given that they had such a long friendship, and we had an important mutual friend, Scotty was predisposed to let me into his life to an extent that he might not have otherwise. One of the tricks of shooting *cinéma vérité* film is becoming part of the wallpaper, as it were. You and your crew become semi-invisible as you slowly embed yourselves into the lives of the subject. Lois, Scotty's wife, in fact, was resistant at the beginning, but the presence of the film crew became soothing to her in a certain way. We were kind of like friends and family after a while, even taking her on the occasional trip to Chico's to go clothes shopping. So, as Scotty might say, you work your way in. Eventually, we were all very welcome at the house on Kew Drive, and it became a very good experience for everyone.

I was astonished to find film footage of Scotty in the act. This came about on a *vérité* shoot one day with the choreographer, Tony Charmoli. In the course of rambling through his house, discussing all things Scotty, Tony mentioned that he had Super 8 footage of Scotty at an orgy that took place at the Charmoli house in the Sixties. Of course, I asked to see that film and Tony was at first resistant, but then we arranged a private screening with Scotty in attendance. The film contained a drag parade around Tony's swimming pool (also in the documentary) and scenes from a sex party in Tony's guest room featuring Scotty and a couple other people. We eventually acquired the rights to the film from Tony. For me it was important to show Scotty in his prime doing what he did best. We had many shots to choose from. In the end we chose two; one of them features Scotty masturbating. It wasn't such a hard decision, the harder decision was whether or not to pixelate the footage, which we ended up doing. Although little is left to the imagination.

You have many close friends of Scotty's in your film as a testament to his good character. Without using names, can you tell me anything about the stars or people you tried to get into the film who declined – and why?

The longtime boyfriend of Raymond Burr declined to appear on camera. We had a long, very pleasant visit with him at the Raymond Burr vineyard in Northern California where he lives. And he confirmed everything about Scotty and his relationship with Raymond Burr and other people in Hollywood from that period. This particular individual did not feel comfortable appearing on camera and cited a particular fear of homophobia as a gay business owner of a winery. I was saddened to hear that he felt he had been a victim of homophobia among potential customers, but of course respected his decision.

Another former sex worker, one of a pair of identical twins who were on Scotty's roster, also declined to be on camera. He simply didn't feel comfortable. However, he confirmed for me a great deal of information, including many names of famous figures with whom Scotty fixed him up.

What legal concerns did you have about stories involving real people, not just stars? I notice that at one point Scotty gives the names of friends in his community of "tricks" and says that some of them are still alive.

I didn't have a great deal of concern. Much of this happened so long ago. I was more struck by how virtually everyone we visited with the camera was willing to speak and how freely they spoke. A lot of the gentlemen interviewed did not live gay or openly gay lives. They, in fact, lived largely heterosexual lives. In some cases, we interviewed them while their children and grandchildren were in the room. But they seemed to have no shame, no regret; in fact, quite the opposite. There seemed to be a great deal of pride about having been an object of desire at one time, of having helped people out. There was also a real pride in their association with Scotty, who clearly is a beloved figure among all of his friends. I never heard anyone say a bad word about him and I met scores of people he has known since the Forties. Ultimately, everyone on camera signs a release, so there's never any concern about people feeling they've been inappropriately recorded.

There is some explicit footage in the film, and there's the occasional explicit dialogue, such as "Charles Laughton liked to suck dick..." But the film seems to shy away from too much physical detail of the lovemaking that people might be curious about where the big stars are concerned. After all, when people are engaged in sex they reveal different or other aspects of their character... For example, there is more than one reference to Scotty's threesome with Cary Grant and Randolph Scott. Or Scotty's long relationship with Spencer Tracy, which I heard about over twenty-five years ago, so I take it to be true enough, but still I would have liked more detail. I wanted more! Was there more that you were reticent to use, or was Scotty reluctant to go into detail?

Scotty frequently went into greater detail about physical and sexual acts with people he "tricked." I found he tended to elaborate or single out particular sex acts or details about sexual relations with particular people, Spencer Tracy among them. With Tracy, he frequently mentioned, and I quote, "He would chew on your cock." It was, in many cases, an editorial choice to eliminate specific details for one reason or another. For example, sometimes it just seemed to cross a line that might alienate a general audience, or even push the movie into "X-rated" territory. On other occasions, it slowed the sequence down and we were aiming for a film not much more than ninety minutes in length. So there just wasn't room for everything.

Two of the more startling moments in the film are when Scotty talks about sex as a youth with farm animals and also his relationships with Chicago priests – defending both of these episodes in his life (including saying very nice things about the priests who paid him for sex when he was young). Both really take one aback. I haven't read Scotty's book yet [Full Service: My Adventures in Hollywood and the Secret Sex Lives of the Stars by Scotty Bowers and Lionel Friedberg, Grove Press, 2012], *although I want to, and most people reading this interview – or seeing your film – will not have read his book either. Are these elements in his memoir? Did you have any qualms about including them?*

Those elements are in the memoir. Scotty doesn't shy away from discussing them. They're definitely a key part of his narrative as he likes to tell it. I didn't feel it was my duty to excise major chapters of his life as he sees fit to tell it. I did my best to include all of the major passages that he deemed important and to explore them in as meaningful a way as possible.

Going back to Scotty's wife for a moment. She is such a compelling character in the film. Starting out, did you know she was going to play such an important role? How hard was it to get those difficult scenes between the two of them? She is as willing as him to bare her soul... what did it take to get them comfortable with you and to capture those scenes?

Lois was at first resistant to the idea of being filmed, if not resistant to the idea of the film in general. At first, she chose not to appear on camera. Eventually, she was willing to be interviewed though she requested that we not film inside the house, which is very cluttered and shows profound evidence of Scotty's hoarding. I don't think Lois wanted that aspect of their lives to be revealed. Eventually, we filmed her singing at a Los Angeles nightclub. I think she enjoyed that experience. Part of the process of *cinéma vérité* filmmaking is working your way in, and the film crew and I, by virtue of showing up so frequently, ended up being almost a

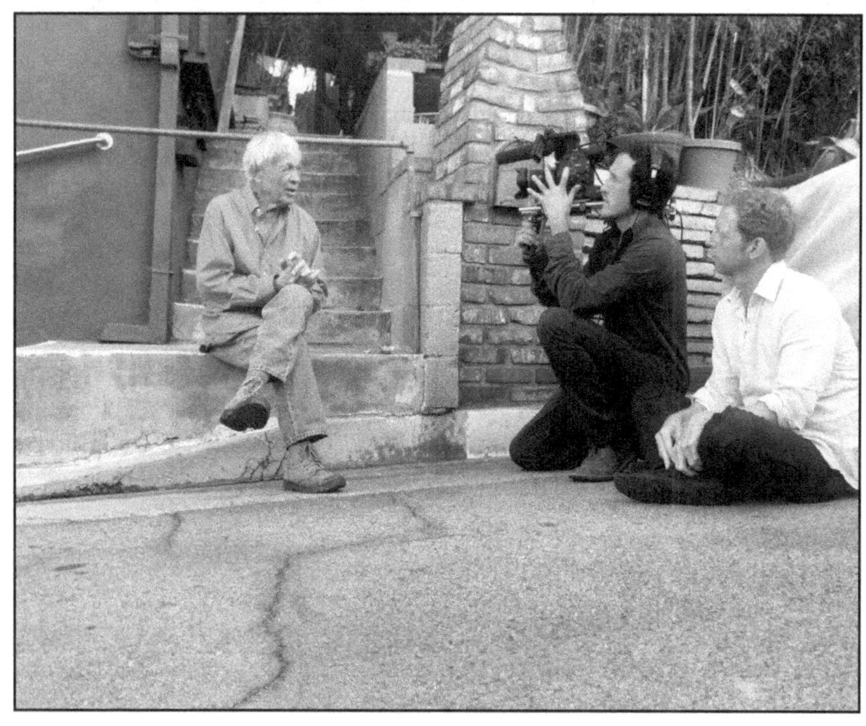

Scotty Bowers in front of his Laurel Canyon house,
being filmed by Matt Tyrnauer
and cameraman Christopher Dapkins
(photo by Jonas Kord).

daily fixture in Scotty's and Lois's lives. The difficult scenes just "happened" in the course of some long shoot days. This is the joy – and frustration – of *cinéma vérité*. You have to log the hours and shoot or overshoot to get the gems. Eventually, I think she felt comfortable with all of us, though as she has not yet seen the movie, I don't know how she feels about the final product.

What was the budget for the film and where did the money come from?

The film was made with private equity financing and the budget was modest, as you can imagine.

I always wonder about films like this one. What was the most expensive piece of footage in the film – either in terms of money spent for rights, or money spent on the time and effort in getting the shot?

The most expensive piece of archival footage was the BBC clip of George Cukor at his home.

This film was made with a small crew, which is the way I like to work when shooting *cinéma vérité*. I find that large camera crews, and especially boom microphones for sound, destroy *vérité* shoots because they make the subjects feel self-conscious. As a result, most of the scenes in the film were relatively inexpensive to shoot because the crew wasn't expensive.

How will the movie make its money back? Can a documentary filmmaker make a living in the US – and if so, how?

The movie has been doing very well at the box office and foreign sales are very strong, as well as TV and all other ancillary sales. It's very possible to make money on documentaries, and there are now more ways than ever to do it. The model with this one involves preserving rights and then splitting rights, and the revenue streams are plentiful. The film has been a huge critical hit and has had massive success in the press worldwide. So to quote Scotty, "That's what you call business, baby."

The audience for nonfiction film and television is bigger than ever and growing by leaps and bounds. I think this is a great time to be making documentaries and even making money off of them, which in the past was an oxymoron.

The film operates on several levels, which I love. For one thing, it is great fun as Hollywood lore that has been all but ignored in other books and films. But certain lore about this hidden Hollywood is harder for audiences to accept as truthful, it seems to me. Cary Grant and Randolph Scott as a couple – OK. While Spencer Tracy's secret sex life with Scotty, for example, upsets some film buffs. Why, do you think?

There have been rumors about Cary Grant for years, and Cary Grant's marriages never captured the public's imagination and were never immortalized by the press in the same way that the supposed (adulterous) relationship between Hepburn and Tracy was. The mythmaking behind the Hepburn-Tracy on-screen/ off-screen romance was industrial-strength, abetted by the studio publicity machines seeking to promote George Cukor's classic films in which they starred; and by Hepburn herself, who in her later years did everything possible to promote the myth that she and Tracy lived as a romantic couple all those years. This supposed romance survives as perhaps the most famous of all from that classic Hollywood period. It captured imaginations around the world and, as is quite clear from the reactions of horrified fans whenever the myth is debunked, it has taken very firm root in the human psyche. For this reason, Scotty's refutation of the Hepburn-Tracy myth is the most disputed of all of his counter-narratives.

The film gradually becomes an intimate portrait of Scotty as a one-of-a-kind human being. Much of his uniqueness (if that is the right word) comes from his sexual identity, of course, but there are also remarkable scenes of him doing things – like climbing ladders (at his age) for home repairs, or sorting through his piles of letters and magazines – that deepen our feeling for him. Did you know, starting out, that the film would eventually become such a contemplative character study?

No. I didn't expect to be able to spend so much time with Scotty, but when I met him I soon saw what a complex character he is, and it became clear to me that this was much more than a production that would seek to debrief him on his ribald tales of old Hollywood. I didn't know that he was a hoarder. I didn't know a lot about his relationship with his wife, Lois, or his previous wife, Bette, and I only knew the basic outline of his biography that is recounted in his memoir. To get to the deeper meaning of Scotty and his story, it became clear that I would have to spend quite a bit of time with him shooting *cinéma vérité*, because he's not a naturally analytical or contemplative sort. He's a natural man of action who lived in the moment, which I admire greatly. But this kind of character doesn't give you a lot of insight into their inner life in the course of interviews. I got it through observation with the camera.

Finally, it seems to me that the film builds to a philosophical defense of sexual freedom. This is explicit in Scotty's own view of himself, in the interviews, but it is implicit throughout the film in the respect you pay to all of his ideas and experiences. Was this larger theme always part of the plan or did it partly evolve in the filming and editing?

I saw in Scotty's memoir some evidence that he was a sexual outlaw and rebel. As I began to interview people who knew him in the old days and began to understand better the environment of gay Hollywood in the old days, it occurred to me that Scotty was extraordinarily brave and had helped a lot of people find their footing in a time of great uncertainty for anyone who did not identify as heterosexual. I've never met anyone so universally admired by all the people who know him, and many of the principal players from his life, decades ago, were able to express to me their deep admiration for him, not only as a friend, but as a uniquely well-adjusted man who longs to make people happy and has fewer sexual hang-ups than maybe anyone ever to live. He was sexually free in a time when most people were not. He's a very brave man for being willing to live a life on his own terms.

Barry Alexander Brown and *Son of the South*

2021

Interview by Patrick McGilligan

Barry Alexander Brown's first major feature, *Son of the South,* is an historical drama that is also entirely of the moment with its true story of a white Alabaman named Bob Zellner, who was drawn into action by shame and outrage, in the early Sixties, over what was happening to Freedom Riders in the burgeoning Civil Rights Movement. Rebuking Ku Klux Klansmen in his own family, Zellner joined the Student Non-Violent Coordinating Committee (SNCC), whose leadership was largely black.

The biopic, freely adapted by Brown from conversations with Zellner and Zellner's memoir *The Wrong Side of Murder Creek* (NewSouth Books, 2008) also reflects the personal journey of its white director, another scion of Alabama, who is best known as the gifted editor of Spike Lee films. Their "joint" credits include *Do the Right Thing, Malcolm X* and a dozen more key films over the years, not counting documentaries and commercials, leading up to *BlacKkKlansman* in 2018, for which Lee won a Best Script Oscar and Brown a nomination for Best Film Editing. *Son of the South* can be seen as a bookend to the true-life *BlacKkKlansman* as well as Brown's 1979 Oscar-nominated documentary *The War at Home*, which chronicled the anti-Vietnam War movement in Madison, Wisconsin.

Like *BlacKkKlansman*, *Son of the South* has KKK scenes, cross -burnings, and a near-lynching that precedes the opening credits. Among its many fine performances are those of Lucas Till as Bob Zellner, Julia Ormond as local civil rights activist Virginia Foster Durr, and Brian Dennehy in his final screen role, as Zellner's KKK activist grandfather. James Forman, John Lewis and Rosa Parks are among the real-life figures in the screen story, which also includes the Reverend Ralph Abernathy as portrayed notably by Cedric the Entertainer (who appeared in *The Kings of Comedy*, another Spike Lee film edited by Brown).

—◦—

How long ago did this project start? When did you get interested in Bob Zellner's book?

The film really began in the Eighties. I was living in New York, and Bob had started going out with a cinematographer, Judy Irola, and Judy and I knew each other. Judy said, "You're from Alabama, right?" She told me her new boyfriend was from Alabama, and I met him, and we got along great. That was Bob Zellner. That was about 1983 or '84. In those early days Bob started telling me stories of the early Civil Rights Movement from a little over twenty years

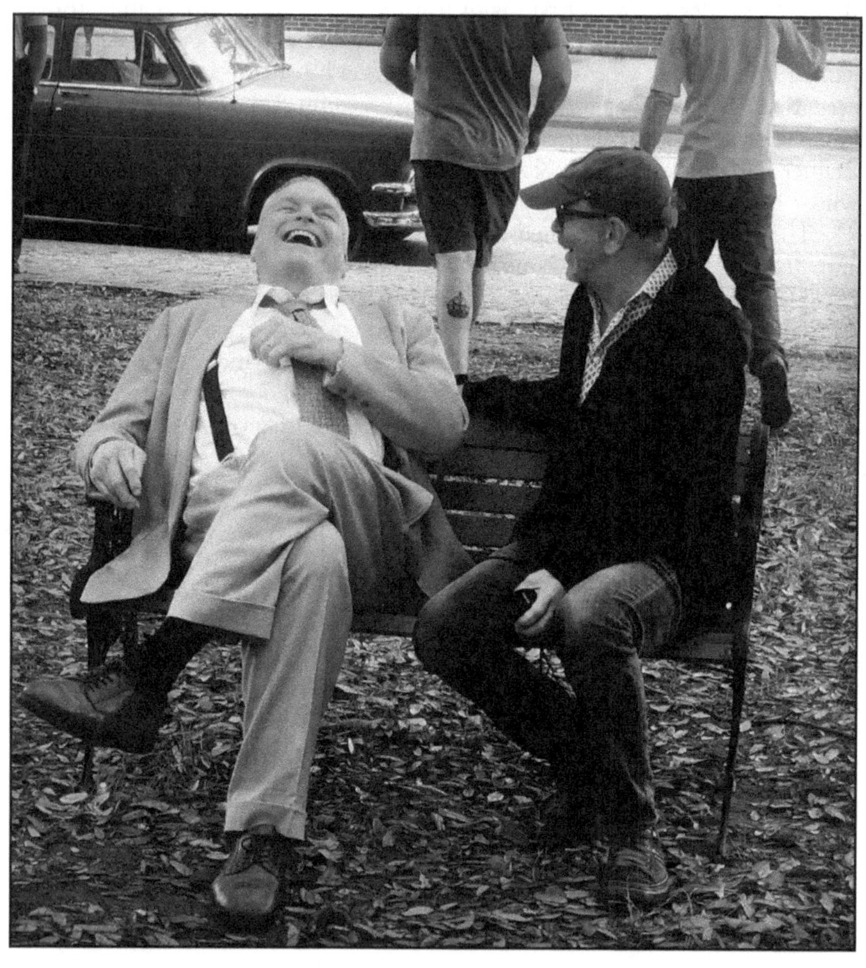

Brian Dennehy (acting in his last screen role) and
Barry Alexander Brown on the set of *Son of the South*
(photograph by Verane Pick).

before, and every story was just jaw-dropping. I knew there was a film in there, somewhere, but the canvas seemed too big.

Over the course of about five years in the Sixties, Bob went to jail seventeen times, but there were many other stories besides his jail experiences. He was the first member of SNCC to arrive in Mississippi after the three young men, Andrew Goodman, James Chaney and Michael Schwerner, went missing. He brought Rita Schwerner [widow of Michael, one of the three Civil Rights activists murdered by the KKK] down to Mississippi, and the story of that first day and night they spent in Mississippi is incredible on so many different levels. But I couldn't figure out how to make his life story, which was just too big, into a movie. It wasn't until over twenty years later, really, that it hit me. I should start in 1961, the year that Bob really got involved in the Civil Rights Movement, and that would allow me to say everything I wanted to say.

My mother's family is from Alabama. Growing up, we lived in many different places because my father was in the Air Force, but much of the time we lived in the Deep South, the panhandle of Florida, Mississippi, and Alabama. We also lived in Madison, Wisconsin for a spell, and that is where I first got my start in filmmaking with *The War at Home,* a documentary about the anti-war movement.

I wanted to make a film that said something about the South of my childhood. That summer of 1961, where Bob transitioned from somebody completely on the outside of the Civil Rights Movement to someone who was pulled into the very center of what was going on, gave me the opportunity. I wrote a script based upon those five months in his life. I found that period of time to be one of the most interesting parts of his story – the person who has to make a choice, the person who doesn't necessarily want to get deeply involved in a political movement because he doesn't want to give his life over to it, he'd rather graduate from college – which Bob did in May of 1961 – and go off to get a master's degree and live his life.

Bob didn't want to throw his whole being into a movement that was incredibly dangerous at that point in time. Each crossroad he came to during that spring and summer forced him to come to grips with what kind of person he was, what kind of man he wanted to be – even, to some extent, what kind of Christian he was. Each crossroad pushed him toward taking a path deeper and deeper into the Civil Rights Movement. So it really wasn't his book that inspired me. It was the stories I heard from Bob, because while I was writing the script, Bob was writing his book.

What were the principal creative hurdles in writing the script?

What I really wanted to do was to write a script that would feel like the South, one in which everybody was a real human being. Even people who did villainous things still had to be people. Certainly, the people I knew when I was a kid in the South, some of them appeared to be great people. Good fathers, good mothers, people with a great sense of humor. The South is a funny place, and I wanted the script itself to be funny – very funny – at times. For me, it was always the hurdle of making every character into a real person and not a cardboard villain. You see that over and over and over in too many other films – these horrible villainous people who don't serve any purpose other than to give viewers a cardboard character to hate.

I find it a lot more disturbing if you get to know somebody, and you get to actually like them, but then discover that there is something very dark in their souls. There's a hate in their souls. Racism is hatred, and I think the hatred of racism is a lot more disturbing than, say, the scene we've watched time and again in films, the Southern cop that pulls a car of black people over, and the cop is just evil incarnate. He's two-dimensional, a cardboard character, he's not real. I actually find the cardboard character, in many ways, less disturbing than the reality.

Is Bob Zellner still around and was he involved?

Yes! While I was writing the script, I would show Bob scenes as I wrote them. And then he would come back to me with his suggestions and criticisms. When turning a real story into a script, part of the process is taking license. Even though something may have really happened, I wasn't around to hear the original dialogue. So, Bob would relate stories and incidents to me, but then I had to write the dialogue to make the scenes flow. After I wrote scenes, Bob would react and tell me, "Well, no, it didn't really quite happen like that. It was more like this…"

When we shot the film, completely in Alabama, most of it around Montgomery, where a lot of the story originally took place, Bob, who lives nearby in southern Alabama, came up during the filming and we were together on the set. He was around a lot. As a matter of fact, he's actually one of the extras in the hanging scene, the scene where the KKK take the Bob Zellner character out to hang him. He plays one of the Klansmen in the crowd. Then in the cut I actually feature him. Bob gets a consulting credit at the end of the film because he deserves it. Without him, I don't think we would be nearly as accurate in telling the story. I don't think this story would be as inspiring without the authenticity Bob helped to give it. When you see this film, it rings true.

What are the most fictionalized parts of the script, and why did you choose to fictionalize these parts?

People assume the character of "Doc" [played by Jake Abel] is fictionalized in the film. But Doc was a real guy; he was really in the boxing club with Bob at Huntingdon College, he really was from McComb, Mississippi, and he really did drive by the march in McComb in his truck and scream at Bob for being a traitor. He really was in the crowd that wanted to hang Bob after that march. The guy was called Doc because he had been a medic in Korea, which is pretty admirable, and Bob had liked Doc. So that is how we played it.

People also assume I fictionalized Bob arriving at the SNCC office in

Atlanta, Georgia, being handed the keys, and then being left alone for weeks without much direction, just taking names and writing up phone messages for SNCC leaders like Bob Moses, John Lewis, and Diane Nash. Then Jim Forman showing up with a tape recorder and recording Bob, because he understands this white guy from Alabama is for real. That also happened exactly like that in real life, right down to Jim Forman showing up with the big Wollensak tape recorder he traveled around with. It's really special for me that we got Chaka Forman, his son, to play his dad in the movie.

Now the characters of Carol Anne [Bob's white girlfriend, played by Lucy Hale] and Joanne [Lex Scott Davis as her black rival for Bob's affections] are amalgams. Huntingdon College had been an all-girls school, but Bob was among the first classes of boys to come into the college, and he did have one particular girlfriend who considered herself an artist. According to Bob, she was quite a good artist and very progressive-minded, but she did not want to get involved in the Civil Rights movement. Carol Anne is not just that girlfriend, however – she is based on several girlfriends Bob had in college.

Joanne is the same way. There were several African-American women, when Bob first joined the Civil Rights movement and started with SNCC, who had a big influence on him – women like Diane Nash, Joanne Grant, and Ella Baker. To create Joanne, his love interest, I took a story that Bob told me about a girl he met at a black college in the South, a girl who had never been around white people at all. She said to him one time that she always had been told that white people's hair smelled like chicken feathers when they got wet and she wanted to smell Bob's hair. He did have a romantic involvement with this girl, and so I married that real-life girl with the African-American women who had such a big influence on him, because the women were very strong in the Civil Rights movement.

Diane Nash was one of the leaders of the Nashville sit-in movement. Joanne Grant was a journalist and activist. The Executive Secretary of the Southern Christian Leadership Conference, Ella Baker, who was such a dynamic person, was the one who met with young college students and told them, "You've got to set up your own organization." She is the one who pushed them to set up the SNCC Committee and helped organize their first meeting. For most of the film, I tried to stay close to what really happened.

Rosa Parks [played by Sharon Lanier] says to Bob in the film, "Something bad is going to happen right in front of you some day, and you have to choose which side you're on, and not choosing is a choice." Rosa Parks really did say that to Bob, and she really did say that to him in exactly the doorway of the church where we shot that scene in the movie.

In an earlier scene in the church, Reverend Martin Luther King, in reality, was present. It was Rosa Parks, Reverend King and Reverend Ralph Abernathy. Spike [Lee] said to me about that scene, "It's going to be difficult to get the King family to give you permission. And Reverend King has gotten a lot of love, a lot of love, and a lot of credit. Reverend Abernathy's gotten almost none. He's been forgotten by many people. Why don't you just have the scene be with Reverend Abernathy and Rosa Parks?" I thought that was a good idea, and then Cedric the Entertainer came in to play Rev. Abernathy, and he was wonderful in the part. He did a beautiful job.

Treating historical figures like Rev. Abernathy, Rosa Parks, James Forman and other real-life characters in the film can be a tremendous responsibility. What research or extra steps did you take to make these characters as true to life as possible?

Much of how I developed these characters – such as Rosa Parks and Jim Forman and Virginia Foster Durr – was based on Bob's recollection of them. The scene with Jim Forman, for example, really took place where it takes place in the movie. From 22-year-old Bob's point of view, Jim is seen as an elder statesman in the movement, even though, at that moment in time, he was only about thirty years old. But there weren't many thirty-year-olds in SNCC. So I wanted Jim Forman to be played as an elder statesman, or at least older than everybody else.

Bob talked about Rosa Parks, Reverend King and Reverend Abernathy as being people with great senses of humor. That's what I wanted to convey in Rosa Parks's character. She seems very shy and quiet in the interviews you can see with her, especially from around the time of the bus boycott, in 1955 and '56. But privately, according to Bob, she could be more effusive, stronger, funny, wry. I wanted to bring that out.

Alabama activist Virginia Durr is someone I was able to meet personally, in the Eighties, and spend some time with her, when I was back down in Montgomery, visiting my parents. Bob introduced me to Virginia, and I was able to get a real feel for her. She reminded me of my grandmother, so perhaps I drew something of her to help build that character. But Julia Ormond came along to incarnate Virginia Durr. She even supplied a great ad-lib in the film – something I did not write – when she says to Jessica Mitford [played by Sienna Guillory], after finding out that Jessica's car has been burned: "I'm glad you came back in one piece because Clifford is going to want to kill you." It is a perfect line. I mean, that is such a Southern thing to say.

In terms of the main character, Bob, it was really, as I've said, a case of spending many years with him. After being Bob's friend for years, I could really write Bob, including that saying of his, which I like a lot – "I'll try anything three times." There's also that moment in the film, when he stops the car and gets out to pick up a turtle in the middle of the road. I was with Bob when he did something like that once, and I said to myself, "I've got to put that in the film." That little moment says something about him. Lucas Till also spent a lot of time with Bob to get his cadence down and capture his essence – because Bob is a guy who appears to be very gentle, but there is also something tough and maybe even mean down inside of him as well – and Lucas got that.

—◦—

Why did it take so long before the cameras started rolling?

It did take a long time, at least ten years, to get this movie made. I believe I finished the first draft of the script in early 2009, and we went into production in 2019. It was hard to get the money, to get people to believe in the project. Over and over, people would read the script, they would get excited, and then they would just go cold on it. There were people that showed up and declared, "Oh, we're going to raise the money…" Then almost always, at some point, they just disappeared.

What finally got the film going was I got a call from Daniel Radcliffe, who had somehow gotten hold of the script and read it. This was in the fall of 2017. Daniel said, "I love the script." At that point, I was very discouraged and thought the film was never going to get made. Then I got this call out of the blue from Daniel saying, "I really want to talk to you about playing Bob Zellner." I was just amazed. Quite frankly, I don't even know how he got a copy of the script. Scripts sometimes float around, and somehow, through the powers that be, or luck, or whatever you want to call it, an actor picks it up and reads it and gets interested.

If Daniel Radcliffe had been able, in 2017, to play Bob Zellner, we would have shot this film in 2018. But Daniel had another film that he had already committed himself to in South Africa, a very similar kind of role, a white attorney who comes along to join the black movement. After weeks of thinking about it and, I think, struggling with the decision, he came back to me and said, "Listen, I've really committed myself to this other film, and I just don't think I can play these two similar roles." As far as I know, that other film never got made. But Daniel – showing up at a time when I was depressed, and telling me, "This a great script and I would like to play the lead role" – that energized everything.

As a matter of fact, Daniel's interest attracted the attention of a lot of other people asking what is this about, when is it going to happen? It just put a lot of energy into the project. And partly because of Daniel, we were up again and running, and gathering new momentum. By 2019, we knew that we could raise enough money. Stan Erdreich, who was one of the producers from Birmingham, started raising money down in Alabama, and a lot of our investors eventually came from Alabama, which is a great thing to think, that this film, which was a real Alabama story, was going to be a real Alabama film, made by people in Alabama, shot in Alabama, about a guy from Alabama, and funded by people in Alabama. That was very encouraging. But going into production, we had one hurdle after another. Six weeks before filming was to start, we didn't have a cast. All of the actors who said they would do it had, for one reason or another, fallen out of the film.

Tell me about the cast, how you found them, where they came from…
Even though six weeks before shooting we really didn't have the actors, the cast we got turned out to be magical. I was the luckiest son of a gun ever to get Lucas Till [noted for his roles as Young Jack Cash in *Walk the Line* and as Havok in the series of *X-Men* films] to play Bob. We got the script to him, and I spoke to Lucas in a Skype call after he read it, and he asked, "How did this role come to me?" It was such a nice thing to hear, that somebody was so thrilled and honored to play the role.

I was just as lucky to get Julia Ormond to play Virginia Durr, who was Southern aristocracy. I'd met Virginia a few times in the Eighties, with Bob. She had this wonderful accent, really the same kind of Alabama accent as my grandmother, because they were from the same part of Alabama. Julia, who's English, said, "I want to try and get that accent." There is a lot of existing footage of Virginia Durr, including one long interview with her from the Eighties where you can really hear her accent. I thought, "Oh boy, this is a tough accent to get. I don't know if Julia can get it. It's a really hard thing to do." Well, Julia went for it with her dialogue coach, and lord, she nailed it. She tried something that could have turned out horrible if she hadn't nailed the accent. But she's such a great actress; she worked on the accent and nailed it.

Lucy Hale embodied Bob's girlfriend Carol Anne, and she and Lex Scott Davis [her rival for Bob's affections] both have an amazing chemistry on camera with Lucas. Dexter Darden, a brilliant actor with subtle depth, came along at the last minute to play John Lewis. There's this one moment where he sings a Civil Rights song, and it's wonderful. We had to wait for Shamier Anderson, because he was doing the television show *Goliath*, and they had to shoot him out of the series in order to get him to Alabama for the filming. Shamier plays Reggie, the guy who really doesn't trust this white guy, Bob Zellner, coming into the Civil Rights movement. And wow, is he so powerful! He's so strong.

Brian Cox was supposed to play Bob's grandfather, and he called me up and said that he had re-read the script and felt he just couldn't play yet another nasty human being. I really appreciated the fact Brian called me personally. I could tell he felt terrible about pulling out. But Nicole Ansari, Brian's wife, with Brian's help, went to Brian Dennehy and showed him the script. Dennehy really liked the script and said he would do it. So I went from Brian Cox to Brian Dennehy, two giant actors – I really felt blessed. Working with Brian Dennehy was fantastic. He wasn't in the best of health, but he was a trooper. At times he had to stand up and address Bob [Lucas Till], face to face, and he needed a physical support, because these were sometimes long scenes with a lot of dialogue. But you don't feel his frailty when you see the performance. He delivered something so good, so powerful, and so disturbing.

I remember watching the scene, between the grandfather and the grandson, when we were shooting it, in which the grandfather explains and justifies his racism. Brian did such a great job of delivering that scene that I thought, who wrote this? I wrote it, disturbingly enough, but in my head it never quite had the power that Brian gave to the words.

Montgomery must have been a divided place, to put it mildly, back in the early Sixties. What kind of support, or blowback, did you get from people who did or did not like the subject of the film?

Overall, Montgomery was incredibly supportive. People really came out for this movie. We didn't really have anywhere close to enough money to make the film, and without all of the help and the support of local people, it couldn't have been made. For the big riot scene of May 20, 1961, as many as two hundred extras came out to work all day. It was hot weather – hot, hot, hot – but they came out the next day too and did it all over again. All in all, Montgomery was very supportive.

One place that had a lot of reservations about the film was Bob's alma mater, Huntingdon College. Huntingdon has come a long way since 1961, and a third of their student body today consists of minorities. The college really has made an effort to diversify. But college officials were really uncomfortable about the scenes we wanted to shoot, which included the Klan marching onto the campus to get Bob and his friends. This was an incident that really happened. A small Klan cross was burned outside his dorm room, and as a matter of fact, Bob told me there were three Klan crosses burned on the Huntingdon campus in '61.

The school that really opened its arms to us was Tuskegee University. So instead, we shot all of the Huntingdon scenes at Tuskegee, which is a gorgeous campus. Tuskegee rolled out the red carpet for us. People were so supportive, open, and happy to have us there, "Klan" and all.

What was the most difficult scene in the movie to direct?

The most difficult scene was the Freedom Riders riot scene, which takes place outside of the Greyhound Bus Depot in Birmingham. We shot in the exact spot where the riot happened in May of 1961, which was special because how often do you get a chance to do that? Right across the street was the Moore Building, where Clifford Durr's office was. He was the attorney who got Rosa Parks out of jail the day she was arrested in 1955 for not giving up her seat on the bus. Clifford Durr's office and that building is still there, and it looks exactly like it did in 1961. We shot in that office, with Clifford [played by Greg Thornton] and Virginia Durr [Julia Ormond] gazing down at the riot from the very windows the real people looked out of that day nearly sixty years ago.

We had the real Moore building, and we had the real Greyhound bus depot, but we were going to have almost no time, only a day and a half, to shoot this complicated scene. I wanted it to feel like a real riot, so it really came down to rehearsing on many of the weekends before shooting. We had rehearsals with the stunt coordinator [William Scharpf], with John Rosario, the director of photography, and with the actors. Rosario stepped up, doing a fantastic job under a lot of pressure. We choreographed as much of the riot as possible so we could just fly through it when the day came. We didn't ever have quite enough extras. I wanted hundreds and hundreds of extras, but we didn't have that many, so wherever I'd put the main camera, we'd put everybody we had in front of that camera.

My son, Nick Brown, was the second unit director, and he had his own crew. While I was shooting scenes with the principal actors, Nick was filming little cameos that are fantastic and filled in a lot of missing action to deliver a first-class cinematic riot. As a matter of fact, Nick wanted to shoot inside the bus while we were shooting the riot outside of it. He wanted to shoot one of the Freedom Riders cringing inside of the Greyhound bus, not wanting to come out. I thought, "I don't know… is that really going to work? I don't think so." I wasn't very encouraging, but John Rosario overheard Nick and I talking about it, and told Nick, once I walked away, "Go ahead and do that. That's a great idea." Rosario was right. As a matter of fact, that moment made the cut and it's very moving. It's one of the most haunting images of that sequence.

I really think it's one of the best riot scenes of all time. You can compare it to any of the other great riots in pictures, like that in *Do the Right Thing*. I edited both of them. At the end of the day, I'm very proud of that sequence because everybody showed up with amazing energy. The actors, the extras, the stunt people, and John Rosario – it was an amazing team effort.

I'd like to say one more thing about that scene. It was tough to get the right kind of Greyhound bus. We got one that wasn't exactly right, and we had to make some adjustments. Without the production designer Eloise Stammerjohn, quite frankly, this movie would not be half of what it is, because Eloise made the sets work under harsh conditions and with never enough money. She took the bus that wasn't quite right and came up with ways to remake the outside of the bus with the image of the Greyhound dog and the authentic wording you'd expect. She constantly wowed me. Eloise is one of the best production designers I have ever worked with, and a surprising thing is she is also from Montgomery. She doesn't live there, she's a very successful production designer who works on all kinds of movies all over the world, but Eloise came back to Montgomery to make this movie, and it made a big difference.

⸺―◇―⸺

I can think of a few important editors who crossed over from editing to directing, among them Robert Wise and Hal Ashby. What have you learned as an editor that was most helpful towards directing?

I learned so much from the years and years and years I've been an editor. I didn't start off as an editor of features. I started off in documentaries. Even on my first film, *The War at Home*, co-producing and co-directing, I had to do a certain amount of the editing because Chuck France, the editor, was working full time with the local PBS station in Madison, Wisconsin. Somebody had to pick up the ball, and I did.

I would say the years and years of working with Spike Lee taught me about pacing, recognizing great performances, planning the coverage for a scene, and recognizing great cinematography. A few years ago, I worked with John Rosario, the young cinematographer for *Son of the South*, on a short film, and I knew right away that he was the real deal. I knew once I did *Son of The South*, he was going to be the DP.

I think I became a better writer just from listening to great performances and working with well-photographed scenes. Editing for Spike taught me when a scene begins and when it ends. I think I became a much better writer, thanks to having edited his films for so many years. If you go back to a film like *Do the Right Thing*, that is an incredible script, and more recently, *BlacKkKlansman* was another great script, for which Spike won the Oscar. You learn about great dialogue by listening to it. Once you can really hear dialogue, I think you can write it.

As an editor, you deal with so many elements of the film finally, in one way or the other, that each and every one of those elements teaches you something and you get better and better and better in every aspect of filmmaking.

Spike Lee is credited as executive producer. What did he do behind the scenes?

I showed Spike the script very, very early on, and he was one of the first people to give me notes on it. There were times, throughout the process, going forward and getting closer and closer and closer to production, that Spike and I had helpful conversations, sometimes about different actors. I would say, "Well, this actor looks more like the real person, but this actor is really the better actor." And he'd say back to me, "Cast the better actor."

Once I finished the first cut of the film, I showed it to Spike and he gave me notes, and at one point he asked me for a favor. There was one character in the film who says, "Don't feel bad about doing the right thing." What the character was talking about was committing a racist act – doing something horrible to somebody. Spike said, after watching the cut, "Please don't have the actor say that." I had never thought about that line in relation to *Do the Right Thing*, but I laughed when he said that and understood right away. I definitely changed the line.

I have learned so much from Spike, because we came along together in the Eighties, and when we first started out making feature films, really going all the way back to *She's Gotta Have It*, we were both learning. I think we've learned from each other. But Spike is a major talent, and there's no way that you can work with one of the greats – and he *is* one of the greats – and not learn from all the hours of working together. I'm blessed to have worked with and learned from Spike.

One more thing I should say is Spike always infuses a certain amount of humor into his films, no matter how serious the film is, because humor is a part of life, no matter what else is going on. Oftentimes films about the Civil Rights movement are incredibly dry; the story becomes two-dimensional, and the people are no longer real. Having learned from Spike, I knew you have to have humor, even in the darkest moments. You see it in *Son of the South* when they're taking Bob out to hang him, and in the scene before, in the car, the guy in the back says, "Are you really a Communist? I never heard anybody speak Communist before. Can you say something in Communist for me?" It's a funny moment. I mean, they're taking him out to hang him, and yet there is this humor. That moment, incidentally, comes from a real story from Bob Zellner's life.

There is a scene in the film where black members of SNCC reproach the Zellner character for the favorable attention he gets from the press because he is white, and they don't get the same type of attention. Spike has at times in the past criticized white directors for taking up film subjects revolving around black people or Civil Rights. How did you face up to this issue going into what is, after all, a picture about the Civil Rights movement?

As I said, I wanted to do a film that would say something about the Deep South that I grew up in. My roots are in the Deep South, and I grew up in the old South. There's a new South, and there was an old South. The old South was harsh and African Americans literally had no rights. Terms that were used in everyday language, which I won't repeat, were just awful, but most white people never even thought twice about using them. I wanted to make a movie about that moment in time. As a white southerner, I felt I could make a film that would be about a white southerner, to take you into that world and make it real, to give it depth.

If you look at the Civil Rights movement, you have got to understand that the real problems existed in the white world and not in the black world. If you really want to understand the conflict, if you really want to understand what had to happen, you had to have an insider's point of view about moving from the white world into a black world. That's exactly what Bob Zellner did in the early Sixties. Having grown up in the white south, he moves from an absolutely white world into a black world.

I was able to give that a very personal point of view, an insider's point of view, because I did the same thing. I came from a very white world, and for the last thirty-five years I've worked for a black company, 40 Acres and a Mule Filmworks, and that place changed me deep down. I understand the difficulty in making a film about a white person in a black movement –

and the Civil Rights movement was a black movement, it had to be – but a handful of allies came from elsewhere, not always just white people but Asian Americans too.

I was not going to be arrogant enough to say, "Well, I can make a film about John Lewis," although John Lewis who was from Troy, Alabama, is a character in the film. I knew Troy, Alabama from when I was in high school. But I don't presume to understand the life of John Lewis, even though I lived in Montgomery and he lived in Troy, only fifty miles apart, and we were not so many years apart in age. But I don't think I could have truly understood his experience.

I grew up a Southern Baptist and Bob Zellner grew up a Methodist. He went to Huntingdon College, and I've had two nieces go to Huntingdon. I know what it's like to grow up in the Deep South as a white person in the old South. I know how racism is instilled in you. And I know what it's like to make a decision to be different, to not follow that road. I know what it's like, deep inside, to still carry those lessons of racism because you never completely get rid of them. As much as you want to say you have, somewhere deep inside of you those lessons are still instilled. I was quite ashamed for a long time of my Southern roots. But I eventually came around to acknowledging them. There's a lot about the South that I do like, and admire, and am comfortable with.

But with *Son of the South*, I have not made a white savior movie. I've made a film about somebody who was saved *by* the Civil Rights Movement. It's an important statement that you don't always have to be the savior. You can be the one saved.

World Class

Pedro Costa

2010
Interview by Patrick McGilligan

Portuguese director Pedro Costa's three bleak immersions into the slum life of Lisbon's Fontainhas neighborhood – his breakthrough *Bones* (*Ossos*, 1997), its follow-up on the bleak life of one of the denizens, *In Vanda's Room* (2000), and the nearly three-hour *Colossal Youth* (*Juventude Em Marcha*, 2006) – have been described as aestheticized poverty, minimalism in the service of avant-garde formalism, and just plain "difficult" or "numbing." The informal trilogy has also been hailed as a "truly incantatory experience" (Kent Jones, *Film Comment*) and "the cinema of the future" (Jonathan Rosenbaum, *Chicago Reader*).

For too long the Costa experience has belonged primarily to film festivals and big-city arthouses, but now the less privileged can see for themselves. Criterion has lovingly packaged the three works into a "Letters from Fontainhas" collection replete with video essays and interviews, photographs, trailers, and outtakes, a booklet of critical appraisal, and two rare, related Costa short films post-2006. A bonanza for Costa's growing fans, the set is a must for political and cinema internationalists.

Costa was interviewed by telephone from Lisbon.

What was your motivation for embarking on this informal trilogy of Fontainhas films? I've heard you say that you woke up one day to realize that you had been living on the wrong side of the circus.

It was never meant to be a trilogy, of course. If I was being completely honest we would talk about four films – not three films. The film just before *Ossos, Casa de Lava,* was the key that opened the door to all the other films.

Casa de Lava was a film I made in Africa, in Cabo Verde, the islands where all the immigrants in the Fontainhas neighborhood come from. They are mostly African and the majority of them come from these islands in the Atlantic Ocean.

I shot *Casa de Lava* in 1994 on one of the islands. The film was supposed to be, in my wildest dreams, a remake of a Jacques Tourneur film called *I Walked with a Zombie* (1943). Of course that was a stupid idea; I was young. But I loved Tourneur, and at that time I was a bit lost and already having a lot of doubts and questions about what was going to be my life in film. Did I want to follow the path of most of my colleagues today, my generation? Doing normal films with crews and producers and scripts, etc.? Having a comfortable life, or something else? If it was "something else," I didn't have a clue how to do it.

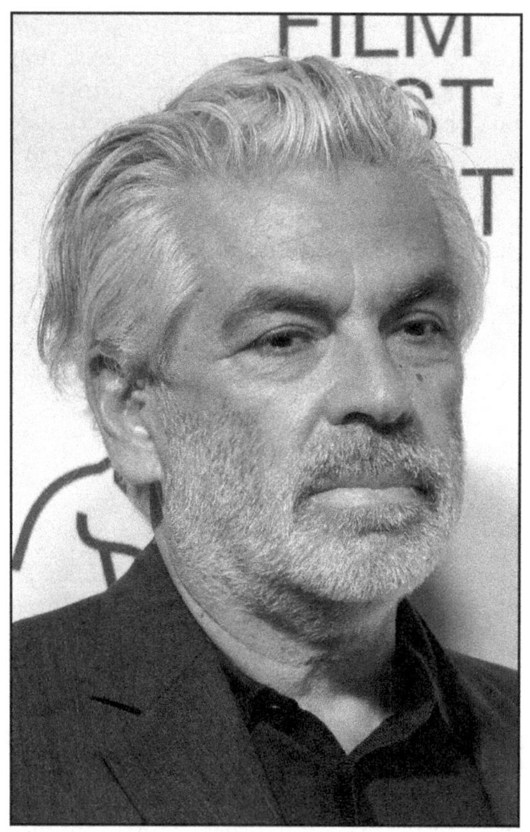

Pedro Costa at Film Fest Gent in 2020
(photo by Joost Pauwels).

So I decided to ask the producer I had at that time to give me some money and I went away, far away, to these islands, with this idea of doing an adventure/ghost/zombie remake of *I Walked with a Zombie*. I had a very good experience there, and I like the film I made – it is a very special film for me – but it goes way beyond artistic satisfaction. This film held the key to my life, to all the choices I've been making since.

After the shooting I called all the people on the islands that I'd been working with, that I took as actors – the non-professionals – and the people that were helping me – to thank them. They gave me, and a lot of other people in the crew, gifts – tobacco and coffee and other items – that I was supposed to give to their friends and family who were immigrants here in Lisbon, in the neighborhood of Fontainhas. So I got on the bus to go to Fontainhas, carrying this big bag of stuff, intending to deliver the goods, and that's how I discovered the neighborhood.

Had you never been there before?

At this time, in 1997, it was really a scary place, a very dangerous area, not completely outside of Lisbon, but let's say it was on the border of Lisbon. It was a big shanty town, very dark, organized in architecture, space and color like an African or even Arab medina – the old town. There was a very secret way in and way out. They even had guards. It was really like a fortress, a castle. I had no reason to go there before and really no one would walk in there unless they wanted to buy or sell something – often drugs.

I was living in Lisbon at that time, far, far from this place, and it felt right to go by bus. I could have taken the train, but the bus was really important because, you know, with the traffic jams and crowds it took time to get there. It was forty-five minutes by bus from my house to this place and it gave me the preparation already. I found myself among the people, and on this kind of bus route to the suburbs they were working people – going to work or coming from work – and you could see at once that it was a different class. They were not only black, they were another social class, and I wanted to be among them.

Everyone knew about this place of course, but I never dreamt of going there, thinking about a film or a project. My life, as I told you, was more oriented towards something normal in a professional way. But that's what happened. I went to this place. They opened all doors to me. It was quite easy because of this key – this password – the gifts that I had brought. I also spoke a little bit of Creole that I learned in Africa, and that is what they spoke there inside this ghetto. They spoke Creole – they never speak Portuguese.

When I delivered the goods and gifts, I was immediately accepted. I became totally fascinated by the place. When I told you that I had wanted to do a remake of Tourneur, well, I confess I have a dark side. I like films that deal with the dark side, the mystical side, the American B-films of Tourneur and [Edgar] Ulmer, which have always been close to my soul. The squalor of the place fascinated me. At the same time it was a very lively and loud place. People talked loud, they were dynamic. So I became a part of their world immediately. I was fascinated by them, and I think they were also fascinated by me. Who is this guy? Why does he speak Creole? Why does he want to be here and he's not even taking drugs?

I think I was there almost a year, just walking around and having dinner and lunch and going to parties – I was invited to everything: marriages, funerals – becoming one of them. Every day was a time of thought and preparation, not really thinking of shots or dialogue at first. Gradually I began sifting through film ideas – realizing that a film could be possible – and that was probably the first political sign or real change in my life. When I began bringing my small camera along, that changed things a lot, because at first I was not very convinced that a small DV [digital video] camera could do what I wanted to do, which was create something that looked like a Tourneur film.

Aesthetically, visually, the Fontainhas films stand apart from everything else I've seen. Your palette is so somber, so dark.

This was part of my changing. Once I decided I would like to do films here with these people I felt completely on their side with the color and the light. The light felt special. It is available light, the sun or the moon or candles in many instances. The light reflects on the faces or bodies. I got this strange idea that there's some sort of light that comes from the people. Vanda or her sister – some of the others – are so white; that's because something inside them reflects light. These were films that were made with the glow or energy that actually comes from them, which is again the Tourneur influence.

In some ways it was a political decision for me to abandon film crews, but I knew I had to in that dangerous place. It would be a mistake to have a crew, because at that time it was such a cruel and deceiving society. Crime all over. Unemployment. Everything that is bad in society. Film crews are a reactionary force anyway. That was my experience, and I had a couple of years as an assistant director before I started directing. A lot of bad things happened on those films, barbaric things, fights between producers and directors, and a lot of union people were not interested in the film at all, just getting the money. We'd end up with many more people than we were supposed to have on the crew. There was always inflation, and that was not the life I wanted.

I knew I had to do a film there almost alone, or with chosen people. I knew I could make a film that way. Everybody can make a film with three or four people. It's sound and image and… it depends on your ambition… but you can do without a lot of the other things. I could forget about actors. I could forget about make-up or costumes and make do with the things here that pleased me, more than aesthetically. Or you can do it as I did – with the help of the people that are around the neighborhood, and that turned out fine. We all got the same money: directors, actors, crew. That changes everything, though it's not much money.

Can you talk about the actors in the first and third films? Are they all amateurs, or non-professionals?

In the first one, *Ossos*, I have two, three actors mixing with boys and girls from the neighborhood. The people from Lisbon in the part that was shot in the city, not in the neighborhood, they were actors – the nurse, the prostitute, these kinds of roles. I needed them because those characters were from the city, from Lisbon, and they were difficult parts. In *Colossal Youth*, there are no professional actors.

Some – not all the slum actors – were really strange, secretive, sometimes aggressive, sometimes not responding to direction. That's what happened with Vanda [who plays a fictional character in *Ossos*], for instance. She would never do what I told her to do, she would do something else, and that was a great lesson for me. I used to say, "Vanda, you come in, you go there, you sit down, you're feeling sad, you stare out of the window" – and she would do the opposite. She'd walk in, go over to a table, stand, drink a beer and start laughing. She used to explain, "You know, I'm not feeing sad. I prefer to laugh. I don't want to sit down. I'd rather stand." So it was – I don't want to say impossible – but with non-actors the basic fundamentals of doing a film are changed. You either open up to it or not. It's difficult, but I choose to work this way and sometimes it doesn't work, of course, and you have to say so. But sometimes, and most of the times, what comes out, or what I hear, is a germ to build on in the story.

Some American critics have talked about the non-actors behaving in a deliberately blank or non-expressive manner – the acting isn't convulsive or emotional. Is that a deliberate style, or did it evolve?

I'm not sure I agree with that – especially not in the case of *Vanda's Room*, because that's the film where I directed the least and there was really very little imposing of anything. What's there are the feelings – the emotions, the sadness or joy – everything you see in that film – comes from the people themselves.

So Bresson is not an influence, as some critics have written?

Yes, he is an influence for me and a lot of people. But the key to what you're asking is this question of what's secret and what's public, what's private and what's not private. The films explore that. There are secrets and private spaces and there is a more extroverted part of the people. They are formed like that. Otherwise they would be dead. They have to hide a lot of feelings and emotions because life has not been very nice to them. So if sometimes they looked a bit blank or mute or whatever, it's more their personality than my direction.

Can you talk about the deliberate pacing of scenes? You take a long time to let something transpire in front of the camera. You don't hurry the film in any conventional way.

It's different for all three films. But yes, you can see that I am searching sometimes. When I was working or shooting, especially *Ossos* – alone more or less, although sometimes I had a friend doing the sound – I felt like – you can choose – either a painter, or a sociologist, or an anthropologist. The process was something between science and art. Everything was interesting for me, artistically as well as sociologically, on human terms. In narrative terms, in fictional terms if you want. I knew I had the material, though I had a lot of work to do. I had a lot to see and to hear. Could I, for example, show the whole neighborhood through Vanda or Ventura, the old guy in *Colossal Youth*? I thought so. That was the idea – that just one of them could speak for all of them.

At different times for the different films, during those long shots you are talking about, you can tell that I'm searching for something. I'm also searching for the correct placement of the camera and the lights, sometimes. In *Ossos* I was waiting for something to happen, while the boys are searching for feelings, or words to describe their feelings. They're young, the film is about young people, and they are sometimes caught in very difficult moments. So I had to give them time. I could not rush.

Ossos was my first amazed gaze at this world. I was amazed at the tricks of the lighting. I was amazed at the way people responded to the light. I was amazed at the secrecy of the place, of the people. I discussed this afterwards with the people when I showed the film. They were puzzled or, some, disappointed, of course, the ones that wanted something more documentary, let's say. I told them, "This is the first one. This is mine. This is my first impression." So *Ossos* has a very special, poetic, free form. For me it was like a prototype.

Did you worry constantly about imposing your vision on this world?

No, never! What worried me were very practical and concrete things. That was a very good and big change in my life because, before, I was always worried about the shots and the dialogue and the *mise-en-scène*. Now there was much more to worry about than the artistic problems. The worries were more organic, not so much a question of true or false, because they accept and want fiction. Even *Vanda* is not really a pure documentary. I think it's very useful when a documentary goes just beyond the plain facts. The work is still evolving for me. But this approach is not new, after all. Flaherty did it – an obvious example. Another filmmaker who did it the same way I am trying to do it, working with people, is Jean Rouche, the French documentarist who worked stin Africa.

What has been the reaction to your films about this neighborhood inside Portugal?

If I have an audience, it's the people themselves. I'm making the films for them. Not all of my colleagues are so lucky as to know their audience. I am doing these films for a small community; I film them, and then I show them to them. They are the first audience always. The first screenings are there; I always find a cinema that is not far from that place, and I have a two-, three-, four-week run for the families and everyone involved. Everyone gets a DVD who wants a DVD. That community is the first audience – that's about six or seven thousand people, so it's not small.

At the same time the film is released in Lisbon and Portugal, but that is another story. The first one, *Ossos*, was a big, big success, strangely. It played for months and months, and everybody wrote about that film, because it was the first time this reality was on the big screen. There was the smell of drugs, danger, lives that were not very cheerful, and at the same time everyone could see that it was a real film, a story yet truthful. *Ossos* was an event; it was new. People knew about this place but it was hidden; nobody had ever showed it before.

After *Ossos* it has been less and less because of course people don't want to see that again, and they saw it already, so they think they will be seeing the same thing all over again.

Has it led to any changes or improvement in Fontainhas?

We did some shorts after *Colossal Youth* – one is called *Tarrafal*, the other is *The Rabbit Hunters* – which are also in the boxed set. The idea of *Tarrafal* [part of the omnibus film *O Estado do Mundo*/State of the World (2007)], which we did two or three years ago, was to do a little film to help one of the guys I know, who works with us all the time, who was going to be deported from Portugal. That's happening throughout Europe. They are putting people on planes back to their *patria*. This guy received a letter from the foreign office of the government saying you'll be put on a plane soon, so pack your bags. We made this 15-minute film to help him: about him, his mother and father. Just the hope and the action of doing the film was enough for him, for us. At least there was an effort, and we hope it may be useful, but the film hasn't stopped his deportation process yet. It didn't change anything.

No, in economic terms it's always the same. My films have not changed lives.

What's next for you?

A film with the same people, the younger kids, not children, but twelve fourteen-year-old guys that don't remember Fontainhas because they were born in the new housing projects [in the northern neighborhood of Casal Boba, where the neighborhood was relocated after Fontainhas was levelled]. I'm starting now, sitting at tables or at the bar, talking about two or three ways of doing it – what would be the story, who will play the parts. It takes a long time, four or five months, just to think through it, and then I start shooting.

Adoor Gopalakrishnan

2011

Interview by Patrick McGilligan

Adoor Gopalakrishnan is a household name for cinema lovers in India and in Indian households around the world. Over the last forty years he has created a personal body of work that is among the richest of his generation, films set in his native Kerala in the Malayalam language that are regionalist yet universal. "Among the many," wrote Professor Peter L. Attipetty, "he is alone and his films are exceptional." Gopolakrishnan has won the prominent National Award of India nine times; the Smithsonian Institution in Washington, D.C. has presented him at a retrospective as the "Poet Laureate of Indian Cinema"; and he has been decorated with the Légion d'honneur and the Commandeur de Ordre des Arts et des Lettres in France.

Few of his films or documentaries are available in DVD in English-speaking countries. Although they evince the quietism of Ozu and the naturalism of Satyajit Ray, and they often protest injustices, his films are also lyrical and poetic and not easily compared to other filmmakers. "Like Kiarostami, Gopalakrishnan is a master of the unsaid," wrote Mark Cousins in *Sight and Sound*; his films are like "silent screams."

Among those available in DVD is the third of his eleven features, *Rat-Trap* (*Elippathayam*, 1981), which concerns a wealthy aristocrat who is trapped by his own manipulations. *Shadow Kill* (*Nizhalkkuthu*, 2002) depicts the inner doubts of a state hangman in the kingdom of Travancore (later part of Kerala) in 1941. *Four Women* (*Naalu Pennungal*, 2007) tells the story of four archetypal women under class or societal constraints at different periods in Kerala history. (His documentary explorations of the Kathakali style of classical dance theater can be found in extracts on YouTube.)

In the U.S. recently to take part in the Maximum India Festival at the Kennedy Center, Gopalakrishnan passed through Milwaukee to speak at the Milwaukee Area Technical College.

—◦—

Can you tell me a little bit about the Malayalam culture and the Kerala state in India?

"Mala" means "the hills." "Alam" is derived from the word Azhi, meaning the sea. It is the land between the hills and the sea. Over time the whole culture became known as Malayalam and that became the name of the language as well.

What happened some time ago is that there was a reorganization of the Indian states on the basis of the languages spoken. We used to have something like three hundred and fifty princely states in the whole country. Some of

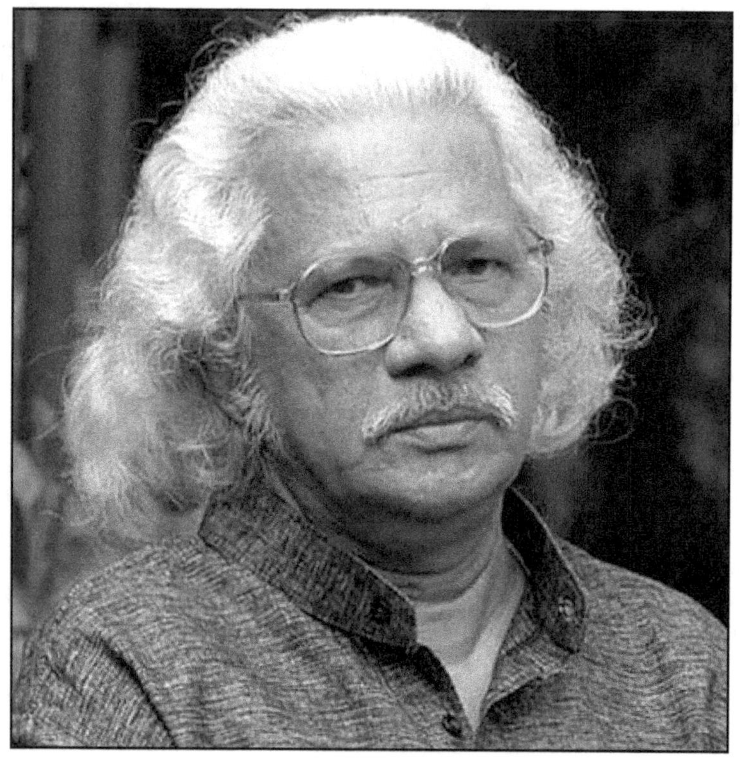

Adoor Gopalakrishnan
(photo from the Gopolakrishnan Archives).

the languages and culture had deteriorated, but on the basis of languages and culture and geographical contiguity some areas were joined together – in the South, for example, the area where Tamil was spoken, and so it became the Tamil state. Mostly in the northern parts they spoke Hindi – and other languages – but Hindi was the most common. Hindi along with English was the national, universal language. Growing up, everyone in a state had to study three languages – your mother tongue, English, and Hindi. In the South we studied these three languages but in the North they did not study a third language, Malayalam. They studied only Hindi and English.

Kerala is the southernmost part of India, a narrow strip of land on the Arabian coast. It's between the hills and the sea, very fertile land with a high concentration of population. It is the most literate state in India. We have Hindus, Christians, and Muslims living together; forty percent are Hindus; each of the others represent thirty percent each. We even had a small Jewish population for a long time. We have a great tradition of living in harmony because there has never been an incursion from the outside and a forcible conversion from one religion to another; these kinds of things happened in the northern regions, but never in Kerala, which is insulated because of the hills and the sea.

We had more contact with the rest of the world. Kerala used to be known as the Malayalam Coast. It used to be a destination in the old days for Europeans, for travel, and for muslin clothing, for example. It was a stopover when people traveled from China on the spice trail. Over the years there has been a lot of cross-fertilization of cultures, languages, and ideas.

It's a very modern state also. If you travel in Kerala now the whole state is almost like one contiguous living place. You almost cannot separate one city from the next; there has been an even growth everywhere. We have modern-day amenities and facilities everywhere – electrification, transportation, telecommunications, roads, social services, health care.

In terms of living standards, the South is far ahead of the rest of the country. In Kerala we don't really have homeless or very poor people, for example. Wages are high, people have jobs. Kerala happens to have been the first state with a local Communist government, and even today Communists are often involved in the coalitions.

You started out making documentaries. You don't make as many anymore, do you?

In the beginning I used to make films on every subject that came my way. In the last few years I have been concentrating on documentaries with subjects that have to do with theater or the classical art forms of Kerala. I don't do many other documentaries anymore but I enjoy the ones I do make because I learn a lot in the process. The research is always very exciting. To learn how or why a particular form of art or theater has advanced in Kerala, how it reached today's growth, this is really exciting for me. In between feature films there are long intervals, so I always make these other kinds of films as a change of pace. And it refills my creative energies.

Making documentaries has influenced me in many ways. In the beginning it was for me almost like being a one-man unit. I used to do my own camerawork. I used to do my own sound. I used to do everything. That kind of discipline and learning helped me.

Documentaries also have affected the reason why, in my fictional films, I don't like to fake any reality. I try to be truthful. What I am saying in the film may have many levels of interpretation, but I always say that at one level, at the basic level, the film has to be a real document of the period, a real place, and people at a certain time in history. Maybe that has come from the documentary experience.

I am not interested in creating a reality that engages the audience just on its surface. I want the audience to explore beneath the surface. I have learned, for example, that holding a shot makes the audience watch more closely what is going on within the frame. In a moving shot, the movement itself becomes important, not always what you are seeing within the frame. The moment you start holding the shot, for some length of time, you start to notice the texture, the composition, and so many other things.

So you prefer static shots?

Not necessarily. It depends on what I am shooting. Of course I do try to keep the camera moving, but not so much that the audience is watching it. I don't want them to see that my camera is moving. I want them to watch the scene, not the camera movement.

Has the impulse towards truthfulness and real documents always been present in your film work?

Always from the very beginning – in film. I used to do plays before film. I used to write, perform, and produce plays in my high school and college days. I had a job also, for a short period. I gave up all that to join the Pune Film Institute, the national film school, when it was started in 1961. This was the first film school in the whole country. I joined the second year. When I passed out of the school in 1965, I realized it was impossible for me to make the kinds of films I wanted to make right away. The traditional way would have been to apprentice myself to someone for years and then slowly, if one is lucky, one gets a chance to make a film. I made documentaries during that period instead, and it took seven years for me to make my first feature [*One's Own Choice/Swavamvaram*, 1971-2].

During that period I also started a film society movement in Kerala. We got outstanding films from other countries and from our own country, and we showed them to young people who were interested in the cinema. The film society movement started as a low-budget escape but it inspired many young people to go and study cinema and then make their own films.

Wasn't the impulse towards realism or truthfulness at odds with your theater background? Your films certainly are not very theatrical or stylized.

When I entered the Pune Film Institute I stopped doing theater and left that behind. But it was important and good for me that I did theater before I did cinema; I learned exactly where theater stopped and where film started.

Film is perhaps innately more realistic than theater. Theater can be realistic too, but it has a different vision of reality. The whole thing is different. If you put a piece of furniture on the stage, it takes on a meaning different from that of a mere object of daily use. Everything is difficult in theater – sound, for example, is different in the theater – while everything is possible in the medium of cinema, and nothing is taken for conventional and attributed meanings.

Were you influenced from the beginning by particular filmmakers that you had watched in school or in the film society years?

There have been many because I studied cinema very formally and watched films from Méliés down to all the great masters. I cannot pick out one or two influences.

The Italian neorealists?

Yes, but my films do not belong to neorealism, not at all.

Do they belong to any school?

No, I don't think so, because my reality – the way I experience reality – is different from others. I cannot transplant someone else's ideas or traditions. The more I watched the great masters, the more I understood you have to have your own way of looking at reality. Your salvation lies in that. Not imitating, not following someone else. All the great masters have taught us how to look at reality, but when each looked at reality their own way, their films become very personal statements.

Cinema has a lot to do with one's own culture – my culture in my case. I'm not just telling a story. It's beyond that. The story is just an excuse. I am trying to make the audience experience many things – not just that one thing, the story. The story is just an excuse to keep the audience inside the hall. Of course there has to be this element of the audience wanting to know what happens next. That's why they stay. Otherwise they'll walk out. The story is what keeps them sitting. But my primary goal is for the audience to share the experience I want to give them, hopefully an experience on many levels.

Does the humble way of life, the village life, still exist in Kerala as is depicted, for example, in your films Shadow Kill *and* Four Women?

Those films take place in the Forties, the British period. Then there were very few amenities. In *Four Women*, for example, I show a very waterlogged area of Kerala. Transportation in the country in those days was by boats. Now things have changed, to a great extent.

You seem very attuned to the rituals of the period.

In some ways. I have to be faithful to the period, and those films are documents of that period. Very truthful documents – I'm proud of that. And the rituals are very important. *Shadow Kill* is about the ritual of killing someone, and in *Four Women*, for example, the coming-of-age or fertility ritual for young women is also very important. That's the whole point of one story in that film, because with the coming of age the relationships change in that house – suddenly the father becomes protective of his daughter; her older sister becomes jealous and selfish; and the brother-in-law sees another man in the picture. The relationships change. The fertility ritual is really important because the lives of the women depend on those relationships – on marriage and the coming of age. The fertility ritual becomes the real ground for the story to take place.

I cannot help but notice that you prefer to set the stories of your films in the past.

My films are devoted to the period I have lived through, yes. I would find it harder to make a contemporary film because I feel you have to have had the perspective of living through a particular time. I don't know what I think about something until I have gone through the experience and some time has passed.

The farthest back I have gone is the Forties, not before, because I was born in the Forties and I grew up in the Forties, so I am physically depicting things I really knew, things I've seen and heard and experienced.

So the films are always, in some sense, autobiographical.

I suppose so.

Are the actors in your films always professionals?

I use both, professionals and non-professionals. The casting is done on the basis of whether the particular actor will look like the character or the role, not based on his fame or popularity. A popular actor can be harmful because some of them have only been seen in a certain mold. If you try to break the mold that can be a problem – for the actors also – if they have been doing a certain type all their life, it can be difficult asking them to change too much.

Normally, if I do not know an actor, I cast him in a small role first, see what he does and if he's good. If I find that he is responsive and can do what I want him to do, then I cast him in a bigger role. With non-professional actors I don't cast them in the main roles, of course. If I see them somewhere – on the stage or in other films or even sitcoms – [I'll cast them if] their look is right.

Do you cast people from seeing them on the street or at the market in town, for example?

I've done that also. Many people come to me, in fact, often when I'm between films, to ask for a role in my next film. I tell them to come back when I'm ready – but only if they have the right look.

Do actors sometimes contribute anything to the ideas in the script? In the case of Four Women, *for example, because it is all about women's lives, I wonder if the actresses contributed anything to the content of the scenes, either in discussion or improvisation.*

I don't want actors to interpret a role on their own. What the actor thinks might lead to a clash of styles. I ask them to follow the script specifically. No improvisation.

I notice that you are rather stingy with music in your films, or that music doesn't play that big a role unless it is integrated into a scene, with characters playing instruments, for example. Is that a reaction to Bollywood?

I don't use music too much, no. I don't use it to heighten a scene. I might use it as a theme, or a leitmotif. But I don't score music under everything on the screen. I don't believe in that. Music can really hurt you unless you use it with real restraint.

In general, sound can contribute a lot. You can listen to so many other alternative sounds in one of my films. And silence also can be effective. In the commercial films, from frame one to frame last, there is a score. People have gotten used to hearing music all the time. Where they don't hear a diagrammed score they think something must be wrong. They grow restless. This is the sad part.

The colors of nature are so lush in your films, sometimes in contrast to the humble lives of the people. Do you put a lot of thought into the color scheme?

One has to think about the colors. You can't always allow the predominant color to be green, for example. And there are many, many shades of green. In fact there are two main monsoons in Kerala, and during the monsoon you see so many shades of green. I love that. I have shot one entire film [*Man of the Story/Kathapurushan*, 1996] during the monsoon because everything is so clear and clean – just waiting for the rains to stop and then shooting. I wanted to catch the many shades of green.

Is there a big tradition in Kerala of noncommercial filmmaking, or are you pretty much the tradition?

[Laughs] There were other filmmakers in Kerala before me but they were not offbeat like me. They were trying to do better films in the framework of the commercial cinema. Their films were not a departure from anything. In the beginning, my films were seen as a departure from what had been there before.

Who is the intended audience of your films? How are they distributed inside India?

They are mainly shown in Kerala, but Kerala has a huge population. We have thirty million people and an educated audience and something like 4,500 cinemas. There are a number of big commercial houses in a number of cities all over India where they also can be shown with subtitles for non-Malayalam speaking people.

In how many other languages are your films subtitled or dubbed within India?

Just English, because almost everyone in an educated audience understands English, and they are the people who go to see this kind of film. There is a whole lot of the other kind of cinema, the popular cinema, where they sing songs and dance dances and there is nonstop action. Those are the big Bollywood kind of films, which is not cinema.

How do you define your cinema?

It is a very personal kind of cinema, which tries to communicate with good audiences anywhere, everywhere.

After Kerala, are the metro cities scattered throughout India a good market for you?

Yes – or I should say, it is a developing market. We also get media exposure on national television.

After the films have been shown theatrically?

Yes, until recently. They used to show "The Best of India" on national television, but for the time being this has stopped. National television also wants to make more money, and they feel these kinds of films don't make enough money, even on national television, which is run by the government. They think they don't get as many advertisements as they do with the other kind, the big films, the more commercial films.

It doesn't sound as though Parallel Cinema is very healthy in India.

I don't promote that term. I don't encourage people to say Parallel Cinema. I don't make Parallel Cinema. I just make cinema. It's a journalist's coinage. You may as well call it "offbeat cinema," because we have no real "parallel" way to screen our films to audiences. We depend entirely on the same cinemas where they show the commercial films to the masses.

Really?

There is nothing like a parallel distribution.

There's no such thing as an art house?

We don't have art houses. We say art house films because that is the term used, but there are no art houses.

So a theater in a metro area might show your film one week and a Bollywood film the next?

Yes. Bollywood and all kinds of films like Bollywood, because other regions make all kinds of bad films too. Each region produces its own bad films, which are very popular with audiences, which follow the ballads of its local heroes and stars. The so-called Bollywood of Bombay – that's the commercial cinema of Bombay – they don't even produce thirty percent of the total production of the films made in India. The bulk of the production comes from the South in four different languages – Malayalam, Tamil, Telagu, and Kannada. Those are not Bollywood but the bulk of them are bad films often very much like Bollywood.

Our films are indeed small films by comparison. It's very difficult to make our films because we don't get the same size audiences. The audience is complexly conditioned by the other kind of cinema. For them, cinema means all those things that we consider nonessentials – singing, dancing, action. The nonessentials become essentials in those films.

Personally, do you struggle to reach an audience?

I do, but my struggle is not very difficult now because I have made so many films and I have a certain reputation. It's not extremely difficult for me to get financing, and normally people don't lose money on my films. Most of the other small films do badly perhaps, but mine cover the costs and are sometimes profitable. I have faithful audiences.

What's a typical budget for one of your films?

It varies. I don't work on so-called shoestring budgets, because I always say I don't want a big budget or a small budget, I want the right budget. I prefer to make my films the way I want to make them and I always have. I never compromise on the film because I don't have the right amount of money.

What was the budget of your last picture, for example?

Ten million rupees. A typical Bollywood picture, by comparison, might cost three hundred million rupees, but some cost ten times more than that.

Do you have to go outside Kerala to get financing?

It's always possible to get financing in Kerala. *Four Women* actually was a production of my own because I was doing it also as a program for national television. *Shadow Kill* was a co-production with France because there are certain advantages to French collaboration. The film is then released in France and Europe.

What's your best market outside of India?

It depends. Each film is different. Some films do well outside of India, other films don't.

What are you working on now? Have you decided on the subject of your next film?

I don't know. I'm not settled on anything yet. It takes a long time for me to decide on an idea. I ask myself, is it a transient subject? Or is it an idea that will have standing value beyond the time when the film is made? I ask myself these kinds of questions over and over before I even start writing a script. An idea has to be very strong, strong enough to sustain and carry me along this whole process of making a film. For myself, it also has to be something new, not repeating something that I've done before, because for me, films are both ruminations and discoveries.

French Connections

Michel Ciment and *Positif*

1993
Interview by Patrick McGilligan

Imagine a film magazine that in place of an editor-in-chief – it has never had an editor-in-chief – relies upon the goodwill of an editorial committee that meets regularly once a week for three-hour meetings. Imagine a film magazine that does not pay fees for the articles it publishes, or for the editorial duties entailed. Imagine that this same film magazine has existed for four decades in precisely this fashion, without any institutional support.

Then again, there's no need to imagine. The magazine exists, its name is *Positif*, and for film critics, students, scholars and buffs its fortieth anniversary in the year just past was a cultural milestone. In *Positif*'s native France and elsewhere in Europe, the occasion was celebrated by press attention and film festival accolades, and in the U.S. by a special tribute sponsored last November by the Museum of Modern Art in New York City.

The first, less-than-forty-page issue in 1952 contained articles about Luis Buñuel, Vittorio De Sica, Jean Cocteau and Claude Autant-Lara. The fortieth anniversary issue (May, 1992), 160 pages, was crammed with columns and departments: obituaries for Richard Brooks and Nestor Almendros, a "transcript" with Maurice Pialat, interviews and articles on Blake Edwards and Edward Yang, a "dossier" on color in the cinema, roundups of film festivals from around the world.

Along with another French film journal, *Cahiers du Cinéma*, *Positif* is the oldest continuous film magazine in the Western world that is not underwritten by a government, college, archive, or parent organization. *Cahiers* (which, to be technical about it, was launched a year earlier) is better known to Americans because it had a short-lived English-language edition in the late Fifties and early Sixties, and because a number of its contributors (Godard, Rohmer, Truffaut, et al.) became leading directors of the *Nouvelle Vague*. But the influence of *Positif* may be more pervasive, especially among film critics and tastemakers. Over four decades, *Positif* has helped write the aesthetic history of Hollywood by championing certain genres and trends and exploring the careers of unsung American filmmakers. It has shed light into dark nooks and crannies of the international cinema. It continues to lead the way in rediscovering the motion pictures of the silent era (its research is sometimes linked to the annual film festival in Pordenone, one of whose directors is the *Positif* correspondent in Italy).

Although the magazine is published in French only, that is part of its cachet. And although the subscription list numbers only about three thousand, many of those three thousand are key people who help shape the verdict on what films and filmmakers get exposure at film festivals and in

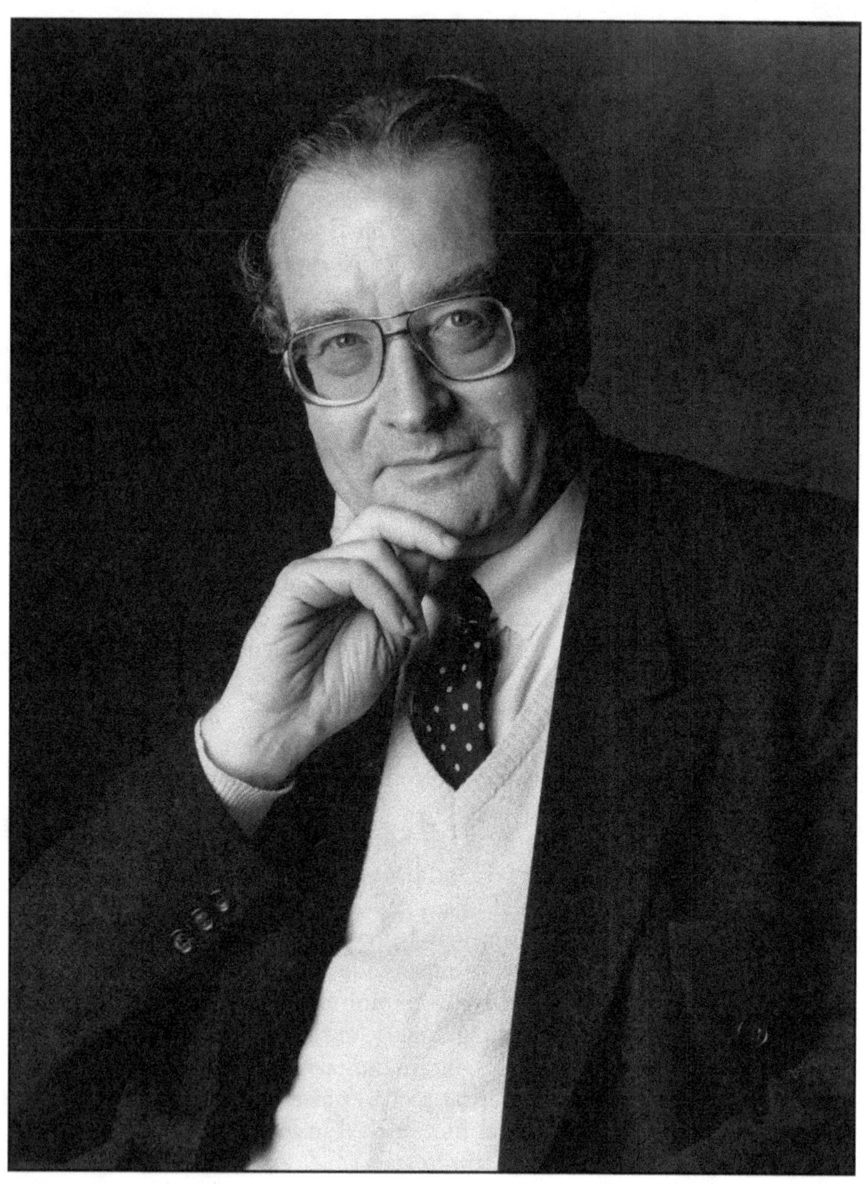

Michel Ciment in 1993
(photo by William B. Winburn).

the best theaters, what receives awards and critical notice, what gets written up in film books (*Positif* seems to breed authors the way *Cahiers* once bred directors).

Says one ultra-key person: "*Positif* helps to form the opinion of the opinion-makers – festival directors, daily or weekly critics, foreign reviewers, heads of film schools, publishers. They get the magazine, read the contents, and suddenly pay more attention to a director who has been featured in *Positif*. The same is true of *Cahiers*. These magazines have an influence that is much bigger than their actual circulation."

The speaker is Michel Ciment, a professor who teaches American studies at the University of Paris. The author of well-known books about Elia Kazan, Stanley Kubrick, Joseph Losey and John Boorman (among the ones translated into English), Ciment has been a contributor to *Positif* since 1963 and a member of the board since 1966.

That is not unusual. One member of the present board, Paul-Louis Thirard, has been writing for *Positif* since 1954 (Thirard has written noteworthy books about Luchino Visconti and Michelangelo Antonioni, and is an expert on Italian cinema). There are board members who date from each decade of the magazine's existence. *Positif* prides itself on its continuity, democratic discussions and teamwork, and a consistent critical policy that reflects a group consensus. In this respect, as in several others, it differs – sometimes bitterly – from its archrival, *Cahiers du Cinéma*.

—◦—

Positif originated in the city of Lyon, with the efforts of a student, Bernard Chardère (later director of the Lumière Institute). When Chardère went into military service shortly thereafter, the magazine had to switch to Paris. It's been in Paris ever since.

"The fact that the magazine was created by provincial people is quite important," explains Ciment, interviewed as a spokesman for the editorial committee (all subsequent quotes are his). "It's a magazine which has always been very much in the movement of ideas and taste, but at the same time it has a reputation of staying free of fads. Paris is a place where the fashions change very quickly. In a way – maybe this is purely psychological – I think the magazine has retained a kind of independence towards what we in France call 'Parisianism,' which is salon snobbism."

In France, in the period after World War II, there was a resurgence of interest in Hollywood movies – which had not been shown there during the war years – and in films in general. Jean Cocteau, Henri Langlois and others put on a Festival de Film Maudit in the town of Biarritz in 1949, and many film societies and journals started up. *Cahiers du Cinéma* was one of the first, most influential of the new publications, but *Positif* made its mark early as well.

Of the two, *Positif* was the more left-wing, according to Ciment, in part because it stood against censorship in France ("which was quite strong in the Fifties because the Church was quite powerful"), against nationalism and the right-wing movement in France, against the colonial wars in Indochina and Algeria. "To write for *Positif* was to have left-wing feelings," says Ciment. At the same time, *Positif* was aligned with the surrealist movement, with André Breton and his faction, which esteemed poetry and painting, comic strips, dreams, slapstick comedy, fantasy, and horror films.

Ideological differences translated into matters of taste. This meant that *Cahiers* often celebrated "the most conservative Hollywood directors" – people like Hawks or Hitchcock or George Cukor – whereas *Positif* championed more authentically nonconformist directors, such as Huston, Buñuel, Losey. Occasionally, the two magazines found themselves in agreement – both were enthusiastic about Robert Aldrich, Frank Tashlin, Richard Brooks and Orson Welles – but more often they diverged. "If you liked skeptical, critical directors," says Ciment, "you'd write for *Positif*. If you enjoyed popular art, if you were more Catholic-oriented, more conservative, more of an aesthete, if you liked Rossellini and Dreyer, you'd write for *Cahiers*."

The first focus on Antonioni outside of Italy was in a special issue of *Positif* in 1959. The little magazine published the first extensive interviews with Roman Polanski and Andrzej Wajda. It actually celebrated popular art more than *Cahiers*, which would defend a genre film only if it bore the stamp of an "auteur." *Positif* was the first magazine to place a certain emphasis on American Westerns, and to hail such masters of the genre as Delmer Daves and Anthony Mann.

"The French were more aware of the importance of people like Daves and Mann," says Ciment, "because we didn't have Westerns on TV. It was much more difficult for an American audience or journalist, seeing B-Westerns all day long on TV, to take a serious look at the Western. The fact that we were not brainwashed by mediocre stuff helped us look at Westerns in a more acute way.

"The reverse is often true. Godard was better appreciated abroad than in France, because we were too close to the sociological aspect of Godard's films, too partisan, too involved. I think *Positif* attacked Godard [as a filmmaker] because we were blind to his cinematographic qualities, and because we were too sensitive to the politics of the man. If you have a certain distance, perhaps you are more capable of objectivity."

Along with *Cahiers*, in the Fifties *Positif* pioneered the transcripted question-and-answer format with distinguished filmmakers (usually writers or directors) that has become a staple of journalism and almost a cliché of film magazines. Several of Ciment's own books are an outgrowth of that style, behind which there is a decided philosophy. "We have always done interviews that way," he says. "People who are being interviewed appreciate it. Keeping the shape in which the interview occurred, keeping even the intonations and the rhythm of the language, the choice of words, is the only protection against manipulation. That is an integrity. As soon as you start to synthesize or compose, the meaning changes."

Transcripted Q. & A.'s were one of the few things *Cahiers* and *Positif* agreed on. From the beginning, the two publications had a hostile relationship. Truffaut wrote strong pieces attacking the *Positif* crowd, and *Positif* responded with articles attacking *Cahiers* for its right-wing aesthetics. If *Cahiers* put something on the cover, it is likely *Positif* would sneer at it, and vice versa.

Auteurism was a particular sore point. "The auteur policy, as it was practiced by Truffaut or Rohmer, was overstated. It said that an auteur can never be wrong. Also, that the later films of a director are always the best – the late Renoir, the late Rossellini, the late Hawks, the late Ford. It was the idea that an auteur has a regular progression, he never fails, and the films of his old age are the sum of his reputation.

"At *Positif*, when we look at a new film, we always take into consideration the themes, the style, and the consistency of a certain director's body of work. On the other hand, it has happened very often that, even with some of the directors we like, we don't like some of their films. There were some very bad reviews in *Positif* of some of John Huston's films, for example. Or take the case of John Frankenheimer, a director we really liked in the Sixties. I remember Bertrand [Tavernier] and myself did forty pages of an article and interview on him in 1970. Probably in the last twenty years we have reviewed only one of his films favorably."

At the same time that *Cahiers* and *Positif* were rivalrous, there was "a certain complicity" in their enmity. "They all loved old films. They were all sitting in the third row of the Cinémathèque, and they were all listening to [Cinémathèque director] Henri Langlois. In a way they were enemies as Trotskyites can be against Communists, but they were all fighting for the same cause, fighting for the cinema like Marxists fighting for the revolution."

In the Sixties, *Cahiers* swung to the left. The fact that *Cahiers* gave birth to so many directors meant that *Cahiers* "felt obliged to laud all the films coming from their ranks, altering their critical judgment to praise their buddies." This damaged the credibility of *Cahiers* somewhat. At the same time, Ciment admits, *Positif* might have felt overly obliged to attack some of the *Cahiers*-alumni directors.

Cahiers swung so far to the left that, by the Seventies, the strong distinctions had re-emerged. *Cahiers* became "ultra left-wing Maoist," in Ciment's words, "while *Positif* had remained rather Trotskyist or liberal." *Cahiers* seemed to hate nearly everything that sprang from Hollywood during this decade. But *Positif* leaped to the defense of the New American

Cinema and became one of the first prestigious film magazines to put on its cover mavericks such as Monte Hellman, Bob Rafelson, Robert Altman, and Martin Scorsese.

Nowadays the policies of *Positif* are more "liberal or along a social-democrat line." That is not so very unlike *Cahiers*, although the rivalry still simmers. When I spoke to Ciment for this article, he was on his way to one of the weekly Sunday meetings to discuss an editorial reply to a *Cahiers* essay lambasting *Positif* for its consensus criticism.

He sums up the present state of affairs: "The decline of revolutionary ideals and the onset of all the crises in Eastern Europe mean the Left is not what it was in the Fifties – which was a very flamboyant and optimistic Left. I would say the Left is in an internationalist period. But *Positif* still looks at films critically, still tries to analyze them in their social and economic backgrounds; it's not purely an aesthetic approach, although of course aesthetics plays a major role.

"Today I would say the differences between *Positif* and *Cahiers* are not as striking. Perhaps the differences today are more in the critical approach rather than in the films [chosen to be] written about. I think *Positif* has kept more of a critical standard, more interest in the history of the cinema, more interest in in-depth criticism. Perhaps *Cahiers* has evolved more toward a magazine-type publication. Not like *Premiere* – that would be nasty! – but they have tended in recent years to become more popular, not only in layout but even the way in which certain articles are written and interviews conducted. They've tried to broaden the audience of the magazine, while *Positif* has remained more hard-core in the film-buff sense."

—◦—

One of the unique aspects of *Positif* remains its policy of reviewing films by group consensus. A half-dozen *Positif* writers converge on the Cannes Film Festival each year, armed with credentials and making a point of seeing the entire lineup. Afterwards, they meet for several hours and average their opinions, later reviewing the entire festival film by film – some sixty or seventy – according to the majority feeling.

"We like the magazine to take a stand," says Ciment. "Of course, we have deep differences – some people do not like Antonioni, others do not like Wim Wenders – but most people like more or less what the magazine represents and defends. We rarely publish a 'pro and con' type of thing. We find that's a kind of cop-out. Although perhaps we should do more."

In Paris, where they are accorded respect by the press agents and distribution outlets, the editorial committee (which fluctuates in number but stands at roughly fifteen) go to screenings in a pack in order to see and assess a new release. Recently, for example, a *Positif* delegation viewed the new

Polanski film *Bitter Moon*. If they had liked it, they would have assigned a "dossier" (or special section) on Polanski's career. As it happens, they disliked it, and "decided just to have a review, a rather negative review, written by the one of us who disliked the film least, but who would write a review that would be more negative than positive."

Among the U.S. filmmakers nowadays, *Positif* gravitates to the "independence movement" – the Coen brothers, Quentin Tarantino or Tim Burton – "which for us is the best of the new American cinema. Of course, there are exceptions like Clint Eastwood, whom we like a lot. But even Eastwood I would say is not, strangely not, mainstream."

Ciment adds: "I think the importance of magazines such as *Cahiers* and *Positif* has increased with the years, precisely because the nature of cinema has changed. In the Fifties, the importance of a film buff magazine was absolutely secondary, because most of the movies were made by commercial companies and didn't need the support of film buff magazines. Today, when there are really two kinds of cinema – either the blockbuster type of film, which of course ignores the specialized magazines, or what I will call the author's cinema, whether it is the Coen brothers, Wim Wenders, Pedro Almodovar, Peter Greenaway, and so on – these [latter] people have to care about these magazines because very often we are the first to pay attention to them."

Surprisingly, Ciment feels that U.S. film magazines compare favorably with the best in France, and that "in general the quality of writing and research seems much higher in America." Among prominent byline critics, he likes reading Michael Sragow, David Ansen, Richard Corliss and Dave Kehr "because I find such a high quality of writing and an attempt at looking at films from every standpoint, from the writing of the script to the acting.

"[If I miss anything in American magazines, it's] the cosmopolitan aspect of the French magazines, the overture towards world cinema. For example, we spoke to Theo Angelopoulos in '73 or '74 for the first time, and he's just starting to become known in America now. That could be said of a great number of world directors. [And I wish that instead of spotting 'trends' there was] more of a critical debate, which did exist in America at the time of *Film Culture*, [the heyday of] the Underground Cinema, and the debate between Andrew Sarris and Pauline Kael. That's the one thing that is missing in American film magazines today."

Bertrand Tavernier on the American Cinema
1992

Interview by Patrick McGilligan

If you happen to have encountered Bertrand Tavernier on one of his swings through the United States, then you probably know that the French director travels with an extra suitcase stuffed with videotapes and laserdiscs of old and rare Hollywood movies that he collects and adds to his trove in Paris. If you happen to have visited Tavernier in the French capital, then probably you have found yourself, somewhat mandatorily, slumped on a pillow in his apartment, at 4 a.m., watching a "rediscovery" or arguing the relative merits of Hawks vs. Walsh.

Apart from being a world-class filmmaker, Tavernier is an insatiable film buff – in general, a buff of many facets of American culture. Long before he became justly acclaimed as the director of such films as *The Clockmaker* (1974), *Let Joy Reign Supreme* (1975), *Coup de Torchon* (1981), *A Sunday in the Country* (1984), *'Round Midnight* (1987) and *Life and Nothing But* (1989), Tavernier had a separate, distinguished body of published work as a film journalist and critic. Mostly, his films do not smack of buffery (let alone flaunt it), but there is the occasional American source material turned Gallic – the Jim Thompson novel (*POP. 1280*) metamorphosed into *Coup de Torchon*, or the jazz expatriate subject of *'Round Midnight* (and the casting of the roles, in particular).

In the Fifties, in Paris, when a number of film journals began to hail certain Hollywood directors, define genres, and champion auteurism, among other critical approaches, Tavernier was launching his first career. He was one of the few Frenchmen who moved easily between *Cinéma* ("the magazine of the film societies – those not only in Paris, but the small villages"), the prestigious and dogmatic *Cahiers du Cinéma*, and the more left-wing *Positif*. "I loved to provoke each of them," jokes Tavernier, "praising [Sam] Fuller in *Positif*, Delmer Daves or Billy Wilder in *Cahiers*, John Ford in *Cinéma*."

One of the first reviews Tavernier wrote was of the 1957 film *Time Without Pity* by Joseph Losey, and one of his first interviews was with Italian director Alberto Lattuada. Later, while working as a publicist in Europe, he did important interviews with many writers and directors passing through Paris, and American exiles living abroad – including victims of the Hollywood blacklist.

It was at *Cinéma* in the late Fifties that Tavernier met the man who became his longtime friend and collaborator: Jean-Pierre Coursodon. Coursodon, who has lived in the States since the late Sixties, has written excellent books about silent and early-sound comedy (Laurel and Hardy, W.C. Fields, Buster Keaton) and coedited and written many of the essays in the two-volume *American Directors* published by McGraw-Hill in 1983. Since Tavernier has emerged as such a prominent director, Coursodon must be content to play I.A.L. Diamond to Tavernier's Billy Wilder, for press purposes. But Coursodon is every bit the equal collaborator on the book that is their seminal contribution to film literature – *50 Ans de Cinéma Américain*.

Actually, there have been three incarnations of this book – the definitive French mirror on Hollywood. The first, modest-sized edition, in 1961, co-written by Coursodon and French critic-director Yves Boisset, was called *Twenty Years of the American Cinema*. Tavernier collaborated just a little on that version. When Coursodon took the book over for a second edition in 1969, he enlisted Tavernier as a full partner. Their expanded volume, called *Thirty Years of the American Cinema*, was published and praised, then disappeared from bookstores, becoming a cult item in France. The third manifestation, the entirely revised and updated *50 Ans...*, was published in the spring of 1991 in France (Éditions Nathan).

Because of their close relationship, Coursodon and Tavernier were able to conduct much of their collaboration – this time, as in 1969 – at long distance: bulky letters, expensive nightly phone calls. "It is amazing that after all this time it is still like osmosis between us," Coursodon remarks. "Almost ninety-nine percent of the time we agree." And when they disagree (Coursodon loves *One-Eyed Jacks*, Tavernier has reservations), the enthusiast pens the entry, while the other appends a modest demurral.

The French title *50 Ans...* is somewhat arbitrary, meaning that Tavernier and Coursodon take as their starting point the Hollywood of 1940, its films, and those filmmakers who were active at the time; but the authors range back over the filmmakers' previous work, and also scrutinize those who have arisen since 1940. The critical essays are all the more provocative in that they reflect a rethinking of some of their creed – shadings of opinions – taking into account everything Tavernier and Coursodon have learned and discovered since *Thirty Years of the American Cinema*.

As they worked on the present edition, it grew to monster size. Yet the double-volume of hardcovers – 1,200-plus pages – was an instant, surprising success in France. The first printing, nearly seven thousand copies, sold out, and the book has gone into a second press run. The leading daily paper, *Le Monde*, hailed it as "both an indispensable reference work and a very personal approach to half a century of American cinema," while the highbrow *Positif* called it "better than a reference book, than a film buff's bible: an absolute model of critical literature."

Dave Kehr of the *Chicago Tribune*, one of the multi-lingual few in the U.S. who have managed to read the two volumes (mostly) through, says, "It's the kind of exploratory criticism – like Andrew Sarris's *The American Cinema*, or Richard Corliss's *Talking Pictures* – that recharges your passion for the medium. It shows you pathways and makes you want to run right down them. At a time when American movies seem almost played out artistically, Coursodon and Tavernier remind us of how creatively rich Hollywood once was, and how it could be again."

French film criticism has long exerted an influence on American film criticism, and to say the least there has been much cross-fertilization and debate across the waters. Unfortunately, it will be some time before an English translation of *50 Ans...* is ready and U.S. publication details are worked out – before, in short, French-language-challenged Americans can read Tavernier and Coursodon's book. Meanwhile, Tavernier – taking time out from editing a new feature film and completing a documentary that explores the role of French soldiers during the Algerian war for independence – agreed to talk about the book that demonstrates his ongoing love affair with the American cinema.

—◦—

What led you to undertake such a massive revision of earlier editions of your book?

For a long time, now and then, we were approached to do another edition, adding just a few pages more. One day the proposition looked serious, and we started thinking about doing a slightly bigger book – but not much bigger. If we had known that it would become *that* book, we never would have agreed to do another edition.

How long did the work take you?

Three years. We decided there were three ways to proceed: Either we were going to keep the original text, in some cases, providing we saw nothing to change. Or we were going to keep the text of the '69 edition and comment on it – saying we had been right or wrong [in our initial critiques]. Or we were going to start from scratch in some cases, especially about many directors whom, in 1969, we knew very little – Borzage, Leisen, Curtiz, etc.

Plus, we decided that directors like Lang, Hawks, Hitchcock or Chaplin – who are much covered elsewhere – did not need overly long essays; it was sometimes easier to condense what we were thinking about them, than in the case of some directors where you have to study less the ensemble of work than a series of films that are all different. Let's say, for instance, Sidney Lumet – he practically needs to be discussed film by film; whereas with Fritz Lang or Chaplin, it's possible to see their work thematically.

We decided – and it was a fatal decision in terms of the amount of work – to see all the important films again and all the films recently rediscovered: for example, in Chaplin's case, the films unearthed by Kevin Brownlow in [the documentary series] *The Unknown Chaplin.*

The first option, in the end, was nearly always rejected – because we always found new things to write about. Sometimes our original perspective had been right, but even so, the essays, which were very short in the first edition – one or two pages – grew to twenty thirty, forty pages. Slowly we got carried away by ourselves.

We wrote it in the same way as we did the first one: Jean-Pierre was in New York and I was in Paris. The meant several hundred letters, practically a long phone call every night. It was a labor of love. I didn't take any money to write it, and I left the advance from the publisher to Jean-Pierre, who needed it more.

This summer [1991] in Paris we talked about certain directors who had risen in your estimation in the intervening years since the 1969 edition, while others had fallen or been diminished. Who is the American director who perhaps rose the highest in your pantheon?

First, I must say it feels strange to comment on a book of opinions and essays. It is like commenting on one's own commentary. But there are certain people whom we more or less condemned, too quickly or wrongly.

Like Robert Aldrich. We said that his career was coming to a dead end, and I think that was a mistake. We were not the only ones; everybody in the world was writing that. Aldrich always had that certain moment where people thought he had lost everything, and he was always rising again like a phoenix. Just after we finished the '69 edition, Aldrich did some of his best work – at least one of his best films, which is *Ulzana's Raid* [in 1972], a stunning Western. And I think we were wrong in saying *The Dirty Dozen* was the antithesis of, let's say, *Attack!* In reappraising him, I think Aldrich never betrayed his political ideas and positions. Sometimes his direction weakens the original ambition, makes the films look ambiguous; but on the whole he is one of the few directors who never changed politically. Just look at the complete version of [his 1977 film] *Twilight's Last Gleaming.* I myself wrote most of the text about Aldrich – and the words that came to mind when I was writing about him were "forcefulness" and "consistency."

That was one case. I cannot say which man climbed the highest. One would be Jacques Tourneur...

Why?

His direction, his style, consists of a very mysterious mixing between a very elaborate lighting and a soundtrack different from the average American film. Tourneur was always making the actors speak very low, in a subdued way, which you can only appreciate in good prints, and not in a dubbed version. Some of the films we wrote about in the '69 edition we saw in bad prints, sometimes dubbed, which always hurt the films, and in the case of directors like Tourneur, totally destroyed the films. You need to see Tourneur's work, especially, in good prints.

Then you have the case of someone like Gregory La Cava. Some of his films were real discoveries... especially in the Thirties. The same with Michael Curtiz. And William Wellman: *Heroes for Sale, Wild Boys of the Road, Other*

Men's Women… real discoveries. When we wrote about Wellman the first time, we were primarily looking at his films of the Forties.

On the other hand, there were films we praised too much, like [the 1954 Don Weis film] *The Adventures of Hajji Baba*, which was a cult film in France. We became a little more dubious about it. Or there were directors we praised a lot, like Tay Garnett. Later on, we saw most of his films – some are good – but when we had seen only a few of them, the totality of the work seemed [as if it must be] more interesting than it is; judging by *Her Man* or *One Way Passage*, you might think you would find the same values in thirty or forty other Tay Garnett films, but that's not the case. The same could be said of [Frank] Tashlin, George Sidney, or the last films directed by Jerry Lewis or Hitchcock, which were overrated in France.

Sometimes we overrated part of the work of a director because we did not know the other part. When we wrote that the best work of Allan Dwan were those films he made with producer Benedict Bogeaus, his last films, it is not true. Some are quite remarkable, and I still like them very much – *Silver Lode* and *Tennessee's Partner*. But when you see some of the films Dwan did in the silent days, with Gloria Swanson, they are even more interesting. I could name a lot of directors like that… whose best period was sometimes unknown, even to us.

Take Douglas Sirk. This time around we had more reservations about some of the big melodramas that people love now – *Written on the Wind, Imitation of Life*. Especially so compared to certain films of John Stahl. In the new book, now that Sirk is a director very much admired by everybody, we expressed reservations about, for instance, the treatment of the black characters in *Imitation of Life* – especially as compared to Stahl's [1934] version. Stahl was better. Stahl was, in a way, more modern and less paternalistic. (Jean-Pierre wrote most of that essay.) And we had fresh reservations about Dorothy Malone [in *Written on the Wind*]… she's not very good… you cannot call that acting.

At the same time, we were laudatory about a [1946] film of Sirk's like *A Scandal in Paris,* which is completely unknown and is a small masterpiece. The direction is as brilliant; but for one thing, the screenplay, by Ellis St. Joseph, is better; the dialogue is terrific; the black-and-white photography is by [Eugen] Schüfftan; the acting – George Sanders in particular – is better; and the cynical aspect of the film makes it something more original.

Some of those melodramas of Sirk's are not only very well made but very personal. Yet when you see the work he did with students in Germany [in the Seventies], three little films – Fassbinder acts in one of them – based on material by Schnitzler and Tennessee Williams… these films are absolutely wonderful. And you wonder if Sirk had been given better material than Fannie Hurst, or a better actor than Rock Hudson, maybe he would have done better films. There are certain films that are good in spite of the material,

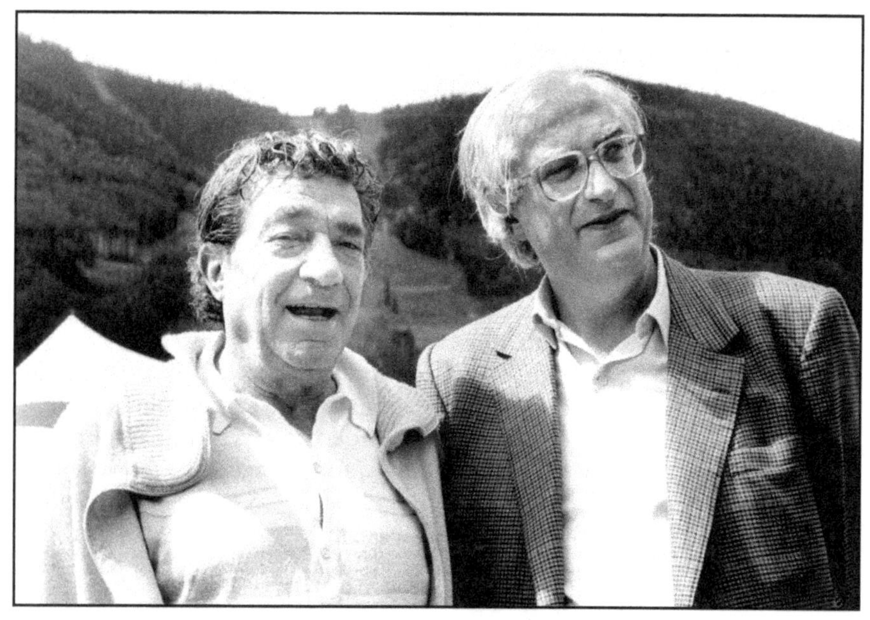

Blacklisted American director John Berry, who acts in the cast
of *'Round Midnight*, with Bertrand Tavernier at the
Telluride Film Festival in 1990.

the actors, the kind of film it is, the studio... Then you have certain other films, like *A Scandal in Paris* or *There's Always Tomorrow*, that are simply good.

Were there other people like Robert Aldrich whom you were unfair to, in the earlier editions?

We were very unfair to the directors who had been the target of the French critics of the Fifties, [critics] who, in order to promote Hawks, Hitchcock, Fuller, and Anthony Mann, violently attacked some directors respected by the Hollywood establishment and the American critics.

Already in the '69 edition we were more open-minded, but still very unfair to somebody like Fred Zinnemann. It took us a while to discover a film like [his 1949 film] *Act of Violence*, and *The Men* [made in 1950] is quite an interesting film. Making some of the films Zinnemann made at a certain time was very, very brave. Becoming a director myself, I began to appreciate more the difficulty of some films. Even if the result is imperfect, the fact that certain films are made implies such energy and real courage.

About Mitchell Leisen we were too severe. I remember the [Leisen] essay in the '69 edition was not too long, because we had only seen three or four of his films. Jean-Pierre, in the intervening twenty years, has seen practically all of his films. So his essay on Mitchell Leisen turned out to be very long. The same for Frank Borzage, Curtiz, Wellman, and others.

[Still], we did not change our minds on a lot of directors. On the contrary, we reaffirmed our views on people like Anthony Mann, Delmer Daves, Billy Wilder...

Did meeting the filmmakers, interviewing them, sometimes help you in revising your opinions of their work?

Yes. And not only meeting the people, but reading things too. In America, certainly, a lot of books exist now that did not exist in the Sixties. Suddenly we had a lot of new information – people talking about unknown films and filmmakers. It's true, meeting different directors and screenwriters helped change our minds – but we tried not to, just because we liked somebody personally, always to find their films interesting.

Sometimes you couldn't help it?

Yes. [Laughs]

—◇—

You told me that sometimes you did not like the people, either, and that that reinforced a negative view. My impression is that you detested Howard Hawks...

No, no. I liked him. You felt that he was forceful, a real auteur, someone who controlled all his films. What I did not like was his politics. By meeting and talking with Hawks, I understood why I liked his comedies so much, and other films like *To Have and Have Not* and *The Big Sleep*, but I could also see very well why certain ideological things in his films did not please me. Because Hawks was very conservative, very right-wing. He wanted to make a film about Vietnam, and he told us he wanted to take some of the scenes deleted from *Sergeant York* and put them into his Vietnam film. That was frightening. It's good for him that he never made that film.

Do your political preferences lead you overboard in certain directions – in terms of praise, or condemnation?

We try very much not to be led by our politics. Someone very right-wing can make a wonderful film. But, for instance, in [Hawks's 1959 film] *Rio Bravo*, I can't help feeling the Mexicans are caricatured and treated in a way I don't like. Someone who was not a left-wing director – Henry Hathaway – treated them better in [his 1954 film] *Garden of Evil*, more respectfully. Not to mention a beautiful Western like [the 1959 film] *The Wonderful Country* by Robert Parrish. We try to study films in terms of content, so we have to deal with politics, but we try not to repeat the mistakes of certain French critics who condemned certain films just for political reasons.

At the beginning of your career as a film critic, you were perhaps less considerate...

Yes, but I was always fighting with *Positif*, which condemned [Sam] Fuller. They were calling his films fascist, which they were not. I saw that as completely mad. I think a lot of political labels put on some directors were very European [labels] and had nothing to do with the real content of the movies. In France a lot of films were labeled progressive just because they were pro-Indian. John Wayne became pro-Indian, suddenly, in [the 1953 John Farrow film] *Hondo*...

The politics of the American cinema is not just a matter of left and right as defined by a European point of view. What we say in the book is that you can distinguish between a liberal director (or writer) by his attitude towards certain notions, certain myths, which are very important in Hollywood films: Nature, Individualism, the Group, Civilization... In the basic American ideology, the first two are usually very positive and redeeming, with Biblical implications of a Lost Paradise. On the other hand, the Group and Civilization contain elements of threat, danger, and corruption – of mobs, lynching posses, urban decay, the mad scientist, corrupt newspapermen. You can even link Nature and Individualism with the West, the other two with the East, and come up with an interesting ideological map of the American cinema. You would discover that *Taxi Driver* and Murnau's *Sunrise* have much the same content, as do *Apocalypse Now* and much of [D.W.] Griffith. Add to that the American attitude toward the intellectual – [Intellectuals] are, most of the time, a real threat – and The Other (another race, another country)...

In a film like *The Purple Plain* by Robert Parrish – which I saw again a few days ago – the attitude toward the Burmese culture is so respectful; the people are dealt with such respect, not only not making fun, but never patronizing. Politics is not only whether a film is pro-war or anti-war, but something that is more deeply felt. If you draw the lines this way, you can see that [John] Ford is not a reactionary director, as Georges Sadoul, a French Communist historian, said so often. For Ford is a director obsessed by collectivity and by group, and not by the hero, the individual, against the rest of the world.

⸺◦⸺

I remember that this summer you also compared meeting Hawks to Raoul Walsh, and that you also compared Hawks's films to Walsh's, saying that in your view Walsh had risen in stature, and that there was much yet to be discovered in his body of his work. You surprised me by saying that Walsh may be the superior director.

I don't like to state that. Jean-Pierre and I tried not to construct a hierarchy. I can say Walsh is a *wider* director; his interests were wide, and he had moments when he could do a nearly metaphysical Western like *Pursued*, that Hawks would never have dared to deal with. On the other hand, Walsh was never able to do anything as controlled as *To Have and Have Not* and some of Hawks's comedies. Hawks is a great director, but narrow; he always did the same three or four films. There are people who have a narrow vision of the world, and Hawks is one. You don't *feel* the world in a Hawks film. You don't *feel* the world as you do in a Walsh film. Hawks was limited. He understood a certain type of person, a type of hero, a type of action – not *job*, *action*. From this range, he made masterpieces. Sometimes he was a genius.

But Walsh did some daring things – very, very early. Walsh is handicapped by his legend. When I met him, I discovered he was much more literate than people think he was. People put him down as a very good action and man's director. It's much more than that. Walsh was sometimes able to experiment. Certain films of his, like *The Regeneration* from 1915, are stunning. It's a film ten, fifteen years ahead of its time. It anticipates Stroheim. Martin Scorsese told me when he saw it that if he was shooting in the Bowery he would not change one shot of that film.

When they would give Walsh something to experiment with, he was immediately ready. Walsh was at ease with the sets, which were very avant-garde, of William Cameron Menzies in [his 1924 film] *The Thief of Baghdad*. He could do *The Big Trail* [in 1930] in 70mm. He made an interesting habit of the diagonal – a geometric figure he used a lot – in the framing, in the camera movement, in the way people moved through the space. We wrote a great deal in the book about that, his filmic texture and pacing, which we compare to Count Basie or Max Roach.

I also insist that Walsh is a woman's director. Most of the time the actresses are terrific in his films; even the intermediate actresses, like Virginia Mayo, who is absolutely stunning in [Walsh's 1949 film] *White Heat*; and when he was working with Ida Lupino, Olivia de Havilland, or Anna Nilsson, the results were flamboyant and expressed a vision that was truly romantic.

—o—

Becoming a director, you mentioned, has somewhat altered your perspective as a critic. Do you find that, in the elapsed time since the 1969 edition, you have become more or less tolerant as a critic?

More tolerant for certain things – like real ambition and the difficulty of setting up certain kinds of productions. You suddenly appreciate the struggle it must have been for certain directors to keep their integrity, sometimes. To protect their work.

And less tolerant of certain things. For instance, as young film buffs we were very enamored of people like Dorothy Malone or Rhonda Fleming, that kind of actress. The bad acting of certain films I became less tolerant of. I became less tolerant of the portrayal of minorities [in many films]. In a way, it's a function of growing older as well as becoming a film director – I became more irritated at the way [other] races were portrayed. Really angry sometimes.

As a director, I grew to admire someone like [John] Huston very much, especially during the last part of his career. At a moment when practically every director past a certain age was repeating himself, doing exactly what they had been doing – sometimes better, much of the time worse… I mean Hawks with *El Dorado* and *Rio Lobo*, even Hitchcock… in Huston's case you have somebody whose last fifteen years included some of his best films, maybe. At least his most audacious projects: *Wise Blood, Fat City, The Man Who Would Be King, The Dead,* even *Under the Volcano*. It's an incredible body of work. Huston's a unique case in the history of the cinema. To end up your career with *The Dead*! Huston was more daring at the end of his life than when he was starting.

When it came to certain directors, I was, for some time, too much under the influence of people like [François] Truffaut. The worst thing for a critic is a lack of a real curiosity and following the general fashion. We did not investigate enough – ten, twenty years ago – about some directors.

For instance, we let somebody like Anatole Litvak die without ever meeting him – and he lived in Paris! Litvak is somebody whose films I've since discovered from the Thirties and Forties, as well as his documentaries for [Frank] Capra. Litvak made the best of the *Why We Fight* series. But in the Sixties, Truffaut, in order to boost [the 1958 Otto Preminger film] *Bonjour Tristesse*, which he loved, knocked other directors who had adapted François

Sagan. One of them was Litvak [who adapted Sagan's novel into *Goodbye Again* in 1961]. And stupidly, we followed Truffaut. Because Litvak's last films were bad, we refused to investigate his career. And his career had started in Russia; then he went to Germany and France, where he made masterpieces in the Thirties like [his 1932 film] *Coeur de Lilas* – which contain scenes and a use of sound as imaginative as Renoir – as well as interesting films like *L'Equipage* [from 1935], which seems to me less dated than [Howard Hawks's 1930 film] *The Dawn Patrol*. So the lack of not being open – being prejudiced – is the worst thing. Film history has suffered a lot from that.

In Huston's case, it's true, I was a little like Truffaut – aloof about Huston. I admired some of his films, but I remember being aloof about *Red Badge of Courage* and some others. When I see *Red Badge of Courage* today, I realize it was not an easy film to do. There are shots in it that now, I say to myself, "My God, I wish I could do that!"

Is there an irreconcilable gap between a film critic like you and one who has never been a filmmaker?

Sometimes the critics are a little bluffed by superficial things, which they think are difficult, and they don't see the really difficult things, which are sometimes the most obvious. There is not a gap, but maybe I wouldn't make the mistake, like some critics who, when speaking of the style of [Robert] Bresson, say he never moved the camera. It makes me laugh. Bresson moves the camera *all the time* – you just don't notice it, because he moves with the characters; you have at least thirty or forty tracking shots in a Bresson film, which is a lot for someone whom a lot of critics describe as a kind of French Ozu. You see a lot of technical mistakes like that from critics, technical mistakes that are also mistakes of reading the films.

Even as a film buff, I hated clans – *chapelles* – a group of critics thinking all the same. Neither Jean-Pierre nor I belonged to any group. And now it is even more infuriating to see young French critics repeat the opinions of Truffaut, Rivette, and Godard, without taking into consideration the discoveries made since that time – the books, the essays, published in America, England, Italy. Since I became a director I have become even less tolerant of that way of thinking.

Very few directors have made the transition from being a film critic. Truffaut did, and he became more tolerant. You can see it clearly in his book about Hitchcock – that he used his experience as a director in his questioning.

Do you mean that sometimes a critic is beguiled by the superficial, but doesn't understand the real obstacles facing the filmmaker?

Yes – but I mean a lot of other things too. As a young critic, I could often identify the responsibility for the visual look of a film, and whether it was much more the cameraman than the director, for example. Don't ask me how! It was instinctual. I could see that a director's style would completely change with another cameraman, while other critics were praising the work of the director. In our '69 edition, we often specified that the visual talent came from the cameraman. Then, later on, we met the actor, writer, or director involved, and found out that what we had written was true. It is important to identify in a film, who or what is the *driving force*.

Not only the cameraman, but the scriptwriter, often.

Already, in the first edition, I think we were the first in the world to have a dictionary of screenwriters. *Film Comment* was second and quoted us very often at that time. Frequently we spoke of the writer when we wrote about certain directors, although we made mistakes at that time, even in that category. We overrated certain people; we underrated some.

For example, we were more lucid on the subject of Philip Yordan than [our colleagues were] – because we said it seemed that Yordan had not written a great number of "his" screenplays. And I wonder why, in '69, we included essays on Jo Eisinger, Martin Rackin, Daniel B. Ullman, Gerald Drayson Adams, or John Twist – which have been taken out of the new edition. We overrated people like Clair Huffaker {whatever happened to him?) and even Burt Kennedy. At the time we said Kennedy was one of the most brilliant screenwriters; he is gifted, but I think now I would tone down the adjectives.

So you try to strike a balance in your discussion of a director's oeuvre – incorporating the contributions of cameramen and writers?

In even our longest essays about directors, we always make a point of citing the writers and what part they played, and so on. In our text about Raoul Walsh, we mention the parts played by certain screenwriters in his career; one of the weaknesses of Walsh is that he used and trusted somebody like [writer] John Twist too much. I don't know why Walsh used Twist on his last two films, when he could have employed better screenwriters. In fact, I do know – it's because John Twist loved to womanize with him... But Twist's writing weakens some of Walsh's films, from *Colorado Territory* [in 1949] to *A Distant Trumpet* [his last film in 1964].

When we talked to Henry Hathaway, he said the screenwriters he preferred working with, whom he found the most talented, were Grover Jones and Wendell Mayes. We tried to mention, therefore, in our essay on Hathaway, what these people brought to his films; or what Ben Hecht brought to the films he worked on for Hathaway. We even mention that the last act of [Hathaway's 1947 film] *Kiss of Death* was rewritten by Philip Yordan – it was Hathaway who told us that – which has never been mentioned elsewhere, even in your book *Backstory*.*

In the U.S., Henry King and Hathaway are given a certain amount of respect, but it seems that in reappraising them you have more than respect – quite a bit of admiration for them.

Yes. I found that sometimes they were very interesting, and sometimes

---

* Philip Yordan is interviewed in *Backstory 2: Interviews with Screenwriters of the 1940s and 1950s* by Patrick McGilligan (University of California Press, 1997).

on a level that people have very rarely spoken about. The fact that *A Fable* by William Faulkner is dedicated to Hathaway is a sign of something. Hathaway told me in an interview that he really tried to originate only two properties in his life: One was *A Fable*, which he asked Faulkner to write as a screenplay – the idea of the coming of Christ during the First World War. Faulkner wrote it as a novel and sent it to Hathaway, ten years later. The second project was a remake of *Of Human Bondage* with Montgomery Clift and Marilyn Monroe – which was, in the early Fifties, just after *Niagara*, a brilliant idea. And in *Niagara*, which is a beautiful film, Hathaway wanted to cast James Mason instead of Joseph Cotten. The association of Mason and Monroe is so modern and interesting that it makes Hathaway much more than just a good craftsman – it gives him a sharpness, a flair, that has never been studied.

Henry King worked a lot more on his screenplays than is generally known. In the Scarecrow Press book about King [*Henry King, Director: From Silents to Scope* by David Shepherd, Ted Perry, and Frank Thompson, Scarecrow, 1996], Gregory Peck says that the last draft of [the 1949 film] *Twelve O'Clock High* was completely written by Henry King – all alone. And Peck also says that for *The Bravados* [in 1958], King changed two things: He made the man whom Peck was chasing innocent of the rape. That was not the idea of the screenplay; it's a beautiful change. Peck said the change was for religious reasons – King hated the ideas of someone seeking vengeance, so he made him guilty by the very idea of revenge. And then King thought of the twist at the end where the Peck character goes to confession, because King was a truly religious man. King made those two changes because of his moral values. They completely altered the film. One of the ideas was a little heavy and sentimental, but one of them was superb – making *The Bravados* one of the rare films where the hero is wrong throughout the film.

Does a director rate higher for you if he could also write?

There are two types of directors who write: The directors who write their own screenplays – [Joseph L.] Mankiewicz, Delmer Daves, many people – *are* writers. And sometimes they are writers on the screenplays where they are not [credited as writer]. Delmer Daves told me he wrote a lot of things on [his 1945 film] *Pride of the Marines*, for instance.

The second type greatly influences the writer, in different ways. It's not as though these directors are actually writing, but they give a kind of direction. That's Hitchcock, Hawks, Lubitsch… It's *nearly* like writing.

Then you have the director who does not write but whose style will change certain things, and whose style, therefore, becomes almost like writing.

When you are watching American movies, what do you regret missing out on the most – in the translation? Not strictly the language, but in the cultural aspects.

It's difficult sometimes. I think we miss less now because we are more used to things and have read a lot. We lose things in the dialogue, of course. Things that we once thought were good lines, we now realize were very used, sometimes very tired, jokes. Maybe we lose certain colloquialisms – although on some subjects we seem to know more than the people making the films… for example, about jazz, or certain facts in Westerns, or films taking place in the South. I have an impression that I could be more accurate in terms of Southern behavior and accents than they were in [the 1960 Vincente Minnelli film] *Home from the Hill* or [the 1958 Martin Ritt film] *The Long Hot Summer.*

How about… just cultural subtleties?

I miss them. Although in some ways I think somebody in Milwaukee is as far away from Hollywood and the people making films there, as a Frenchman. [Laughs] The Americans created a lot of genres that had codes that could be read immediately by everybody in the world – at least, the important things. Sometimes we broke the codes before most Americans. The Western, for example, was being written about seriously in Italy, England, and France before the U.S.

You always miss things. You miss things most of all in the most literate films – an adaptation of a well-known book when some screenwriter had a good sense of colloquial dialogue.

Why is it that American critics took Hollywood pictures so much for granted for so long? There was a dearth of serious appraisal. I know from the book I just finished about George Cukor that Cukor was revered by the French in his lifetime, but was apoplectic about being ignored by film festivals in his own country. In the Sixties he had to hire a publicist to promote his name…

I think the Americans were late. I don't know why. The serious criticism started in England and even in France.

Even your book of interviews with screenwriters comes so late – look how little information there is about the Thirties, how much is lost! Because, in America, Hollywood was entertainment; it was not to be taken seriously.

But some of the filmmakers were taking films seriously. Somebody like [W.S.] Van Dyke was writing theoretical articles, in '34, '35, and a book about the making of *Trader Horn* [*Horning into Africa*, 1931]. A cameraman, John Alton, was writing what might be the first book by a cameraman, *Painting with Light* [Macmillan, 1949].

This is a subject I wondered about when I wrote my essay about Robert Florey in the book. I studied a [1936] film of Florey's called *The Preview Murder Mystery.* The film is full of flaws, but sometimes brilliant and visually, sometimes extremely brilliant. Why, I ask in my article, did a man like Florey, doing that little B film at Paramount, why was he shooting a scene with a cop questioning a subject, with a circular tracking shot, the people all in shadows, except for a few moments when there is a lamp in the middle of everything that gives off flashes of light according to the camera movement? It's a shot that is complicated, very expressionistic. The public that would see that film on a double bill would never notice. Practically no serious critic – *Variety*, yes – was even mentioning the B film. Why was Florey doing that? Was it to prove something to himself?

Was Florey an artist?

I don't know if you could use that word. Let's say he had moments where he was inventive, inspired, and moments when he thought he was an artist, but he was not, because the ideas were ludicrous. I don't think he was very lucid or sharp about the elements of a screenplay; the ones he wrote are incredibly uneven, with some very bright ideas, as in the case of [his 1936 film] *Hollywood Boulevard*. Florey had a love of show business and movies. Sometimes he had good and bad things in the same movie. But it's an interesting question: What pushes somebody, who will not even be noticed by the critic of the *New York Times*, to do that?

⎯⎯◦⎯⎯

According to your opinion, which was the best studio in the Golden Age?

Warners and RKO, I think. I cannot say they were the best, but they made the films I prefer. For comedies, Paramount was also prestigious – because of Ernst Lubitsch and Billy Wilder. But Warners had so many good films… and you have the impression that you can still discover hidden treasures [from that studio], especially in the Thirties. RKO – because there were a lot of very good screenwriters there. The studios without stars were the best sometimes, for me, because they had to compensate with other good actors and screenwriters.

Do you take producers into account in your book?

Of course, although we did not have enough information to do a separate dictionary of producers. But when, for example, we write about Warner Bros., we talk about the parts played by Hal Wallis, Jerry Wald, and – somebody that everybody seemed to respect and find creative – Henry Blanke.

Who were the great producers at RKO?

I would say, of course, Pandro Berman and Dore Schary. Maybe Adrian Scott. Certainly Val Lewton, one of the most creative producers. But it was mostly a studio full of very interesting writers – the ones who worked with Robert Wise and Val Lewton, and a lot of the left-wing writers.

You are so busy these days, making films yourself. Do you still find time to indulge yourself as a critic and buff?

Just before calling you, I was trying to watch again a film I once enjoyed for the camera movements: *Rome Adventure*, [a 1962 film] by Delmer Daves. But if I were revising my opinion, I'd say I found the acting – not only Troy Donahue, but Suzanne Pleshette and Rossano Brazzi – unwatchable. Bad acting is something I have become less tolerant of, as I said. I couldn't finish watching it.

I just received a laserdisc of *The Searchers*, and watched the beginning of it, this evening, too. The disc is in widescreen. I read the notes, which they say matched the widescreen from the original VistaVision negative. It looks very beautiful, but it's *wide*screen – like a CinemaScope shape. In our book you'll find many things like this coming from me, which are really directorial questions. In the video version, *The Searchers* looks like a 1.85 ratio [i.e., 1:1:85]; now, in laserdisc, it's more like CinemaScope. I remember seeing the original film in VistaVision. What would be the proper ratio? They cannot put VistaVision on laserdisc, but the VistaVision negative is really closeup CinemaScope. This proves the film we are seeing is not the true film.

In the case of Fritz Lang, I ask in what ratio exactly were his last two American films shot – *While the City Sleeps* [from 1956] and *Beyond a Reasonable Doubt* [also 1956]? I myself have seen them in 1.33, 1.85, and even in SuperScope. I know that Lang was a tyrant with the framing of a film. So I would love to have that question investigated. What is the original shape, the frame, Lang used for those films? The real one. Because SuperScope was sometimes a process done in the lab.

The same is true of *The Incredible Shrinking Man* [a Jack Arnold film made in 1957] and other films done at Universal [in the Fifties] – Sirk's *Sign of the Pagan*, for example, which I have seen in 1.33 and CinemaScope. Sirk said that sometimes he was doing two versions at the same time, but there must have been one that had his preference, and there must be one that was better lit than the other. It's very interesting to ask that kind of question.

What American films have you seen most often, most regularly?

I think *The Searchers* – maybe twenty-five times. Most of John Ford. *The Grapes of Wrath*. At one point, *The Hanging Tree* [a 1959 Delmer Daves film] and *Moonfleet* [Lang, 1955], some Billy Wilder and Ernst Lubitsch comedies. Even Blake Edwards. I used to watch *One, Two, Three* [Wilder, 1961] and *The Party* [Edwards, 1968] once a year.

Incidentally, *One, Two, Three* was a very good political commentary, and a film incredibly in advance of its time about the destruction of Communism. Incredibly accurate. The same with *Ninotchka* [Ernst Lubitsch's 1939 film]. The scene where they go to the station to find the comrade: they go up to a man thinking it must be him; the man turns and salutes – he is a fascist! And *Ninotchka* was finished, I think, one month before the Hitler-Stalin pact! It proves that Billy Wilder and Ernst Lubitsch were always right historically and politically. [Laughs]

Did you have any personal disappointments, re-seeing favorite films?

I saw a film that I had last seen when I was eleven years old: *Gung Ho!* [Ray Enright, 1941], a war film with Randolph Scott. I was horrified, because it was a most jingoistic film, with racist depictions of the Japanese. I remember loving it when I was a boy.

On the other hand, I re-saw a film I'd seen when I was fourteen – *Wake of the Red Witch* [Edward Ludwig, 1948]. I still love it. I adore that film. Here is a director I would like to know more about: Edward Ludwig, a quite mysterious and interesting director. I said to myself, "Oh, I was right to see it three times when I was fourteen!" I have seen it three times since.

If you do another edition of your book – ten, twenty years hence – who are your subjects for further research, whose films have eluded you until now?

They would be people in the Thirties – screenwriters and directors. And silent films, of course. I would love to see certain silent Walsh films, because Ford told me that one of the films that impressed him most was *The Honor System* [a Walsh film from 1917]. And I heard – though I was not there – that at the Italian film festival devoted to silent movies [in Pordenone], the great discovery was not only the silent films of Cecil B. DeMille, which people now know are great, but the films of his brother William. A few people told me these films are absolutely stunning, and nobody has ever written about them.

There are many, many people whom we do not know enough about and did not include much about in the book. There are now some directors practically all of whose films we have seen; but with even those directors I have one, two, or three films I have yet to see that look promising or interesting or were, at some point, well received. That goes from John Ford to Gregory La Cava to… Stuart Heisler: It took me a long time to catch up with Heisler's [1940 film] *The Biscuit Eater*, and Martin Scorsese just wrote me that he's sending me a video of *Journey into Light* [Heisler's 1951 film], with Sterling Hayden, because he thinks the film's terrific…

The task seems almost infinite.

It is infinite. I think we are just starting the story of the cinema. A lot of territory still has to be explored…

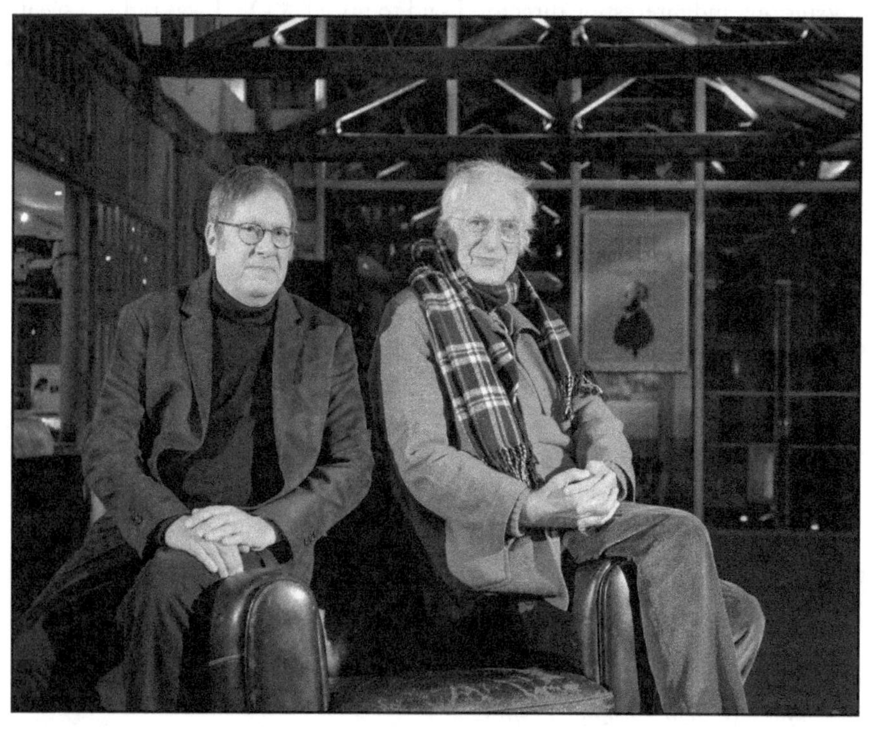

Patrick McGilligan and Bertrand Tavernier
at the Institut Lumière (Hangar du Premier-Film) in 2018
(photograph by J.L. Mège).

Bertrand Tavernier on the French Cinema

2020
Interview by Patrick McGilligan

For lovers and admirers of Bertrand Tavernier's *My Journey Through French Cinema*, made in 2016, the good news is that there is a sequel: an eight-part, three-and-a-half-hour series called *Journeys Through French Cinema*, which was lauded when first broadcast on French television in 2017, and is now available, as a DVD, in the U.S. through the Cohen Media Group.

This new documentary is, like *My Journey Through French Cinema*, comprised of rare archival interviews mixed with meticulously selected highlights from favorite films, while Tavernier, speaking directly to the camera, takes Francophiles on a personal tour of the films and directors he has discovered and rediscovered in his life's journey as not only an auteur par excellence, but also as a film historian whose experience, knowledge, observations, and convincing passions are second to none.

—o—

Do I detect, in this wonderful new series, a retrospective apologia to some extent for what the Positif *and* Cahiers du Cinéma *critics – and perhaps yourself in the past – wrote about certain French filmmakers in the Fifties and Sixties, appraisals that long tarnished some reputations? How and why you have changed your views about some of the filmmakers you now celebrate?*

In the first two episodes I speak mainly of Jean Grémillon, Max Ophüls and Henri Decoin. A retrospective apologia? Not at all. Very early, I discovered *Douce* (1943), *La vérité sur Bébé Donge* (1952), *La traversée de Paris* (1956) and *Le corbeau* (1943), and loved those films. During the same period, I supported *Breathless* (1960), *The 400 Blows* (1959), *Les Mistons* (1957), and saw *Hiroshima mon amour* (1959) six times. With a few friends, it seemed possible to enjoy the films of both Jean-Luc Godard and Claude Autant-Lara *and* Henri-Georges Clouzot. Supporting the New Wave did not mean we had to excommunicate the directors belonging to a previous generation, people like Grémillon and Julien Duvivier. We were at the Cinémathèque for the first retrospective dedicated to Duvivier and discovered *Allo Berlin? Ici Paris!* (1932), a very ebullient comedy. I wanted to avoid any references to the critical wars, sometimes very dated, between those two clans.

Both *Positif* and *Cahiers* were sometimes right, but often wrong, and because of their disagreements they misunderstood many films as well. *Cahiers* missed Grémillon and René Clément; *Positif*, Robert Bresson and Sacha Guitry; and both missed Decoin, Anatole Litvak, Maurice

Tourneur, Raymond Bernard and Edmond T. Gréville. I wanted to start from scratch, from my memories, from the emotions I felt when I first discovered some of those films – especially *Douce, Casque d'Or* (1952), *Pattes blanches* (1949), *Les croix de bois* (1932), *Coeur de lilas* (1932) and Gréville's *Remous* (1935) – or rediscovered others, such as *Le corbeau* (1943). Sometimes, it is true, I was re-evaluating and reacting against a previous trend in critical thinking. This is true of my enthusiasm for *Le corbeau* or *Forbidden Games* (1955); those films, when I saw them again, did not correspond with their prior reputation. I made quite a few mistakes when I was under the influence of one of those clans, never meeting Litvak, André Cayatte, or Charles Spaak.

So I decided to refer only to what was for me still fresh, true, and good in, for instance, the opinions of François Truffaut when he was fighting for Guitry, Marcel Pagnol and Jacques Becker. By the way, Truffaut was always more inspired, sharper, and more accurate when he was writing about the directors he loved – Lubitsch or Hitchcock – than when writing about the directors he despised – Ford, Huston, or British cinema. He pilloried Michael Powell, David Lean, Carol Reed, Alberto Cavalcanti and Alexander Mackendrick, even going so far as to say that the British cinema did not "exist." As I say in my series, however, Truffaut allowed me to understand the real importance of Guitry and Pagnol, how sometimes they were ahead of their time.

The French critics mostly saw them as playwrights who were only preoccupied with filming their own plays (*théâtre filmé*), forgetting that Pagnol was one of the first directors who decided to shoot virtually an entire film on location, building farms and sometimes using an abandoned village as a setting. He also recorded the sound on location. Guitry, who was an important playwright – the French Noël Coward – nevertheless was the only person who, by a stroke of genius, decided to take a camera with him to film the artists he loved – Auguste Renoir, Rodin, Saint-Saëns, Monet – in 1914. He, who was constantly attacked for only documenting his own plays – a false statement because he wrote original screenplays that are among his best work, among them *Bonne chance!* (1935) and *La poison* (1951) – was the only director to have this kind of revolutionary vision. He was the only director who evoked the Occupation in a melodrama, *Donne-moi tes yeux* (1943). There is an allusion [in that film] to the black market and more openly to the blackout in the streets, showing only people's feet illuminated by a flashlight. It predates the New Wave. Nobody in America, England or later on in France was as open-minded.

I show, in this series, that those two geniuses confronted some very serious themes. One easily relegates Pagnol, for example, to the atmosphere of the cycle of films he made with Raimu, which are funny, emotional, and warm. But one forgets many provocative and sometimes dark films like *Jofroi* (1934), *Angèle* (1934) and his splendid version of *Manon des sources* (1952).

What Truffaut said about those two impressive creators was very intelligent and ahead of its time. I loved the clip I found that shows Truffaut talking on the phone about Guitry, in a bizarrely staged conversation – who had this strange idea? … and to whom is he supposed to be talking? …very amusing. On my own I found myself liking some of the films of Pagnol and Guitry, but Truffaut helped me to understand them more deeply.

In My Journey Through French Cinema *you spoke movingly of your interactions with Jean-Pierre Melville, which helped you to form your high opinion of his career. I wonder if you ever met Henri Decoin, about whom in this series you reveal biographical traits that helped you to appreciate his body of work. When you met with these directors personally, got to know them, how did it help you to understand their films?*

Melville and Claude Sautet were my two godfathers in the cinema. Jean-Pierre helped me in many ways. Not so much in my tastes. I disagreed often with his opinions. Sometimes I was wrong – he had a tremendous admiration for William Wyler, for instance, and it was only later that I rediscovered this great director – and sometimes I resisted his negative views. He hated *Johnny Guitar* (1954), *Time Without Pity* (1957) and *Moonfleet* (1955), for example, three films I still like. I did learn a lot of things about directing from him, however – how to be economical; how to create an interesting space with just a chair, a table, a lamp, and a curtain; and how to light some shots. But, more importantly, I decided I would never behave like Jean-Pierre with the crew, never humiliate anyone publicly. He was a dictator on the set and a warm human being afterward. Like Henry Hathaway. And knowing him allowed me to understand the reasons behind several of his visual choices. I am a director, and I wanted to talk about those people not with the knowledge of a critic or film historian, but from a director's point of view or sensitivity.

Alas, I never met Decoin, a filmmaker I really began to appreciate more and more in recent decades. His early life was astonishing, with a horrible and very poor childhood (he would swim in the Seine at Christmas to bring back some money for his parents); then he broke several records in swimming, won a few decorations in the trenches during the war [World War I], became a pilot and shot down eleven planes. He never mentioned any of this in an interview.

I kept discovering films he made. His first [in 1934], which he wrote and directed, *Toboggan,* is a superb film whose first ten minutes are autobiographical with a tough depiction of a shantytown. It is a boxing film, not romantic or glamorized. The corruption is shown as if it is something obvious, natural, that you do not have to underline. Decoin had been a sports reporter, and everything in this film looks authentic. I rediscovered one masterpiece, *Non coupable* (1947), as well as fascinating details or ideas even in his more commercial films. In *La chatte* (1958) – a kind of pre-*Army of Shadows* – Decoin asked his composer, Joseph Kosma, to avoid any kind of melody and to substitute strange, abstract sounds. He was also the only director who worked with the greatest avant-garde composer, Pierre Henry, on *Maléfices* (1962), and twice with Henri Dutilleux, one of the greatest composers of the twentieth century. Decoin was a real rediscovery for me, above all his *Retour à l'aube* (1938), which starts as a traditional comedy, becomes a bittersweet romance, and ends as a rough, stark film noir.

I also felt closer and closer to Duvivier as I watched more of his films. I should have tried to meet him too, and the same is true of Litvak, who made a string of fascinating and challenging films in the Thirties. Decoin was very often a feminist director, and so was Autant-Lara, the only French filmmaker who had the courage to make two moving and very militant films – *Le Journal d'une femme en blanc* (1965) and *Une femme en blanc se révolte* (1966) – both of which strongly defended the right to abortion, which was in those years a crime. Those two films are priceless and stand up very well. Autant-Lara was also very feminist in all the films written by Jean Aurenche and made during the war, including *Le mariage de Chiffon* (1942) and *Douce*, and in his adaptation of Simenon, *En cas de malheur* (1958).

Meeting some directors – including Melville, Sautet, Jean Renoir, Claude Chabrol, Éric Rohmer, Godard, Agnès Varda, Pierre Schoendoerffer, Pierre Granier-Deferre, and screenwriters like Aurenche, Jacques Prévert, Pascal Jardin, Pierre Bost and the widow of Henri Jeanson – certainly helped me to understand them and gave me some rare insights. Sometimes, with Jean Delannoy, for example, it did not help. But alas, for many directors, I had to investigate their careers without meeting them, to try to understand why I was touched by some scenes, and what elements made their films so indispensable. I am thinking especially of films directed by Max Ophüls, Grémillon, Duvivier and Becker – all of whom I did not meet.

I was incredibly moved by what the screenwriter Charles Spaak [*La grande illusion, Panique, La fin du jour, La belle équipe, Le ciel est à vous*] said of Grémillon. I had thought Spaak was a cold and cynical writer, but instead I discovered somebody who was moving, emotional, and deeply articulate. I totally re-evaluated Spaak after seeing so many of his films. He wrote a great number of superb screenplays for underrated directors, including Albert Valentin on *L'Entraîneuse* (1938) and *La terre qui meurt de vallée* (1936). Recently I saw again the incredible body of work he did with the underrated André Cayatte – *Justice est faite* (1950), *Nous sommes tous des assassins* (1952), *Avant le déluge* (1954), *Le dossier noir* (1955) – the last a tough, challenging depiction of France after the Liberation. These films deal powerfully with anti-Semitism, the corruption of justice and of the police, and directly attacked capital punishment at a time when more than fifty-eight per cent of the public defended the guillotine. Contrary to many American films, Cayatte and Spaak attacked the death penalty through characters who were guilty, sometimes of horrible crimes, such as killing a baby who cries during the night, or strangling a young girl. I show only one scene from a Cayatte/ Spaak film in the series, the moment in *Retour à la vie* (1949) – his episode in a portmanteau film – where Bernard Blier tries to convince his aunt to sign a legal document the family forged while she was in a concentration camp. She has just come out of Buchenwald, sleeps on the floor, and does not utter a word during the episode. It is incredibly strong for the period. I think it is the first film to show a real concentration camp victim.

Just as My Journey Through French Cinema *sang the praises of several rugged male icons of the past, including Jean Gabin, it seems in this series you are rediscovering less celebrated figures, too often demeaned as light entertainers, such as Maurice Chevalier and Danielle Darrieux. Chevalier, it seems, almost became a caricature of himself in Hollywood films. Darrieux had only limited exposure in America. Which French films of theirs should cinephiles seek out to appreciate their artistry?*

I dedicated a special section to Jean Gabin because he was one of my favorite actors and performed in many masterpieces, and not only before the war. His postwar period, with *Touchez pas au grisbi* (1954), *La traversée de Paris, En cas de Malheur, La vérité sur Bébé Donge* (1952), *La nuit est mon royaume* (1951), *Le Chat* (1971), *Des gens sans importance* (1956) and *Le président* (1961), was neglected. Gabin was always not just good, he was great, never playing or singing a wrong note, just like Charlie Parker or Bing Crosby. Yet, just as important, he was really instrumental in the production of those films: he bought the rights with Duvivier to *La Bandera* (1935); helped with the production of *La grande illusion*; bought the novel *Gueule d'amour* (1937) and gave it to the producer who hired Grémillon, who made a masterpiece. Gabin co-produced *Le Chat,* a very tough and challenging subject, where he does not play a nice character. He was responsible for helping bring many films to life. No other actor did that, especially before the war.

Gabin before and during the war was brave. Curtis Bernhardt, who directed him in one interesting film before the war, *Le tunnel* (1933), wrote in his memoirs that Gabin protected him in Germany from the Gestapo, which wanted to question and deport him because he was Jewish. Gabin always called the French ambassador or consul, and each time prevented Bernhardt's deportation. And Gabin enlisted, and fought in Italy and France. He never forgave Universal – or the U.S. government – which forced him to buy back his contract in order to free him to fight for his country, and for that reason he refused to return to America even when they wanted to give him the David O. Selznick [Lifetime Achievement] Award [from the Producers Guild of America].

Chevalier was a wonderful actor in all the first Lubitsch musicals and in *Love Me Tonight.* He was funny, charming, very at ease with all the inside jokes, the double entendres, and innuendos that were very provocative for the period. It was in his last American period that he became a kind of caricature of himself. In a few French films, like Robert Siodmak's *Pièges* (1939) – later remade by Sirk – he was fresh and good. That was his best film, along with the marvelous and cynical *Avec le sourire* (1936), directed by Maurice Tourneur.

And Darrieux – who was always superb, deep, challenging, graceful, and moving in *all* her roles, in *all* her films – was as modern as Gabin. But she never originated a single project. She just acted in them. Beautifully. Darrieux has at least fifty great films in her career – all kinds of films, including romantic comedies where she is the ingénue, breezy, sexy, and quick. She sings beautifully in *Un mauvais garçon* (1936), *Battement de coeur* (1940) and *Premier rendez-vous* (1941). She never sang a wrong note, and even in her last period she sang beautifully in Demy's *Les Demoiselles de Rochefort* (1967) – she was the only one who was not dubbed. She performed a beautiful version of Louis Aragon's poem "Il n'y a pas d'amour heureux"– dedicated to my mother* – in *8 Femmes* (2002), and a delicate rendition of a Francis Poulenc composition in one of her records. She was just as organic and truthful in tough dramas; I am thinking, in particular, of the last part of Decoin's *Retour à l'aube*, where she is incredibly impressive. Among her greatest performances are her roles in *La vérité sur Bébé Donge*, Ophüls's *Le Plaisir* (1952), and *The Earrings of Madame de…* (1953) – which is her masterpiece – Duvivier's *Pot Bouille* (1957), *Battement de coeur*, *Occupe-toi d'Amélie!* (1949) and *Le rouge et le noir* (1954), this last in spite of the pedestrian direction.

I was particularly fascinated by the episode about music in the films, learning that so many French filmmakers wrote lyrics and were sophisticated composers of songs in their own films. This was totally new to me, and a revelation. Why do you think this was true in France at that time? Is it as true today? Why is it not at all the case with American directors? It is almost unheard of in Hollywood.

I explained in *My Journey Through French Cinema* that the relationships between directors and composers were totally different in France and in the United States. Many French composers had written serious music before writing for the cinema, among them Saint-Saëns, Jacques Ibert, Arthur Honegger, Maurice Jaubert and Georges Auric. In America in the Thirties, the studio hired mostly arrangers and orchestrators of European musicals, in the case of Max Steiner – Strauss, Lehár – or Broadway hits for Adolph Deutsch. The studios were panicked by the fact that some composers could be "intellectual"– this is explained in a very good book, *The Composer in Hollywood* by Christopher Palmer [Marion Boyars, 1990]. For instance,

* See "Confluences, Tavernier, Aragon and others" by Bruno Thénenon, *Le Progrés* (July 10, 2013). Aragon and his wife, the writer and translator Elsa Triolet, were sheltered in Lyon by Tavernier's parents – his father, the poet, journalist and literary critic René Tavernier and his mother Geneviève – during the German Occupation, from 1941-43. Aragon dedicated his famous poem to Tavernier's mother.

before *King Kong*, Steiner had never written an original piece of music. The American studios always assigned orchestrators to control the composers, especially to watch over someone like Franz Waxman, who was the most educated and ambitious of the Hollywood composers.

In France, the great directors – [René] Clair, Renoir, Duvivier, Jean Vigo, Litvak – chose their composers. There was a real friendship between Clair and Jaubert, and with George Van Parys; between Duvivier and Jaubert; Jacques Ibert and Jean Wiener; Renoir and Kosma; Vigo and Jaubert; Cocteau and Auric; Sacha Guitry and Adolphe Borchard, and Luigy; Pagnol and Arthur Honneger. There are many letters between those musicians and directors. Something I say in this series that had never been said before is that many of the French directors boasted a real musical sophistication and collaborated with the composers by writing lyrics for the songs and even, sometimes, the music for the entire film.

Grémillon co-wrote the waltz for *Quatorze Juillet* (1933). Grémillon was a very good composer, and in the series there are clips from *Le 6 juin à l'aube* (1946) and *André Masson et les quatre éléments* (1958), for which he wrote the score. Duvivier wrote the lyrics for many songs in his films. For filmmakers to write good lyrics, you must understand rhythm and syncopation. René Clair worked on all the songs in all his films, as did Guitry, Carlo Rim, and the underrated Jean Boyer before the war, who wrote marvelous songs, many of which were hits. Decoin was often fascinating in his choice of composers and in his relationship with them; he is the only director who twice picked Henri Dutilleux, the greatest composer of the time. Jacques Becker and Pierre Chenal loved jazz – Chenal dating from the Thirties – and the same was true of Grémillon, which you can see in the clips from *Daïnah la métisse* (1932).

In the United States the composer, at least until the mid-Fifties, was most often imposed by the studio or the producer. There are a few notable exceptions, not often analyzed or commented upon. Lewis Milestone hired Aaron Copland three times, I think; Wyler did the same thing once; Ford took a lot of time to talk to Steiner for *The Informer* (1935) – not always for the best, since Steiner's music is sometimes tedious. Most of the composers, however, spoke only with the heads of the music departments who, very often, were intelligent and educated. Elmer Bernstein said that in the Fifties the only directors he met and spoke with for a long time before composing their scores were Otto Preminger and Cecil B. DeMille, and both were precise and intelligent about what they wanted in terms of music. Very few American directors before John Carpenter could write music. Victor Schertzinger wrote the music for several Lubitsch films and a few songs before becoming a director; Allan Dwan wrote new lyrics for folk songs; and Richard Quine wrote a number of songs – one can hear one of them in the [1958] Western *Gunman's Walk*.

The more I investigated the subject, the more I found that music was a good way to understand the world and the mind of a director, a good key to entering into his world. This insight is almost always neglected by film historians. It was fascinating to discover how Decoin or Duvivier worked with their composers. Duvivier, who wanted to make a musical drama out of *Casque d'or* in the Sixties, very quickly spotted Lalo Schifrin, who had written only one French film up to that time, and asked Schifrin to work on the score. We recently found two of those compositions. There were similar important collaborations between Vigo and Jaubert, Godard and Georges Delerue or Antoine Duhamel, and Jacques Demy and Michel Legrand. I always say that the composer is the first critic of the film. The music he writes is an emotional response to the power of the images, of the direction, of the way the story has been visually translated.

You discuss in the series how some French filmmakers – Clair, Renoir, and others – came back from World War II exile in Hollywood and were treated poorly in France; they were seen as professionally "defeated," I think the subtitle says. Would you say something about how some French filmmakers adjusted in Hollywood, doing either well or badly, and why it varied among the individuals? Who fit in the best, or was shrewdest? And how were their careers affected or revived upon returning to their native land?

Clair and Duvivier, who came back first, were accused of having deserted their country. Both had Jewish wives. Duvivier had turned down, as Gabin did, the generous proposals of the Vichy government for films he should make. Those postwar attacks were violent, unfair, shameful, and led by people who were not among the real *résistants*. It hurt Duvivier a great deal. That explains the violence, the pessimism, the bitterness of *Panique* (1946), one of his masterpieces, where an innocent man is lynched just because he does not seem to behave properly; or the lyrical anger of *Au royaume des cieux* (1949). I would have loved to have shown clips from this great film, but it had not been restored, where a bunch of young girls guilty of crimes are exploited by the woman at the head of a reform school – I think you can find a subtitled print in America through Don Malcolm's Midcentury Productions – or, for contrast, the cheerful invention of *La fête à Henriette* and [*The Little World of*] *Don Camillo*, his rare optimistic films.

Duvivier was deeply unhappy in Hollywood – "Duvivier's emmerde" [i.e., bored stiff] is what he wrote in a letter. He did learn how to be less tyrannical on the set, which the American crews did not like. There are a few good episodes in [the 1942 film] *Tales of Manhattan* – the first is brilliantly directed – but there is another with Paul Robeson that is rather shameful. *Flesh and Fantasy* (1943) is sometimes inspired and beautiful, but Universal cut the first episode – one of the best, which they put into a Reginald LeBorg B flick without crediting Duvivier – changed the order of the stories and added a few jokes. Duvivier was very bitter, as Ellis St. Joseph, who worked on the screenplay, told me. Duvivier sleepwalks in *The Impostor* [aka *Strange*

Confession] (1944). But Duvivier came back to France with several hits and his work became more inspired than ever. He directed his darkest masterpiece in 1952 or '53, *Voici le temps des assassins…* (1956), aka *Deadlier Than the Male*. Then, with the exception of *Pot Bouille* (1957), and the well-crafted *Marie-Octobre* (1959), he did become more erratic.

Ophüls also came back later because of the commercial failure of his last films in America, which are among the best directed by a foreign filmmaker. Ophüls was more at ease with the studios after the disaster of *Vendetta* (1950) – he was fired by Howard Hughes after a few days, then replaced successively by Preston Sturges, Mel Ferrer, Stuart Heisler, and, ultimately, Hughes himself. I have not recently seen *The Exile* (1947), but I love *Caught* (1948), shot very quickly and economically, out of anger against Hughes; *Letter from an Unknown Woman* (1948) is a masterpiece; and *The Reckless Moment* (1949) transforms a soap opera, a melodrama, into a rather tough examination of American familial values. Ophüls got along very well with John Houseman and Walter Wanger and came back to France only because his last film had been a real commercial failure. But his first French film, *La Ronde* (1950), was a hit.

Renoir came back a few years after the war, and everyone but Gabin had forgotten his shameful behavior in 1940, which I discuss in *My Journey Through French Cinema*. You must read the wonderful biography written by Pascal Mérigeau, which has been translated into English [*Jean Renoir: A Biography*, Running Press, 2017]. It destroys a lot of clichés about Renoir and corrects a lot of mistakes. In Hollywood, Renoir did not speak English very well and his relationship was not great with Zanuck. And even Dudley Nichols, one of his best friends, became a kind of dictator on that bad film with Charles Laughton, *This Land Is Mine* (1943), forbidding Renoir the use of a crane, and refusing to make cuts in the dialogue. His best American films are a few good scenes in *The Southerner* – which also has a very bad performance by Beulah Bondi – and the second half of *Diary of a Chambermaid*. After Hollywood, Renoir was acclaimed for [the 1951 film] *The River* (which was transformed in the editing room by him and Ellis St. Joseph), and in France for *French Cancan* (1954), his biggest hit, but he was not entirely successful in readapting to France. Some of his films were overpraised by the New Wave, which had reevaluated *La chienne* (1941) and *Boudu [Saved from Drowning]* (1932) and are rather bad, except for *Le caporal épinglé* (1962). *Elena et les hommes* (1956) is a disaster and now looks ten times more dated than Clair's *Les grandes manoeuvres* (1955).

As for the New Wave's attacks on the French cinema's "tradition of quality," when you went back to rewatch so many of those films, did you feel was there any validity to those critical attacks? Can you describe how they*

---

* A highly polemical article in the January 1954 issue of *Cahiers du cinéma*, "Une certaine tendance du cinéma français" ("On a Certain Tendency of French Cinema"), written by the 21-year-old critic François Truffaut, attacked many of France's leading screenwriters and directors and generated a major controversy at the time.

hurt or damaged filmmakers you knew?

In the series, I deliberately avoided those questions. Talking about them is the best way to avoid a real analytical approach to the films and to the contributions of the directors and writers. I also avoided mentioning the term "New Wave" because such labels become more important than the work. Talking about New Wave filmmakers as a group prevents you from examining the huge differences between the directors. Can you tell me what are the artistic, literary, political, and visual values shared by Jean-Luc Godard and Eric Rohmer? They have nothing in common, beginning with their placement of the camera. Or Chabrol and Truffaut? Jacques Rivette and Godard? Their sensibilities, their styles, the emotions they try to capture, are totally different, even diametrically opposed. There are more links among the British directors like Karel Reisz, Lindsay Anderson, and Tony Richardson, or among the Americans like Scorsese, Paul Schrader, William Friedkin, John Milius and Francis Coppola. Rather quickly, in fact, Truffaut and Godard came to hate one another.

So instead, I to try to analyze what moved me so deeply in their films, including their innovations, such as the way Godard used music and space in *Pierrot le Fou* (1965). Putting different artists into the same box is the best way to be blind and dogmatic. It is the same with "poetic realism," which is where the critics have assigned Duvivier, Marcel Carné, Renoir and Grémillon. They were different in so many ways – visually, politically, and emotionally. The label "French Quality" was sometimes relevant. It described films that were well-crafted, well-photographed, and well-acted in a rather anonymous, studio-bound style. It describes well some MGM directors like Jack Conway, Richard Thorpe. They were films in which you did not feel the personality, the voice, or the feelings of the director. This label was stuck on the work of a lot of different directors sharing, at least at first sight, a classical style, sometimes rightly – half of the films by Delannoy, most of the late films of Carné – but often dogmatically and stupidly.

For instance, Autant-Lara is a very classical director, and his historical films in color are stiff and conventional, not like his first ones in black and white. But you always recognize his convictions – pacifist, anti-Establishment, against religion and the oppression of women – his anger and his voice. You feel his presence in many scenes. He is the only director to have made a film about conscientious objectors during the Algerian War. Alas, he was forced by French censors to shoot it in Yugoslavia, and it hurt the film. The same can be said for a more inspired director like Clouzot, who is now totally rehabilitated. I know that, among others, Decoin and Clément suffered from these kinds of attacks, especially Clément, who directed *La Bataille du rail* (1946) on location with non-professional actors and also filmed, on location in Italy, *Au-delà des grilles* (1949) – the only film shot with live sound in Italy during this period. Clément experimented in many of his films, shooting *Monsieur Ripois* (1954) in the streets of London with a hidden camera long before the New Wave. For some obscure reason, Truffaut hated Clément and refused to see how bold and challenging *Forbidden Games* or *Les Maudits* (1947) were. Many years afterward, when he discovered *Le Jour et l'heure* (1943) on television, he wanted to write a letter to Clement to praise that film and to apologize.

The reality is always more complex. The critics who claim they are disciples of the New Wave always forget that Truffaut praised two films by Autant-Lara – *La traversée de Paris* and *En cas de Malheur* (1948) (Autant-Lara stubbornly refused to believe it). He put two or three stars on *Douce*, and wrote that *Voici le temps des assassins…* was a real masterpiece – he and Duvivier wrote to each other – and Truffaut also praised *Pot Bouille*. As I say in my film, Chabrol also admired Duvivier; the openings of his films were always imaginative and innovative. Yes, those attacks hurt many people. Before *The Clockmaker* (1974), nobody wanted to hire Aurenche or Bost, two incredibly talented screenwriters. I myself was accused of fighting the New Wave, one of the dumbest statements ever. If you want to criticize the New Wave, you write an article; you do not make a film that will take two years of your life. I had actually fought for many New Wave directors, including Chabrol, Godard, Varda, and Demy.

I just wanted to work with Aurenche and Bost after looking at their films and discovering that their dialogue, their political and social ideas, their style, were fresh, biting, and impeccable. I wanted to know the people who wrote, in *Douce*, made in 1942-43, the line spoken by the Countess to a very poor woman, "I wish you patience and resignation"– two words used by Pétain in all his speeches – to which a farmer responds, "You should have wished impatience and revolt!"

The series restores reputations and celebrates neglected filmmakers. After re-seeing many films, were there filmmakers – perhaps without mentioning specific names – for whom your earlier, youthful enthusiasm no longer seemed as deserving?

I decided to forget those films. I am not a prosecutor. I did not want to say that after the beautiful *French Cancan*, the films of Renoir went downhill, because I am so grateful for *La règle du jeu* (1939), *La chienne* and *La grande illusion* (1937).

Would you say something about the great French scenarists who weave through My Journey Through French Cinema *and now this series, people such as Charles Spaak, whom it seems you appraise differently now, after getting to know more about him and re-seeing his films, than when you were a younger cinephile? When someone like Spaak writes for different directors, what does he bring of himself to disparate French filmmakers? Or did they come to him to tap his distinct qualities?*

Many French scenarists played important roles over the decades.

Somebody like Henri Jeanson, especially in his last films, could sometimes overpower the director, but not the talented and tough ones like Duvivier. Writers like Jeanson were successful and powerful, and the New Wave, which wanted to impose the preeminence of the director, liked to put them down – sometimes rightly, but most of the time, not. Some of those French scenarists were not only writing or co-writing screenplays. One forgets they also worked on the casting. They knew actors very well. Jacques Prévert did the entire casting of all the films he made with Carné, with whom he fought over *Les portes de la nuit* in 1946. After Gabin, influenced by [Marlene] Dietrich, abandoned the project, Prévert had the inspiring and luminous idea to cast the young Simone Signoret in the lead role. Carné, who wanted to assert his independence, refused this brilliant suggestion, and chose instead a very bad actress who ruined the film. Aurenche cast Jacques Tati in Autant-Lara's *Sylvie et le fantôme* (1946); and supported Gabin and Bourvil against Autant-Lara, who wanted to hire [Yves] Montand, a bad choice, and Bernard Blier for *La traversée de Paris*. Pierre Laroche supervised the casting of all of Jacqueline Audry's pictures.

Many of those scenarists were fascinating people. Jeanson was a talented journalist, pacifist, and anarchist who wrote for *Tribune socialiste* and the satirical weekly *Le Canard enchaîné*, writing political articles and films reviews – sometimes of his own films, which he castigated. He defended Tunisian peasants against the French colonial system, and supported the young Polish Jew, Herschel Grynszpan, who had killed a Nazi official, Ernst vom Rath, in 1938. Like Ben Hecht, Jeanson fought all his life against anti-Semitism, supported the Republican side in the Spanish Civil War, and was twice condemned to many years of prison – before the war for anticolonialism, pacifism, and supporting the killer of the Nazi; and during the war for writing that "Nothing is more shameful than an anti-Semite." Some French journalists denounced him to the Germans.

He was one of the rare people in the French cinema, along with Jacques Prévert, who signed the manifesto in 1933 against Hitler and defended Clouzot against the Communists and the Catholics during the Liberation. Until his death, Jeanson remained a pacifist and was against the death penalty; he was an anticommunist, very witty – he said to a painter, André Derain, a collaborationist who usually was very dirty but was wearing a nice suit to go to the German Embassy – "So, Derain, the spot's inside?" – and sharp. His best screenplays are *Pépé le Moko* (1937), [the 1938 film] *Hôtel du Nord* (with Jean Aurenche), *La fête à Henriette* (1952), *Au royaume des cieux* (1949), *Le garçon sauvage* (1951), *Un revenant* (1946) and *Les amoureux sont seuls au monde* (1948).

My admiration for Jeanson grew a lot, especially with regard to his courage. He was sometimes difficult to work with, writing pages and pages of dialogue. Duvivier was constantly cutting, recutting, and rewriting him;

they quarreled and split up many times, but then they would go back to being best friends. Pierre Bost was another fascinating person, a wonderful novelist who wrote the novella *A Sunday in the Country*. We discovered many talented writers during our research.

But my real discovery was Charles Spaak because he wrote a tremendous number of great screenplays, a lot of them totally underrated, among them *La terre qui meurt* (1936) and *L'Entraîneuse* (1939), a very feminist melodrama with Michèle Morgan, who was very convincing as a brunette. As I said earlier, I was mistaken in thinking he was cold and cynical and discovered he was a warm, emotional person when speaking about Grémillon. That changed my point of view. Later on, I rediscovered the great, challenging films he made with André Cayatte: *Nous sommes tous des assassins,* which takes a stand against the death penalty at a time when fifty-eight percent of the French public was in favor of it; *Avant le déluge* (1954), against anti-Semitism; and *Le dossier noir* (1955) and *Justice est faite,* (1950) about the inequities of the legal system. All those films explore with a real inventiveness a variety of social classes – the bourgeois, workers, and peasants – and deal with a tremendous number of characters, who make the films very lively. They offer a challenging portrait of France after the war.

Spaak was also hated by Truffaut, who tried to ignore the fact that Spaak had co-written *La grande illusion,* choosing to believe Renoir, who pretended to have improvised many scenes, which in fact were in the version co-written by Spaak. I regret never having met him. Spaak is one of the characters in my film *Safe Conduct* (2002), the one who writes a Maigret screenplay while in jail. I discovered in my research that he transformed a crooked Jewish banker [from Simenon's novel] into a crooked French banker [in his screenplay] – a very simple act of resistance that moved me tremendously. This was for him so self-evident that he does not mention it in his memoirs.

As an example of the many neglected filmmakers that you highlight in the series, would you talk a little about Jacqueline Audry and her importance as a pioneering female director at a time when there were so few female filmmakers in France? First, did you ever meet her? What kind of obstacles did she face in her career? Her films are not well known in the United States. For example, not a single Criterion title is available of any of her films.

Alas, no, I never met her, just her husband Pierre Laroche, a talented screenwriter who worked twice with Jacques Prévert, on *Les visiteurs du soir* (1942), a very stodgy film for me, and the often moving *Lumière d'été* (1943), well-directed by Grémillon. Laroche was an anarchist and pacifist, a rather left-wing person. When I met him, we talked only about the films of Georges Lautner that he had just written. Jacqueline Audry was not at all a fashionable director in those years; she was under constant attack by the New Wave. I must say her last pictures – including an adaptation of Sartre's *Huis Clos* (1954) – were misfires, but at the time I was unduly influenced by Truffaut and his friends. A few years later, I discovered some of her earlier films, which were not easy to see. Audry was not trendy at all, even if some of her titles were highly praised by a good critic and friend of mine, Jacques Lourcelles, who was instrumental in the rehabilitation of many directors. I found some of them to be funny, daring, and sexually provocative, especially *Olivia* (1951), which now has been restored. It is quite a beautiful film with an Ophülsian atmosphere – great sets and costumes – and it deals, without being exploitative or voyeuristic, with a lesbian relationship. It is the frankest French film on this subject, and very well-acted.

Some of Audry's pictures were great successes, but she really had to fight to impose herself on them, most of the time working without big budgets. I find her warm and touching, especially in the clip in my film where she says, with great simplicity, "If I had been a man, I would have directed many more films, at least eight or nine more." She has been rehabilitated now, and a book, alas not a very good one, has been written about her. Most of her films are owned by René Chateau, who put them out on DVD when nobody was interested, but who did not restore them or work from new prints. The only ones that have been restored are *Olivia* and one of her first, *Les Malheurs de Sophie* (1946), a feminist adaptation of a very famous children's novel written by la Comtesse de Ségur.

Would you talk a bit about the archival footage that is so important to the series, how you found it and the difficulties involved? I am thinking not only of the Charles Spaak interview that is used several times but also the television panel show that interviewed actors and actresses, and which was obviously of a high intellectual quality, asking serious questions about filmmakers and films. Such a television show seems emblematic of the gulf between the way the cinema is treated in French culture and how it is treated in American culture. No television show like that could survive here. It would never claim a big enough audience.

During the Fifties, Sixties, and Seventies, there were a few shows on public television – only one channel for many decades – dedicated to the movies. They were produced by people like Armand Panigel, François Chalais, and Claude-Jean Philippe. Some of them were badly edited, and sometimes the interviews – such as those with [Cecil B.] DeMille and [Billy] Wilder – were superficial, but you could also find many wonderful moments, such as the interviews with Charles Spaak, a real discovery; another with Duvivier by Chalais, the only interview with this director; and another with Henri Jeanson. You could also find Truffaut speaking about Jacques Becker, Guitry, or Pagnol; Panigel talking about Clouzot; or Chalais interviewing Alain Delon. Wonderful stuff. Panigel's outtakes must contain treasures, but the footage must be restored digitally and that is expensive.

There was also a very demanding show called *Cinéastes de notre temps*, produced by André Labarthe and Jeanine Bazin, with each episode devoted to one director – Fuller, Ford, Godard, Ophüls, Renoir. In later decades, there was a great show called *Cinéma, Cinémas*, which was mostly about American films with rare interviews with Budd Boetticher, Richard Brooks and Sam Fuller, most of them done by Philippe Garnier. On Canal+, they had *Le cinéma club*, created by Jean Ollé-Laprune, who collaborated with me on *My Journey Through French Cinema*. On that show they talked about films shown on that channel, each time inviting as guests a director, screenwriter, actor, or actress. I found treasures there.

Alas, in this new century, most of those shows – as well as shows about jazz and classical music – were cancelled by the new presidents of the public services. Ignorance became quickly contagious. All this was done for commercial reasons, forgetting that many of those shows, despite all predictions, were successful in their time.

I see the series as a visual correlative akin to Andrew Sarris's The American Cinema, *while concentrating mainly on your enthusiasms and not dwelling on negative examples. Anyway, is the series finished now? Do you have any more documentary excursions into the French cinema planned? I had a feeling you might sometime in the future delve into the French New Wave and your own successive generations of French filmmakers.*

I was not thinking of Andrew Sarris, but more of Martin Scorsese making his films about the American cinema and Italian directors.[*] I found those films very moving and personal. I loved the fact that a very highly regarded director took all this time to speak of other directors, to fight for them, and to rehabilitate some of them. I loved the fact that in his film about Italian directors he spoke in the first person and did not pretend to be objective. As Victor Hugo wrote, "Il y a dans l'admiration je ne sais quoi de fortifiant qui dignifie et grandit l'intelligence." ["There is in admiration a force I can't describe, which dignifies the intelligence and causes it to grow."]

---

[*] *A Personal Journey with Martin Scorsese Through American Movies* (1995) and *My Voyage to Italy* (1999).

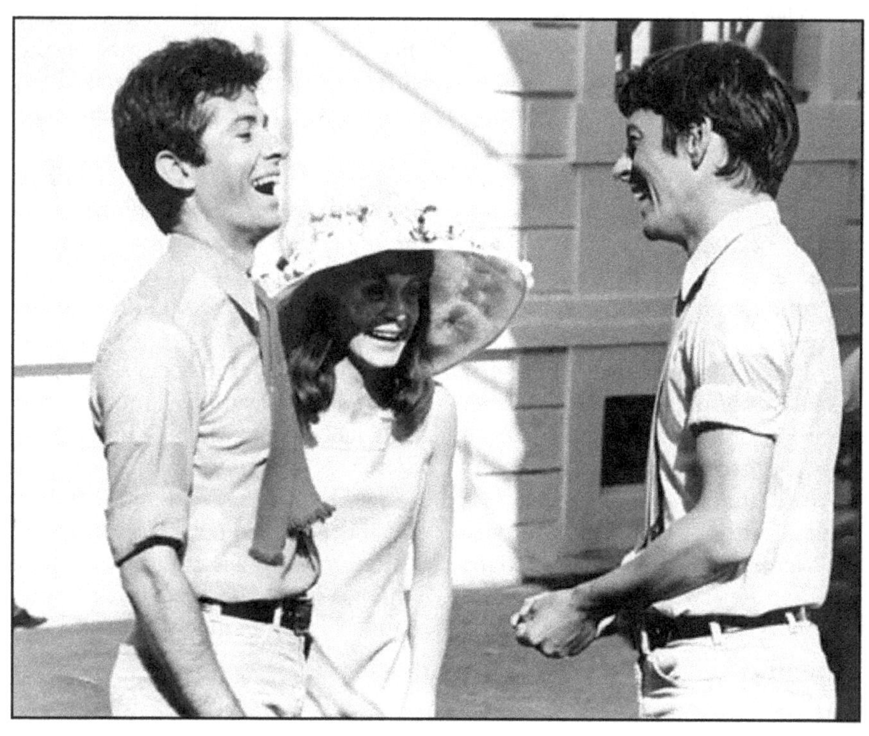

George Chakiris, François Dorléac, and Grover Dale on the
set of *The Young Girls of Rochefort*.

Grover Dale!

2021

Interview by Patrick McGilligan

One day, not long after interviewing George Chakiris for a book I was working on about Woody Allen – believe it or not, they appeared together long ago on the stage of Caesar's Palace in Las Vegas – I watched Jacques Demy's *Les Demoiselles de Rochefort* a.k.a. *The Young Girls of Rochefort* from 1967, which I barely remembered from a previous viewing, and that I wanted to see for Chakiris's performance. My attention was drawn by the other equally handsome American lead, whose magnificent jetés share the screen with Chakiris's. However, Grover Dale does not receive equal billing, due to Chakiris having appeared as Bernardo in the film version of *West Side Story*. On impulse, I contacted Dale, in his late 80s.

The first thing you need to know about Dale is he speaks in exclamation marks! His dance moments in movie musicals are also like exclamation marks. His genius was fleetingly and memorably glimpsed in three pictures in the Sixties, with *The Young Girls of Rochefort* by far his biggest showcase, after which the unmistakably tall, loose-limbed dancer unaccountably disappeared from film. Dale devoted the rest of his career to experimental dance, collaborating closely with Jerome Robbins on various projects, and to choreographing and directing Broadway plays and television shows. He was Tony-nominated twice for directing and choreographing Broadway productions and shared a Best Director Tony with Robbins for *Jerome Robbins' Broadway*. Dale was also Emmy-nominated for choreographing Barry Manilow's 1985 TV special, and for most of the Nineties he served as publisher and editor of *Dance & Fitness* magazine, which evolved into the top-ranked on-line forum Answers4dancers. com. Dale was instrumental in establishing a foundation to champion rights and recognitions for choreographers, including launching the Bob Fosse Awards.

Nowadays Dale is working on his autobiography, which is bound to interest people for his personal life as well as his professional journey and achievements. For much of the Sixties, Dale was involved in a secret marriage without certificate to actor Anthony Perkins of *Psycho* fame. After separating from Perkins in 1973, Dale married the actress, singer, and dancer Anita Morris, who played many screen roles and was Tony-nominated on Broadway for Best Featured Actress in *Nine*. Dale and Morris fathered a son – James Badge Dale, who is also an accomplished actor – and the two remained wed until her untimely death in 1994.

My interview with Dale focused on his involvement in the enduring *The Young Girls of Rochefort* directed by Demy, the French poet of musicals, whose death from AIDS came too soon at age 59 in 1990.

—◦—

How did you get connected with The Young Girls of Rochefort?

I was on Cape Cod when it happened. Harvesting clams. This was during my secret long-term relationship with Tony [Anthony] Perkins, and we were about to spend a whole month there together, finally away from the prying eyes of the media and public. I was so excited; I was planning a welcome-home feast to celebrate Tony's arrival that night.

I was in the cottage's driveway when the phone rang. Hoping it was him, I raced inside to grab it. But it wasn't Tony. It was Eric Shepard, my agent.

The first thing he asked was if I had a passport. Of course I did. But I was about to spend a month on Cape Cod, gosh darn it! I wasn't going anywhere. So, I laughed him off, saying the passport was in New York.

"Too bad," he responded, "because a passport is the only thing that's going to get you to London where you've been invited to co-star in a French musical with Gene Kelly."

Gene Kelly! Gene Kelly was my idol. This sounded too good to be true.

Apparently, a lead actor had dropped out at the last minute and the director needed an immediate replacement. The musical was *The Young Girls of Rochefort* and the director, of course, was Jacques Demy. As Eric continued to lay out the details of my performing alongside Catherine Deneuve, Françoise Dorléac, Jacques Perrin, and George Chakiris, I was flabbergasted.

"How did Demy pick me?" I asked.

Turned out, [long-time MGM composer and producer] Roger Edens had screened *The Unsinkable Molly Brown* for him, and before it was even over, Demy requested "the dancer in the red socks"– no audition, interview, or screen test necessary.

Sight unseen, I'd landed a dream job.

However, it would mean boarding a flight to London that evening – and forfeiting my long-awaited alone-time with Tony. Sigh. But this was an opportunity I couldn't pass on. Tony certainly wouldn't, Eric reminded me. And Eric was right. When I called Tony, it turned out he was also about to bail on our stay to do his own film [Claude Chabrol's *Ten Days Wonder*]. It would work out perfectly, he assured me, because his shoot was less than a hundred miles from Rochefort.

What did Demy see [in The Unsinkable Molly Brown*] that made him want you?*

You can see for yourself in this clip on YouTube: https://www.youtube.com/watch?v=kH6nWfDEdqY

My part in *Molly Brown* – which I also secured with no audition (and again, I was in shock!!) – was as Debbie Reynold's character's brother Jam.

There was a freedom and abandon in my dancing that Demy probably caught. After all, I was dancing as if my life depended on it – and it kind of did. Going back to Demy's "guy in the red socks" comment, while filming *Molly Brown* I walked on set one day wearing red socks. Debbie Reynolds demanded an explanation – which, as lead actor, she had every right to do. I explained that wardrobe hadn't provided any socks, but bare feet in shoes become sticky so I'd provided my own.*

"And they just *happen* to be red?" Debbie remarked.

I offered to change into normal black socks. "But 'Jam' wouldn't wear anything that normal," I argued.

Debbie punched my shoulder playfully. But she didn't let me off the hook just yet.

"You'd better dance your ass off," she said. Otherwise, she promised to personally shove the red socks down my throat!

So, for five straight hours I delivered every move and every step without holding back. That kept me out of trouble and, apparently, impressed Demy. My small-town country-boy look may have also played a role. He wasn't looking for slick and professional. I'm guessing he saw an engaging, goofy, eager quality about it that evoked the innocence needed for *The Young Girls of Rochefort.*

One more funny tidbit: Eric had assured me the *Rochefort* script would be waiting for me on my first-class seat on Air India, to study on the way over. And it *was*. But it was in French! Still, I figured that was a mistake – in London I'd get my English script. But nope. That's when I learned *Rochefort* would be rehearsed, staged, and shot entirely in French.

And how did that go?

On Day One, I fumbled my way through every scene without understanding a single word coming out of anybody's mouth – including my own! The look on Jacques Demy's face was pure panic.

It was clear I'd have to dance my ass off to keep this part too! And thankfully, I did a better job with Norman Maen's choreography than with my French. I *was* assigned a dialect coach, but in the end, they completely dubbed me. I think they dubbed all the Brits and Anglos, except maybe for Gene Kelly, or at least, in his case, not every one of his scenes.

Can you describe your first meeting with Jacques Demy – how he struck you? What you liked about him?

Our first meeting happened when the opening scene of the film – our

---

* The song, "He's My Friend," was added by composer Meredith Willson to extend the score for the film version of *The Unsinkable Molly Brown*. With choreography by Peter Gennaro, the "wildly exuberant" dance number, in the words of A.H. Weiler, writing in *The New York Times*, featured Dale, fellow dancer Gus Trikonis and Debbie Reynolds. Dale is the one in the red socks he wore to the set from his hotel room drawer.

arrival at the river – was being shot. A quick hello – welcome-and-glad-to-see-you. Then he asked how I managed to get there on such short notice. We laughed about the miracles that happen when actors drop out of movie roles! As I described driving fervently back to New York to retrieve my passport, he said that some actors have all the tools needed to pull off a winner. "Now that you got yourself here," he assured me, "let's see what this day delivers!"

From that moment, my impression of Demy was sweet, caring, and reliable. And I was right.

You worked with an amazing cast, which is one of the pleasures of the movie. I want to ask you about some of them. First, George Chakiris. I know you were in the original Broadway cast of West Side Story *(and he was not). But did you know George before* Rochefort?

Before *Rochefort*, I didn't know George directly, but I knew a few things about him. For the London production of *West Side Story*, he was cast as Riff, the leader of the Jets. Months later, [director-choreographer] Jerome Robbins saw the potential for a role change. George might be the perfect Bernardo. By darkening his skin a bit, the casting switch was pulled off. For the movie, George's new role as Bernardo was celebrated, as we all know, at Oscar time.

Back at the opening river scene, George arrived and almost immediately initiated a disagreement with Jacques about the "silly" stingy-brimmed hat he was assigned to wear. I stood by silently, wearing my own, even sillier, hat. Hat-wearing was a signature aspect of the film. No compromise was offered. So, what to do?

When the cameras started rolling, I leapt out of our truck to direct it onto the transporter bridge, then I casually removed my hat and tossed it into the cab. Then I held my breath, fearing an explosion. But nothing happened. Demy let me get away with it.

As soon as George exited the truck, he did the same. We remain hatless throughout the film. A year later, when *Rochefort* was released, a *New York Times* critic specifically praised the elegance of my hair while dancing.* Yet more proof that potential blunders can transform into miracles.

George Chakiris was already very well-known and established. I suppose it is for that reason he is billed high above you in the cast, even though your parts are virtually equal. I couldn't stand it when George got pilloried, during all the pro and con that eventuated about the remake of West Side Story, *for not being Puerto Rican enough casting in the original. He's great in* West Side Story *and in* Rochefort *too. So you got to know him a little during the filming…? Tell me about him as a personality and a performer.*

Like Demy, George could be sweet and charming. But he had a few anxieties some of us weren't prepared for.

* Renata Adler, April 12, 1968, *New York Times*: "Some of the best dancing, again, is by Grover Dale, in a minor part; even his hair joins in the general elegance with which he moves."

Outside of the raucous times spent with Catherine, Françoise, and myself, George leaned towards pensive, thoughtful moments. Laughter was often followed by a tendency to nitpick. Complaining about his hat in the opening scene was just the start. Y'never knew when a grumble was going to come out of him. I'll add that, although George never brought it up, I'm sure he was grateful for my solution of discarding our hats.

I'd like to ask the same question about Gene Kelly, whom you have also mentioned as an idol. This is one of his great last dancing roles, a big and good role. How much did you interact with him?

Definitely he was a major idol of mine. Hey, we both discovered tap dancing in the hills of Pennsylvania. That doesn't happen in every neck of the woods.

One day early in the shooting of *Rochefort*, we were filming in the town square and George noticed that Gene was watching us dance. *What?! THE Gene Kelly has his eyes on us?* I couldn't believe it. But there he was, standing next to the camera, talking to Demy. As it turned out, Gene was telling Demy he wanted to stage a dancing scene with George and me. *Oh my god!* In less than an hour, we were strutting next to a legend. The magic moment was interrupted by Demy, though, when he realized the three of us dancing together wouldn't work with the storyline and would ruin the ending, which was already shot. But he managed to keep the new sequence in the movie by replacing George and me with two unnamed dancers.

George and I were crushed. But as I told George – who accused me of being a hopeless romantic – no one can *ever* take away from us the twenty minutes of dancing with Gene Kelly. And I stand by that.

Gene was everything you'd hope your idol to be: laidback, likeable, sweet, ambitious, and smart as a whip. I was too shy to tell him I hailed from Pittsburgh, as he did. On set, he was a class act. He spoke multiple languages and had an easygoing swagger about him. But he wasn't showy or flirtatious. Unfortunately, though, his time in Rochefort was limited due to his upcoming project, *Hello, Dolly!*, which he was about to direct with Barbra Streisand for 20th Century-Fox. So he was usually in a rush. Most of his downtime was spent with Françoise Dorléac, with the exception of group meal gatherings at the local eatery. And even then, he was rushed. But I treasure the time I did get to spend with him.

My heart soared when he offered me a part in *Hello, Dolly!* But even that invitation was rushed! He asked me to play the role of Ambrose in the film [eventually to be played by Tommy Tune]. Wow! What a dream! But I had to say no. Eric Shepard, my agent, couldn't get me out of a contract with Paramount Pictures for *Half a Sixpence*. Gene offered to advise Eric how to deal with Paramount, but I knew it was useless. Eric was afraid of Paramount. Gene's response to that was that I should "get another agent." In the end, I sacrificed Ambrose for my loyalty to Eric, which was a very high price to pay.

Bertrand Tavernier told me that Danielle Darrieux was the only performer allowed to sing her own songs in Rochefort. *True? She is one of France's legendary names. Can you give me any insight into her talent and the way she worked with Demy or yourself in scenes?*

Danielle was a star player. Singing, dancing, or acting, she celebrated every note and line she was given. It didn't matter if it was day one, two, or ten – whenever Danielle Darrieux performed, your eyes and ears were in for a glorious experience. I'm not surprised they decided to dub everyone else's singing…

She was also a team player. She showed up for everyone – stars, extras, bit players, crew members, you name it. It would be fair to say that like everyone else, she embraced the family ambiance that Jacques and his wife, Agnès Varda, established on day one.

Finally, the sisters – Catherine Deneuve and François Dorléac. In the case of the former, still alive, one of the great professionals of French film, still doing admirable work. In the case of the latter, Rochefort *was her penultimate picture. It must have been a joy to watch them so playful in their scenes together. How well did you get to know them?*

Very well. And, yes, they were delightful. Catherine was also everything you'd want in a movie star. Her English was good, and she had a great sense of humor. But she also graciously sat back to give her sister space to shine.

Catherine and I, the two of us, goofed around a lot. On set and at the hotel. Catherine's gorgeous, so men were naturally attracted to her, but knowing about my relationship back then with Tony, she wasn't worried about *me* crossing the line. She was married to David Bailey, a famous English photographer, at the time. I had a precious last moment with Françoise. We were in the hallway, outside her room, when she had an idea: "Why don't you drive back to Paris with me?" But I had to decline. I had a flight to London the next day to start shooting *Half a Sixpence*. The following morning, I loaded my bags into a cab and headed to the airport. Reflecting on the beautiful time I had in Rochefort, I drifted off. Minutes later, I was awakened by a loud, persistent honking. When the crazy car zoomed by, I saw Françoise at the wheel, blowing me a kiss.

My driver shook a fist at her, ranting about people driving too fast.

It was the last time I ever saw her. About a year later, I woke up to the news of Françoise's tragic death – in a car crash. Rushing to the airport, she lost control of her vehicle and hit a signpost. Her car caught on fire and witnesses saw her struggling to get out. But she was unable to open the door. It was a devastating loss for everybody, especially her family. And I never reconnected with Catherine or Demy after that. I wish I could explain why.

Can you talk about how the dances were choreographed and how they were technically performed? In front of huge crowds that were being held back behind the camera? In the actual physical locations? What are the unusual demands of performing your dances in real places rather than a theater?

We had no rehearsal halls. The dances were choreographed on location. And Norman Maen worked in an unusual manner: He wrote out his dances, and we learned them exactly as he envisioned them. No feedback. No experimentation. Just do whatever's written on the darn piece of paper.

Then everything was filmed out in the open, visible to everyone. There were no major barricades that I can recall. I have one photo in my scrapbook that shows one of the local kids watching me, and you can see the curiosity and hunger in that kid's eye. He was right there with us, thinking "film acting" is the way to go. I wonder if he ever went anywhere with it.

Dancing in the streets of Rochefort was the best performing experience I've ever known. Reacting to real sunshine, breezes, cafés and streets was miraculous. My emotions suddenly became as accessible and real as the world around me. I wished I could dance on location forever.

Were the dance chorus entirely French? Or were some also raided from Broadway shows?

Chorus dancers were hired in London, so most were English.

Why didn't you do your own singing? What was the technical process of lip-synching? Were all the songs pre-recorded by others? And while you were singing, were the songs blaring out from a record player?

Songs were pre-recorded in French. On set, we sang out loud, following along with the playback, whether we knew what the words meant or not. We had no idea we'd be dubbed. It may have been decided after the film wrapped, when the results of our crash-course-French-training became evident.

How much contact did you have with the composer Michel Legrand? I'd love to have your word-picture of him.

Unfortunately, I don't have words about Legrand. I don't think we ever met.

You mentioned Agnès Varda. Of course, she too is a legendary figure, married at the time to Demy. Can you expand on her role during the making of this film, how you interacted with her, and how she functioned with Demy?

Agnes supported her husband every step of the way. Together, she and Jacques were the best caretakers I ever worked with. She treated everyone like family, always receptive, kind, and generous. She reminded me of my Grandma Ammon, who was such a major influence during my childhood – which wasn't the happiest. Except that when doling out wisdom, Grandma never sugar-coated anything. Agnes was like my Grandma Ammon except on "sweet pills"!

Agnes, like Jacques, was a modest person, in personality as well as appearance. She was probably quieter than most creative types. Her wardrobe and behavior choices were very simple, for example, similar to her husband's – I don't recall even seeing her wear make-up. And on the set of *Rochefort,* she acted like a spouse rather than a colleague. She was there to support her husband.

How about Demy himself.? How well did you get to know him? How closely did he follow his own script? How planned out was he, and how much was improvised?

Jacques gave off a down-to-earth air of confidence and humility. He was a T-shirt-and-Levi's kind of guy. And not only did he look like a kind, sweet man, he *was* a kind, sweet man. Both he and Agnes were always present, along with their seven-year-old daughter, Rosalie. By nature, they did not come across as aggressive or ambitious. They were like your favorite neighbors in the village where you grew up, quiet and unobtrusive.

Jacques wielded power, but I never knew it. He was like the brother or father I always wished for. In my mind, his hand was always resting on my shoulder. Patting me gently.

He never asked for improvisation, but we felt trusted and free enough to volunteer it anyway. If I went too far (which I did, more than once!), I knew just a glance or two from him would get me back on track. I trusted his every instinct.

One case of "going too far" was after George's and my disappointment over losing our dance with Gene Kelly. Maybe to make it up to us, Jacques had Legrand write us a new number – a duet in the town square café. During its filming, I was so amped up, my head broke through the Plexiglas ceiling! Production had to shut down for hours to fix it. During lunch, Kelly pointed out the lump on my head and joked with Jacques about dancers' energy going through the roof… I think that's actually what inspired Kelly to offer me the role of Ambrose in *Hello, Dolly!*

You are also a showstopper in Half a Sixpence… including "Money to Burn," which folks can watch in this excerpted version on YouTube:
https://www.youtube.com/watch?v=FdL5_df5Iy4

After those three amazing performances in film musicals in a row, all acclaimed at the time, you virtually stop dancing in movies. Why?

The reasons are sort of threefold.

First off, I was just honestly hard on myself. I never thought I had a serious chance in movies.

Secondly, as my agent warned me, the industry was changing. Movie musicals were on the downturn, as they were considered too much of an investment in time and money.

Finally, something happened on the set of *Sixpence* that changed my course.

On movie sets, scene and lighting changes eat up a lot of time. There's

---

* In the film version of *Half a Sixpence*, directed by George Sidney, Dale was recreating the role of Pearce he had originated on Broadway. One highlight is Dale's dancing in the huge, sprawling "Money to Burn" number, choreographed by Gillian Lynne. "He manages to outdance everyone else on the screen," wrote Joe Baltake in his Passionate Moviegoer blog, "and in this scene, there are dozens."

a lot of sitting around. So, Tommy Steele came up with a perfect solution: poker-playing. And I got totally sucked in. The time just flew by.

One day, I'm sitting there with a pair of kings and a wild card in my hand. I'm about to go in for the kill. But suddenly, an assistant director informs me I'm wanted on set. *What?* I'm filled with resentment over the interruption. Then I catch myself. *Here I am, with the thrill – and incredible pay – of co-starring in a major movie, and I'm resentful of doing my job? What am I thinking?*

That was a huge wake-up call. Recognizing poker as damaging – my first taste of understanding the addiction I'd seen in others – I stood up from the table and vowed never to come back. And I kept that vow. Instead, I retreated to my trailer, spending my breaks writing, instead of playing poker. That started me down a path that I'm still on to this day – about to publish my first book!

The very first thing I wrote, during *Half a Sixpence* breaks, was a musical that was produced and aired live on a CBS show called *Look Up and Live* on August 6, 1967, under the title "Inner Feelings, Outer Forms." That led to an opportunity, in the late Sixties, to collaborate with Jerome Robbins for a second time (the first being my role in the original production of *West Side Story*). This time it was on a project involving experimental dance called American Theatre Lab. It changed my life completely. From then on, performing was replaced with directing and choreographing.

I understand you're working on a memoir. Do you have a tentative title? And can you practice your dustjacket prose by telling me, in a nutshell, what the book will be about?

Thank you so much for asking! The working title is *A Boy Like That: Hits, Misses, Messes, and Miracles as I Danced Across the Stages of Broadway and Hollywood.* The book is told in a series of anecdotes that recount the ups and downs – both personal and professional – of my seven-decade theater career. I don't hold back on sharing my struggles (including a scandal or two!) in hopes that my journey from a three-room shack on a dirt road to showbiz success will inspire readers to follow their dreams, and that they'll find my behind-the-scenes revelations, including my failures and foibles, entertaining.

Notes and Acknowledgements

Grateful acknowledgement is made to the following journals and magazines, which originally published many of these interviews: *Take One*, *Film Comment*, *Focus on Film*, *Sight and Sound*, *Cineaste*, and *Film International*. Thank you also to Gerald Peary and Danny Peary for permission to reprint my interview with Ralph Bakshi from their book *The American Animated Cartoon: A Critical Anthology* (Plume, 1980).

Thank you to the editors who helped shape the pieces when they first appeared in print, suggesting pertinent changes and fine-tuning the results with their editing: Stuart Byron, Harlan Jacobson, and Richard Jameson of *Film Comment*; Philip Dodd and Nick James, *Sight and Sound*; Allen Eyles, *Focus on Film*; Richard Porton and Gary Crowdus, *Cineaste*; Daniel Lindvall and Matthew Sorrento, *Film International*.

Photographs courtesy of: Barry Alexander Brown (and Verane Pick); Aaron Schmidt, Pictorial Collection, Boston Public Library; Grover Dale (and Jennifer Thomas); Peter Davis (and Alicia Anstead); Michael Elias (and Ron Colby); Clark Graphics; Gopolakrishnan Archives, University of Wisconsin-Milwaukee; Historic Images; Max Knowlton-Sacher; J.L. Mège, Leslie Pichot, and Thierry Fremaux, Institut Lumière (Lyon, France); Joose Pauwels; Matt Tyrnauer; and William B. Winburn.

This is the first publication of my interview with Gregory A. Kolp, who passed away in Las Vegas, Nevada, in 2018.

Whenever possible, the interview subjects collaborated, making emendations and clarifications, on the final form of their interviews. I have spared trees and omitted long filmographies with details (and post-interview updates), which the reader may find on imdb.com.

A special nod of gratitude to the Interlibrary Loan Department at the Raynor Memorial Library of Marquette University in Milwaukee; and to Mary Huelsbeck and her staff at the Wisconsin Center for Film and Theater Research in Madison, Wisconsin. Huelsbeck was a saint, fielding my many requests for published material and photographs.

Index

3 Women (Altman), 171
6 juin à l'aube, Le (Grémillon), 253
8 Femmes (Ozon), 252
20th Century-Fox, 68-9, 73, 76-7, 92, 123, 176-6, 267
40 Acres and a Mule Filmworks, 196
50 Ans de Cinéma Américain (Tavernier/Coursodon), 230
84 Charlie MoPic (Duncan), 44
400 Blows, The (Truffaut), 247

Aaron, Henry, xi, 144
Abernathy, Ralph, 185, 189-90
Abraham Lincoln Brigade, 126
A Bridge Too Far (Attenborough), 78
Ackroyd (Feiffer), 177
Act of Violence (Zinnemann), 235
Actors Studio, 143
Adams, Gerald Drayson, 240
A Distant Trumpet (Walsh), 240
Adventures of Hajji Baba, The (Weis), 233
A Fable (Faulkner), 241
A Face in the Crowd (Kazan), 124
A Fistful of Dollars (Leone), 136-7, 142
A Hard Day's Night (Lester), 95
A King in New York (Chaplin), 98
Ainslee, Marian, 118-9
Alamo, The (Wayne), xi
Aldrich, Robert, 224, 232, 235
Alien (Scott), 46
Alland, Bill, 112
Allen, Irwin, 77
Allen, Woody, 36, 55, 263
Allied Artists, 106

Allo Berlin? Ici Paris! (Duvivier), 247
All the King's Men (Rossen), 91
All the President's Men (Pakula), 70, 76
Almendros, Nestor, 221
Almodovar, Pedro, 227
Alsino and the Condor (Littin), 162
Altman, Robert, xii, 63, 169, 171-6, 226
Alton, John, 242
Alvarez, Kiki, 59
André Masson et les quatre éléments (Grémillon), 253
Andrews, Julie, 2, 9, 99
Angèle (Pagnol), 248
Ann-Margret, 1, 9-10, 172-3
Anna Lucasta (Yordan), 151
Ansari, Nicole, 192
American Cinema, The (Sarris), 230, 261
American Civil Liberties Union (ACLU), 111
American Madness (Capra), 67
American Theatre Lab, 271
American Theatres Corporation, 68
American Film Theatre, 7
Amoureux sont seuls au monde, Les (Decoin), 258
Anchors Aweigh (Sidney), 161
Anderson, "Bloody Bill," 139
Anderson, Lindsay, 256
Anderson, Shamier, 192
…And Justice for All (Jewison), 56
Angelopoulos, Theo, 227
Ansen, David, 227
Antonioni, Michelangelo, 223-4, 226

A Personal Journey Through American Movies (Scorsese), 261
Apocalypse Now (Coppola), 45, 56, 61, 174, 236
Aragon, Louis, 252
Are Husbands Necessary? (Taurog), 123
Arkin, Alan, 172
Army of Shadows (Melville), 249
Arrabal, Fernando, 61
Arzner, Dorothy, 122
A Scandal in Paris (Sirk), 233, 235
Ashby, Hal, 43, 46, 171, 194
Ashley, Ted, 70, 74-5, 78
A Touch of Class (Frank), 115
A Tree Grows in Brooklyn (Smith), 117
A Tree Grows in Brooklyn (Kazan), 117, 123
Attenborough, Richard, 115
Attipetty, Peter L., 209
ATV (television station), 69
Au-delà des grilles (Clément), 256
Audry, Jacqueline, 258-9
Aurenche, Jean, 250, 256-8
Auric, Georges, 252
Au royaume des cieux (Duvivier), 254, 258
Australian Broadcasting Company, 32
Autant-Lara, Claude, 221, 247, 250, 257-8
Avant le déluge (Cayatte), 250, 259
Avec le sourire (Tourneur), 252
A Woman of Uncertain Character (Sigal), 105

Back Lot (Rapf), 120
Bailey, David, 268
Baker, Ella, 189
Baker, Lenny, 143
Baker, Mary, 106-7, 111, 113
Baldwin, James, xiii
Baltake, Joe, 270
Band Wagon, The (Minnelli), 177
Bandera, La (Duvivier), 251
Bank Shot, The (Champion), 2
Barbarosa (Schepisi), 25, 39
Barry Lyndon (Kubrick), 76
Barzman, Ben, 95, 112
Bataille du rail, La (Clément), 256
Battement de Coeur (Decoin), 252
Bazin, Jeanine, 260
B.C. (comic strip), 14
Beagle, Peter S., 21
Beatles, The, 95, 166

Beatty, Warren, 44, 63, 173
Becker, Jacques, 248, 250, 253, 26
Becker, Leon, 95, 100
Beetle Bailey, 14
Begelman, David, 73, 75, 77
Beguiled, The (Siegel), 140, 144, 146
Belle équipe, La (Duvivier), 250
Belushi, Jim, 44, 59
Benedek, László, 136
Benjamin, Ben, 110
Ben-Hur (Wyler), xi
Berenger, Tom, 45, 62
Beresford, Bruce, 25, 39
Bergen, Candice, 172-3
Bergerman, Stanley, 123, 125
Berkeley, Martin, 124-5
Berman, Pandro, 243
Bernard, Raymond, 248
Bernhardt, Curtis, 251
Bernheim, Alain, 129
Bernstein, Elmer, 253
Bernstein, Leonard, 8
Bernstein, Walter, 128
Best Years of Our Lives, The (Wyler), 67, 95
Betrayal, The (Micheaux), 149-51, 155-7
Beverly Hills Cop II (Scott), 162
Beyond a Reasonable Doubt (Lang), 244
Big Chill, The (Kasdan), 45, 51, 54
Big Sleep, The (Hawks), 236
Big Trail, The (Walsh), 237
Birth of a Nation, The (Griffith), 149
Biscuit Eater, The (Heisler), 245
Bitter Moon (Polanski), 227
Blackhawk, The (Bennet/Sears), 27
BlacKkKlansman (Lee), 185, 195
Black Sunset (Sigal), 105, 112-13
Blade Runner, 46
Blair, Betsy, 94, 98
Blanke, Henry, 126, 243
Blaustein, Julian, 124
Blazing Saddles (Brooks), 2
Blier, Bernard, 251, 258
Blue Velvet (Lynch), 162, 167-8
Body and Soul (Micheaux), 96, 149
Boetticher, Budd, 261
Bogeaus, Benedict, 233
Boisset, Yves, 230
Bolt, Robert, 55
Bondi, Beulah, 255
Bonjour Tristesse (Preminger), 238

Bonne chance! (Guitry), 248
Bonner, Raymond, 57
Boorman, John, 223
Borchard, Adolphe, 253
Borges, Jorge Luis, 44, 58
Born Free (Hill), 95
Born on the Fourth of July (Stone), 44, 56-7
Borzage, Frank, 231, 235
Bost, Pierre, 250, 257, 259
Boston Globe, The (newspaper), x-xiii
Bourvil, 258
Boyer, Jean, 253
Boyfriend, The (Russell), 1
Boy from Oklahoma, The (Curtiz), 125-6
Boy with Green Hair, The (Losey), 161, 164
Boyle, Richard, 44, 56-60, 62
Brando, Marlon, 143
Bravados, The (King), 241
Brazzi, Rossano, 244
Breaker Morant (Beresford), 25
Breathless (Godard), 58, 247
Breezy (Eastwood), 144, 146
Bresson, Robert, 205, 239, 247
Breton, André, 224
Bride Wore Red, The (Arzner), 122
Brooks, Richard, 221, 224, 261
Brown, David, 101
Brown, Nick, 194
Brown, Oscar, 151
Brownlow, Kevin, 231
Brustein, Robert, 176
Boudu sauvé des eaux (Renoir), 255
Buchman, Sidney, 91, 96, 100
Bugs Bunny, 14
Bunny Lake is Missing (Preminger), 95
Buñuel, Luis, 119, 221, 224
Burns, Lillian, 163
Burr, Raymond, 180
Burton, Richard, 99
Burton Tim, 227
Butler, Hugo, 125
Buz Sawyer (comic strip), 14
Bye Bye Birdie (Sidney), 10

Cahiers du Cinéma (magazine), 221, 223-7,
    229, 247, 255
Callenbach, Ernest, x
Cagney, James, x, xiii, 137-8, 142
Caine, Michael, 44
Campbell, Robert, 92

Canal+ (TV), 261
Canard enchaîné, Le (newspaper), 258
Cannes Film Festival, 18, 161-2, 226
Caporal épinglé, Le (Renoir), 255
Capra, Frank, 67-8, 238
Carabatsos, James, 44
Carnal Knowledge (Nichols), 10, 169, 172-3,
    176-7
Carné, Marcel, 256, 258
Caro, Robert, 101
Carpenter, John, 253
Cars That Ate Paris, The (Weir), 25
Carter, Forrest, 134
Carter, Jimmy, 56
Casablanca (Curtiz), 81, 110
Casa de Lava (Costa), 201
Case of Mrs. Wingate, The (Micheaux), 151
Caspary, Vera, 98
Casper, 15
Casque d'or (Becker), 248, 254
Caught (Ophüls), 290
Cavalcanti, Alberto, 248
Cayatte, André, 248, 250-1, 259
CBS Television, 15, 135, 145, 271
Cedric the Entertainer, 185, 190
Chabrol, Claude, 250, 256-7, 264
Chacón, Juan, 59
Chacon, Rene, 56
Chakiris, George, 263-4, 266
Chalais, François, 260
Chamberlain, Wilt, 144
Chaney, James, 187
Chaplin, Charles, 5, 11, 28, 36, 96, 98-9, 231
Chardère, Bernard, 223
Charmoli, Tony, 179
Chasen, Dave, 91, 102
Chat, Le (Granier-Deferre), 251
Chatte, La (Decoin), 249
Chateau, René, 260
Chauvel, Charles, 27
Chekhov, Michael, 142
Chenal, Pierre, 253
Chessman, Caryl, 111
Chetwynd, Lionel, 44
Chevalier, Maurice, 251
Chicago Reader, The (newspaper), 201
Chicago Tribune, The (newspaper), 230
Chienne, La (Renoir), 255, 257
Ciel est à vous, Le (Grémillon), 250
Cimino, Michael, 43, 46-7, 49-50, 56, 61

Cinéastes de notre temps (TV), 260
Cinéma (magazine), 229
Cinéma, Cinémas, 261
Cinéma club, Le, 261
Cinemation, 17
CinemaScope, 244
Cinerama, 69
Citizen Kane (Welles), 3, 108, 112
Citron, Steve, 94
Clair, René, 253-5
Clapton, Eric, 10, 162
Claudia and David (Lang), 123
Clément, René, 247, 256-7
Clift, Montgomery, 241
Clockmaker, The (Tavernier), 229, 257
Clouzot, Henri-Georges, 247, 256, 258, 260
Cocteau, Jean, 221, 223, 253
Coen Brothers, 227
Coen, Franklin, 124, 128-9
Coeur de Lilas (Litvak), 239, 248
Coffee, Lenore, 98
Cohen Media Group, 247
Cohen, Mickey, 108
Cohn, Harry, 105
Cohn, Sam, 171
Cohn, Sidney, 93
Cole, Lester, 93-5, 98
Coleridge, Samuel Taylor, 1
Collier, John, 96
Colorado Territory (Walsh), 240
Colors (Hopper), 167
Colossal Youth (Costa), 201, 205-7
Columbia Pictures, 1, 8, 68-9, 73-7, 79, 105, 107, 111
Comden, Betty, 177
Composer in Hollywood, The (Palmer), 252
Compulsion (Fleischer), 161
Compulsion (Levin), 161, 164
Comtesse de Ségur, 260
Conan the Barbarian (Milius), 46
Conkling, Chris, 21
Conrad, Joseph, 45
Conway, Jack, 256
Coogan's Bluff (Siegel), 139
Coonskin (Bakshi), 19-21
Cooper, Gary, 138
Copland, Aaron, 253
Coppola, Francis, 63, 162, 256,
Corbeau, Le (Clouzot), 247-8
CORE (Congress of Racial Equality), 19

Corliss, Richard, 227, 230
Cotten, Joseph, 108, 241
Count Basie, 237
Count Vim (Weir), 32
Coup de Torchon (Tavernier), 229
Coursodon, Jean-Pierre, 229-31
Cousins, Mark, 209
Cover-Up (Stone), 55
Coward, Noël, 248
Cox, Brian, 192
Crazy World of Julius Vrooder, The (Hiller), 2
Croix de bois, Les (Bernard), 248
Crosby, Bing, 251
Crumb, Robert, 17
Cukor, George, xiii, 179, 183, 224, 242
Cummings, Ruth, 118
Curtiz, Michael, 125-6, 231-2, 235

Dafoe, Willem, 45, 62
Daïnah la métisse (Grémillon), 253
Dale, James Badge, 263
Daley, Bob, 134, 144
Daly, John, 57
Daltrey, Roger, 1, 10
Dance, Girl, Dance (Arzner), 122
Danton (Wajda), 36
Darden, Dexter, 192
Darrieux, Danielle, 251-2, 268
Dassin, Jules, 96
Daves, Delmer, 224, 229, 235, 241, 244
Davis, Clive, 73-4
Davis, Lex Scott, 189, 192
Dawn Patrol, The (Hawks), 239
Day, Doris, 126
Dead, The (Huston), 238
Dean, James, 22, 143
Death of a Salesman (Miller), 139
Decoin, Henri, 247, 249, 250, 252-4, 256
Deer Hunter, The (Cimino), 56, 61
Defiance (Stone), 57
de Havilland, Olivia, 238
Delannoy, Jean, 250, 256
De Laurentiis, Dino, 46, 50
Delerue, Georges, 254
Delon, Alain, 260
DeMille, Cecil B., 91, 245, 253, 260
Demme, Jonathan, 162, 168
Demoiselles de Rochefort, Les (Demy), 252, 263-9

Demy, Jacques, 252, 254, 257, 263-70
Deneuve, Catherine, 264, 268
Dennehy, Brian, 185, 192
De Palma, Brian, 25, 43, 46, 50
Depardieu, Gérard, 177
De Quincey, Thomas, 1
De Sica, Vittorio, 136, 221
Derain, André, 258
Des gens sans importance (Verneuil), 251
Detective Story (Wyler), 95
De Toth, André, 128
Deutsch, Adolph, 252
Devils, The (Huxley), 10
Diary of a Chambermaid (Buñuel), 255
Dietch, Gene, 14
Dietrich, Marlene, 113, 258
Diamond, I.A.L., 230
Dies, Martin, 123
Directors Guild, 149
Dirty Dozen, The (Aldrich), 232
Disney, Walt, 18, 27, 72, 76, 161, 169, 176
Dmytryk, Edward, 107
Doctorow, E.L., 175-6
Donahue, Troy, 244
Don Camillo (Duvivier), 254
Donne-moi tes yeux (Guitry), 248
Don Quixote (Cervantes), 26
Don't Raise the Bridge, Lower the River
    (Paris), 95
Dorléac, Françoise, 264, 267-8
Do the Right Thing (Lee), 185, 194-5
Douce (Autant-Lara), 247-8, 250, 257
Douglas, Kirk, 95, 113
Dreyer, Carl, 224
Dr. Max (Weir), 28
Dr. Strangelove (Kubrick), 28, 58
D'Aubuisson, Roberto, 51
Duarte, José Napoléon, 59
Duellists, The (Scott), 46
Duhamel, Antoine, 254
Dulac, Edmund, 15
Dune (Lynch), 162, 167
Durr, Clifford, 193
Durr, Virginia, 185, 190, 192,
Dutilleux, Henri, 250, 253
Duvall, Shelley, 169, 171
Duvivier, Julien, 247, 250-8, 260
Dwan, Allan, xi, 233, 253
Dylan, Bob, 163

Earrings of Madame de..., The (Ophüls),
    252
Easy Rider (Hopper), 79, 172
Edel, Leon, 101
Edens, Roger, 264
Edwards, Blake, 99, 221, 244
Eiger Sanction, The (Eastwood), 146-7
Eight Million Ways to Die (Ashby), 43, 51
Eisinger, Jo, 240
Eisenstein, Sergei, 3
Ekberg, Anita, 143
El Dorado (Hawks), 238
Elena et les hommes (Renoir), 255
Elias, Michael, 114
Elliot Loves (Feiffer), 177
En cas de Malheur (Autant-Lara), 250-1, 257
Entraîneuse (Valentin), 250
Equipage (Litvak), 239
Erdreich, Stan, 191
Evans, Robert, 169, 171, 174
Exile, The (Ophüls), 255
Exorcist, The (Friedkin), 2

Famous Artists, 110
Farber, Manny, 161-2
Farrow, John, 236
Fassbinder, Rainer Werner, 233
Fat City (Huston), 238
Faulkner, William, 241
Feldman, Charlie, 110
Ferrer, Mel, 255
Festival de Film Maudit, 223
Fête à Henriette, La (Duvivier), 254, 258
Fields, W.C., 229
Film Comment (magazine), xii, 201, 240
Film Crazy (McGilligan), xii
Film Culture (magazine), 227
Film Quarterly (magazine), x
Fin du jour, La (Duvivier), 250
Fink, Harry Julian, 141
First Traveling Saleslady, The (Lubin), 142
Flaherty, Robert, 124, 206
Flaubert, Gustave, 177
Flesh and Fantasy (Duvivier), 254
Fleischer, Max, 18, 169
Fleming, Eric, 135
Fleming, Rhonda, 238
Florey, Robert, 242
Flynn, Errol, 108
Fonda, Henry, xiii

Forbidden Games (Clément), 248, 257
Ford, Harrison, 25-6, 34, 38
Ford, John, 174, 225, 229, 244-5, 248, 253, 261
Forman, Chaka, 189
Forman, James, 185, 189-90
Foreman, Carl, 94-5, 128
Four Women (Gopalakrishnan), 209, 213-4, 217
France, Chuck, 195
Frank Capra: The Man and His Films (Glatzer), 68
Frankenheimer, John, 128, 225
French Cancan (Renoir), 255, 257
French Connection, The (Friedkin), 49-50
Fresh Air (radio), ix
Freud, Sigmund, 26, 33
Frida (Taymor), 114-5
Friedkin, William, 49, 56, 63, 256
Fritz the Cat (Bakshi), 15, 17-9
Front de l'art, Le (Valland), 129
Fuller, Sam, 229, 235-6, 261
Full Metal Jacket (Kubrick), 44
Full Service (Bowers/Friedberg), 181
Funicello, Annette, ix

Gabin, Jean, 251-2, 254-5, 258
Gable and Lombard (Furie), 246
Gaines, Harris, 151
Gallipoli (Weir), 25, 28, 34, 36,
Gang, Martin, 107, 111
Garbo, Greta, 99
Garçon sauvage, Le (Delannoy), 258
Garden of Evil (Hathaway), 236
Gardens of Stone (Coppola), 162, 168
Gardner, Ava, 114
Garfield, David, 93
Garfield, John, 92, 96
Garfunkel, Art, 172
Garland, Judy, 91, 101
Garnett, Tay, 136, 233
Garnier, Philippe, 261
Geiger, Peter, 70
General Cinema, 69
Gennaro, Peter, 265
George White's Scandals, 163
Gentleman's Agreement (Kazan), 161
George Cukor: A Double Life, 179 (McGilligan)
Gersh, Phil, 108

Giannini, A.P., 67
Gibson, Mel, 26, 114
Girl of My Dreams (Davis), 117, 125, 127
Gladstone Gander, 27
Glatzer, Richard, 68
Godard, Jean-Luc, 44, 58, 221, 224, 239, 247, 250, 254, 256-7, 261,
Going Away (Sigal), 105, 113
Goldfarb, Bob, 106-7, 112-4
Gold, Lee, 98
Gold Rush, The (Chaplin), 11
Gold, Tammy, 98
Goliath (TV), 192
Gone With the Wind (Fleming), 101
Goodbye Again (Litvak), 239
Good Earth, The (Buck), 120
Good Earth, The (Franklin), 122
Goodman, Andrew, 187
Good, The Bad and the Ugly, The (Leone), 133, 136, 141
Gordon, Bernard, 112
Gould, Elliott, 172
Grade, Lew, 69
Grahame, Gloria, 111
Grande illusion, La (Renoir), 250-1, 257, 259
Grandes manoeuvres, Les (Clair), 255
Granger, Farley, 110
Granier-Deferre, Pierre, 250
Grant, Cary, 181, 183
Grant, Joanne, 189
Grapes of Wrath, The (Ford), 244
Greatest Story Ever Told, The (Stevens), 78
Greed (von Stroheim), 118
Green, Adolph, 177
Greenaway, Peter, 227
Grémillon, Jean, 247, 250-1, 253, 256, 259
Gréville, Edmond T., 248
Griffith, D.W., 3, 36, 149, 236
Group Theatre, 93
Grynszpan, Herschel, 258
Gueule d'amour (Grémillon), 251
Guillory, Sienna, 190
Guitry, Sacha, 247-9, 253, 260
Gulf + Western, 72
Gung Ho! (Enright), 245
Gulpilil, David, 33
Gunman's Walk (Karlson), 253
Guns of Navarone, The (Thompson), 95

Hale, Lucy, 189, 192
Hall, Ken G., 27
Half a Sixpence (Sidney), 267-8, 270-1
Hamburger Hill (Irvin), 44
Hand, The (Stone), 44, 63
Hang 'Em High (Post), 144
Hanging Tree, The (Daves), 244
Hanoi Hilton, The (Chetwynd), 44
Hardy, Oliver, 58, 229
Hathaway, Henry, 236, 240-1, 249
Hawks, Howard, xi, 25, 45, 224-5, 231,
    235-9, 241
Hays Office, 137
Hayes, Billy, 43, 51
Hayden, Sterling, 143, 245
Head, Heart and Hand (Weir), 35
Healey, Dorothy, 108, 113
Health (Altman), 175
Heartbreak Ridge (Eastwood), 44
Hearts and Minds (Davis), 117, 129
Heavy Traffic (Bakshi), 17-9
Hecht, Ben, 128, 240, 158
Heims, Jo, 144
Heiress, The (Wyler), 95
Heisler, Stuart, 245, 255
Hellman, Jerome, 38
Hellman, Monte, 226
Hello, Dolly! (Kelly), 76, 267, 270
Hemdale, 57-8
Hemingway, Ernest, 114-5
Henreid, Paul, 110
Henry, Pierre, 250
Henry King, Director (Shepherd), 240-1
Hepburn, Katharine, xiii, 183-4
Her Man (Garnett), 253
Heroes for Sale (Wellman), 232
Hertz, David, 122
Hey, Good Lookin' (Bakshi), 20
High Plains Drifter (Eastwood), 134-5, 139
Hi and Lois (comic strip), 14
Hill, George Roy, 176
Hindenburg, The (Wise), 76
Hiroshima mon amour (Resnais), 247
Hirschfield, Alan, 73-5, 77
Hitchcock, Alfred, 36, 147, 224, 231, 233,
    235, 238-9- 241, 248
Hitler, Adolf, 6, 224, 258
Hobbit, The (Tolkien), 13, 21
Ho Chi Minh, 56
Hoffman, Dustin, 171

Holden, William, 146
Hollywood Boulevard (Florey), 243
Home from the Hill (Minnelli), 242
Hondo (Farrow), 236
Honegger, Arthur 252
Honor System, The (Walsh), 245
Hoover, J. Edgar, 108, 127
Hopper, Dennis, 161, 163, 167
Horning into Africa (Van Dyke), 242
Hôtel du Nord, 258
Houseman, John, 255
House Un-American Activities Committee
    (HUAC), 91-4, 96, 98-100, 102, 105,
    108, 112, 123, 125-7
Howard, Jim, 81
Howard, Robert E., 46
Hudson, Rock, 233
Huffaker, Clair, 240
Hughes, Howard, 162, 255
Hugo, Victor, 261
Huis Clos (Sartre), 259
Human Highway (Young/Stockwell), 162
Hunter, Marian, 124
Hurst, Fannie, 233
Huston, John, 67, 224, 238-9, 248
Huston, Walter, 67
Huxley, Aldous, 10

Ibert, Jacques, 252
Iceman (Schepisi), 25
Imitation of Life (Sirk), 233
Impostor, The (Duvivier), 254
Incredible Shrinking Man, The (Arnold),
    244
Indian Fighter, The (De Toth), 127-8
Informer, The (Ford), 253
In Love and War (Attenborough), 114-5
Irola, Judy, 185
I Walked with a Zombie (Tourneur), 201,
    203
I Want to Go Home (Resnais), 177-8

Jackson, Glenda, 155
Jaglom, Henry, 167
Jarre, Maurice, 26
Jaffe, Sam, 105-8, 111
James, Henry, 101
Jardin, Pascal, 250
Jarrico, Paul, 98, 106-7, 112-3
Jaubert, Maurice, 252-4

Jaws (Spielberg), xi, 70, 79, 147
Jazz Singer, The (Curtiz), 126
Jean Renoir (Mérigeau), 255
Jeanson, Henri, 250, 258, 260
Jerk, The (Reiner), 144
Jerome Robbins' Broadway, 263
Jesus Christ Superstar (Jewison), 3
Jewison, Norman, 56
Jofroi (Pagnol), 248
John, Elton, 1, 10
Johnny Guitar (Ray), 249
Johnson, Lyndon, 53
Jones, Grover, 240
Jones, Kent, 201
Jour et l'heure, Le (Clément), 257
Journal d'une femme en blanc, Le
    (Autant-Lara), 250
Journey into Light (Heisler), 245
Joyce, James, 30
Jung, Carl, 26, 32
Justice est faite (Cayatte), 250, 259

Kael, Pauline, 62, 227
Kadish, Ben, 127-8
Kahane, B.B., 105-7, 111
Kahlo, Frida, 114
Karmitz, Marin, 177
Kasdan, Lawrence, 54
Kate: The Woman Who Was Hepburn
    (Mann), 179
Kaufman, Charles, 124
Kaufman, Philip, 134
Kazan, Elia, 117, 123-4, 223
Keaton, Buster, 229
Keats, John, 1
Kehr, Dave, 227, 230
Kelly, Gene, 94, 264-5, 267, 270
Key, The (Reed), 95
Kilpatrick, Dick, 124
Kilpatrick, Thomas, 119, 122
Kim (Saville), 161
King, Henry, 240-1
King Kong (Cooper/Schoedsack), 253,
King, Martin Luther, 189-90
Kings of Comedy, The (Lee), 185
Kiss of Death (Hathaway), 240
Kopelson, Arnold, 57
Kosma, Joseph, 249, 253
Kovic, Ron, 44, 56
Kroeger, Wolf, 173

Kubrick, Stanley, 28, 35, 44, 223
Kyne, Peter B., 118

Labarthe, André, 260
Lancaster, Burt, 128
La Cava, Gregory, 232, 245
Landau, Ely, 7
Lang, Fritz, 3, 231, 244
Lang, Jennings, 145
Lang, Walter, 123
Langlois, Henri, 223, 225
Lanier, Sharon, 189
Lantz, Walter, 22
Lardner Jr., Ring, 107, 120
Laroche, Pierre, 258-9
Lastfogel, Abe, 110
Last Movie, The (Hopper), 167
Last Unicorn, The (Rankin, Jr./Bass), 21
Last Wave, The (Weir), 25, 32-4
Last Year in Marienbad (Resnais), 177
Lattuada, Alberto, 229
Laughton, Charles, 180, 255
Laura (Preminger), 110
Laurel, Stan, 58, 229
Laurents, Arthur, xii
Lautner, Georges, 259
Lawrence, Stanley, 126-7
Lawson, John Howard, 107
Lazar, Irving Paul "Swifty," 110
LeBorg, Reginald, 254
Lederer, Charlie, 106
Le dossier noir (Cayatte), 250, 259
Lean, David, 248
Lee, Spike, 185, 189, 195-6
Legrand, Michel, 254, 269-70
Lehár, Franz, 252
Leigh, Vivien, 91, 101
Leisen, Mitchell, 231, 235
Lenz, Kay, 146
Lennart, Isobel, 98
Leone, Sergio, 47, 135-7
Letelier, Orlando, 51
Let Joy Reign Supreme (Tavernier), 229
Letter from an Unknown Woman (Ophüls),
    255
Levien, Sonya, 98
Levine, Joe, 78
Lewis, Jerry, 177, 233
Lewis, John, 185, 189, 192, 197
Lewton, Val, 243

Life and Flight of the Reverend Buckshotte, The (Weir), 30
Life and Nothing But (Tavernier), 229
Lighton, Louis, 123
Li'l Abner (comic strip), 14
Lisztomania (Russell), 2, 11
Little Audrey, 15
Little Murders (Arkin), 172, 177
Litvak, Anatole, 238-9, 247-8, 250, 253
Loew's, 69
London, Jack, 151-2
Lone, John, 49
Long Day's Journey Into Night (Lumet), 161, 168
Long Hot Summer, The (Ritt), 242
Look Up and Live (TV), 271
Lord Jim (Conrad), 45, 52
Lord of the Rings, The (Bakshi), 13, 21
Lorre, Peter, 110
Los Angeles Times, The (newspaper), 117, 128
Losey, Joseph, 96, 98, 161, 164, 223-4, 229
Lost Horizon (Capra), 1
Lourcelles, Jacques, 260
Love Me Tonight (Mamoulian), 251
Lubin, Ronnie, 107-8, 113
Lubitsch, Ernst, 241, 243-4, 248, 251, 253
Lucas, George, 27
Lucky Me (Donohue), 126
Lucky Lady (Donen), 70, 76
Luigy, 253
Luis Buñuel: The Red Years: 1929–1939 (Gubern/Hammond), 119
Lumet, Sidney, 231
Lumière d'été (Grémillon), 259
Lumière Institute, 223
Lupino, Ida, 238
Lynch, David, 262, 267
Lynne, Gillian, 270

Macbeth (Shakespeare), 38
Machen, Yvonne, 151
Mackendrick, Alexander, 248
Mad (magazine), 15
Mad Men (TV), 110
Madame Tussaud, 36
Maen, Norman, 265, 269
Mahler (Russell), 1, 3, 6
Mahler, Anna, 5
Mahler, Gustav, 3, 5-7

Malcolm, Don, 254
Malcolm X (Lee), 185
Maléfices (Decoin), 250
Malheurs de Sophie, Les (Audry), 260
Malone, Dorothy, 233, 238
Malpaso, 133, 144
Mame (Saks), 2
Mamoulian, Rouben, xi
Manilow, Barry, 263
Man in the Maze, The (Sigal), 114
Mankiewicz, Joseph L., 241
Mann, Anthony, 95, 224, 235
Mann, William J., 179
Man of the Story (Gopalakrishnan) 215
Manon des sources (Pagnol), 248
Man Who Would Be King, The (Huston), 238
March, Fredric, 67, 108, 113
Marchenko, Joy, 162
Mariage de Chiffon, Le (Autant-Lara), 250
Marie-Octobre (Duvivier), 255
Married to the Mob (Demme), 162, 168
Marsh, Reginald, 15
Marty (Mann), 94
Masaryk, Jan, 107
Massey, Raymond, 108, 113
Mason, James, 241
Maudits, Les (Clément), 257
Mayes, Wendell, 240
Mayo, Virginia, 238
Mazursky, Paul, 143
MCA, 68, 110, 164
McBride, Joseph, xi
McCabe and Mrs. Miller (Altman), 173
McCarthy, Joseph, 95, 100, 103, 105
McCoy, Tim, 118
McGuinness, James Kevin, 125
McGuire, Dorothy, 123
McKenney, Eileen, 122
McQueen, Steve, 38, 78
Medrano, Jose, 56
Melville, Jean-Pierre, 249-50
Men, The (Zinnemann), 235
Menuhin, Yehudi, 99
Menzies, William Cameron, 237
Mérigeau, Pascal, 255
MGM, x, 68, 69, 118-20, 122, 124, 161, 163-4, 256, 264,
Michelangelo, 22
Mickey Mouse Club, The (TV), x

Midcentury Productions, 254
Middletown (TV), 117
Midnight Express (Parker), 43, 51, 53, 56, 62
Midway (Smight), xiii
Mighty Heroes, The (TV), 15
Mighty Mouse, 14
Milestone, Lewis, 253
Milius, John, 43, 46-7, 256
Mini-Squirts (Bakshi), 15
Minnelli, Liza, 70, 145
Minnelli, Vincente, 242
Missing (Costa-Gavras), 44, 58
Mistons, Les (Truffaut), 247
Mitford, Jessica, 190
Monde, Le (newspaper), 230
Monet, Claude, 248
Monogram, 106
Monroe, Marilyn, 241
Morris, Anita, 263
Monsieur Ripois (Clément), 257
Montand, Yves, 258
Monty Python (TV), 32, 58
Moonfleet (Lang), 244, 249
Morgan, Michèle, 259
Mork & Mindy (TV series), 171
Morrison, Jim, 55, 62
Morrison, Van, 37,
Moses, Bob, 189
Mosquito Coast, The (Weir), 25, 28, 37-40
Mostel, Zero, 127
Mouse that Roared, The (Arnold), 95
Mr. Smith Goes to Washington (Capra), 91
Mumbo-Jumbo (Reed), 13
Murnau, F.W., 236
Museum of Modern Art, 19, 221
Music Lovers, The (Russell), 6
My Favorite Year (Benjamin), 177
My Journey Through French Cinema
    (Tavernier), 247, 249, 251-2, 255, 257,
    261
My Voyage to Italy (Scorsese), 261

Naming Names (Navasky), 125
Nash, Diane, 189
National General, 69
Navasky, Victor, 125
Negative Space (Faber), 161
Newman, Paul, 78
New York Times, The (newspaper), 57, 117,
    149, 243, 265-6

New York University, 44, 54-5
Next Stop, Greenwich Village
    (Mazursky), 143
Niagara (Hathaway), 241
Nichols, Dudley, 255
Nichols, Mike, 172, 177
Nicholson, Jack, 1, 161-2, 172-3
Nietzsche, Friedrich, 6
Nilsson, Anna, 238
Nilsson, Harry, 169, 171, 173
Nine (stage production), 263
Ninotchka (Lubitsch), 244
Nixon, Richard, 53, 55, 105, 144
Non coupable (Decoin), 249
North, Edmund, 118
Nous sommes tous des assassins (Cayatte),
    250, 259
Nuit est mon royaume, La (Lacombe), 251

O'Connor, Donald, 110
Occupe-toi d'Amélie! (Autant-Lara), 252
Odets, Clifford, 122-3
O Estado do Mundo (Costa), 207
Of Human Bondage (Maugham), 241
Olivia (Audry), 260
Olivier, Laurence, 95
Ollé-Laprune, Jean, 261
On the Waterfront (Kazan), 143
One-Eyed Jacks (Brando), 230
One Flew Over the Cuckoo's Nest
    (Forman), 21
One, Two, Three (Wilder), 244
One Way Passage (Garnett), 233
Ophüls, Max, 247, 250, 252, 255, 260-1
Orbison, Roy, 162
Orion, 57
Ormond, Julia, 185, 190, 192-3
Ornitz, Sam, 112
Ossos (Costa), 201, 205
Othello (Shakespeare), 38
Other Men's Women (Wellman), 232-3
Outlaw Josey Wales, The (Eastwood), 133-4,
    139
Ozu, Yasujiro, 209, 239

Pacino, Al, 51, 56
Pagnol, Marcel, 248-9, 253, 260
Paint Your Wagon (Logan), 145
Painting with Light (Alton), 242
Palance, Jack, 113

Panigel, Armand, 260
Panique (Duvivier), 250, 254
Paramount Pictures, 15, 17, 20, 72, 169, 171, 243, 267
Paris, Texas (Wenders), 162
Parker, Alan, 46, 52, 56
Parker, Charlie, 251
Parks, Rosa, 185, 189-90, 193
Parrish, Robert, 236
Parton, Dolly, xi-xii
Party, The (Edwards), 244
Pattes blanches (Grémillon), 248
Patton (Hill), 118
Peary, Gerald, x
Peck, Gregory, 241
Peckinpah, Sam, 46
Penn, Arthur, 128
Pépé le Moko (Duvivier), 258
Perkins, Anthony, 263-4
Perkins, Millie, 161
Perrin, Jacques, 264
Pétain, Marechal Philippe, 257
Petrie, Daniel, 56
Phantom, The (comic), 27
Philippe, Claude-Jean, 260
Pialat, Maurice, 221
Picker, David, 145
Picnic at Hanging Rock (Weir), 25, 32, 34
Pièges (Siodmak), 252
Pierrot le Fou (Godard), 256
Plaisir, Le (Ophüls), 252
Platoon (Stone), xii, 44-6, 51, 55-7, 60-2
Playgirl (magazine), xi
Play Misty for Me (Eastwood), 144-5, 147
Pleshette, Suzanne, 244
Plumber, The (Weir), 25, 32
Poison, La (Guitry), 248
Polanski, Roman, 224, 227
Pollock, Jackson, 14
POP. 1280 (Thompson), 229
Popeye (Altman), 169, 171, 173-8
Porky Pig, 14
Portes de la nuit, Les (Carné), 258
Poseidon Adventure, The (Neame), 77
Postman Always Rings Twice, The (Garnett), 136
Positif (magazine), 221, 223-7, 229-30, 236, 247
Pot Bouille (Autant-Lara), 252, 255, 257
Powell, Michael, 248

Powell, Robert, 10
Premier rendez-vous (Decoin), 252
Preminger, Otto, 253
Président, Le (Verneuil). 251
Presley, Elvis, 10
Pressman, Edward, 46
Prévert, Jacques, 250, 258-9
Preview Murder Mystery, The (Florey), 242
Pride of the Marines (Daves), 241
Price, Vincent, 100
Prince Valiant (comic strip), 14
Producers Guild of America,. 251
Proust, Marcel, 53
Pryor, Thomas M., 249
Psycho (Hitchcock), 147, 263
Psych-Out (Rush), 162
Public Enemy, The (Wellman), 142
Pune Film Institute, 212-3
Purple Plain, The (Parrish), 236
Pursued (Walsh), 237
Puttnam, David, 56
Pyle, Howard, 14

Quatorze Juillet (Clair), 253
Quine, Richard, 253

Rabbit Hunter, The (Costa), 207
Rackham, Arthur, 15
Rackin, Martin, 240
Radcliffe, Daniel, 191
Rafelson, Bobm, 226
Raiders of the Lost Ark (Spielberg), 82
Raimu, 248
Rainer, Luise, 122
Rains, Claude, 108, 113
Rambo (Cosmatos), 61
Rapf, Maurice, 120
Rat-Trap (Gopalakrishnan), 209
Rawhide (TV), 135, 137
Reagan, Ronald, xi, 59-60, 91, 101-2, 108, 110, 176
Reagan, Nancy, 102
Reckless Moment, The (Ophüls), 255
Red Badge of Courage (Huston), 239
Red Channels, 100
Reds (Beatty), 44, 63
Redford, Robert, 70, 137
Reed, Carol, 248
Reed, Ishmael, 13
Regeneration, The (Walsh), 237

Règle du jeu, La (Renoir), 257
Reisz, Karel, 95, 256
Rembrandt, 22
Remember the Day (King), 123
Remous (Gréville), 248
Renoir, Auguste, 248
Renoir, Jean, 25, 36, 63, 124-5, 225, 239, 250, 253-7, 259, 261
Republic Pictures, 106
Resnais, Alain, 176-8
Retour à l'aube (Decoin), 250, 252
Retour à la vie (Clouzot), 251
Reynolds, Debbie, 265
Richard III (Shakespeare), 50, 59
Richards, Robert L., 127-8
Richardson, Tony, 256
Rim, Carlo, 253
Rio Bravo (Hawks), 236
Rio Lobo (Hawks), 238
Ritt, Martin, 242
River, The (Renoir), 255
Rivette, Jacques, 239, 256
RKO Pictures, 161, 243
Roach, Max, 237
Robbins, Jerome, 263, 266, 271
Roberts, Marguerite, 98
Robertson, Dale, 110
Robeson, Paul, 149, 254
Robinson Crusoe, 26
Rodin, Auguste, 248
Rogers Jr., Will, 125-6
Rohmer, Eric, 221, 225, 250, 256
Rome Adventure (Daves), 244
Romero, Oscar, 60
Ronde, La (Ophüls), 255
Roosevelt College, 149
Roosevelt, Franklin D., 52
Rosario, John, 194-5
Rosenbaum, Jonathan, 201
Rosenberg, Julius and Ethel, 105, 107, 114
Rosenberg, Meta, 108
Rossellini, Roberto, 224-5
Rossen, Robert, 91-3, 95-6
Rossetti, Dante, 1
Rouche, Jean, 206
Rouge et le noir, Le (Autant-Lara), 252
'Round Midnight (Tavernier), 229
Rourke, Mickey, 49-50
Russell, Alice B., 151-1
Russell, Shirley, 11

Ryan, Cornelius, 78
Rydell, Mark, 140

Sabatini, Rafael, 27
Sadoul, Georges, 237
Safe Conduct (Tavernier), 259
Sagan, Françoise, 238-9
Saint-Saëns, Camille, 248, 252
Salvador (Stone), 44-6, 51, 55-60, 62-3
Sanders, George, 233
Sarris, Andrew, 227, 230, 261
Sartre, Jean-Paul, 259
Sautet, Claude, 249-50
Searchers, The (Ford), 244
Secret Defector, The (Sigal), 105
Segal, Alex, 139
Segal, George, 115
Sembene, Ousmane, x
Semenenko, Serge, 67-8
Scarface (De Palma), 43, 49-52
Scharpf, William, 194
Schary, Dore, x, 243
Schepisi, Fred, 25, 39
Schertzinger, Victor, 253
Schifrin, Lalo, 254
Schlöndorff, Volker, 178
Schneider, Abe, 79
Schneider, Bert, 79
Schnitzler, Arthur, 233
Schoendoerffer, Pierre, 250
Schrader, Paul, 26, 38, 54, 256
Schüfftan, Eugen, 233
Schulberg, Budd, 124
Schwarzenegger, Arnold, 47
Schwerner, Michael, 187
Schwerner, Rita, 187
Scorsese, Martin, 36, 44, 46, 54, 63, 226, 237, 245, 256, 261
Scott, Adrian, 243
Scott, George C., 2
Scott, Randolph, 181, 183, 245
Scott, Ridley, 46
Scotty: The Secret History of Hollywood (Tyrnauer), 179
Searchers, The (Ford), 244
Segar, E.C., 169, 171, 176
Selznick, David O., 106, 251
Sergeant York (Hawks), 236
Shadow Kill (Gopalakrishnan), 209, 213, 217
Shakespeare, William, 38, 57

Sharif, Omar, 3
Shaw, Irwin, 99
Sheen, Charlie, 45, 61,
Shelley, Percy Bysshe, 1
Shenson, Walter, 95
Shepard, Eric, 264, 267
Shiga, Shigeo, 35
Ship, Reuben, 94
Short-Timers, The (Hasford), 44
Sidney, George, 233, 270
Siegel, Don, 136, 139-41, 145
Sight and Sound (magazine), 209
Sign of the Pagan (Sirk), 244
Signoret, Simone, 258
Silverberg, Bob, 114
Silver Lode (Dwan), 233
Simenon, Georges, 250, 259
Simon (Brickman), 177
Singin' in the Rain (Kelly/Donen), 177
Siodmak, Robert, 252
Sirk, Douglas, 233, 244, 252
Sloan, John, 15
Smith, Betty, 117
Smith, Dick, 69
SNCC (Student Non-Violent Coordinating
    Committee), 185, 187-90, 196
Snow White and the Seven Dwarfs
    (Disney), 161
Snyder, Tom, 11
Solow, Herbert, 120
Southerner, The (Renoir), 255
Southern Christian Leadership Conference
    (SCLC), 189
Southey, Robert, 1
Spaak, Charles, 248, 250-1, 257, 259-60
Spielberg, Steven, 27, 36
Springfield Rifle (De Toth), 128
Sragow, Michael, 227
Stahl, John, 233
Stammerjohn, Eloise, 194
Stanislavski, Constantin, 142
Stanton, Harry Dean, 162
Stanton, Myra, 151, 157
Stanwyck, Barbara, 108, 110
Steele, Tommy, 271
Steiner, Max, 252-3
Sterile Cuckoo, The (Pakula), 145
Stevens, George, 78
Stewart, James, xiii, 140
Sting, The (Hill), 70

St. Joseph, Ellis, 233, 254-5
Stockwell, Betty Veronica, 163
Stockwell, Harry, 163
Story of Will Rogers, The (Curtiz), 125
Strasberg, Lee, 166
Strauss, Richard, 10, 252
Strangers on a Train (Hitchcock), 110
Stross, Raymond, 99
Student Prince, The (Thorpe), 30
Stulberg, Gordon, 145
Sturges, Preston, 255
Sunday in the Country (Tavernier), 229, 259
Sunrise (Murnau), 236
Superfly (Parks Jr.), 19
SuperScope, 244
Survivors, The (Edwards), 101
Swanson, Gloria, 233
Swayamvaram (Gopalakrishnan), 212
Sylvie et le fantôme (Autant-Lara), 258
Symbol of the Unconquered (Micheaux), 149

Tales of Manhattan (Duvivier), 254
Talking Pictures (Corliss), 230
Tamarind Seed, The (Edwards), 2
Tarantino, Quentin, 81, 227
Tarrafal (Costa), 207
Tashlin, Frank, 224, 233
Tati, Jacques, 258
Taxi Driver (Scorsese), xi, 54, 236
Taylor, Elizabeth, 99
Taylor, Robert, xi
Tchaikovsky, Pyotr, 3, 6-7
Temple, Shirley, 91
Ten Days Wonder (Chabrol), 264
Tender Comrades (McGilligan/Buhle), xi-iii
Tender Mercies (Beresford), 39
Tennessee's Partner (Dwan), 233
Terre qui meurt, La (Vallée), 250, 259
Terrytoons, 13-5
Thalberg, Irving, 120
There's Always Tomorrow (Sirk), 235
Thief of Baghdad, The (Walsh), 237
Thirty Years of the American Cinema
    (Coursodon/Tavernier), 230
This Land Is Mine (Renoir), 255
Thomas, Danny, 126
Thompson, Jim, 229
Thornton, Greg, 193
Thorpe, Richard, 256
Tidwell, Janice, 114

Till, Lucas, 185, 190, 192
Time Without Pity (Losey), 229, 249
Time: The Present (Slesinger), 120
Thirard, Paul-Louis, 223
Toboggan (Decoin), 249
Today Show, The (TV), ix
To Have and Have Not (Hawks), 236-7
To Live and Die in L.A., 162
Tomlin, Lily, 171
Tomorrow Show, The (TV), 11
Tommy (Russell), 1, 6, 8-10
Tom Terrific, 14
Top Gun (Scott), 61
Tora! Tora! Tora! (Fleischer), 76
Touchez pas au grisbi (Becker), 251
Tourneur, Jacques, 201, 203-4, 232
Tourneur, Maurice, 247-8, 252
Towering Inferno, The (Guillermin), 73, 77
Townshend, Pete, 8-10
Tracks (Jaglom), 167
Tracy, Spencer, 181, 183-4
Trader Horn (Van Dyke), 242
Train, The (Frankenheimer), 128-9
Traversée de Paris, La (Autant-Lara), 247, 251, 257-8
Trevanian, 147
Tribune socialiste (newspaper), 258
Trikonis, Gus, 265
Truffaut, François, 221, 225, 238-9, 248-9, 255-7, 259-60
Trumbo, Dalton, 107, 112
Tucker (Coppola), 162
Twelve O'Clock High (King), 241
Twenty Years of the American Cinema (Coursodon/Boisset), 230
Twilight's Last Gleaming (Aldrich), 232
Twist, John, 240
Two Mules for Sister Sara (Siegel), 145
Two Years Before the Mast (Dana Jr.), 52

UCLA, 107, 127
Ullman, Daniel B., 240
Ulmer, Edgar, 204
Ulzana's Raid (Aldrich), 232
Under Fire (Spottiswoode), 44, 58
Under the Volcano (Huston), 238
Une femme en blanc se révolte (Autant-Lara), 250
United Artists, 72, 75, 78, 145

Universal Pictures, 68, 70, 72, 75, 92, 106, 112, 134, 139, 144-7, 244, 251, 254
Unknown Chaplin, The (Brownlow), 231
Un mauvais garçon (Boyer), 252
Unpossessed, The (Slesinger)
Un revenant (Christian-Jaque), 258
Unsinkable Molly Brown, The (Walters), 264-5

Valentin, Albert, 250
Valentino: The Last Emperor (Tyrnauer), 279
Valland, Rose, 129
Vanda's Room (Costa), 201, 205
Van Dyke, W.S., 118, 242
Van Parys, George, 253
Varda, Agnès, 250, 257, 268-9
Variety (newspaper), 76, 125, 243
Velikovsky, Immanuel, 32
Venice Film Festival, 178
Vérité sur Bébé Donge, La (Decoin), 247, 251, 252
Victors, The, 95
Vidal, Gore, 179
Vigo, Jean, 253-4
Viertel, Salka, 99
Visconti, Luchino, 30, 223
Visiteurs du soir, Les (Carné), 259
VistaVision, 244
Viva La Muerte (Arrabal), 61
Viva Zapata! (Kazan), 58
Voici le temps des assassins... (Duvivier), 255, 257
vom Rath, Ernst, 258
von Stroheim, Erich, 188
Vorhaus, Bernhard, 95

Wake of the Red Witch (Ludwig), 245
Wagner, Cosima, 5, 6
Wagner, Richard, 2
Wajda, Andrzej, 36, 224
Wald, Jerry, 243
Walk the Line (Mangold), 192
Wall, The (Parker), 52
Wallach, Eli, 133
Wallis, Hal, 243
Walsh, Raoul, xiii, 229, 237-8, 240, 245
Wang, Wayne, 43
Wanger, Walter, 255

War at Home, The (Silber/Brown), 185, 187, 195
Warner Bros., 2, 17, 68-70, 72, 74, 77-8, 87, 93, 106, 110, 125-6, 133, 140, 146, 143,
Warner, Jack, 125
Wasserman, Lew, 110, 145
Waxman, Franz, 253
Wayne, John, xi, xiii, 38, 46-7, 70, 110, 137-8, 236
Weakness and Deceit (Bonner), 57
Weekend in Dinlock (Sigal), 105
Weiler, A.H., 265
Weill, Kurt, 10
Weis, Don, 233
Welcome to the Club (Shenson), 95
Welles, Orson, 113, 224
Wellman, William, xiii, 232-3, 235
Wenders, Wim, 162, 226-7
West, Mae, xiii
West, Nathanael, 122
West Side Story (Robbins/Wise), 263, 266, 271
While the City Sleeps (Lang), 244
White Heat (Walsh), 56, 238
Who, The, 8
Why We Fight (Capra), 238
Wiener, Jean, 253
Wild Boys of the Road (Wellman), 232
Wilde, Cornel, 110, 235
Wilder, Billy, 229-30, 235, 243-4, 260
William Morris Agency, 110
Williams, John, 147
Williams, Robin, 169, 171, 174-5
Williams, Tennessee, 233
Willson, Meredith, 265
Wind from Nowhere, The (Micheaux), 149, 151
Wise, Robert, 194, 243
Witches, The (De Sica), 136
Within Our Gates (Micheaux), 149
Witness (Weir), 25-8, 34, 36, 37, 38, 40
Wizard of Oz, The (Fleming), 40
Wizards (Bakshi), 13, 19, 21
Where Eagles Dare (Hutton), 145
Whitman, Stuart, 110
Wise Blood (Huston), 238
Women, The (Cukor), 63
Woman on the Beach, The (Renoir), 124-5
Wonderful Country, The (Parrish), 236
Woods, James, 44, 58-9

Wordsworth, William, 1-2
Wrangell, Isabelle Fair, 124
Wright Brothers, 18
Writers Guild of America, 43, 118, 122-3, 125, 128
Written on the Wind (Sirk), 233
Wrong Side of Murder Creek, The (Zellner), 185
WUSA (Rosenberg), 78
Wyeth, N.C., 14
Wyler, William, 67, 95, 249, 253

X-Men films, 192

Yang, Edward, 221
Yankee Doodle Dandy (Curtiz), 142
Year of Living Dangerously, The (Weir), 25-6, 36, 40
Year of the Dragon (Cimino), 43, 49, 55
Yojimbo (Kurosawa), 137
Yordan, Philip, 112, 240
Young Frankenstein (Brooks), 73
Young, Neil, 161-3
Young, Robert, 123

Zaentz, Saul, 21
Zanuck, Darryl, 123, 255
Zanuck, Richard, 101
Zellner, Bob, 185, 187-93, 196-7
Ziegler, Evart, 106, 113
Ziegler, Ziggy, 114
Zinnemann, Fred, 235
Zone of the Interior (Sigal) 105

Books by Patrick McGilligan

As author
Woody Allen: A Travesty of a Mockery of a Sham (forthcoming)
Funny Man: Mel Brooks
Young Orson: The Years of Luck and Genius on the Path to Citizen Kane
Nicholas Ray: The Glorious Failure of an American Director
Oscar Micheaux: The Great and Only
Alfred Hitchcock: A Life in Darkness and Light
Clint, The Life and Legend: A Biography of Clint Eastwood
Fritz Lang: The Nature of the Beast
Jack's Life: A Biography of Jack Nicholson
George Cukor: A Double Life
Robert Altman: Jumping Off the Cliff
Cagney: The Actor as Auteur

As editor
Tender Comrades: A Backstory of the Hollywood Blacklist (with Paul Buhle)
Film Crazy: Interviews with Hollywood Legends
Six by Robert Riskin
Backstory: Interviews with Screenwriters of Hollywood's Golden Age
Backstory 2: Screenwriters of the 1940s and 1950s
Backstory 3: Interviews with Screenwriters of the 1960s
Backstory 4: Screenwriters of the 1970s and 1980s
Backstory 5: Interviews with Screenwriters of the 1990s

www.ingramcontent.com/pod-product-compliance
Lightning Source LLC
Chambersburg PA
CBHW051500030726

47592CB00006B/2024